A PHILOSOPHICAL GUIDE
TO CONDITIONALS

A PHILOSOPHICAL GUIDE TO CONDITIONALS

Jonathan Bennett

CLARENDON PRESS · OXFORD

This book has been printed digitally and produced in a standard specification
in order to ensure its continuing availability

OXFORD
UNIVERSITY PRESS

Great Clarendon Street, Oxford OX2 6DP

Oxford University Press is a department of the University of Oxford.
It furthers the University's objective of excellence in research, scholarship,
and education by publishing worldwide in

Oxford New York

Auckland Cape Town Dar es Salaam Hong Kong Karachi
Kuala Lumpur Madrid Melbourne Mexico City Nairobi
New Delhi Shanghai Taipei Toronto
With offices in
Argentina Austria Brazil Chile Czech Republic France Greece
Guatemala Hungary Italy Japan South Korea Poland Portugal
Singapore Switzerland Thailand Turkey Ukraine Vietnam

Oxford is a registered trade mark of Oxford University Press
in the UK and in certain other countries

Published in the United States
by Oxford University Press Inc., New York

© Jonathan Bennett 2003

The moral rights of the author have been asserted

Database right Oxford University Press (maker)

Reprinted 2006

ISBN 978-0-19-925887-1

To the memory of David Lewis

fruitful philosopher, helpful teacher, good friend

PREFACE

Perhaps a 'Guide' should cover its field in an even-handed manner, whereas the present work takes sides in some active debates. Still, I try to be informative about positions that I reject, fitting them into the picture and giving them their hour in court; so this book can serve as a guide to as much of the literature as I have been able to understand.

Why should anyone want to be helped to manage the literature on conditionals? My answer appears in §1.

There is more original work here than is usual in guides. I make no apology for that. I venture to remark that Chapter 22 is, in my opinion, my weightiest original contribution to the understanding of conditionals.

Conditionals had a regular place in my tutorial teaching in Cambridge (1956–68), and I lectured on them a little at the University of British Columbia (1970–9). At Syracuse University (1979–97) they were the subject of five semester-long graduate seminars, the book-length notes for which grew through four rewritings to resemble a book in other ways too. Since retiring from teaching, I have consulted more philosophers, read more, thought harder and more carefully, and kneaded the material into better shape. Here it is, the best I can do, though Iris Murdoch was right: 'No philosophy book is ever finished, it is only abandoned.'

This *Guide* is aimed primarily at graduate students and senior undergraduates, but it may have something to offer also to their teachers.

Much philosophical writing on conditionals is, to put it vaguely, technical, and its authors have a facility with such things that has been denied to me. My painful crawl towards understanding may have helped me to be useful. In the literature as it stands, moves are often made with a swiftness that declares them to be obviously sound, whereas for many of us they are not *obviously* anything. My own struggles warn me against cutting expository corners in that way.

They also limit what I can tackle. My sad consciousness of the range of daunting technical logical work by van Fraassen, Thomason, Stalnaker, Skyrms, Pollock, Nute, McGee, Lewis, Levi, Jeffreys, Harper, Hall, Hájek, Gupta, Gibbard, Adams, and others has intensified through the years. I cannot get this work under my belt securely enough to be able to report on it decently, but two thoughts console me. Even if I did master those materials, to expound them for my intended readers would require an intolerably long book; and I do understand

and perhaps adequately expound the logical work that bears most directly on the philosophical themes that are my book's topic.

The last half-century's work on conditionals has been collegial. Joining in this tradition, I have shown parts of late drafts to people whose work I discuss, and they have been generous with help. I am grateful to Michael Tooley, William Lycan, Mark Lance, Richard Jeffrey, Frank Jackson, Allan Gibbard, Hartry Field, Brian Ellis, Wayne Davis, James Cargile, John Bigelow, Stephen J. Barker, and Ernest Adams. I should especially mention Dorothy Edgington, Adam Elga, Alan Hájek, the late David Lewis, Barry Loewer, and Robert Stalnaker, each of whom gave me what amounted to a series of tutorials which have enabled me to improve the work greatly. Although I have rejected some of my collaborators' offerings, and must take the final responsibility for everything in the book, I proclaim it as a joint effort.

Whenever I report what someone 'told me', 'warned me', or the like, I always mean that he or Dorothy did so in a personal communication.

Like my books *The Act Itself* and *Learning from Six Philosophers*, this one was composed in Nota Bene. This word-processing system, in which I have no financial interest, put at my finger-tips all the symbols that I needed. It is also faster, more powerful, more rational, more adult, and better adapted to academic needs than anything else on the market.

Critical and other remarks can be sent to me at jfb@mail.com.

CONTENTS

1

Introduction

1. SOME QUESTIONS

'If the American ambassador had understood her instructions, Iraq would not have invaded Kuwait.' 'If Shackleton had known how to ski, then he would have reached the South Pole in 1909.' 'If rabbits had not been deliberately introduced into New Zealand, there would be none there today.' These are probably all true, and we can hear, think, and say such things without intellectual discomfort.

Philosophy teaches us how to inspect familiar things from an angle that makes them look disturbing and problematic. What Locke wrote of stones and iron also holds for thoughts and statements: 'Though the familiar use of things about us take off our wonder; yet it cures not our ignorance' (*Essay Concerning Human Understanding* III.vi.9). What first drew philosophers' attention to conditionals like the three above was the question: how can we know whether they are true? If any of the three is true, it is contingently so: it is a truth about what happens to be, not what must be, the case. We discover contingencies by examining the actual world; but how are we to do that for conditionals that concern what *would* have ensued if something *had* been the case that in fact *was not* the case? How can we learn about such matters by investigating how things stand in actuality?

It easy to gesture vaguely towards the right answer to this question. But getting the details right, and finding the best theory in which to express and explain them, proves to be difficult and rewarding.

Other conditionals are not openly and explicitly about what would have ensued if things had been different. 'If they have chains on their tyres, there must be snow in the pass.' 'If he learned that from Alice, then she is smarter than I thought.' 'If they scheduled the meeting for Wednesday, I must be losing my memory.' These also raise a problem about verification: when we beam our senses on the actual world, we learn unconditional things—P, Q, and R—and it is not obvious how these discoveries guide our judgements on conditional matters, how they tell us that if S, then T.

To answer this we must become clear about what these conditionals mean—a formidable task. Any conditional in this second group is false if its antecedent (the part between 'If' and the comma) is true and the consequent (the part after the comma or after 'then' if that occurs) is false. Does that yield the whole story about what such a conditional means? If so, then

> If he learned about that from Alice, then she broke a promise to me

simply means

> It is not the case that: he learned about that from Alice and she did not break a promise to me.

Some philosophers have accepted this account of what the conditional means, but nearly everyone now rejects it (§9). Well, then, what *else* does the meaning of such a conditional contain? We shall explore that in Chapters 3 and 6–7.

The first three examples all contain '. . . had . . . would . . .', whereas the second trio do not. This reflects the fact that conditionals are of two principal types. To see how different they are, consider this pair: (1) 'If Booth did not shoot Lincoln, someone else did.' (2) 'If Booth had not shot Lincoln, someone else would have.' These are both of the form 'If A, C'; each A concerns Booth's not shooting Lincoln, and each C concerns someone else's doing so. Yet every informed person accepts 1, whereas 2 is disputable.

It has not been easy to understand exactly where the line falls between the two types, and what puts it there; and philosophers have disagreed about this. In Chapter 22 below, I shall support one of the views by disproving the only rival that has seemed plausible to anyone; but that proof lies on the far side of a large philosophical terrain.

Some difficult questions that an analytic philosopher might tackle are not worth the trouble. Paul Grice told me that a discussion group of J. L. Austin's wrestled with this question:

> For some adjectives, the phrase 'very [adjective]' can be changed, with no significant change of meaning, to 'highly [adjective]'; for other adjectives the 'highly' version sounds wrong. What generates or explains the line between the two classes of adjectives?

In the first class we have 'excited' and 'intelligent', in the second 'bored' and 'stupid'. It may occur to you that some adjectives have an *up* or *down* element in their meanings, suggesting that 'highly' can stand in for 'very' with the up adjectives but not the down ones. Not so, however; 'highly conceited' is all right, but 'highly vain' is not. Nobody has found the answer to this question, it seems, and I know of no reason to care. One could tackle such a problem only for the mountaineer's reason, *because it is there.*

The pursuit of a good analytic understanding of conditionals is doubly unlike that. In many philosophical areas we *use* conditionals as load-bearing parts of theoretical structures, and sometimes our use of them reflects assumptions about how they work—assumptions that could be challenged by a good analysis. Also, working through the central problems about conditionals forces one to learn things in many philosophical areas: the metaphysics of possible worlds, probability and belief-change, probability and logic, the pragmatics of conversation, determinism, ambiguity, vagueness, the law of excluded middle, facts versus events, and more. After each of the five graduate seminars on conditionals that have I taught, several students told me, in almost exactly these words, 'This was the hardest seminar I have ever taken, and the most profitable.' I report this in praise of my topic, not of my teaching.

Having admitted difficulty, I add that this book ought to be manageable by any student who has some solid analytic philosophy behind him or her. The literature on conditionals is harder than it needs to be: many contributors to it take such work in their stride, and neglect the needs of the less well muscled, who must struggle to keep up. I have needed much time, effort, and help from friends and colleagues, to get on top of various things that others manage more easily. My travails warn me against cutting corners fast when explaining things to others.

I aim to work through the main parts of the fairly recent philosophical literature on conditionals, showing what goes on in them and helping the reader to see that this topic is—like philosophy in general—tough but manageable. For some account of earlier work, see Sanford 1989: 13–45.

2. DEFINING 'CONDITIONAL'

We encounter a conditional through a sentence expressing it, that is, a sentence whose meaning it is. How can we tell whether a given sentence expresses a conditional? One might look to its superficial features for an answer:

> S: An item is a conditional if it is expressed by an English sentence consisting of 'If' followed by an English sentence followed by 'then' followed by an English sentence.

Conditionals are often expressed without 'if'—for example, 'Had the civil war not been fought, American slavery would have continued into the twentieth century'. Still, the meaning of that sentence could be expressed in the 'If . . .' form; so we might replace S by:

S*: An item is a conditional if it is *expressible* by an English sentence . . . etc.

This does not read off conditionalness purely from the surface of the sentence, but it comes close to that. The changes needed to get something into the 'If . . .' form are trivial and obvious.

S* fails to cover all the ground, because some conditionals have 'If' but not 'then', and some of those differ significantly from all that do contain 'then' (§91). Also, conversely, S and S* both count as conditionals some items that are not so. In response to someone's assertion of S, James Cargile devised a counterexample (unpublished). Let 'Only Joe would come to the party bringing his wife who always says at first that she won't come' be the first sentence, and let 'She does come' be the second. Assemble those according to S and you get:

If only Joe would come to the party bringing his wife who always says at first that she won't come then she does come.

This undistinguished English sentence is plainly not a conditional, but rather an optative, like 'If only she would let me kiss her!'

To explain why it is not a conditional, we have to go further down from the surface. Every conditional applies a binary (= two-place) conditional operator to a pair of propositions; that is, it means something of the form $O_2(A,C)$. Cargile's optative, on the other hand, applies the singulary (= one-place) operator 'If only [it were the case that] . . . ' to a single proposition; that is, it means something of the form $O_1(P)$. It may look like 'If A, then C', but that is an illusion.

Perhaps, then, we can define 'conditional' as 'item expressible in a sentence of the form "If [sentence A], then [sentence C]", the effect of the whole being to apply a binary operator to propositions expressed by those two contained sentences'. If this were the best we could do, our recognition of conditionals in other languages would depend upon our translating items in those languages as meaning what 'if' does in English. That seems to go backwards: the best way to discover that some Turkish word means the same as our 'if', one would think, is to learn how the Turks use it in expressing conditionals. Still, this English-dependent account might be about the best we can do at this preliminary stage. It lets me capture in my net swarms of obviously genuine conditionals, perhaps indeed all of them (if I adjust it to cover conditionals that do not contain 'then'); and with luck it does not capture too much else. A stronger, deeper account can emerge from the analysis (or analyses) that we eventually come up with. In philosophy we often have to start with rough criteria—or even a mere ostensive list—to pick out a lot of members of some class, develop an analytic account of how they work, and treat that as implicitly defining the class.

Admittedly, that preliminary account does capture some items that we would rather exclude. For example, 'She was always home before midnight: if she missed the bus, then she would walk' (Dudman 1984a), where 'if' means about the same as 'whenever'. Again, when my colleague hears me say that I have applied for leave, he may say 'If you have applied, I'm going to apply too' (Akatsuka 1985). This is not a conditional, either. My colleague means 'Because you have applied, I'm going to apply', and he uses 'if' because he is still digesting the news about my application. Had he known about it for a month, that use of 'if' would be unnatural. Having noted these two kinds of sentence, we can avoid tripping over them; but they do imply a further imperfection in my preliminary account of what a conditional is.

My rough, preliminary account of what I take 'conditional' to mean fails to fit one large class of conditionals unless it is pulled into shape around them. That is because of a fact that was (so far as I know) first described in Gibbard 1981b: 222–6. In the conditional:

If the British did not attack Suez, the Israelis rigged the situation to make it look as though they had,

we find the two sentences

The British did not attack Suez
The Israelis rigged the situation to make it look as though they had,

each of which occurs in the conditional with the same meaning that it has when it stands alone. Contrast that with the following:

Con: If the British had not attacked Suez, Soviet troops would not have entered Hungary a few weeks later.

This has nested within it these two sentences:

Con$_1$: The British had not attacked Suez
Con$_2$: The Soviet troops would not have entered Hungary a few weeks later.

Though Con$_2$ is a complete sentence, it is hardly usable except in compounds with other sentences. Con$_1$ clearly has a stand-alone meaning, but not the one it bears as an ingredient in that conditional. Standing alone, it involves the notion of a *past past*—a time that was already past at some understood past time. For example: 'Before you criticize his naivety, remember how things stood when he entered the Foreign Office. The British had not attacked Suez

. . .' and so on. The conditional does not use this *past past* tense. (See also Dudman 1984*a, b*.)

I share the common opinion that Con should be represented as having the form $O_2(A,C)$, but Gibbard's point warns us that its A and C are not Con_1 and Con_2, the sentences appearing on its surface. I take Con to mean something of the form

> O_2(The British did not attack Suez, Soviet troops did not enter Hungary a few weeks later).

We can even use those sentences to express what Con expresses, by writing 'If it had been the case that . . . it would have been the case that . . .'. I shall revert to this matter in §6.

When I speak of the 'antecedent' (or 'consequent') of a conditional, I mean the first (or second) sentence that occurs *when we represent it in the form $O_2(A,C)$*. So I shall say that the above two conditionals have the same antecedent, though it does not appear on the second conditional's surface.

3. CHALLENGING THE TERNARY STRUCTURE

My loose account of what conditionals are would be rejected by Gilbert Harman (1979), who has argued that 'if' never stands for an operator on a pair of propositions. His alternative account of it, significant and challenging though it is, seems not to have won acceptance. What motivates it is Harman's desire for a unified treatment of 'if' that covers its use in conditionals and also in sentences like 'He asked her if she would marry him'. Unity is always worth wanting, but in this case, I believe, it cannot be had.

V. H. Dudman (forthcoming) also denies that 'if'-sentences (as he calls them) mean something of the form $O_2(A,C)$. Rather than seeing 'If the bough breaks, the cradle will fall' as having a 'ternary' structure in which one item ('if') links two other items (constituent sentences), Dudman argues for its being a two-part item, the first part of which is 'If the bough breaks', which he calls 'a string beginning with "if"', or an '"if"-string', for short:

Examples like the following demonstrate that an 'if'-sentence has a *string beginning with 'if'* for a constituent:

> . . . the moment for such frivolities, if it had ever existed, was now past. . . .

> The knowledge that there was a leak, if it became public, could be more damaging than the leak itself. . . .

In them we descry that string interrupting a *prior sentence* ('The moment for such frivolities was now past', 'The knowledge that there was a leak could be more damaging than the leak itself') which it could synonymously have preceded or followed: there is no doubting its integrity. And then the point is simply that the commonplace ternary structure would sunder this undoubted constituent. (Dudman (forthcoming))

This is part of Dudman's basis for his theory about how 'if'-sentences work grammatically, and what their role is in our lives. I share the fairly general disbelief in this theory, and can devise no way of engaging with it that would profit you or me. However, you may take a sceptical view of my attitude, for either of two reasons. If Dudman's theory were correct, most of this book would be wrong; and Dudman sometimes decorates his theoretical themes with a descant of amused contempt directed at other writers on conditionals. So you may suspect that my rejection of his theory arises from fear or from indignation.

Perhaps in part it does, but it also has rational support. In §137 I shall briefly cast doubt on Dudman's account of what the two kinds of 'if'-sentences are *for*. Chapter 22 as a whole will constitute a decisive argument against a main pillar of his position, namely a thesis about where to draw the line dividing 'if'-sentences into two main groups (§6). And right now I shall comment briefly on his grammatical 'demonstration', reported above.

Dudman writes that 'the commonplace ternary structure would sunder this undoubted constituent', namely the 'if'-string. Would it? That depends on what you mean by 'sunder'. When we regard the string as consisting of two constituents—'if' and a sentence we call the 'antecedent'—we need not deny that in certain transformations the string holds together. However strong its integrity, there are things to be said about its 'if' component, and others to be said about the remainder of the string; it would be astonishing if there were not. The things that are separately sayable constitute much of the literature on 'conditionals', as we call them; all of that could not be destroyed by Dudman's point about the 'integrity' of 'if'-strings.

Lycan 2001: 6–15 is like Dudman's work in adducing syntax in partial defence of a semantics of conditionals. Lycan does not contend that any rival semantic analysis conflicts with the syntactic facts, but I think he holds that some of the latter can be explained by his analysis and not by any other. I am not convinced of that, but those pages are worth study.

The syntactic facts that Lycan emphasizes seem to have no overlap with the ones highlighted by Dudman.

4. TWO TYPES OF CONDITIONAL

Like most students of them, I hold that conditionals fall into two importantly different species. We have met one sample pair, and here is another:

Did-did: If Shakespeare did not write *Hamlet*, then some aristocrat did.

Had-would: If Shakespeare had not written *Hamlet*, then some aristocrat would have.

Without having a full analysis of either, I have committed myself to understanding Had-would as meaning something of the form:

O_2(Shakespeare did not write *Hamlet*, Some aristocrat wrote *Hamlet*);

and Did-did also means something of that form, with the same antecedent and consequent. Since the two are plainly not equivalent—one being probably true and the other daft—they must use different conditional operators (thus Adams 1970).

There are countless other such pairs, for example: 'If this tyre did not get a puncture, it had a blowout'; 'If this tyre hadn't got a puncture, it would have had a blowout'. The members of each pair are strikingly alike, yet they differ in what it takes to make them true or acceptable. In my examples so far, the Did-did conditional is acceptable while the Had-would one is not, but it can be the other way around. The Department wants the eulogy for our honorary graduand to be written by either Alston or Bennett, and we two decide that he will do it. Asked later who wrote the eulogy, I reply that I think Alston did, adding 'If not, I don't know who wrote it.' I would reject 'If he didn't, I did', because I know that I didn't; but I may well accept 'If he hadn't, I would have'.

We want a good analytic understanding of each of the two kinds of conditional. One might hope to find a Y-shaped analysis of them—first stating what is common to the two kinds and then bifurcating in order to describe the differences. That they have much in common seems clear. Each involves a binary operator on propositions; and we shall see that the two operators share most of their logical properties (§69). This nourishes the hope for a Y-shaped analysis with a long, thick stem.

In my final chapter I shall expound a Y-shaped account by Wayne Davis, and another by Robert Stalnaker. Each gives for the two types of conditional a unified account that is nearly complete, lacking only a choice between two settings of a single parameter, one for each type. These are rival analyses, which cannot both be right; and I shall argue that each is wrong.

Can some other Y-shaped analysis succeed? Allan Gibbard, in an important paper, answers No. He goes further: the two types of conditional, he startlingly suggests, differ so deeply that their logical similarities are 'little more than a coincidence' (1981b: 211). Robert Stalnaker has argued powerfully against that (1984: 111–13), and I agree with him. In §69 I shall *explain* the logical likenesses between the two, not generating a Y-shaped analysis, but at least exorcizing the 'coincidence' spectre.

One kind of conditional is the topic of my Chapters 2–9, the other of 10–21. So the main dividing line through conditionals, with Did-did on one side of it and Had-would on the other, is this book's central organizing feature. I need, therefore, to place the line correctly. If I put some conditionals on the wrong side of it, I may try to make my analyses do impossible things.

Here is an attractive project: (1) develop criteria for sorting conditionals into two groups, then (2) sort them on the basis of those criteria, then finally (3) analyse the two sorts of conditionals. But we ought not to assume that this can be done. One important writer on conditionals has written that a sorting criterion 'might more properly be expected to *accompany* and not to precede the formulation of an adequate theory' of one of the sorts of conditionals (Adams 1975: 104). If so, then our (2) sorting of individual conditionals—our decisions about which belong to which type—cannot look back to (1) superficial recognitional criteria, and so must look ahead to (3) the final analyses. The procedure will be to start with what we hopefully take to be paradigm members of each sort of conditional, get analytic ideas about how they work, and then find out how far each analysis extends—that is, which other conditionals it fits.

Even if we must proceed in that way, it would be nice if our launching paradigms were at least marked off by some reliable rules of thumb. Here is an example of what I mean. H. P. Grice (1957) offered an analysis of the concept of 'non-natural meaning', as he called it. That is the concept that is most relevant to language, and is at work in

Those three rings on the bell (of the bus) mean that the bus is full

and not in

Those spots mean that he has measles.

We have an intuitive sense of the difference, but Grice did more than offer examples and appeal to our intuitions. He pointed out that in the first example, (1) one could go on to say 'But in fact it is not; the conductor made a mistake'; (2) it is all right to talk about 'what was meant' by the three rings; (3) the statement implies that by making the three rings *someone* meant that the bus is full; (4) the statement could reasonably be expressed in the form 'Those three rings mean "The bus is full"'; (5) the statement is not equivalent to 'The fact that the bell has rung three times means that the bus is full' (the bell might have rung three times because of a short-circuit). Those five truths about the first example—which are also, *mutatis mutandis*, true of most examples that Grice wanted to group with it—are all false of the second. You cannot properly say 'Those spots mean that he has measles, but he does not have measles', or 'What is meant by those spots is that he has measles', or 'By those spots someone means that he has measles', or 'Those spots mean "He has measles"'; and you *can* say 'The fact that he has those spots means that he has measles'. Grice offered those five differences as drawing the line separating the uses of 'mean' that his analysis aimed to cover from ones it did not. Then he proceeded to the analysis. His way of demarcating his topic is not verbal and mechanical—it does go into meaning, but not far enough to be controversial.

I have nothing as substantial as that. For initially segregating conditionals into two main groups I can offer only something almost purely verbal and superficial:

> In every conditional of one group, and in no conditional of the other, the sentence expressing the consequent has 'would' as the auxiliary of its main verb.

In my examples up to here, the verb 'had' has occurred in the antecedent, but that is not essential. Sometimes it is 'were': 'If he were to reduce taxes by that much, the country would be bankrupt within a decade.' Sometimes neither word occurs: 'If the Palestinians declared statehood now, the Israelis would retaliate'. The common thread through all these is just 'would' in the consequent (strictly, in *expressing* the consequent, but I shall sometimes cut that corner). This is not purely verbal, because it requires recognizing an operator on two propositions, the antecedent and consequent.

The criterion as stated is not quite correct, because some uses of 'would' do not put a conditional in the 'would' group, and recognizing those requires going below the surface a little. Some involve the idiom 'would like'. What is the word 'would' doing in 'I would like to go for a swim'? The thought might be a conditional one: 'If I were to go for a swim, I would like it', but more often it will categorically express a desire, meaning 'I want to go for a swim'. Now, it could be used in this way in the consequent of a conditional, such as 'If you will come with me, I would like to go for a swim'; and I do not classify this along with the main bulk of 'would' conditionals. I expect agreement about this. I wish I had a neat way of saying why it is right.

There can also be trouble from uses of 'would' to express the notion of a *past future*, as in 'Some day he too would stand upon that scaffold' and 'She announced that they would be married in the following month'. That use of 'would' could also be built into the consequent of a conditional that does not belong in the 'would' group. Not knowing how Ambrose Bierce died after he disappeared into Mexico in 1913, someone might write: 'If he was jauntily setting off for Mexico intending to spy on Pancho Villa, then he would die a violent death within the next two months.' That is the past-future use of 'would', not the use that puts a conditional into the 'would' group.

The imperfections in my gesture towards a line of demarcation are not fatal. The final line will emerge out of the analyses of the two types of conditional.

5. LABELS FOR THE TWO TYPES

We need labels for the two kinds of conditional. It would be good to label each in a way that helpfully describes it, rather than being stipulated and meaningless ('Type One', 'Type Two'), or meaningful and false. Unfortunately, we have no labels with this virtue.

One popular nomenclature calls the 'would' group *subjunctive conditionals* and the other *indicative conditionals*, with those adjectives often used as nouns. John Pollock wrote a book about the former, entitled *Subjunctive Reasoning.*

The conditionals that are called 'indicative' under this proposal are indeed all in the indicative mood, but that does not make the label a good one because most and perhaps all of the others are in the indicative mood also. The subjunctive mood has some slight use in English, in expressions of wishes such as 'God help you', and 'Would that he were here!', but English has never worked it hard, as do Latin and French. In 1860 a textbook on English said: 'The subjunctive is evidently passing out of use, and there is good reason to suppose that it will soon become obsolete altogether' (see *OED*, 'subjunctive'). Seventy years later the prediction was almost fulfilled: 'The word "subjunctive" is almost meaningless to Englishmen, the thing having so nearly perished'; 'As a matter of grammar, the instinct for using subjunctives rightly is dying with the subjunctive' (Fowler 1931: 163, 166; see also Zandvoort 1963). I have found no grammatical authority supporting the claim that the conditionals of the 'would' type (as I am provisionally calling them) employ the subjunctive mood. When we move to nearby languages that do have a robust subjunctive, we find that in German the equivalents of the 'would' conditionals are indeed expressed with the *subjunctive mood* but that French and Spanish do the work with something different, the *conditional tense.*

The other popular label for conditionals of the 'would' type is 'counterfactual', used both as an adjective and as a noun. David Lewis's book on them bears the title *Counterfactuals.* This comes from the idea of the antecedent's being false (counter to fact), but exactly *how* that idea is involved is not obvious. You can easily satisfy yourself that it is not that someone who asserts the conditional thereby commits himself to the antecedent's being false, or that the truth of the conditional requires the falsity of its antecedent. It may be nearer the mark to say

that someone asserting the conditional ordinarily expresses his confidence that
the antecedent is false without outright saying so. 'If you had called 911 when I
asked you to, the ambulance would be here by now' would normally be said only
by someone who thought the hearer had not made the call. Without his actually
saying this, his form of words does somehow imply or suggest his confidence in
the falsity of the antecedent.

Even if that were right for all conditionals in the 'would' camp, it would not
make 'counterfactual' a good label for them. It would be based on a feature that
has nothing to do with the antecedent's being contrary to fact, but only with the
speaker's thinking that it is so. Also, secondly, 'counterfactual' is not matched by
a corresponding label for the other type of conditional, which nobody has called
'factual' or 'profactual' or the like. Thirdly, it is unsatisfactory to base a label for
a class of conditionals on a fact about what is merely implied or suggested rather
than asserted outright in its instances. (In this I agree with Woods 1997: 8 n.)

A better basis for 'counterfactual' comes from the fact that conditionals in the
'would' camp can properly be accepted and asserted by someone who is absolutely certain that the antecedent is false. Even, indeed, by someone who would not
accept the conditional if he thought its antecedent to be true; that will not always
be so, but the 'would' form of words leaves the door open to it. Nothing like that
holds for conditionals of the other type, in which 'would' does not occur.

Although this is solider than the simple 'speaker's disbelief' basis, it still does
not make the label 'counterfactual' a good one; and we still have no good matching label for the other type of conditional. Furthermore, much analytic work is
needed properly to explain and justify this latest contrast between the two kinds
of conditional (§88).

Holding my nose, I adopt the labels 'subjunctive' and 'indicative'. Fortunately,
their defenders never claim that 'subjunctive' helps us to understand conditionals of the type to which they apply it—what its analysis is, the roles of such conditionals in inferences and in our lives. The word serves only to remind them of
the primacy of 'would' in (most of) the conditionals to which the label is applied,
and that reminder works well enough, despite reflecting an error about what the
subjunctive is.

In Chapter 12 and thereafter, I shall sometimes need to focus on subjunctive
conditionals whose antecedent is false—not assumed to be false by someone, but
actually false. I shall use 'counterfactual' as a label for those. When others use the
word in passages I shall quote, they always mean what I mean by 'subjunctive'.

6. THE RELOCATION THESIS

Some students of conditionals deny that the word 'would' helps to draw the principal line. They group the conditionals that I call 'subjunctive' together with many that I count as 'indicative', namely ones like:

Does-will: If you swim in the sea today, your cold will get worse.

If conditionals of this Does-will type belonged in the same hopper as the subjunctives, my use of the label 'subjunctive' would be indefensible, and my preliminary drawing of the line would be wrong.

I used to be a *relocator*: I wanted to relocate the main line through conditionals so as to put the 'would' conditionals and also the Does-will ones together on one side of it (Bennett: 1988b). I have since seen the error of my ways. My first defence of my switch (1995) went off at half-cock, but I got it right in 2001. In §§134–5 below I shall, developing material in the latter paper, prove that the relocation thesis is wrong. (Because the labels 'indicative' and 'subjunctive' are intolerable if the relocation thesis is correct, I once coined the terms 'straight' and 'corner' for the two kinds of conditional, on a hint from symbols that are often used to express them, namely → and >. A few writers have followed me in this. I apologize.)

It will help me, tactically, to expose the relocation thesis if I first expound two of the most persuasive arguments in its favour.

The first has to do with conditions of acceptability. Suppose the facts are such that I am right when I say to you:

Does-will: If you swim in the sea today, your cold will get worse.

Suppose further that you do not swim in the sea today, and that tomorrow I tell you:

Had-would: If you had swum in the sea yesterday, your cold would have got
            worse.

It seems reasonable to think that my Does-will conditional was acceptable at the earlier time if, and only if, my Had-would conditional is true at the later time: the two stand or fall together. So perhaps they are merely two wordings for a single conditional, differing only in tense, in which case Does-will belongs with the subjunctives, despite its not containing 'would'.

That plausible line of thought has seduced many of us. In §§134–5 I shall show what is wrong with it.

The other argument cannot be so briefly stated, and is harder to dislodge (Dudman 1983, 1984*a*, *b*). Consider four ways for a statement to pick out a moment or period of time. (1) *Past past*. In the sentence 'We were rolling up the tent, and Charles had doused the camp fire', the verb phrase 'had doused' puts the action at a time earlier than the past time that is primarily being spoken of. (2) *Simple past*. In 'We were rolling up the tent' or 'We rolled up the tent', reference is made to a past time, but not as past relative to some other past time that is also spoken of. (3) *Present*. (4) *Future*.

The verb forms that normally refer to past past time in simple sentences can also do so in the antecedents of conditionals. For example: 'We were wondering whether Charles had doused the camp fire, and I still do not know whether he had. *If he had doused the fire, he had been very quiet about it.*' In some antecedents, on the other hand, the 'had'-plus-participle form pertains not to (1) the past past but to either (2) the simple past: 'If Hitler had invaded England instead of Russia, he would have won the war'; or (3) the present, as in 'If Antoinette had been here, we would not be drinking ale'; or (4) the future: 'If the auditors had come tomorrow, they would have found the books in perfect order.'

The verb forms that normally refer to simple past time can also do so in the antecedents of conditionals. For example: 'I do not know whether it was Charles who made the anonymous gift. *If it was, I have misread his character.*' But in some antecedents those same verbal forms take us not to (2) the simple past but rather to (3) the present, as in 'If the Provost was [or: were] plotting against the President, he would be on campus now rather than sunning himself in Florida'; or (4) the future, as in 'If the Provost plotted against the President, he would lose'. In this last, other readings are possible, but 'plotted' *can* be understood as taking us to the future.

Finally, the verb forms that in simple contexts take us to the time at which the utterance is being made can also do so in antecedents of conditionals, as in: '*If John loves Mary, he has a funny way of showing it*', where 'loves' clearly has to do with John's feelings about Mary at the time of utterance. Present-tense forms, however, serve in certain other antecedents to refer not to (3) the present but only to (4) the future, as in: 'If it rains tonight, the river will be in flood tomorrow': 'If you swim in the sea today, your cold will get worse'. Each of those antecedents contains a present-tense verb—'rains', 'swim'—referring to the future.

This is the phenomenon of *forward time shift*, in which a 1 verb form does the work of 2, 3 or 4, a 2 form does the work of 3 or 4, and a 3 form does the work of 4. Some conditionals force a forward time shift on the principal verb in the antecedent, others do not.

Dale and Tanesini (1989) argue for taking this lightly. The time-shift criterion, they contend, appears to be a localized English phenomenon, not appearing in Italian or—they assume—in other languages. They conjecture that it is explained by the idiosyncratic willingness of English to 'allow the present tense in simple non-compound sentences which clearly express propositions about the future: John is taking his exam tomorrow, John takes his exam tomorrow'. Yet Spanish, French, German, and Turkish all have this feature, as no doubt do other languages; though not all of these have a time shift in some conditionals. Gibbard may be right in suggesting that time-shift conditionals 'form a significant grammatical class' (1981b: 226).

Dudman has proposed the line between time-shift conditionals and others as a basis for separating the two great classes of conditionals. It has the effect, as did the previous point about what conditionals stand or fall with what others, of grouping the Does-wills with the 'would' conditionals that I call 'subjunctive'. (Or rather: grouping the time-shift Does-wills in that way. Some Does-wills lack the time-shift feature—for example 'If he loves her, he will marry her' (Thomason and Gupta 1980: 299).) Whether the grammatical distinction has that semantic effect, however, is controversial. Among those who think it does not, Edgington (1995b: 314) is alone in offering a different and milder suggestion for what the time shift signifies.

The forward time shift was first described in detail by Gibbard (1981b: 222–6). He uses it as a basis for calling Does-will conditionals 'grammatically subjunctive', while apologizing for the label, and reserves 'grammatically indicative' for conditionals that lack the time-shift feature. But he does not use that to reorder the domain of semantic enquiry. On the contrary, he announces that he will 'leave aside' the Does-wills (229), while defending one semantic analysis for the remaining indicatives and another for subjunctives. Despite this caution, at p. 228 he gives a good reason for putting the Does-wills semantically with the ones he calls 'indicative'.

Without having got to the bottom of the time-shift phenomenon, I decline to follow Dudman in allowing it to force a change in how we classify conditionals.

For the next eight chapters my topic will be indicative conditionals, considered on their own. I shall regularly use → to express the operator of such a conditional, so that 'If you swim in the sea today, your cold will get worse' can be expressed as 'You will swim in the sea today → Your cold will get worse', or as 'Swim → Cold', for short. Mostly, though, I shall combine the arrow with dummy letters, writing 'A→C' to stand for any indicative conditional.

7. INDEPENDENT CONDITIONALS

A different line through conditionals also helps to shape this book. It has both subjunctives and indicatives on each side of it. Here are two subjunctives, one on each side of this new line:

(1) If the river were to rise another two feet, the subway system would be flooded.

(2) If the river were to rise another two feet, it would be two feet higher than it is now.

Of these, 1 is contingent, 2 is necessary; but that is not the essence of the distinction I am drawing. What I care about is that in 1 the consequent is reachable from the antecedent only with help from unstated particular matters of fact, while in 2 one can get the consequent from the antecedent without input from any matters of particular fact. I shall say that 1 is a *dependent* conditional, 2 an *independent* one.

An independent conditional may not be logically necessary; it may depend on causal laws alone. In contrast to

If that cyclist had been on the other side of the mountain two hours ago, he would not have been here now,

which depends on unstated particular matters of fact, we have the independent conditional

If that particle had been two light years from here a month ago, it would not have been here now,

which holds as a matter of sheer physics. The other basis for independent conditionals is morality. As well as fact-dependent conditionals such as

If she had told her husband about his prognosis, she'd have acted very badly,

we have independent ones like

If she had tortured a child just for the fun of it, she'd have acted very badly.

Those are the three categories of independent conditionals: logical, causal, and moral. Most examples in the conditionals literature are logical.

Those contrasting pairs are all subjunctives, but the line also cuts across the indicatives. Thus, logical:

If the closing date is Tuesday the 14th, then we shall have to hurry with the paper work.

If the closing date is Tuesday the 14th, then the closing date is a Tuesday.

Causal:

If two more people get into the dinghy, it will sink.

If the dinghy and its contents come to weigh more than the same volume of the water they are floating in, the dinghy will sink.

Moral:

If you lied to him about that, you did him the worst disservice you possibly could.

If you lied to him about that, you did something morally questionable.

Solidly independent causal and moral indicative conditionals are hard to come by, but that does not matter. What matters is to grasp the difference between dependent and independent, and not to identify it simply with the line between contingent and necessary.

Whereas the indicative/subjunctive line cuts through the middle of this book, the dependent/independent line runs around its perimeter. I plan to keep independent conditionals out of sight, and out of mind except as unloved exiles, occasionally mentioning them at places where I think one might be tempted to readmit them to the arena.

One reason for this attitude is that in various parts of our philosophical terrain, useful truths about dependent conditionals do not fit the independent ones. For example, many philosophers believe, in my opinion correctly, that an indicative conditional is useful, acceptable, worth asserting or at least considering, only to someone who regards its antecedent as having some chance of being true. 'If I am at this moment sitting in the visitors' gallery of the House of Commons . . .'—I can do nothing with this, because I am dead certain that I am sitting at my desk looking out at Bowen Bay. But now consider: 'If I am at this moment sitting in the visitors' gallery of the House of Commons, then I am sitting somewhere.' Whatever my doubts and certainties, doesn't that one take me by the throat and command assent, on the grounds that logic warrants it? Yes. I suppose it does. But it is a nuisance, spoiling an otherwise good bit of philosophy, and offering nothing by way of recompense.

That brings in a second reason for snubbing independent conditionals: outside the realm of logic (broadly construed), they are not useful or interesting; any work they do can as well be done in other ways. The examples I have given can be replaced by: rising by two feet makes a river two feet higher; no particle can travel faster than the speed of light; it would always be wrong to torture a child for fun; Tuesday 14th is a Tuesday; things sink in liquids that weigh less than they do; lying is always morally questionable. Nothing in these gives the conditional form serious work to do, whereas in dependent conditionals that form does work that we have no other convenient way of doing.

With one class of exceptions, which I shall note in §113, virtually every conditional that occurs outside logic texts, philosophy books, and classrooms depends for its truth or acceptability on beliefs about particular matters of fact. This fact-dependence is what makes them useful to us; it is also the source of the provocative problems that they raise, and is central to the most powerful solutions of them.

I do not hold that as between dependent and independent conditionals 'if' is ambiguous; that would be absurd. So I owe you some other account of how those two sorts relate to one another, and I shall pay that debt when the ground has been prepared—for indicative conditionals in §62, for subjunctives in §95.

8. IDIOMS

The conditional 'if' combines in regular ways with certain other words, and one may be tempted to treat such a phrase as an idiom, that is, an expression whose meaning cannot be read off from the meanings of its constituents. In every case the pull should be resisted.

One philosopher offered to explain the meaning of 'Even if . . .' in an account that makes that an idiom; but all recent workers on that topic have been sure—rightly, in my opinion—that the meaning of 'Even if' comes directly and regularly from the meanings of 'even' and 'if'. This will appear when we explore that topic in Chapter 17.

Similarly, 'Only if . . .' gets its meaning from 'only' and from 'if'. Very roughly: put an 'Only' in front of 'The boys were allowed to play soccer' and you get a statement meaning that no one who was not a boy was allowed to play soccer. Similarly, put an 'Only' in front of 'If the board asks me to resign, I will resign' and you get a statement meaning that no condition that does not involve the board's asking me to resign is one in which I shall resign. No one could doubt that the very same 'only' operates in both of these.

It is one thing to be sure that in the meaning of an 'Only if . . .' conditional the meaning of 'only' intersects with that of 'if'; it is quite another to understand the exact geography of the intersection. The latter is tricky, and I shall not discuss it. For three resolute shots at it, see Appiah 1993, Barker 1993, and Lycan 2001. I have pondered these materials, but not to the point where I feel entitled to report on them.

The case of 'If . . . then . . .' is peculiar. David Sanford wrote a book entitled *If P, Then Q*, presumably intending it to be about all conditionals, not just ones that put 'then' between antecedent and consequent. Many of us used to assume—if we thought about it at all—that the decision to include 'then' was stylistic, with no effect on meaning; but Wayne Davis (1983, listed in Sanford's bibliography but not mentioned in his text) has taught us otherwise. Any good conditional containing 'then' between its antecedent and its consequent remains good if 'then' is dropped; but the converse does not hold, because some good conditionals lacking 'then' turn bad when 'then' is inserted into them (§91). 'If war breaks out tomorrow, the tides will continue to rise and fall' is acceptable. You might prefer the wording '*Even* if war breaks out tomorrow, the tides will *still* continue to rise and fall', but the conditional passes muster just as it stands. On the other hand, 'If war breaks out tomorrow, then the tides will continue to rise and fall' implies that the tidal rise and fall depends somehow on the outbreak of war, which is absurd.

That gives significance to 'then' between antecedent and consequent, but leaves open the question of whether 'If . . . then . . .' is an idiom. Lycan (2001: 8) convincingly argues that it is not. He contends that 'If A, then, C' means something that could be expanded into 'If A, *in that eventuality* C'. This is comparable with 'When she leaves, then I will leave', which can be expanded to 'When she leaves, *at that time* I will leave'. In each sentence, 'then' does similar work.

2

The Material Conditional: Grice

9. THE HORSESHOE ANALYSIS: → IS ⊃

We understand perfectly the truth-functional or 'material' conditional operator that is standardly expressed by the horseshoe symbol. We define this so as to make P⊃Q equivalent to ¬(P&¬Q), that is, to

It is not the case that: P and it is not the case that Q.

This operator is *truth-functional*, meaning that the truth value of P⊃Q is determined solely by the values of P and Q; the horseshoe stands for a function to single truth values from pairs of them; feed in values for P and Q and out rolls the value of P⊃Q.

We know exactly what the material conditional is, or what operator ⊃ is; its truth-functional properties constitute its whole intrinsic nature. Its verbal role in plain English and everyday thought is another question, however. Some philosophers have held that it shows up in informal thought and speech in the indicative conditional, because → is ⊃. I shall call this 'the horseshoe analysis' of indicative conditionals.

According to the horseshoe analysis, 'If Booth didn't shoot Lincoln, someone else did' means the same as 'Either Booth shot Lincoln or someone else did'. This offers us a comfortingly secure hold on conditionals of that sort. We understand ⊃ as well as we do anything in our repertoire; if we found it at work in ordinary speech and thought, firmly linked to one major way of using 'If . . .', that would be a large step towards understanding our conceptual structures. So we have reason to want the horseshoe analysis to be right. There are also reasons to think it is.

The superficially most persuasive of them has occurred to many people and has been presented with helpful clarity by Jackson (1987: 4–6). It concerns something that I call 'the or-to-if inference', and it runs as follows.

You believed Vladimir when he told you 'Either they drew or it was a win for white'; which made it all right for you to tell Natalya 'If they didn't draw, it was a win for white'. That was all right because what Vladimir told you entailed what you told Natalya. Quite generally:

(1) PvQ entails ¬P→Q.

If 1 is correct, then so is the horseshoe analysis, as the following shows. In 1 substitute ¬A for P and C for Q, and you get:

(2) ¬AvC entails ¬¬A→C,

which is equivalent by definition to:

(3) A⊃C entails A→C.

Furthermore, → is at least as strong as ⊃, that is,

(4) A→C entails A⊃C.

The conjunction of 3 with 4 is equivalent to:

(5) A→C is logically equivalent to A⊃C,

which is the horseshoe analysis.

Most of this argument is elementary formal logic, and unquestionable. One might challenge the second premiss (line 4) by suggesting that A→C could be true while A⊃C is false; but this looks like a forlorn hope. With one exception (§61), nobody believes that A→C can be true when A is true and C false. All that remains is to challenge the first premiss (line 1). Your or-to-if inference, from what Vladimir told you to what you told Natalya, was clearly acceptable, and line 1 embodies a *theory* about that—a conjecture about why the inference was all right. In §18, when the time is ripe, I shall argue that the facts are better explained by something that does not imply the horseshoe analysis.

Famously, the latter is open to hosts of seeming counterexamples. They come from the fact that P⊃Q is true for *every* false P and for *every* true Q, so that the horseshoe analysis implies that the likes of these:

If I ate an egg for breakfast this morning, you ate a million eggs, and
If there are no planets anywhere, the solar system has at least eight planets,

are true, though each would be a silly thing to say. Most writers in this area have declared them false, contending that the meaning of A⊃C lacks, while the meaning of A→C includes, the notion of A's being suitably *connected* with C. But specifying the kind of connection has not been easy, and some friends of the horseshoe analysis have stood firm, arguing that the apparent counterexamples can be explained away, leaving their preferred analysis standing.

Let us look first at Grice's way of explaining them away, and then, in the next chapter, at Jackson's different one. Neither succeeds (I shall argue); but each leads through territory that is worth exploring on its own merits, apart from its relevance to our present concerns.

10. CONVERSATIONAL IMPLICATURE

H. P. Grice held that $\rightarrow$ is $\supset$, so that A$\rightarrow$C can be true even when A is not connected with C in any way. The two conditionals displayed above, he would say, are unsatisfactory but nonetheless true; and he sought to explain why they strike us as defective, through a powerful theory which everyone now sees to have much truth in it. (He began this work in his 1961, and developed it further in some 1967 lectures that were later published in his 1989. See his 1967a for the theory in general, and his 1967b for its application to indicative conditionals. Some of it seems to have been arrived at independently by James Thomson (1990: 67–8; written in about 1963).)

The theory concerns *conversational implicature*—a phrase in which the noun points to a certain linguistic phenomenon, the adjective to a way of explaining it. The phenomenon, implicature, occurs when a statement conveys, suggests, signals, or implies something without outright asserting it. I now confess: *In February 1952, in the faculty common room at Auckland University College, I disconcerted my colleagues by spilling hot tea into the lap of the newest assistant lecturer.* You picture me spilling tea on someone else, but you are wrong. Nervous and shaky in my first day in the job, I fumblingly dumped tea into my own lap. You thought otherwise because my report suggested (signalled, implied) that my victim was someone else, and Grice's theory explains how it did so—this being where the adjective 'conversational' comes into play. It is unusual—even a touch peculiar—to refer to oneself through a definite description rather than a pronoun; you assumed that I was not speaking in an off-beat fashion; so you took my phrase 'the newest assistant lecturer' to refer to someone other than myself. Still, I told you the truth. I planned to mislead you, and succeeded; but what I said was true.

So we do distinguish what a statement says from what it 'implicates' (as Grice put it), that is, what it more weakly implies or signals or conveys other than by outright assertion. Of the many sources of such implicatures, Grice focused on one cluster, namely some broad rules of conduct governing civilized discourse:

Be appropriately informative (give enough news but not too much).
Be truthful (say only what you believe, and try to have only true beliefs).

Be relevant.
Be orderly, brief, clear, etc.

These, Grice said, fall under the super-principle 'Be helpful'. They create implicatures because when someone asserts something, we can draw conclusions not
only from what he outright asserts but also from other things that must be true
if he is playing by the normal rules of civilized discourse. I now give four examples, three of them uncontroversial.

If I say to you 'IBM shares will go up' you will infer that I believe they will go
up. Why? Not because 'IBM shares will go up' entails that the speaker thinks
they will, for obviously it does not. Grice's ideas provide an explanation (though
not the whole story). When I say 'IBM shares will go up', you are entitled to
assume that I am playing by the rules, including the one enjoining us not to say
what we do not believe; so you can reasonably infer that I believe IBM shares will
go up, inferring this not from *the proposition I assert* but rather from *the fact
that I assert it*. The proposition itself remains chaste, unsullied by any content
about my beliefs.

If someone says 'He saw Lobatchewsky's proof of the theorem, and published
his own', this conveys that he saw Lobatchewsky's proof first. How? Some
philosophers used to attribute it to the sentence's meaning, contending that 'and'
in this sentence means 'and then'. The sentence-joining 'and' sometimes conveys no thought of temporal sequence—'Nine is three squared and there are
nine planets'—so these philosophers had to call 'and' ambiguous. It is usually
bad in philosophy to postulate a multiplicity of senses of a word, and Grice
offered an escape from this. He held that the sentence-joining 'and' is truth-
functional: a sentence using it is true if each of the joined sentences is true, and
otherwise false; so its meaning contains nothing temporal, and thus the
Lobatchewsky sentence does not mean anything about temporal order. It *suggests* to us that the person saw the other proof before publishing his own because
we assume that the speaker is presenting his narrative in an orderly manner,
which usually involves making *its* order correspond to that of the reported
events. Because this is a general rule of good conversational conduct, we are
entitled to expect a speaker not to depart from it without signalling the departure
('Meanwhile, back at the ranch . . .', 'Before all this . . .'). In the absence of such a
signal, we are inclined and entitled to infer that the narrative order matches the
order of the narrated events, which explains the temporal suggestion of
the Lobatchewsky sentence, and of 'They got married and they had a baby' and
the like. (This kind of orderliness may be flouted for artistic purposes, as happens
in unsignalled flashbacks in some of Vargas Llosa's novels.)

Some philosophers have thought that the sentence-joining 'or' is not ∨, because it is not strictly truth-functional in its meaning. If it is, then 'P or Q' is true just so long as P is true or Q is true, so that I am speaking truly when I say 'Either my father was F. O. Bennett or my father was Stafford Cripps'. Some would hold that this statement is not true, given that I know my father to be F. O. Bennett. It is part of the meaning of the sentence-joining 'or', they have said, that the speaker does not confidently believe, or confidently disbelieve, either disjunct.

This might explain why we wrinkle our noses at a disjunction that someone asserts just because she believes one disjunct. It has drawbacks, though, including a renewed threat of ambiguity. In playing games, giving tests, teasing, etc., it can be proper to assert a disjunction when you know which disjunct is true. For example, an acquaintance cannot remember when we first met, and I tease him with a hint: 'It was either at the Eastern Division meetings in 1956 or in Cambridge in 1963.' This is wholly proper; yet it involves asserting a (slightly compacted) disjunction when one knows which disjunct is true. So even if 'or' sometimes means that the speaker is not sure which disjunct is true, it plainly sometimes does not; so it must be ambiguous.

Grice explained the facts differently. The injunctions 'Be informative' and 'Be brief' tend to pull in opposite directions, and sometimes we have to compromise. But if someone asserts 'P or Q' when she is sure that P, she offends against both rules at once: she could be more informative *and* briefer; or, if she believes both disjuncts, she could say 'P and Q', thereby saying much more at no greater length. This entitles us to expect, normally, that someone who asserts a disjunction is not confident of either disjunct taken on its own; so we do in general expect this; so in asserting a disjunction one implies or signals that one is not confident of either disjunct. If the context provides a special reason to be less informative than one could be—e.g. because one is testing, teasing, playing, or the like—the implication of uncertainty drops out. So the sentence-joining 'or' has only one meaning, namely the truth-functional one, and we can explain all the intuitive evidence seeming to go against this.

Now, fourthly, we come to the thesis that → is ⊃. You can guess how a Gricean defence of that will go. We generally think it absurd to assert A→C purely on the grounds that one is sure that ¬A or sure that C; but this is consistent with (A→C)'s being true in such a case (and thus with →'s being ⊃), its unsatisfactoriness coming from a different source. Grice based this on the same points about brevity and informativeness that we saw at work in arguing that 'or' is ∨. That is to be expected, because according to the horseshoe analysis A→C really is a disjunction. On this account, it would be absurd but not untruthful to say 'If the speed of light is finite, then bananas are usually yellow'. This conditional is true because its consequent is true; but it would ordinarily be a silly thing to say because one could say something stronger yet shorter: 'Bananas are usually yellow.'

I shall need §12 to set the scene for explaining in §13 why the theory of conversational implicature fails in the task of reconciling the horseshoe analysis with our intuitions. Before all that, I shall discuss an aspect of Grice's theory that is too important to neglect.

11. SEMANTIC OCCAMISM

In all but the first of my four examples, Grice's *general* theory of conversational implicature offers to explain facts that would otherwise have to be explained through the meanings of *individual* words. So if we have grounds for attributing thin meanings to those words—taking 'or' to mean ∨, and 'and' to mean &—Gricean theory enables us to defend those semantic views against seeming counter-evidence, thus keeping the meanings thin. In some of his work, Grice contended that if we *can* keep the meaning of a word thin then we *should*. His theory of conversational implicature, he held, can do more than merely defend something arrived at on other grounds; it provides a positive reason for holding that the meanings of 'or' and 'and' are purely truth-functional, and thus thin.

He based this on a variant on Occam's Razor: *Sensus non sunt multiplicandi nec magnificandi praeter necessitatem*; don't postulate more senses, or thicker ones, than you have to. The two constraints are connected: if you put too much into the meaning of a word in some of its uses, you will have to plead ambiguity—'multiplying senses'—to cope with other uses from which some of this meaning is absent (Grice 1987: 47–9). We have already seen this illustrated. If 'and' sometimes means 'and then', then it must be ambiguous because sometimes it plainly does not mean that. Similarly with 'or' and uncertainty. The unspoken premiss here is that ambiguity claims in philosophy and semantics are a source of danger, and should be avoided as far as possible.

When Grice urged us to assign thin meanings to words, this was not only so as to keep down attributions of ambiguity. *Sensus non sunt magnificandi . . .*—he meant this injunction to stand on its own feet. Suppose we have two rival accounts—call them Lean and Fat—of the meaning of some word W. Fat attributes to W all the meaning that Lean does, plus some more. Lean explains certain facts about W's role in discourse partly through the meaning it attributes to W and partly through general principles of language use. Fat, on the other hand, explains all those facts through the meaning it attributes to W. In Grice's view, this difference counts in favour of Lean, because it makes less appeal to the highly specific—the idiosyncrasies of the individual word—and handles more of the data in terms of what is highly general; and that leads towards greater understanding and intellectual control. A full account of any language must, of course, include facts about individual words. How people might use or respond to 'There's a snake in that bush' depends in part on what 'snake' means, as distinct from 'steak' or 'rhinoceros'; you cannot get the whole story out of general principles. This need to come down to the level of specificity marked by individual words makes language study unlike physics, say. But the scientific spirit commands us to keep such specificity to a minimum; which encourages and perhaps justifies Grice's preference for thin single-word meanings, assigning much of the work to general rules governing civilized discourse.

('Why do you contrast the relatively *specific* facts about individual words with *more general* facts about language use, rather than contrasting *particular* facts about individual words with *general* facts about language use?' Because the words in question are universals, not particulars. The facts about what 'snake' means are facts about what many tokens of the word—instances of that universal—mean. So the needed contrast is not of particular with general, but of less with more general.)

Strawson (1986) has criticized Grice's treatment of indicative conditionals by attacking the Occamism it involves. The criticism, though wrong, is instructive. In its background is Strawson's conjecture that A→C means something like:

There is a connection between A and C which ensures that: A⊃C.

Because of what comes before the colon, this gives to → a stronger meaning than Grice accorded it. Strawson calls his 'if' a first cousin to 'therefore'. At the end of the paper he offers two counter-arguments of which one—in the final paragraph—seems to relate wrongly to Grice's theory and to Strawson's other argument. The latter goes as follows. Whatever the actual truth about 'if', there *could* be a connective that means what Strawson thinks 'if' means, whereas Grice's line of thought implies that there *could not*. Grice should predict that if a language contained a Strawsonian conditional operator, all its extra strength would be drained off into the principles 'Be informative' and 'Be brief', leaving the operator itself with no need to carry (and therefore, according to semantic Occamism, *not* carrying) any more meaning than ⊃. Grice's position is guilty of overkill, Strawson concludes, and so must be wrong.

Strawson does not remark that if his point is sound, it counts not just against Grice's account of → but against his Occamism generally. It could equally well have been brought against the Gricean cases for equating 'or' with v and 'and' with &. It generates things like this:

> There could be a connective 'uns' such that 'P uns Q' conventionally meant 'P and Q are not both false, but I am not sure about the truth value of either taken separately'. Grice's Occamism, however, implies that no connective could retain such a thick meaning. All the meaning of 'uns' beyond its truth-functional v component could be—and therefore according to Grice should be—explained in general conversational terms, and not assigned to 'uns' in particular.

This is disturbing, because Grice was plainly right about 'or', and yet 'uns' as described seems to be *possible*.

Fortunately, Strawson is wrong about Grice's commitments. Grice might have to say that we, with our actual practices and forms of life, could not have a Strawsonian 'if'; but he could comfortably allow that there could be societies that had it. Suppose a society where people often give disjunctive information— something meaning 'Either A is false or C is true'—although they knew which disjunct was true. They might do this, for example, in games, intelligence tests, initiation rites, or teasing. Given enough of this kind of disjoining, work could be done by a connective whose conventional meaning was that of 'It is not the case that A is true and C false, *and this is not one of those deliberate withholdings of information*'. That could be 'uns', or the Strawsonian 'if'.

Strawson may have meant his argument to have the premiss that we—in our actual language, with our actual ways of life—could have a conditional connective that is a first cousin to 'therefore'. But *that* premiss is far from self-evident, and Grice gave reasons for thinking it false.

Semantic Occamism, important and true as I think it is, turns out to have little direct bearing on the horseshoe analysis of indicative conditionals. The Occamism debate turns on this question:

> If the facts about the use of expression E—including ones about what uses of it would be found peculiar or unsatisfactory—can be explained either by (1) attributing to E a fat meaning or by (2) attributing a thin meaning and bringing in Gricean conversational principles, are we intellectually obliged to adopt 2?

This question gets a bite on the horseshoe analysis of → only if the facts about the latter *can* be explained by equating it with ⊃ and bringing in Gricean principles. They cannot. Grice thought otherwise because he had not considered enough of the data. A certain thesis about the propriety of indicative conditionals, now widely accepted, gives us a sounder idea than Grice had of what he needed to explain; and in the light of this we shall see that his theory of conversational implicature falls short.

12. THE RAMSEY TEST

The thesis in question was first presented by Frank Ramsey in 1929. Ernest Adams has greatly developed it in the past twenty years, and Frank Jackson—one of many who accept it—has actually called it 'Adams'. What happens when one considers whether to accept an indicative conditional? In a famous footnote Ramsey said this:

If two people are arguing 'If A will C?' and are both in doubt as to A, they are adding A hypothetically to their stock of knowledge and arguing on that basis about C. . . . We can say they are fixing their degrees of belief in C given A. (Ramsey 1929: 143)

The core of what is going on here has been compactly stated by Gibbard, who attributes to Ramsey

the thesis that, in whatever ways the acceptability, assertability, and the like of a proposition depend on its subjective probability, the acceptability, assertability, and the like of an indicative conditional A→C depend upon the corresponding subjective conditional probability . . . (Gibbard 1981a: 253)

. . . and then he uses a formula that I shall introduce later, meaning 'the amount of credence one gives to C on the supposition of A'. The phrase 'acceptability, assertability, and the like' is deliberately open and vague; we shall later pin it down.

So the core idea is that of conditional probability: the probability one assigns to C on the supposition of A. This is what Ramsey's phrase 'degrees of belief' points to, and we shall see that the concept of conditional probability has dominated most thinking about indicative conditionals since Grice.

Gibbard, like many others, calls the Ramseyan procedure for evaluating a conditional 'the Ramsey test'. Some of us have been encouraged in this usage by thinking that in Ramsey's procedure, as one writer has put it, 'we take our stock of beliefs, add the belief that A to the stock, and see whether our new stock of beliefs contains C'. This is a *test*, all right. Drop some of that liquid into this, stir, and see whether it turns blue; drop A into your belief system, stir, and see whether you turn C. However, it gives the wrong answer for some indicative conditionals, and it does not quite capture the spirit of Ramsey's remark.

This is shown by a certain class of examples that van Fraassen (1980: 503) says were first adduced by Richmond Thomason. I might accept 'If my business partner is cheating me, I will never realize that he is'; but when I pretend to accept 'My partner is cheating me' and whatever flows from that in my belief system, I find myself also pretending to accept 'I am aware that my partner is cheating me'. So the conditional fails the quoted version of the Ramsey test, yet the conditional may be perfectly all right. What has gone wrong, obviously, is that in this case my pretended belief that I am aware that he cheats has been produced as a by-product of my thought-experimental method, and not as a result of inferring 'I believe he cheats' from 'He cheats'. So it has no bearing on the evaluation of the conditional, and we should state the Ramsey test in a way that allows for this.

The statement of it that I have criticized has been common in the literature, and I have been guilty of it myself. There have also been better versions, but I have not found any that with perfect clarity steer around the difficulty created by the Thomason examples, though Harper (1981: 5) comes close. Here is my attempt:

> To evaluate A→C, I should (1) take the set of probabilities that constitutes my present belief system, and add to it a probability = 1 for A; (2) allow this addition to influence the rest of the system in the most natural, conservative manner; and then (3) see whether what results from this includes a high probability for C.

This does not involve pretending to believe A. Rather, it is a matter of seeing what results when A is added to a certain system of assignments of probabilities to propositions. The word 'test' is not entirely inappropriate even now, and I shall retain it for old time's sake.

The Ramsey test, as well as not being a matter of pretending to believe anything, is also not a matter of considering what you *would* believe if . . . It is easy to get this wrong, and to think that the Ramsey test amounts to this: to evaluate A→C, consider what probability you would accord to C if you became certain of A. We were first warned against this by Ramsey himself (1926: 82). If it were right, according a high probability to C on the supposition of A would be—roughly speaking—being such that if one came to accept A one would also come to accept C. It is not hard to see the flaw in this. As an atheist I accord a low probability to the proposition that God exists; and my probability for *God exists* on the supposition that I have terminal cancer is equally low, of course. Yet if I came to be sure I had terminal cancer, perhaps my weakness and fear would seduce me into religious belief. If so, then what I would believe if I came to believe A is irrelevant to my probability for A→C. I shall return to this in §49.

Most theorists of conditionals accept the Ramsey test thesis for indicatives. Two dissenting voices should be mentioned.

Peter Gärdenfors has argued against a version of the thesis: he conjoined it with some assumptions about belief revision generally, and derived a contradiction. Dorothy Edgington (1995a: 73–4) has challenged one of the assumptions, namely:

> (P) If a proposition B is accepted in a given state of belief K, and A is consistent with the beliefs in K, then B is still accepted in the minimal [viz. rational] change of K needed to accept A. (Gärdenfors 1986: 82)

Gärdenfors accepts this, Edgington says, only because he is thinking only of all-or-nothing acceptance and rejection, without giving play to degrees of acceptance or subjective probability. When the latter comes in, thesis P loses its plausibility. It can easily happen that you learn something A that is consistent with your present belief state, and that this discovery brings your confidence in B from ≈ 1 to ≈ 0. I shall not pursue this matter here, but for a certain light on it see my explanation of 'monotonic' in §32. For helpful discussion, and references to more of the Gärdenfors literature, see Hansson 1992, 1995.

Levi (1996: 8–15) contends that most of us have misunderstood what Ramsey meant. This is part of a larger concern of Levi's with different things that may be going on when one reasons from premises that are supposed 'for the sake of argument'. His formidable work on this topic has defeated me. I hope my main conclusions in this book are not undercut by it.

The Ramsey test thesis does not hold for subjunctive conditionals. I think that if Yeltsin had been in control of Russia and of himself, Chechnya would have achieved independence peacefully; but for me this conditional does not pass the Ramsey test. When I take my present system of beliefs, add to it the proposition that Yeltsin was firmly in control of Russia and of himself at the time in question, and allow this to ramify through the rest of the system in the most natural and conservative manner, the result does *not* accord a high probability to 'Chechnya achieved independence peacefully'. The supposition about Yeltsin will make differences, but not that one. Rather, it will lead to changing my views about the unreliability of the media, the subtlety of the concept of control, and so on.

13. RAMSEY AND GRICE

The literature on indicative conditionals is a parade of attempts to explain why the Ramsey test is a valid criterion for their acceptability. This—the Ramsey test thesis—is not explained by the conjunction of the horseshoe analysis and Grice's theory of conversational implicature. Indeed, it conflicts with that conjunction, serving to refute it. Because the Ramsey test thesis is true, we cannot equate →

with ⊃ and explain the apparent counterexamples through conversational implicature.

The failure of match between Grice and Ramsey is not total. Both condemn the asserting of A→C *just* on the grounds that one believes C, or disbelieves A, or both, without giving much credence to C on the supposition of A. My confidence that Polynesians didn't come from India convinces me that *Polynesians originally came from India ⊃ Most Maori speak Sanskrit*, and thus, according to the horseshoe analysis, that *If Polynesians originally came from India, then most Maori speak Sanskrit*. Grice would frown on my asserting this, because I could in fewer words say something stronger, namely: *Polynesians did not originally come from India*. The Ramsey test frowns also, because the supposition that Polynesians originally came from India, when added to the rest of my belief system with suitable adjustments made, does not generate a high probability for *Most Maori speak Sanskrit*. In this case, then, Grice and Ramsey pass the same judgement.

But they do not coincide across the board, and the discrepancies all suggest that Grice's theory of conversational implicature, though shiningly true, cannot defend the horseshoe analysis against apparent counterexamples. Perhaps the earliest solid attack on this project was that of Brian Ellis (1978: 114–19); it was followed up by Frank Jackson (1979: 112–19), Brian Skyrms (1980: 83–7), and Dorothy Edgington (1986: 181–3). I shall be guided by Jackson's attack, presenting five of its highlights in my own words.

(1) If I am sure that ¬A, Gricean principles automatically proceed to frown on my asserting A→C, because I could say more in fewer words. In fact, however, it can be acceptable to assert an indicative conditional whose antecedent one is pretty sure is false. I am virtually certain that the Polynesians didn't originally come from India; but it is all right for me to think and say 'If the Polynesians did come from India, there have been inhabitants of India whose language was not Indo-European'. What makes this all right is its passing the Ramsey test: in my belief system, the consequent is highly probable on the supposition of the antecedent. Score one for the Ramsey test over the Gricean approach.

(2) Grice is also committed to saying that A→C is not very assertible by someone who is sure that C is true, because it would be more informative and less wordy for him to assert C outright; but no such thing results from the Ramsey test. Suppose I am sure that C is true, and am also sure of C given A; that means that for me A→C passes the Ramsey test. In at least some examples of this divergence Ramsey is clearly right and Grice wrong. 'I'm sure he means well by me.' 'Even if it was he who persuaded them not to promote you?' 'Even then.' This reply here means 'Even if he persuaded them not to promote me, he means well

by me'; the respondent (implicitly) says this so as to indicate that the consequent is, for him, highly probable even on the supposition of the antecedent. Ramsey takes account of this, while Grice does not, so once again Grice's approach does not do justice to the data.

If Grice's regulative principles failed to condemn something bad, a Gricean might be able to amplify them, making the theory more condemnatory. But when, as in these two objections, Gricean theory condemns something innocent, there is no rescue.

(3) Jackson's third argument against the Gricean defence of the Ramsey test amounts to the point that every logical truth is entirely uninformative, telling us nothing about the actual world, and yet some logical truths are assertible while others are not. This point has no special relevance to conditionals, and draws little blood from Gricean theory, which does not offer 'Be informative' as the whole truth about how discourse should be conducted. In my opinion, *any* theory of speech and communication must handle the assertibility of logical truths with cautious delicacy—this challenges all of us.

(4) Jackson usefully compresses some of Grice's principles into this: 'Assert the stronger instead of the weaker (when probabilities are close).' He remarks that this does not distinguish among logically equivalent sentences so far as assertibility is concerned, since they are all equally weak; yet they can differ in assertibility. He instances a pair of statements related as $\neg A \, \& \, (A \rightarrow C)$ is to $\neg A \, \& \, (A \rightarrow B)$, which are logically equivalent according to the horseshoe analysis—because each is equivalent to the shared antecedent $\neg A$—but which differ in how assertible they are. Jackson cites the examples 'The sun will come up tomorrow, but if it doesn't it won't matter' and 'The sun will come up tomorrow, but if it doesn't that will be the end of the world'. This point of Jackson's seems to be sound.

Some of the best evidence for it has to do with contraposition, that is, the relation that holds between $A \rightarrow C$ and $\neg C \rightarrow \neg A$. According to the horseshoe analysis these are strictly equivalent, because $A \supset C$ and $\neg C \supset \neg A$ are so. But it often happens that $A \rightarrow C$ is acceptable or assertible for someone for whom its contrapositive is not. I accept that *even if the Bible is divinely inspired, it is not literally true*; but I do not accept that if it is literally true, it is not divinely inspired (§59).

Grice's 'Assert the stronger' cannot explain the difference between the members of a contrapositive pair; and, although his account of conversational implicature contains other elements, none of them do—none *could*—explain how a conditional can be preferable to its contrapositive. This explanatory job, it seems clear, requires us to credit 'if' with more meaning of its own than $\supset$ has; general principles could not do it.

(5) Jackson also has an argument from classroom experience. Gricean theory offers parallel explanations for two supposed facts: that 'if' as used in indicative conditionals seems not to be truth-functional though really it is, and that the sentence-joining 'or' seems . . . etc. Students easily accept the story about 'or', Jackson remarks, whereas most of them strenuously resist the story about 'if'. This does indeed suggest that Gricean theory is less than the whole story, and that a convincing answer to 'Why does → seem not to be truth-functional?' cannot be expected from general principles, and must owe something to the meaning of → in particular.

Jackson's attack on Grice's attempt to defend the horseshoe analysis wholly succeeds, I think. Among those it converted was David Lewis. He offered a partial explanation of the validity of the Ramsey test through Gricean principles, but later said that for the test's basis he no longer looked to Grice but rather to a theory of Jackson's to which we now turn. (Lewis 1976: 142–3; 1986e: 152–4. Like Appiah (1985: 178–9), I have had to struggle to grasp how Lewis meant his explanation to work.)

3

The Material Conditional: Jackson

14. SETTING THE SCENE

Jackson also accepts the horseshoe analysis according to which → is ⊃. Or, more carefully now, he holds that the truth conditions of A→C are those of A⊃C, and what is outright asserted by someone who says one is the same as what is asserted by someone who says the other. Grice said this too, but Jackson handles the apparent counterexamples differently, giving primacy to the Ramsey test thesis (1987: 22–32).

In presenting these materials, I shall follow Jackson's use of the technical term *robust*. This word stands for a concept that is present in the Ramsey test: to say that for me Q is fairly (very) robust with respect to P is to say that I accord Q a fairly (very) high probability on the supposition that P is true. In these terms, the Ramsey test thesis says that A→C is acceptable or assertible by me to the extent that for me C is robust with respect to A.

When Jackson first launched this concept he had in mind cases where someone assigns a high probability to C as well as to C-given-A; this person's fairly confident belief in C is 'robust' because the confidence can survive his also coming to believe A (Jackson 1979: 115). In later work Jackson expressed respect for 'a more general account' in which the robustness of C with respect to A requires only a high probability for C-given-A (Jackson 1987: 22). That is what we need; the restricted version does not belong in any general account of indicative conditionals. Although 'robust' does not carry well the meaning the more general account gives it, I shall continue to use it; but I shall always be working with the more general account.

Jackson helps us to get the Ramsey test in focus by exhibiting the role of robustness in our linguistic lives generally, and not only in relation to conditionals. For example, he remarks that usually a disjunction is assertible only if it is robust with respect to the falsity of each disjunct, because disjunctions are commonly used in inferences of the form 'P or Q; not P; so Q', which are useless if one accepts the first premiss only because one rejects the second. Through an elegant example on p. 23 he shows how his approach—emphasizing the need for robustness so that certain inferences will go through—can explain facts which Gricean principles about brevity and informativeness cannot.

We mainly want indicative conditionals, Jackson says, for use in Modus Ponens—that is, arguments of the form:

$$A \rightarrow C, A \therefore C$$

—but a given instance of A→C fails for this purpose if one accepts it mainly because one rejects A or accepts C. Think of A→C as serving in Modus Ponens like a ticket for a particular rail journey: while you reject A, you are not at the place where the journey starts; while you accept C, you are already where it ends. Either way, the ticket gets you nowhere. So it suits our purposes to frown on indicative conditionals, even true ones, if their consequents are not robust with respect to their antecedents.

Robustness is needed for an indicative conditional to be acceptable, but, Jackson points out, it is not in itself sufficient (pp. 15–16). Some assertings of conditionals that pass the Ramsey test are nevertheless unsatisfactory for Gricean reasons; so the Ramsey test thesis does not make the Gricean approach irrelevant to indicative conditionals—it merely blocks it from reconciling the horseshoe analysis with all the data. Up to here, I entirely agree with Jackson.

15. CONVENTIONAL IMPLICATURE

Why does the Ramsey test hold good for indicative conditionals? Having shown that this cannot be answered through purely general principles of discourse, Jackson concludes that the test's validity must come from the meaning of 'if' as used in those conditionals. The semantic truth about the 'if' of indicatives, he holds, is not exhausted by the thesis that → is ⊃; there is more to its meaning than this. That will be warmly endorsed by those who reject the horseshoe analysis, but Jackson *accepts* that analysis: according to him, someone who asserts A→C *asserts* only A⊃C, so that if the latter is true he has spoken truly. But, he adds, the speaker also conveys to his hearers something further that he does not assert but merely implicates—suggests or signals or implies. Grice said that much; but the two disagree about the source of this further implicature or suggestion. Grice traces it to the hearers' expecting the speaker to abide by certain general rules; Jackson traces it to the conventional meaning of the indicative 'if' in particular. It is, he says, borrowing a term from Grice, a matter of '*conventional* implicature'.

This phrase names a real phenomenon. For an uncontroversial instance of it, compare these two sentences:

(1) Noam Chomsky would be a good Commencement speaker, and he is the country's most famous radical left-winger.

(2) Noam Chomsky would be a good Commencement speaker, but he is the country's most famous radical left-winger.

Each conjunction is true so long as both its conjuncts are true. They differ, however, because 2 suggests, as 1 does not, that the two conjuncts stand in some kind of contrast. (One might have to work out what contrast it is. Many of us followed Frege in thinking that '... but ...' always suggests that the first conjunct makes the second surprising, but Dummett (1973: 86) has shown this to be wrong. Someone who utters 2 may mean to contrast a good feature of a Chomsky visit with a bad one; or—thinking that Chomsky's fame would prevent his acceptance—to contrast the visit's being desirable with its being unachievable.)

Other words in our language also serve to suggest things without their being outright asserted. One such is the word 'even', according to the majority view about it. If someone says 'Bertrand Russell was an even more boldly athletic thinker than G. E. Moore', this is defective because it falsely suggests that Moore was a boldly athletic thinker (Russell was 'even more' so), but what it actually says is true, for Russell was a more boldly athletic thinker than Moore. (Not all students of 'even' take that view of it: for reasoned dissent, see Lycan 1991 and 2001. I shall return to 'even' in Chapter 17.)

So we can distinguish what is said from what is more weakly implied; and if a speaker implies something false, we characterize his statement not as false but as infelicitous, potentially misleading, or the like. Grice has called our attention to things that an assertion may weakly imply because of general principles of discourse—these are *conversational* implicatures. Now we encounter weak implications arising from special facts about the conventional meanings of individual words such as 'but', 'even', 'although' and so on—these are *conventional* implicatures.

How do we decide that the two Chomsky sentences have the same assertive force? If in 2 you do not see any significant contrast between the conjuncts, you will find 2 inappropriate or misleading, but you should not call it false unless you reject one of the conjuncts. Or so I say, but on what evidence? What *shows* that the contrastive element in the meaning of 'but' is a matter of implication rather than outright assertion? When a Gricean theorist declares a given utterance to be false in what it *conversationally* implicates but not in what it outright says, he sometimes has a firm, structural answer to the question: 'On what basis do you decide that the communicated falsehood is only implied and not said?' He can reply:

> If you assert something false, the falsehood comes from a relation between reality and the sentence you have uttered; it depends strictly on what *that one sentence* means. But when I say that the utterance of an indicative conditional involves falsehood by way of conversational implicature rather than assertion, that is because there falsehood enters the picture only through certain *general principles* to which the speaker is taken to be subject.

This is clear-cut and objective. Now return to my question about 'but'. The obvious basis for maintaining that 'She was poor but honest' is defective only in what it implies, not in what it says, is the fact that the most natural dissent would not be 'That is not true' but rather 'You may be right that she was poor and honest, but I wouldn't put it the way you did'. Similarly with sentences that do not have truth values—questions, for example. I might ask 'Did John make a donation?' or 'Even John made a donation, did he?'; each asks the same question though the latter insinuates something that the former does not.

These intuitive responses, which Jackson acknowledges to be the only evidence for judgements about conventional implicature (1981: 133; 1987: 40–1), are a fragile basis for theoretically distinguishing assertion from conventional implicature (§106). That the distinction *is* a matter of theory is shown by the fact that one theorist has questioned it (Appiah 1985: 190–1). But Jackson puts it beyond serious question, in my opinion, in the convincing fifth chapter of his 1987 book, where he explains why we should have conventional implicature at all—what role it plays in our linguistic lives. This chapter establishes that conventional implicature does exist and that the standard account of it describes it correctly.

In discourse, says Jackson, we primarily aim to affect one another's beliefs; the asserted content of what someone utters fixes the belief she wants to communicate, and conventional implications can help her to achieve this by removing obstacles:

> If I say 'Hugo is bad at mathematics; nevertheless, he is a fine chess player', what I want you to believe is that Hugo is a fine chess player, not something else. The role of 'nevertheless' is to guard against your refusing to accept my word because you think I am ignorant of the general, but not universal, connection between ability at mathematics and at chess, or even perhaps your thinking that I am in the process of revamping my system of beliefs. (Jackson 1987: 94)

What belief I want to communicate determines what I outright say or assert, according to Jackson; and what my statement conventionally implies or signals helps me to get this belief across smoothly and without needless fuss. This is in the spirit of Locke, who wrote that two of the three 'ends of language in our discourse with others' are: 'First, to make known one man's thoughts or ideas to another. Secondly, to do it with as much ease and quickness as is possible' (*Essay Concerning Human Understanding* III.x.23).

These ideas of Jackson's help to round out and solidify our notion of conventional implicature. Let us now see whether it helps Jackson in his use of that concept to explain why the Ramsey test holds for indicative conditionals.

(Jackson says that 'but' is governed by a special rule of *assertibility*, against which Woods (1997: 61n) made the point that there is more to it than that. The special flavour of 'but' is at work in 'If she was born in Turin, but left when she was three, she doesn't know Italy well', though the clause containing it is not asserted. Apparently unlike Woods and Edgington (1997a: 103–4), I do not see this as greatly harming Jackson's basic position, but a related point by Read (1992: 11–12) has power. Kent Bach (1999) emphasizes the behaviour of 'but' and its kin in indirect quotation ('He said that she was poor but honest') in an attack on the entire category of conventional implicature. The attack, though considerable, does not convince me that my dissent from Jackson should start earlier than it does.)

16. THE CASE AGAINST JACKSON'S THEORY

When someone asserts A→C, Jackson maintains, he *says* only that A⊃C but he *implies* that for him C is robust with respect to A. This is a conventional implicature, he contends, belonging to the class of phenomena he describes so well in his fifth chapter. Speaking of the parallel between how A→C relates to A⊃C and how 'but' relates to 'and', Jackson says that 'the parallel . . . is intended to be exact' (1987: 9, 37).

He needs it to be exact. We have asked what connects indicative conditionals with the Ramsey test. What fact *about* them makes it the case that A→C is satisfactory only for someone for whom the probability of C given A is high? Jackson answers that the two are linked by the meanings of the conditionals. The Ramsey test need not be deduced from general principles: it sits there, in a lump, in the meanings of the conditionals for whose assertibility it is a valid test. Jackson's explanation of *how* it sits there brings in a concept of conventional implicature for which he offers a general theory. Without the latter, his account of how indicative conditionals come to have the Ramseyan property would be empty, or at least ad hoc and unexplanatory. So he really needs there to be an 'exact' or at least a close parallel between his treatments of 'if' and of the likes of 'but' and 'even'.

Jackson does acknowledge one awkwardness of fit, though he does not describe it as such (pp. 38–9). With each of his other examples of conventional implicature, he acknowledges, what a speaker conventionally implies may be true even if what she asserts is improbable: 'Even my cousin could easily beat Jimmy Connors at tennis'; 'Wittgenstein was not a deep thinker; however, he had a strong influence on thinkers who knew him well'. These are unassertible by me, because I regard each as false; but they satisfy the special 'conventional implicature' requirements that they involve: my cousin is a duffer at tennis, so that 'even my cousin' is apt; those who influence other thinkers tend to be deep thinkers themselves, so 'however . . .' is apt. In contrast with this, Jackson acknowledges, the Ramsey test gives 'the whole story' about the assertibility of A→C: such a conditional cannot pass the test but be unassertible on grounds of improbability or falsehood. Jackson calls this 'an unusual property' of the Ramsey test, an 'exception' to what 'usually' happens with conventional implicature.

I shall now describe four other ways in which Jackson's account of conventional implicature as the source of the Ramsey test's validity fails to fit his account of conventional implicature generally. The resulting quintet—his one and my four—undermines his theory of indicative conditionals.

(1) Jackson explains conventional implicature as helping a speaker to get truths to glide smoothly into people's souls, but the supposed Ramseyan conventional implicature of A→C cannot be doing that. If it were, the following would be right:

> When I tell you 'If (A) Nixon's top aides were not blackmailing him into defending them, then (C) he gave them more loyalty than they deserved', I signal to you that my probability for C on the supposition of A is high. I signal this to you, choosing words that conventionally imply it, because this may help me to get across the belief I am primarily trying to communicate, namely that *either Nixon's top aides were blackmailing him into defending them or he gave them more loyalty than they deserved*. The conventionally implied robustness will improve your chances of acquiring precisely this belief rather than being distracted by irrelevant side-issues.

What irrelevant side-issues? What are the threatening distractions, and how does the implication of robustness remove them? I can find no answer to this. The above story is wholly incredible; yet it needs to be true if A→C is to relate to

A⊃C as 'but' does to 'and'. Jackson illustrates his thesis about the transfer of belief with examples using 'even' and 'nevertheless' but not with any using 'if'.

David Lewis, aiming to present Jackson's ideas on this topic, offered a more complex and believable story about the point of implying that for the speaker C is robust with respect to A. It does not, however, concern the removal of obstacles to getting the hearer to believe A⊃C. In his account, the speaker disbelieves A, believes C, and asserts A→C because he wants the hearer to accept C even if he, unlike the speaker, believes A:

Maybe you (or I in future) know something that now seems to me improbable. I would like to say . . . something that will not need to be given up, that will remain useful, even if a certain hypothesis that I now take to be improbable should turn out to be the case. If I say something that I would continue to believe even if I should learn that the improbable hypothesis is true, then that will be something that I think you can take my word for even if you already believe the hypothesis. (Lewis 1986e: 153)

In confining himself to cases where the person who asserts A→C believes C and disbelieves A, Lewis doubly narrowed the range. Also, his account does not concern getting the hearer to acquire the belief one supposedly wants him to acquire, namely that A⊃C. Lewis's account bears little resemblance to Jackson's comparison of ⊃/→ with 'and'/'but', being concerned rather with the durability of the belief in various vicissitudes. It is a good story; but it leads away from Jackson and towards the theory of Adams that I shall come to in Chapters 6–7.

Something like this also occurs in Jackson 1981: 135. Having recounted how 'but', 'even', and the rest help the hearer to absorb the speaker's message, Jackson moves on to a Lewis-like story about the point of the implication of robustness of an indicative conditional. He does not note how greatly it differs from what has gone before, and merely introduces it as 'a second example of the problems attendant on an apparently simple speaker-hearer exchange'.

(2) The misfit shows up also in a formal way. In his fifth chapter Jackson mentions these vehicles of conventional implicatures: 'but', 'nevertheless', 'yet', 'anyhow', 'however'. In the relevant senses of these, the following holds for each:

When W links two sentences, it can be replaced by 'and' without affecting the truth conditions of what is asserted; when used as an operator on a single sentence, it can be deleted without affecting the truth conditions of what is asserted.

Because a sentence-joining 'and' can always be deleted in favour of a full-stop, without affecting the truth conditions, it follows that each of those five words can be dropped without altering the asserted content. Jackson's only other example in his fifth chapter is 'even'. When used in the relevant sense, that too can be deleted, as can his two earlier examples (p. 49), namely 'anyway' and 'at least' as used in 'He is a communist, or at least left-wing'. All of Jackson's examples are deletable: each can be simply omitted (perhaps with a little repunctuation) without affecting what is asserted. Nothing like that holds for 'if'. In indicative conditionals, as everywhere else, 'if' is structural: delete it at your peril! 'If' is not alone in this, Jackson has written to me, because it holds also for 'unless'. I am not persuaded by this defence, which relies on Jackson's associating 'unless' with conventional implicature in the same kind of way that he associates 'if' with it. 'P unless Q' conventionally means the same as 'not-Q ⊃ P', he holds, and conventionally implicates that for the speaker P is robust with respect to not-Q. (Thus, I am not to say 'I'll be miserable unless she kisses me' purely because I am sure she will kiss me.) I reply that the awkwardness of fit between Jackson's account of 'if' and his chapter 5 account of conventional implicature applies equally to 'unless' on this view of the latter.

(3) In his general account of conventional implicature, but before offering to apply it to indicative conditionals, Jackson asks '. . . why tone, why conventional implicature?' (p. 91), and speaks of '. . . the words that are responsible for conventional implicatures, that carry tone . . .' (p. 93). Dummett brought the word 'tone' into this, replacing words of Frege's that mean 'colouring' and 'illumination' (1973: 2, 83–8). It fits some of his examples—'dead' and 'deceased', 'sweat' and 'perspiration'—and countless others, such as 'defecate' and 'shit', 'intellectually challenged' and 'mentally retarded', and so on. These do perhaps involve a difference in what is implied or suggested, but that is not the heart of them; and Jackson was right to ignore them in his account of conventional implicature. As for 'but', 'although', 'even', and the others that he does mention, 'tone' is a less apt label for what they add to the asserted content, but it is still a possible one. If someone said 'Even teaching assistants don't get paid a million dollars a year', it would not be absurd to remark that he had said something true with a wrong tone (because of its implication that TAs are notably well paid). In contrast with this, when a materially true conditional fails the Ramsey test, as when someone says 'If snow did not fall on Mount Rainier last year, the US national debt was halved', the diagnosis 'True assertion, wrong tone' misses the mark.

(4) When a true assertion conventionally implies something false, how should we characterize this? In the context of his theory of indicative conditionals, Jackson repeatedly implies that in such a case the assertion is not 'justified or warranted', explaining that he means epistemic rather than pragmatic justification (pp. 8–10). An assertion may be pragmatically unjustified because pointlessly hurtful or in breach of a promise, or the like, to all of which the Ramsey test is irrelevant. The test does involve something like epistemic justification, as

Jackson says, but what does the latter have to do with 'but', 'even', 'although', and the rest, and with Jackson's general theory of conventional implicature? Nothing, so far as I can see, though Jackson evidently thinks otherwise. In claiming to be employing a single concept of implicature or signalling, he implies that 'He wasn't educated at Eton but he is a civilized human being' is defective because not epistemically justified. This strikes me as untenable. When Jackson uses the phrase 'epistemic and semantic considerations, *widely construed*' (p. 19, my emphasis), he may be countering this difficulty by backing off from linking 'but' and 'even' etc. with epistemic justification ordinarily construed. But he does not tell us *how* he means to widen the construal. This point connects with an objection that Edgington (1986: 186) brings against both Jackson's theory and Grice's, namely that they purport to explain the *assertibility* of something when their topic ought to be its *acceptability* or *believability*. She writes elsewhere: 'There simply is no evidence that one *believes* a conditional whenever one believes the corresponding material implication, and then is prepared to *assert* it only if some further condition is satisfied' (see also 1995*b*: 287 n. 50). Actually, Jackson knew that 'assertibility' is wrong quite early in the piece: 'It is, indeed, better labelled "assentability"—but it is too late to change now' (Jackson 1984: 72).

In five ways, then, Jackson's general account of conventional implicature misfits his application of that concept to indicative conditionals. The last two failures may not matter much; but the first three—Jackson's own and my 1 and 2—are structural, serious, and in my view fatal. A sixth will be presented in §39.

17. THE UNITY POINT

At one place Jackson hedges his claims for his account of conventional implicature. Having asked 'Why tone, why conventional implicature?', he writes: 'Perhaps it is wrong to expect the answer to be the same for each example, but, in many cases at least, it seems that the reason . . .'—which launches him into his general theory of conventional implicature (p. 91). This is cautious; it creates wiggle room. Perhaps Jackson means to allow that indicative conditionals may not be among the 'many cases', and may thus not fall under his general theory. If so, one wonders why a book entitled *Conditionals* should devote a chapter to an account of conventional implicature that applies to some parts of language but not to conditionals.

A little later, Jackson seems poised to confront the problem. Right after completing his (general?) account of conventional implicature, he writes: 'We now have answers to why conventional implicature exists in natural languages . . .

and to why it affects meaning without affecting content . . . But why did we need to turn to conventional implicature . . . in our . . . theory?' (1987: 95–6). Put like that, it is a good question, but Jackson does not put it just like that. More fully, he asks: 'Why did we need to turn to conventional implicature, *rather than conversational*, in our . . . theory?' (my emphasis). Instead of considering for the first time how conventional implicature succeeds in explaining how indicatives work, he considers for the second time why conversational implicature fails in this. The earlier point that the Gricean approach must accept Contraposition for indicative conditionals, that is, must regard ¬C→¬A as being no less assertible than A→C (§10, argument 4), now becomes the point that the Gricean approach must endorse not only Modus Ponens:

A→C, A ∴ C

but also Modus Tollens:

A→C, ¬C ∴ ¬A.

It is a sharp point against Grice; perhaps it deserves to be presented twice in these two guises. But it serves here merely to displace the question Jackson should be asking: '*Did* we really "turn to conventional implicature" as this has just been described?' I answer, No, we did not.

Why did Jackson come at things in this way? Given the story as I have told it, one might think:

Jackson rightly says that the Ramsey test is valid because of the meaning of 'if' as used in indicative conditionals. He ran into trouble because of *where* in the meaning of 'if' he located the Ramseyan element. If he had put it into the core of asserted content, rather than the conventionally implied penumbra, he would have escaped the troubles exhibited here.

I agree with this, but the matter is tricky. As we shall see in chapter 6, the two most obvious ways of building the Ramseyan property of indicative conditionals into their conventional meaning are demonstrably wrong. The right way to do it is somewhat elusive, and still a matter of controversy. So Jackson had reason to want conventional implicature to provide him with a solution.

18. THE OR-TO-IF INFERENCE

The horseshoe analysis of → should be rejected, because of the failure of the only two attempts (it seems) that can be made to reconcile it with the intuitive data. Before finally turning away from it, we should revisit the or-to-if inference (§9) in order to see how feebly it supports the analysis. The attempt to get support from it went like this:

> You believed Vladimir when he told you 'Either they drew or it was a win for white'; which made it all right for you to tell Natalya 'If they didn't draw, it was a win for white'. Why was this all right? The explanation is that what Vladimir told you entailed what you told Natalya, because quite generally PvQ entails $\neg P \rightarrow Q$.

If this is right, then $A \supset C$ entails $A \rightarrow C$, which secures the horseshoe analysis.

Considered as support for the horseshoe analysis, this fails twice: the analysis is not needed, and does not suffice, to explain why it was all right for you to say what you did to Natalya.

Here is why it is not needed. Vladimir was behaving badly unless he was more confident of the disjunction than of either disjunct; and Grice's theory about con-versational implicature explains why (§9). If he was not misbehaving, therefore, he accepted the disjunction independently of whether one disjunct (either one) turned out to be false; so for him Q is robust with respect to $\neg P$. That would make it all right by the Ramsey test for him to assert $\neg P \rightarrow Q$; and your trust in him makes it all right for you to assert this also. This explanation has nothing to do with the horseshoe analysis. It is given by Stalnaker (1975), who calls the trans-action a 'reasonable inference' of one assertion from another, not the entailment of one proposition by another. In §58 we shall see that the or-to-if inference can also be explained in another way.

Anyway, whether or not some rival to the horseshoe analysis *does* explain the acceptability of the or-to-if inference, the analysis itself *does not*. It contributes only the thesis that PvQ entails $\neg P \rightarrow Q$, and thus that the *truth* of what Vladimir told you guarantees the *truth* of what you told Natalya. But it is a famous fact that a true material conditional may be an absurd thing to say; so this entailment thesis does not imply or explain the fact that if you *accepted* what Vladimir told you, then it was *all right for you to say* what you did to Natalya.

The or-to-if inference haunts the literature on indicative conditionals. In §41 we shall see a valid special case of it being used in a powerful argument for a sig-nificant conclusion.

4

The Equation

19. OTHER APPROACHES

The horseshoe analysis having failed, we must look further. Four other avenues of approach to indicative conditionals have been proposed.

One is indicated by the view, attributed to Strawson in §11, that A→C means something like:

Because of a connection between A and C: A⊃C.

This arises from the natural thought that the horseshoe analysis fails because it does not provide for a link between A and C. It certainly *is* defective; A→C may entail A⊃C but is not entailed by it. However, although it is plausible to suppose that the missing ingredient is the idea of A's being connected with C, there are obstacles in the way of developing this into something solid. For one thing, many respectable indicative conditionals involve no such link. Not just jokes like 'If he repays that debt, I'm a monkey's uncle', but sober conditionals like 'If she apologized to him, then he lied to me', which would not ordinarily be based on a view about a direct link between her apology and his lie (§133); and ones like '(Even) if he apologizes, I shall (still) be angry', which rests on the *lack* of connection between his apology and my anger. Unsurprisingly, nobody has worked hard on trying to turn this 'connection' idea into a semantic analysis of indicative conditionals.

A second avenue of approach is lined with possible worlds. These have enjoyed much success in analyses of subjunctive conditionals (Chapters 10–13); so it is natural to hope that they can also cope with indicatives, through the idea that A→C means that C obtains at a certain possible world at which A obtains. This hope is encouraged not only by a desire for theoretical economy, but also by the hope for a Y-shaped analysis of conditionals—one that first sets out what the two kinds of conditional have in common and then goes on to say what differentiates them (§4). Wayne Davis and Robert Stalnaker have both approached indicative conditionals in this second way; this might be a natural place to discuss those endeavours, but for reasons that will appear I choose to postpone them until §§138–9.

A third avenue has been explored by William Lycan (2001). I shall say what I have to say about it in §37 and §84.

The fourth avenue leads, I believe, to the truth about indicative conditionals. It starts from the Ramsey-test thesis that the assertibility or acceptability of A→C for a person at a time is governed by the probability the person then assigns to C on the supposition of A. Jackson used this to marshal facts about usage that are not explained by the horseshoe analysis aided by Gricean conversational implicature. It served that negative purpose well, but with the right soil and climate it can grow into a positive theory.

First, we should focus on acceptability rather than assertibility. They are linked, because you ought not to assert what you do not accept; but still they are different, and acceptability is the concept we need. If I do not think that C is probable given A, I ought not even to *think* A→C let alone to assert it. So we should attend to the Ramsey test thesis considered as saying that A→C is *acceptable* by you in proportion as your probability for C on the supposition of A is high.

Perhaps acceptability is just subjective probability: for something to be acceptable by you is for you to find it probable. If not, then at least we can agree that acceptability depends upon probability and nothing else: you ought not to accept what you do not find probable, and there is no obstacle to your accepting what you do find probable. So we can move to the thesis that the *probability* for you of A→C is proportional to your probability for C on the supposition of A.

20. KINDS OF PROBABILITY

Before moving further into conditionals, I should provide a setting for the Ramsey test by distinguishing different kinds of probability. This will be routine stuff, probably bringing you no news; but I choose to play safe by laying it out explicitly.

Objective probabilities hold independently of what anybody thinks about them. They divide into two kinds.

Absolute: This kind attaches to a single proposition, considered in itself; the proposition's absolute probability is often called its 'chance' of being true. If determinism holds, then the objective absolute probability of any proposition at any time is either 0 or 1. (Or so it is often and plausibly said, but Loewer (2001) disagrees. He holds that a deterministic theory of statistical mechanics makes room for intermediate probabilities that are not merely subjective. His arguments take me out of my depth.) If on the other hand some basic laws of physics are probabilistic, then there are objective chances between those extremes; it may be an objective, absolute, fundamental fact about the proposition that *this atom will decay during the next seven years* (referring to a particular atom) that it has a 50 per cent chance of being true. If such chances also show up on the macroscopic scale, there may be such a thing as the objective, absolute chance that exactly two branches will fall from my trees during the next million seconds, or that more water will flow through the Grand Canyon in 2009 than did in 1987. A statement about *objective* absolute probability has the form $R_3(P,t,n)$, with triadic R_3 relating proposition P to a time t and to a number n (or other measure of probability); it says what probability of truth P has at that time. If P concerns a time earlier than T, then the probability of P at T is either 0 or 1; intermediate objective probabilities all concern the future.

Relative: Even if determinism is true and there are no non-extreme objective chances, there are objective facts about what probability a proposition has relative to certain others—for example, about what probability a body of evidence confers on an hypothesis. These are reportable in statements of the form: 'Given Q, the probability of P's being true is . . .'. It is objective, but whereas chance is absolute, this is relative; it accords P a probability relative to Q. Given that he will fairly deal seven cards from a normal pack, the probability that he will deal at least one ace is 0.538. A statement about *relative* objective probability has the form $R_3(P,Q,n)$, relating proposition P to a second proposition Q and to a measure of probability. The mention of time ('t') drops out because true propositions of this kind are logically or causally necessary, and so do not change truth values over time.

Often enough we will speak of Q's being made probable by . . . and then we express only a part of the total P relative to which Q is probable. 'Given that he will deal seven cards from a normal pack, the probability that he will deal at least one ace is 0.538', with nothing said about the fairness of the deal; or 'Given that he will fairly deal seven cards from this pack, the probability that he will deal at least one ace is 0.538', with nothing said about the pack's being normal. Taking such statements just as they stand, we judge them to be neither causally nor logically necessary; but nor, taken just as they stand, are they true. They are stand-ins for something that is true (and, indeed, necessary), the remainder of their antecedents being supplied by the charitable hearer or reader.

Subjective probabilities are people's degrees of belief. A subjective *absolute* probability of a proposition P is some person's degree of belief in P's truth at a particular time. A statement about P's subjective absolute probability has the form $R_4(P,x,t,n)$, which relates P to a person x, a time t, and a number n. Even if there are no objective chances between 0 and 1, their subjective counterparts will exist so long as people are uncertain. A subjective *relative* probability is the probability or belief level that someone accords to P on the supposition that some other proposition Q is true. The basic form of a statement about P's subjective relative probability has the form $R_5(P,Q,x,t,n)$, which relates P to a second proposition Q and to a person x, a time t, and a number n. Here we retain the mention of time ('t') because the subjective relation between one proposition and another depends upon the person's intellectual frame of mind, which can change.

Isn't this madly unrealistic? How often are we in a position to express our levels of credence in numbers? 'Are you sure they will make the film?' 'No, one cannot be *sure* of such a thing; but I give it a probability of 0.827.' Absurd! Even such approximate values as 'about 0.3' and 'somewhere near 0.6' have little place in our everyday subjective probabilities. We can realistically assign 0 (or 1) to something we know for sure to be false (or to be true); but apart from those two termini, and apart from the contrived set-ups of betting on cards or the like, we have little use for the numerical apparatus. Yet the formal, numerical idea of probability informs many of our thought processes. The formal logic of probability (§21) needs to be able to handle probabilities arithmetically, working on the assumption that they all have numerical values; and this logic is normative for us all—it implies things that *do* apply directly to our actual ways of thinking. Without being able to assign precise numbers to our levels of credence, we have thoughts of the forms:

> I have more faith in P's truth than in Q's.
> P now strikes me as more likely than it did a week ago.
> I am almost entirely sure that P is true (≈ 1).
> The more likely P is, the less likely Q is.

These and their like are familiar elements in the life of the mind; and in a rational mind they will be governed by the principles of probability logic.

Of these everyday thoughts involving probability, the kind that will chiefly concern us is (subjective) relative probability. I imagine you don't think either of these is likely:

> Public: Not later than the year 2084, public executions will be common in the United Kingdom.

> Fascism: Some time in the twenty-first century, an outright fascist government will come into power in the UK.

But I am sure that your (subjective) probability for *Public given Fascism*, or *Public on the assumption of Fascism*, is higher than your (subjective, absolute) probability for Public.

Your probability for Public is absolute—not a probabilifying relation between some other proposition and Public. You do base it on other propositions that you accept, and if you are thinking impeccably it is equivalent to your relative probability for *Public given everything else you believe*. Still, it is not itself a relative probability. Your thought in assigning it has the form 'It is not likely that . . .' and not the form 'The evidence that I have does not support . . .'. Similarly, if you say 'It will probably rain tonight' your topic is rain, not evidence.

21. ELEMENTS OF PROBABILITY LOGIC

I shall now expound some elements of probability logic. A knowledge of them will be needed at certain points in the next five chapters, and we should prepare for it now. Even if you dislike logic and shrink from symbols, it will be worth your while to go patiently through this material. There is little of it; it is not formidable; and it could vivify what is to follow. Throughout these chapters, I use the form 'P(x)' to name the probability—objective or subjective—of x.

We start with three axioms:

(1) If Q is logically equivalent to R, P(Q) = P(R).
(2) If Q is inconsistent with R, then P(QvR) = P(Q) + P(R).
(3) If Q is necessarily true, then P(Q) = 1.

(Alan Hájek reminds me that P must be understood as a function, so that it cannot assign different values to the same proposition; and that we should somehow secure that no probability lies outside the interval from 0 to 1.) A little reflection shows these axioms to be reasonable when understood in terms of objective probability or the subjective probabilities of an idealized thinker.

These axioms require us to pair ¬(A&¬A) with 1, to pair A with 0 if ¬A is absolutely necessary, to pair *It is not the case that sea-water is usually salty* with 0.93 if we pair *Sea-water is usually salty* with 0.07. And so on.

The 'idealized thinker' to whom I have referred does not represent a humanly achievable ideal. Mark Lance, in warning me about this, gives a good example:

Consider the claim that *if the position on the chess board is P and the rules of chess R, then S: white has a winning strategy*. Say P is the position, R are the rules, and white does have a winning strategy. Then since chess is a finite determinate game, P&R entails S. But there are many such P and R where the winning strategy is unknown and indeed, in which, given our best understanding of chess theory, we are led to think the position drawn.

The fact remains that someone who assigns a probability < 1 to what is in fact a necessary truth thereby makes a mistake. My idealized thinker is simply someone who knows all the logical truths and makes no logical mistakes.

Of the theorems derivable from axioms 1–3, I shall present seven, numbered 4–10. Of these, 7 and 10 will be prominent in Chapter 9; the others are needed to prove those two.

Because $Qv\neg Q$ is a necessary proposition, we get

(4) $P(Qv\neg Q) = 1$ (from 3).

This, combined with axiom 2, tells us that if $P(Q) = 0.7$ then $P(\neg Q) = 0.3$, and quite generally that

(5) $P(Q) = 1 - P(\neg Q)$.

Because $Q\&R$ is inconsistent with $Q\&\neg R$, we get

(6) $P((Q\&R) \lor (Q\&\neg R)) = P(Q\&R) + P(Q\&\neg R)$ (from 2).

Because $(Q\&R \lor Q\&\neg R)$ is logically equivalent to Q, and so (by 1) has the same probability as Q, we get the Addition Theorem:

(7) $P(Q) = P(Q\&R) + P(Q\&\neg R)$ (from 6).

This says that the probability of Q's being true is the probability of its being true while R is also true plus the probability of its being true while R is false. This obvious truth is important, as we shall see.

Hartry Field has warned me that (7) the Addition Theorem fails if the Law of Excluded Middle fails. If it can happen that neither R nor $\neg R$ is true, then the probability of Q will be equal to $P(Q\&R) + P(Q\&\neg R) + P(Q \& \text{Neither-R-nor-}\neg R)$. I believe that all my uses of 7 could be reconstructed so as to survive the denial of the law of excluded middle; but this is only a guess, and I am not competent to put it to the test.

Continuing: if Q entails R, then Q is inconsistent with $\neg R$; and so we get

(8) If Q entails R, then $P(Qv\neg R) = P(Q) + P(\neg R)$ (by 2),

from which it follows that

(9) If Q entails R, then $P(Qv\neg R) = P(Q) + 1 - P(R)$ (by 5).

Now suppose that Q entails R and that $P(Q) > P(R)$. Then it follows (by 9) that $P(Qv\neg R)$ is equal to *P(Q) plus 1 minus something smaller than P(Q)*, which means that $P(Qv\neg R) > 1$. But no probability can be > 1; this upshot is absurd. What led to it, namely the supposition that $P(Q) > P(R)$, must be false. So we get:

(10) If Q entails R, then $P(Q) \leq P(R)$.

Considered as a thesis about subjective probability, 10 might be false of an individual person. Someone might be thick-headed enough to be more sure that Smith is a cannibal than that he is a carnivore, not realizing that being a cannibal entails being a carnivore. But a probability *logic* is normative: it sets constraints on how people's degrees of closeness to certainty should behave and combine, as do the laws of ordinary logic and arithmetic. When Dummkopf grasps that being a cannibal entails being a carnivore, he *ought* to stop being more sure of Smith's being a cannibal than he is of his being carnivorous. This is the spirit in which we must understand all the axioms and theorems. (Thus, to someone who has no ideas about what probability to assign to Q, which entails R, theorem 10 says: 'If you do arrive at an opinion about Q, you had better not accord it a higher probability than you give at that time to R.')

Other parts of the foregoing fragment of probability logic can also be normative for a thinker whose probabilities are not expressible in precise numbers. The Addition Theorem, for instance, passes judgement on anyone who is almost certain of P while giving low probabilities to P&Q and to P&¬Q.

22. THE RATIO FORMULA

That fragment of probability logic concerns only absolute probabilities, whether objective or subjective; I have not yet presented any logic of relative probabilities—or, as I shall henceforth call them, *conditional* probabilities—though these will be our chief concern. In discussing them we need a shorthand for 'the probability of C given A'. I shall express this by $\pi(C/A)$, which can be pronounced pi-C-on-A. In this notation, $\pi(\ /\ )$ is a binary operator on two propositions, C and A. Do not slip into reading π as a singulary operator on a proposition C/A, for there is no such proposition. Some writers use P( ) for unconditional and P(/) for conditional probability, but I join with those who think it safer to have a greater notational difference. In quoting others I shall silently bring their usage in line with mine.

How should subjective conditional probability be explained? You might think: 'Subjective relative probability is simply what someone believes about objective relative probability. Explain the latter, and the former will fall into place.' Not so! Consider a geographer who, as evidence accumulates, becomes ever more confident that *the Ross ice shelf will lose at least half of its surface area by 2025*; his subjective probability for—or degree of credence in—that proposition has grown steadily for the past decade. Throughout this time, he has firmly believed that the objective probability of the shrinkage proposition is either 1 or 0, this being a belief that is not responsive to evidence, because it comes straight from his meteorological determinism. Similarly with subjective conditional probability, which is not a firm opinion about an objective conditional probability, but rather a degree of credence accorded to one proposition on the supposition of another.

You can explore your value for $\pi(C/A)$ through the Ramsey test (§12). According to this, your value of $\pi(C/A)$ is high to the extent that the result of adding $P(A) = 1$ to your system of beliefs, and adjusting conservatively to make room for it, generates a high value for $P(C)$.

Thus understood, conditional *probabilities* are properly so called, because they can be proved to conform to the logic of unconditional probabilities, and for other reasons. For a helpful development of this point, see Edgington 1996: 620–3. Responding to an ill-aimed attack, Edgington writes memorably: 'Like any technical notion in logic, mathematics, science or philosophy, you come best to understand [conditional probability] by working with it, not by reading about it' (p. 618). When you work with it, you find that it really is probability properly so called.

The most useful bridge between conditional and absolute probabilities is a formula that has been known and employed for more than two centuries, but which seems to have no standard name. I adopt the name Hájek gives it (forthcoming):

the Ratio Formula: $\pi(C/A) = P(A\&C) \div P(A)$,

subject to a proviso which I shall explain at the start of §23. Throughout this book, I use the form 'n ÷ m', which strictly names an arithmetical procedure, as though it named the fraction resulting from the procedure. The reason is aesthetic.

According to the Ratio Formula, the probability of C given A is the probability of A&C divided by the probability of A—it is not an unconditional probability, but rather a ratio of two such probabilities. This view was presented by Ramsey (1926: 82). I learn from Edgington (1995*b*: 262) that it was presented by Bayes and then by Laplace in the eighteenth century.

We are, as I have noted, hardly ever in a position to express our subjective probabilities in numerical terms, and few of my uses of the Ratio Formula will require me to do so. Its real thrust is its implication that $\pi(C/A)$ is large in proportion as $P(A\&C)$ is large and in proportion as $P(A)$ is small.

Let us pause to see intuitively why this looks true. For a reasonable person like you, $P(A\&C)$ cannot be higher than $P(A)$—you will not regard A&C as more likely to be true than A is. Now let us consider three cases.

Suppose $P(A\&C)$ is only slightly lower than $P(A)$, and look at the two sides of the Formula on that basis. On the left: your regarding A&C as almost as probable as A is means that you think A's truth is likely to bring C's truth with it, or to leave C's truth standing, which means that for you $\pi(C/A)$, as understood through the Ramsey test, is close to 1. On the right: a certain number, namely P(A&C), is divided by something nearly as great as it is, namely P(A), the result being close to 1.

Now suppose that P(A&C) is much lower than P(A), and look again at the Formula. On the left, $\pi(C/A)$ as understood through the Ramsey test comes out as having a low value, and so does the division on the right.

If we try it out again for the case where P(A&C) = P(A), it is easy to see that we get the value 1 on the left and on the right. The Ratio Formula looks right, does it not? For a more rigorous and grounded defence of it, see Edgington 1997a: 108–9.

I do not offer the Ratio Formula as *defining* conditional probability, for it does not. The best definition we have is the one provided by the Ramsey test: your conditional probability for C given A is the probability for C that results from adding P(A) = 1 to your belief system and conservatively adjusting to make room for it.

Given that in the Ratio Formula the right-hand side does not define the left, one would not predict that it is always one's route to the left; and clearly it is not. A person's value for $\pi(C/A)$ can often not be estimated by finding her values for P(A&C) and P(A) and dividing one by the other. Ellis, Edgington, and Mellor have all presented convincing cases of someone's having a value for $\pi(C/A)$ but none for P(A&C).

Indeed, to arrive at a value for P(A&C) one often has to proceed *through* a value for $\pi(C/A)$ or for $\pi(A/C)$, which means that we cannot use the right-hand side of the Ratio Formula to calculate the left (thus Blackburn 1986: 227–8). A better guide to evaluation is given by something which, though arithmetically equivalent to the Ratio Formula, starts in a different place. I shall call it the Multiplying Variant of the Ratio Formula:

MVRF: $P(A\&C) = \pi(C/A) \times P(A)$.

This will come to the fore in §25. In the meantime, we shall employ the Ratio Formula—not as an analysis or definition or procedural guide, just as a truth.

Hájek (forthcoming) argues fiercely and lavishly against the Ratio Formula. His arguments, however, do not cast doubt on any of my dealings with it. (These include my approval of its use in various technical bits of work, including the beautiful arguments of Hájek 1994 and 1989, which I shall expound in §28 and §31 respectively.) I now explain why that is so.

In his new paper Hájek relies upon examples of four kinds. Two involve probabilities of zero and infinitesimal probabilities respectively, and concern things like a mathematically continuous surface at which an infinitely fine dart is thrown. The probability that the dart will land on a given point on the surface is smaller than any assignable fraction, so that although such a landing is possible its occurrence has a probability that is either zero or infinitesimal (your choice). I contend that no such theoretical possibility could have any bearing on our lives; we could not possibly have a practical use for the notion of a *point* on a physical surface. If you think otherwise, try to take an infinitely less bold step: try to think of having a practical use for the difference, on a physical surface, between two regions which differed only at the 99th decimal place when measured in square centimetres.

The third of Hájek's four kinds of example concerns vague probabilities. When for a given person P(A) and P(C) are both vague, the right-hand side of the Ratio Formula must also be vague; and yet, for that person at that time, $\pi(C/A)$ may be precise. In some of Hájek's examples A entails C, so that $\pi(C/A)$ is 1, exactly and precisely, however vague P(A) and P(C) are. This counts against the Ratio Formula considered as an item of probability theory; but it is negligible when our main focus is on conditionals that are not 'independent' in the sense laid down in §7. That the Formula fails for those is a reason not for dropping it but rather for keeping independent conditionals off our screen. I also set aside conditionals that are *falsified* without help from any particular facts, as in Hájek's other examples, where $\pi(C/A) = 0$ because A logically contradicts C. (These remarks are not confined to conditionals whose truth or falsity is settled by logic alone. This challenge of Hájek's could arise in cases where A leads to C purely through causal laws.)

Fourthly, Hájek examines cases where the person has no value for either P(A) or P(C), using these to show that the Ratio Formula cannot be correct as an *analysis* of conditional probability. With this, as I have said, I agree,

23. INDICATIVE CONDITIONALS ARE ZERO-INTOLERANT

The Ratio Formula must be understood as confined to cases where P(A) > 0. If P(A) = 0, then the right-hand side of the Formula has the form n ÷ 0, which has no solution. The right hand side of MVRF—as Alan Hájek has pointed out to me—has the form n × 0, which = 0 for every n. Thus, $\pi(C/A)$ is undefined by one formula and unconstrained by the other, which means that neither formula has any use when P(A) = 0.

Rather than being a flaw in the Formula, this result sheds light on its left-hand side, bringing into view an important consequence of the fact that indicative conditionals are devices for intellectually managing states of partial information, and for preparing for the advent of beliefs that one does not currently have. For an A that you regard as utterly ruled out, so that for you P(A) = 0, you have no disciplined way of making such preparations, no way of conducting the Ramsey test; you cannot say what the upshot is of adding to your belief system something you actually regard as having *no* chance of being true; so you have no value for π(C/A). Given the Ramsey test thesis, tying your value of π(C/A) to your value for P(A→C), it follows that someone for whom P(A) = 0 cannot find A→C in any degree acceptable, whatever C may be. There is abundant intuitive evidence that *nobody has any use for A→C when for him P(A) = 0*. I call this property of indicative conditionals their *zero-intolerance*. The point is widely known; for a good exposition of it see Warmbröd 1983: 250–1.

To see its rightness, combine the Ramsey test thesis with the Ratio Formula, implying that the acceptability to a person of A→C is given by his probability for A&C divided by his probability for A: 'Believe A→C to the extent that you think A&C is nearly as likely as A' (Edgington 1991: 189). You can do nothing with this in the case where your P(A) = 0.

Having boldly said that indicative conditionals are (always) zero-intolerant, I now take it back, acknowledging the existence of three sorts of counterexample to that. Each can be explained without detriment to the Ramsey test thesis.

(1) There are conversational stretches, as I call them. I know I visited Spain last year. If someone expressed doubts about this, I might say 'If I didn't visit Spain, then I am obviously a shameless liar, so if you doubt me, why should you believe anything I say?' This is a conversational stretch: although for me P(I didn't go to Spain) = 0, I assert a conditional with that as its antecedent in order to accommodate my speech to the doubter's beliefs. In this case, where I make the stretch for the sake of argument, I could as well have said '*You ought to be sure that* if I didn't visit Spain then I am a shameless liar, so . . . etc.'. In other cases I might make a stretch out of courtesy, tact, or embarrassment, and in many of those it would not suit my turn to state my whole thought explicitly. But there too I silently base the value of π(C/A) on the upshot of adding A not to my belief system but rather to that of the person(s) to whom I am adapting my speech. This counterexample succeeds because in it I base A→C on the Ramsey procedure as applied not to my system of beliefs but to someone else's.

(Stalnaker, to whom I owe that example and much of my understanding of stretches, holds that A→C is put out of business for me not only when for me P(A) = 0 but also when I *presuppose* A's falsity, being in a frame of mind where its truth is not in question for me. That might be because for me P(A) = 0, but it might have other sources and rationales. I agree about this, but it will suit my purposes to forgo this bit of generality, and attend to the special case where for the speaker $P(A) = 0$. So I shall retain the term 'zero-intolerance'.)

(2) Even if for me $P(A) = 0$, I may be forced to accept A→C—or anyway forbidden to write it off as a non-starter—because it follows from something that is more directly acceptable. This is an 'inferential exception' to the zero-intolerance of indicative conditionals. I believe that if *anyone* admires the Rolling Stones, he (or she!) will never be Pope; and this belief does not run into trouble from zero-intolerance. But it pretty clearly entails that if any member of the Roman Curia admires the Rolling Stones, he will never become Pope, so I am committed to this too. Yet it offends against the unqualified zero-intolerance thesis, on the most natural construal of the latter, because I give a zero probability to the proposition that some member of the Roman Curia admires the Rolling Stones.

The thesis that indicative conditionals are zero-intolerant should be confined to ones that stand on their own feet, and not applied to inferred ones. An 'inferred conditional' in my sense is one that someone accepts only because he accepts a general conditional that entails it. It is easy to explain the inferential exception to zero-intolerance. The latter's source is the Ramsey test: if for me $P(A) = 0$, I have no disciplined way of adding A to my belief system and conservatively adjusting the rest to make room for this. But the Ramsey test is not needed for inferred conditionals; their basis does not involve adding $P(A) = 1$ to one's belief system, but rather inferring A→C from a different conditional whose antecedent does not have a zero probability.

The moon is always more than ten thousand miles from Detroit, so if anything is ever on the moon then at that time it is that far from Detroit, so *if I have been on the moon I have been over ten thousand miles from Detroit*. This conditional is one of the 'problems for the Ramsey Test' adduced by Sanford (1989: 143–4); but it is plausible only considered as an inferred conditional, and so it does not score off the Ramsey test, properly understood.

(3) Then there are counterexamples that succeed because in them the Ramsey test is at work in a simplified fashion which skirts around the usual trouble of supposing $P(A) = 1$ when in fact for you $P(A) = 0$. All these cases have special features which enable one to go from A directly to C without having to consider how the rest of one's beliefs should be adjusted to make room for $P(A) = 1$. This genus has three species that I know of.

(*a*) One involves conditionals that are *independent*, meaning that in them the route from A to C needs no help from matters of particular fact. I said in §7 that these conflict with various useful general principles concerning conditionals, and now we see that one such conflict concerns the zero-intolerance of indicatives. If you can get from A to C purely through logic or general causal laws, or through general morality, your Ramsey test for A→C is a simplified affair: rather than having to accommodate P(A) = 0 by adjusting your other probabilities, you can just dump it in there and go straight to P(C) = 1.

(*b*) Secondly, there are *non-interference* conditionals (§50), which are accepted on the ground that the person holds C to be true and thinks that A's being true would not interfere with that. In *some* of these cases, the irrelevance of A to C is so obvious that one can arrive at A→C in one fell swoop, without having to look into changes that might need to be made in one's belief system if A were to be added to it. Even if I didn't go to Spain last year, Gibraltar still faces the Mediterranean.

(*c*) A third species was brought to my attention by Alan Hájek. An utterly convinced theist, for whom P(atheism) = 0, can accept '(Even) if there has never been a God, the first sentence of the Book of Genesis (still) says that in the beginning God created the heaven and the earth', this being a non-interference conditional. Without having the faintest idea of how he would change his doxastic scheme if it had to include atheism, he is sure that his belief about how Genesis begins would not alter. Then on that basis he can establish a conditional that does not fall into the non-interference category because its consequent is actually false (he thinks)—namely, the conditional 'If there has never been a God, then the opening sentence of Genesis is false'. Another example (for me): 'If there are Hobbits, then Tolkien's most famous novel refers to real beings as its heroes.' In every conditional A→C belonging to *c*, the person accepts A→B as a non-interference conditional, where B asserts the existence of some item having a certain meaning or content, and C assigns to B a relational property ('is true', 'does not refer to anything', etc.) which it must have if A is true.

Several writers have offered purported examples of acceptable indicative conditionals whose antecedents are known to be false, but their examples have all been suspect. A typical one is this: 'If I put my hand on this stove it will be burned.' One naturally thinks of this as said with reference to a hot stove, and as based on the belief that hot stoves can be depended on to burn hands that touch them. This is starting to sound like a subjunctive conditional—'If I were to . . . it would . . .'—which makes it risky to use as a counterexample to a thesis about indicatives. There is a complex story involved here, which I shall tell in §134.

24. THE EQUATION

Back in §12 I said that we ought to agree that your probability for A→C is measured by your value for $\pi(C/A)$. Thus:

For any person x at any time t, x's probability for A→C at t = x's value for
π(C/A) at t,

or, for short:

P(A→C) = π(C/A), where P(A) > 0.

This powerful, simple, and attractive thesis was first made widely known by
Stalnaker (1970), and it has been called 'Stalnaker's Hypothesis'. But he tells me
that Ernest Adams and Richard Jeffrey propounded it before he did; and Adams
says that Brian Ellis deserves equal credit; so I shall leave personal names out of
it, and follow Edgington in calling it the Equation.

On the face of it, the Equation looks like a possible starting point for an analysis
of indicative conditionals. If we know that someone's level of credence in the truth
of A→C is to be measured by his credence level for C on the supposition of A, this
might be a first step towards finding out what proposition A→C is. It is not a bad
start: it has → on the left and not on the right, and it strikes one as being central
and deep, not marginal and shallow. An apparent drawback is its having on the left
not A→C but P(A→C); and we have no way of getting rid of that 'P( )' and arriv-
ing at a solidly old-fashioned analytic formula: A→C is true if and only if . . .

Stalnaker showed one way to go: 'Conditional propositions are introduced as
propositions whose absolute probability is equal to the conditional probability of
the consequent on the antecedent. An axiom system for this conditional connective is recovered from the probabilistic definition' (1970: 107). So we are to start
with the Equation, and work out what the logic of A→C would have to be for the
Equation to be right. So much for the logic of →, but what about the account of
what → is? the truth-conditions for A→C? the desired analytic biconditional
with A→C on the left and something helpful on the right? In 1970 Stalnaker
thought he was on the way to having such an analysis—the one involving
'worlds', mentioned early in §19—and hoped to be able to show that this analysis and the equation are in harmony, so that each could illuminate the other.
Those of us who reject the 'worlds' approach to indicative conditionals can still
build on the Equation, though in a different spirit. We can contend that A→C
means *whatever it has to mean* such that P(A→C) is π(C/A)—that it means
whatever satisfies the logic that has been built on this foundation. Do not dismiss
this as evasive; it might be the entire fundamental truth about indicative conditionals. We like helpful analytic biconditionals, but nothing guarantees that
they are always to be found.

In the case of indicative conditionals, there is a positive reason why they cannot be found. The ultimate obstacle to laying out the truth conditions for A→C

in an analytic biconditional is that it does not have truth conditions. A central thesis of this book—one in which I am in agreement with many contemporary workers in the field—is that indicative conditionals are not ordinary propositions that are, except when vagueness or ambiguity infects them, always true or false.

A recognizably philosophical case for this will be made in Chapters 6 and 7. Before coming to that, however, I shall devote a chapter to laying out reasons of a different and more technical kind for the same conclusion. They all take the form of arguments against the Equation, purporting to show that the probability of a conditional cannot always be the relevant conditional probability; but they all assume that indicative conditionals are normal propositions whose probability is a probability of being true. Some make other assumptions that might also be challenged, but one thing whose denial undercuts them all is that A→C is a proposition with a truth value.

Some of Chapter 5 is fairly tough going, but I advise you to engage with this material. If you pass it by you will be left—as I was until I knuckled down to it—with a sense of skulking around the periphery of exciting but forbidden territory. My guide to it, though hard enough, is easier than anything the previous literature offered to me.

5

The Equation Attacked

25. LEWIS AGAINST THE EQUATION

In 1976 David Lewis set a lively cat among some previously contented pigeons by devising a proof that there is no propositional operator O_2 such that the probability for any given person of $O_2(A,C)$ is, for any A and C, proportional to that person's value for $\pi(C/A)$. This challenge to the Equation came like a bolt from the blue. There have subsequently been other arguments to the same conclusion from ever weaker premises and assumptions. Lewis's first proof, like Hillary's Everest and Bannister's mile, made it easier for others to follow. Disproving the Equation has become a flourishing light industry.

To get a sense of Lewis's first proof, start with the idea of a *probability function* P. This, sometimes called a 'probability distribution', is a function from propositions to numbers between 0 and 1, which could describe the probabilities or credence levels that some thinker assigns to the propositions on which he has opinions. It can be thought of as containing a list of propositions, each paired with a number between 0 and 1. We are describing a probability function chosen at random from all the possible ones, so we can pair propositions with numbers as arbitrarily as we like. For example, we can suppose that for our thinker P(Bananas are usually purple) = 0.999 and P(Sea-water is usually salty) = 0.07. The only limits are set by the probability axioms we have been exploring.

Your probability function at time T is utterly specific: it represents a set of credence levels for a set of propositions: it is not a concept, technique, or theory that can be repeatedly used or applied in changing circumstances in the light of new evidence; rather, it is the total result of your applying at T all your theories etc. to the evidence you have encountered up to then. You move to a new probability function every time the weather surprises you, or your suspicion that you are due for a tax audit is confirmed, or you learn that the reovirus—which you had never heard of—prevents the development of some cancers. If your probability function does not constantly alter, you should get yourself a livelier life.

Perhaps some functions do not represent the state of belief of a possible thinker, although they conform to the axioms. We are concerned with belief functions—probability functions that *could* represent the beliefs of a person. For purposes of Lewis's proof, we can be as generous as we like in what we count as belief functions, except for one substantive requirement which I now explain.

It involves the deriving of one probability function from another by *conditionalizing on a proposition A*. Here is some new notation: if A is some particular proposition, and P is a belief function,

P_A is the new function that results from P through a rise in the probability accorded to A,

$P_A(Q)$ is the probability of Q in P_A, and

$\pi_A(Q/R)$ is the probability of Q given R in P_A; that is, according to the Ratio Formula, it is $P_A(Q\&R) \div P_A(R)$.

A's probability may rise to something less than perfect certainty ($= 1$), and we shall consider this in §26. But first let us attend to how an idealized thinker's becoming certain of some proposition A resonates through the rest of his belief system, affecting his other probabilities. The process is governed by this principle:

Conditionalization: For any proposition C, $P_A(C) = \pi(C/A)$.

Let us go through that slowly. P is a long list of pairings of propositions with numbers between 0 and 1. We now want to create a different list P_A of pairings of the same propositions with (partly different) numbers, by conditionalizing on proposition A. We decide what number to pair with a given proposition C in either of two ways. Relying on the Ratio Formula: we find P(A&C) if that occurs in the list of proposition-number pairs that constitutes P; find P(A), if that occurs in the list; and divide the former number by the latter. Alternatively, dispensing with the Ratio Formula: we conduct the Ramsey test within P, adding P(A) = 1 to it, conservatively adjust to make room for that, and see what value emerges for P(C). Either way, we get $\pi(C/A)$, and that, according to Conditionalization, gives us $P_A(C)$. For a complete account of P_A we must repeat this for every value of C. It can be proved arithmetically that if P obeys axioms 1–3 of §21 then so does P_A.

Lewis showed that the demands of the axioms, conjoined with Conditionalization and the Equation, lead to absurdity. More specifically, they lead to results that could be correct only in a system of beliefs in which no change in any proposition's probability affects any other's. Such a system would be trivial in a certain sense, and so Lewis is often said to have disproved the Equation by means of a 'triviality result'.

Several writers have reproduced the essence of Lewis's proof in versions that are easier to grasp than his—for example Adams 1975: 34–5 (he had seen Lewis's proof in manuscript), and Edgington 1995*b*: 275–6. I shall present the one that has helped me most, namely Blackburn 1986: 218–20.

The proof needs a lemma which we should establish first. This name for it is mine:

If-and: $\pi((Q{\to}R)/A) = \pi(R/(Q\&A))$, when $P(Q\&A) > 0$.

In English: the probability of a conditional on a certain assumption A is the probability of its consequent on the assumption of (A & its antecedent), as long as the latter conjunction has a non-zero probability. Combining this with the Equation we get

$P(A \to (Q{\to}R)) = P((A\&Q) \to R)$.

For example, my probability for 'If the play was performed at the Barbican, then if she saw it, so did I' is my probability for 'If the play was performed at the Barbican and she saw it, so did I'. As Blackburn remarks, the effect of If-and together with the Equation 'is to roll iterated conditionals into one: $B \to (A{\to}C)$ is evaluated as $(A\&B) \to C$' (p. 220).

Doubts about If-and will be aired in §40, where I shall argue that it survives them. It is certainly intuitively plausible, and Stalnaker (1976: 303) has offered a proof of it. Alan Hájek has given me a much simpler one, which I gratefully reproduce here.

$\pi((Q \to R)/A) = P_A (Q \to R)$ by definition of P_A, and Conditionalization

$\qquad = \pi_A R/Q)$ by the Equation

$\qquad = P_A(R\&Q) \div P_A(Q)$ by the Ratio Formula

$\qquad = \pi((R\&Q)/A) \div \pi(Q/A)$ by definition of P_A, and Conditionalization

$\qquad = [P(R\&Q\&A) \div P(A)] \div [P(Q\&A) \div P(A)]$ by the Ratio Formula

$\qquad = P(R\&Q\&A) \div P(Q\&A)$ by cancellation of $P(A)$

$\qquad = \pi(R/Q\&A))$ by the Ratio Formula.

Taking it from top to bottom,

$\pi((Q{\to}R)/A) = \pi(R/Q\&A))$

which is If-and. QED.

With that in hand, we find that Blackburn's version of Lewis's proof is fairly easy to take in. It is another chain of equivalences, starting with:

(1) P(Q→R)

This is equivalent (by the Addition Theorem (§21)) to

(2) P(R & (Q→R)) + P(¬R & (Q→R)).

Apply formula MVRF to 2 and we get:

(3) [π((Q→R)/R) × P(R)] + [π(Q→R)/¬R) × P(¬R)]

Now apply If-and to the first and third of the four items on line 3, and that line turns out to be equivalent to

(4) [π(R/(Q&R) × P(R)] + [π(¬R/(Q&R)) × P(¬R)]

which is equivalent to

(5) [1 × P(R)] + [0 × P(¬R)]

which simplifies to

(6) P(R).

Thus, from our starting point of P(Q → R) we have arrived through equivalences at P(R). This deprives conditionals of all their force: my probability for *I shall kill myself*, according to this, must be the same as my probability for *If I become terminally and painfully ill, I shall kill myself*. For some people, no doubt, those are the same, but not for me! Something must be wrong in the argument leading to this result, and its most vulnerable premiss is the Equation.

Blackburn would not agree. Having presented his version of Lewis's proof, he criticizes it for its dependence on If-and, which he rejects (1986: 220–9). His philosophical attack on If-and is interesting and challenging, but he does not say where he faults the Stalnaker proof of it. I shall not pursue that question here, because we shall soon meet three disproofs of the Equation that do not involve If-and (§§26–7, 29, 31). And in §40 I shall offer support for If-and independently of Hájek's and Stalnaker's arguments for it.

26. IMPROVING ON CONDITIONALIZATION

Lewis's first proof, like Edgington's 'simplified and relatively informal version' of it and like Blackburn's, has what may be an Achilles heel, namely its reliance on a principle about what should happen when someone comes to be absolutely certain of something. Many (most?) of our belief changes are not like that: we may have an experience that raises our probability for some proposition from about 0.6 to about 0.9. It might be maintained that underlying this is a proposition—perhaps one describing the intrinsic nature of the experience—whose probability does rise to 1, but that is disputable and probably false. For a useful discussion see Jeffrey 1983: 167–8.

The mere fact that many rational belief changes do not involve acquiring any absolute certainty does not harm the Lewis proof or its variants, which require only that such changes *can* happen in the intellectual life of a rational thinker. They show that the Equation leads to trivializing results when we consider a couple of belief changes of that sort, whatever else may also happen in the mind in question.

However, some philosophers—for example, Appiah 1985: 94–7—maintain that rational belief change *never* involves becoming perfectly certain, that is, raising a probability to 1. To see why someone might say this, consider the fact that if for me $P(A) = 1$ at some time, then I have no way back: no intellectual considerations can lead me to $P(A) < 1$. For suppose the contrary: then we have $P(A) = 1$, and at a later time $P_B (A) < 1$—my probability for A has fallen because I have come to assign to B the probability 1. That implies that $\pi(A/B) < 1$, which by the Ratio Formula means that

$$P(B\&A) \div P(B) < 1.$$

That is impossible, however, if $P(A) = 1$; for in that case $P(B\&A) = P(B)$, so that the fraction simplifies to

$$P(B) \div P(B)$$

which $= 1$.

Still, that line of argument is not decisive, for there may be a 'way back' not by inference from other probability changes but by the sheer impact of experience. If I settle on $P(A) = 1$, then I cannot rationally have $\pi(A/Q) < 1$ for any Q; but some Q may force its way into my system of beliefs and non-rationally cause me to become less sure of A (thus Edgington 1991: 191–2).

For all that, it may be that in a fully rational belief system only necessary propositions get probability $= 1$. A probability function that satisfies this:

For all A, if $P(A) = 1$ then Nec(A)

is said to be 'regular'. Carnap invented this use for the term (1950: 294), presumably meaning it as an honorific of the kind that logicians express with 'normal', 'classical' . . . and 'regular'. I shall perforce go along with it, using the name 'Regularity' for this thesis that every probability function for any ideal thinker has this property. Regularity, then, is the converse of §21's axiom 3. It is controversial, as 3 is not, at least when understood as a partial definition of 'ideal thinker'.

If Regularity is true, Conditionalization is idle. Of several reasons for that, here is one. According to Regularity, $P(A) = 1$ only if $Nec(A)$, but in that case our idealized thinker will always accord that probability to A; his value for $P(A)$ will never change, and so *a fortiori* it will never rise to 1 from something lower.

Lewis did not accept Regularity (1986f: 107–8). In theorizing about subjective probability, he held, we should concern ourselves with a thinker who is 'ideal' not only in being free of logical error or ignorance, but also in never 'mistaking the evidence'. When such a person changes his probability function in the light of evidence, Lewis thought, it is always by becoming completely certain of some proposition, such as that he currently has a certain quality of sensation; and later discoveries will never give him a need to scramble back from $P(A) = 1$ when A is a proposition of that kind. Lewis also offered an argument—a puzzling one to me—purporting to show why this is the right account of a fully idealized thinker.

So Conditionalization can do work for such a thinker, and thus Lewis's proof applies. But he conceded—'if not whole-heartedly, at least for the sake of argument'—that even if his proof holds for *that* thinker, the gap between the latter and us may be so great as to deprive the proof of most of its interest. If the Equation fails only at the outer limit of idealized rationality, remote from the actual human condition, then we can safely accept it for ourselves.

So we need to start thinking about belief changes initiated by the raising of some probability to something less than 1, our first need being for a principle governing such changes. Richard Jeffrey has supplied one, which he calls 'Generalized Conditionalization', or GC for short (1983: 166–71). He derives it, through elementary arithmetical moves, from what I call 'Jeffrey's premiss', namely the thesis that getting a new probability for A does not affect one's value for $\pi(C/A)$ for any value of C. That seems right. Conditional probability is a relation between a pair of propositions, a relation that holds steady as one of them changes in probability. (Alleged counterexamples will be discussed in §49.) So Jeffrey starts here:

$$\pi_A(C/A) = \pi(C/A)$$

from which, by substitution, it follows that

$$\pi_A(C/\neg A) = \pi(C/\neg A).$$

Expand the left-hand side of each of those equations by applying the Ratio Formula, and multiply both sides of the first equation by $P_A(A)$ and both sides of the second equation by $P_A(\neg A)$. Those two routine operations yield:

$P_A(A\&C) = \pi(C/A) \times P_A(A)$ and
$P_A(\neg A\&C) = \pi(C/\neg A) \times P_A(\neg A)$.

Now add the first of these two equations to the second. The left-hand sides add up to $P_A(C)$—the probability of C is its probability of being true while A is true plus its probability of being true while A is false (that is the Addition Theorem). The right-hand side does not simplify. The result of this addition, then, is:

$P_A(C) = (\pi(C/A) \times P_A(A)) + (\pi(C/\neg A) \times P_A(\neg A))$.

This is Jeffrey's principle GC, a way of calculating a new probability for C, symbolized as $P_A(C)$, consequent upon some rise in the probability of A, perhaps to less than 1. Jeffrey calls it Generalized Conditionalization because it has Conditionalization as the special case where $P_A(A) = 1$. Let $P_A(A)$ have that value in GC, and you will find that the right-hand side simplifies down to $\pi(C/A)$; and the equation of that with the left-hand side, namely $P_A(C)$, is simple Conditionalization.

As well as being derivable from secure premises, GC makes good intuitive sense. Conditionalization reflects the idea that in the new probability function P_A the proposition A, now having a probability of 1, gives to $P_A(C)$ as much of its weight as $\pi(C/A)$ allows it. If my probability for A goes up to something < 1, it does correspondingly less for $P_A(C)$. How much less? Well, if $P_A(A) = 0.5$, then it would seem that the new probability for C will get a shove from A, but only half as much of a shove as if $P_A(A) = 1$. More generally, if $P_A(A) = n$, then one might expect that $P_A(C) = \pi(C/A) \times n$. That is not quite the whole story, though. Our idealized thinker assigns some new positive probability to $\neg A$ (because his new probability for A < 1); if he also assigns a positive probability to C given $\neg A$, then his total new probability for C gets a shove from this too— a shove that is large in proportion as $\pi(C/\neg A)$ is large and in proportion as $P_A(\neg A)$ is large. So we add this shove to the previous one. That is exactly what GC says we should do.

From the mere premise that a change in the probability of A does not bring a change in the conditional probability $\pi(C/A)$ for any C, Jeffrey has derived in a few simple steps a thesis about probability dynamics that is substantive, helpful, and true. I am awed by this performance.

Given its intuitive rationale and its proof, GC seems to be undeniable. Nobody could say about it, as some do about simple Conditionalization, that it hardly applies to our intellectual doings. That makes it notable that the endlessly fertile and ingenious Lewis reconstructed his triviality proof on the basis of GC (Lewis 1986*f*).

27. CARLSTROM AND HILL AGAINST THE EQUATION

Lewis's trail-blazing work satisfied many people that, alas, no proposition A→C satisfies the Equation except in trivial systems. Once that result was known, it evidently became easier to reach that same result by simpler moves and from weaker premisses. One such is the proof of Carlstrom and Hill (1978: 156–7), which I understood after studying Edgington's version of it (1995*b*: 274–5).

Whereas Lewis's two proofs are dynamic, arising from principles about changes in belief, the Carlstrom–Hill proof is static. It says nothing about how belief states should change, and argues merely that there cannot be a proposition X such that: $P(X) = \pi(C/A)$ for every legitimate assignment of probabilities to the elements of X, that is, every assignment that satisfies the axioms of probability logic. The proof depends on supposing two people and a proposition A such that: their total assignments of probabilities agree on the value of $P(A)$ and of $P(A\& \ldots)$ for every contingent filling of that blank, including $P(A\&X)$; but they disagree in their values for $P(\neg A\& \ldots)$ for every filling of that blank.

The stipulated range of agreement involves the protagonists' agreeing in their values for $P(A\&C)$ and for $P(A)$, whatever C may be. This, by the Ratio Formula, implies that *they assign the same value to $\pi(C/A)$*, whatever C may be.

On the other hand: their disagreements over everything of the form $P(\neg A\& \ldots)$ means that they assign different values to $P(\neg A\&X)$. But they assign the same value to $P(A\&X)$, and so *they assign different values to $P(X)$*. Why? Because $P(X) = P(A\&X) + P(\neg A\&X)$, by the Addition Theorem (§21).

Since they assign the same value to $\pi(C/A)$ for every C, and different values to $P(X)$, it cannot be the case that $P(X) = \pi(C/A)$.

The argument also requires that ¬A neither entails X nor is inconsistent with it. I leave it to you to work out why the argument collapses without those. It is not difficult.

Blackburn (1986: 215–18) argues that two *rational* people could not have probability distributions that relate to one another as do the two in the disproof. Two people might agree about everything on the supposition of (A) atheism, including the likelihood of A itself, but be led in opposite directions—disagreeing on *everything*—by the supposition that (¬A) there exists at least one god. This seems to be humanly possible. But Blackburn holds that their agreement on $P(Q)$ and $P(R)$ and $P(Q\&R)$, all given A, leaves them no space in which rationally to disagree in their probabilities for P(Q→R) given ¬A. If they do disagree in that way, they are guilty of irrationality.

A milder complaint would be this: the Carlstrom–Hill scenario and the Equation are indeed inconsistent, so that accepting either requires one to reject the other; but Carlstrom and Hill have merely exhibited the inconsistency, without giving independent reason to accept one side of it. For all they have shown to the contrary, the Equation might support a good argument showing that there cannot be two probability functions that differ in the manner they suppose.

That seemed to me right until I encountered—and eventually came to understand—a dazzling paper in which Alan Hájek presents a successor to the Carlstrom–Hill argument that is invulnerable to anything like Blackburn's or my criticisms (Hájek 1994: 116–20). I now present it.

28. HÁJEK'S REINFORCEMENT OF THAT ARGUMENT

Consider two particular propositions A and C, and a proposition A→C built out of them with a two-place connective →. Assume nothing about what connective it is. 'A' and 'C' do not function as variables here: we are concerned with two particular propositions and the result of applying → to them. We are to look at these propositions in relation to a probability function (a probability distribution, a set of probability assignments) P in which the probabilities of ¬A, A&C, and A&¬C are all greater than zero, and a probability function P* which differs from P in some relevant manner. (What counts as relevant will emerge shortly.) Notice how weak, safe, tame, the initial assumptions are.

Hájek distinguishes two ways in which A→C may relate to A and A&C. First: A→C is a Boolean combination of A and A&C, meaning that it involves those elements in such a way that its truth value depends strictly on theirs. This does not mean that → is truth-functional across the board; we are considering merely the possibility that the truth value of this *particular* proposition A→C is determined purely by the values of A and A&C. Second: A→C is not a Boolean combination of A and A&C. Each possibility breaks into three sub-cases, in each of which—Hájek shows—something can happen that falsifies the Equation. In each of the first trio, probability can shift from one proposition to another in a way that produces a different conditional probability while leaving the probability of the conditional unchanged. In each of the second trio, a probability shift changes the probability of the conditional while leaving the conditional probability unchanged. The whole argument floodlights the relevant changes in probability, leaving no shadows in which accusations like Blackburn's or doubts like mine can lurk.

First possibility. A→C is a Boolean combination of A and A&C. Write down the truth table for A and A&C, strike out the third line (A=F, (A&C)=T), which cannot be satisfied, and you are left with three lines from which can be constructed six combinations, each representing a possible equivalence for the truth of A→C. That is, A→C may be true on line 1 alone, or on 1–2, or on 1–3, or on 2 alone, or on 2–3, or on 3 alone. (It is satisfied on *some* lines because it is not a contradiction; it is not satisfied on *all* because it is not a tautology.) Hájek takes the six possibilities in pairs.

(i) A→C is A&C, or A→C is ¬(A&C)—that is, A→C is true on line 1 or on lines 2 and 3 of the table.

P* might differ from P in assigning a lower probability to ¬A and a correspondingly higher one to A&¬C. You can see that this has no effect on the probability of A→C in either disjunct of i; but it raises the conditional probability. The conditional probability for P is π(C/A) = P(A&C) ÷ P(A); in P* the value for A has gone up (because the value for ¬A has gone down), but the value for A&C has stayed the same. So a lowering of the conditional probability is not accompanied by any change in the probability of the conditional.

(ii) A→C is A, or A→C is ¬A—that is, A→C is true on lines 1 and 2 or on line 3 of the table.

P* might assign a lower probability to A&C than P does, and a correspondingly higher one to A&¬C. For neither disjunct of ii does this alter the probability of the conditional; but it lowers the conditional probability P(A&C) ÷ P(A) because it lowers the numerator and leaves the denominator unchanged.

(iii) A→C is A⊃C, or A→C is ¬(A⊃C)—that is, A→C is true on lines 1 and 3 or on line 2 of the table.

P* might assign a lower probability to A&C and a correspondingly higher one to ¬A. For neither disjunct of iii does this affect the probability of the conditional, because it is a change that takes place either wholly within the conditional's being true (first disjunct) or wholly within its being false (second disjunct). But, again, this difference between P and P* does yield a difference between P(A&C) ÷ P(A) and P*(A&C) ÷ P*(A)—it removes the same amount from both numerator and denominator, so that the value of the fraction goes down.

So much for the possibility that A→C is a Boolean combination of A and A&C. If it is so, then, whatever such combination it is, a plainly innocent shift of probability from one proposition to another that is inconsistent with it can leave the probability of A→C untouched while lowering the value of π(C/A).

The argument goes through equally if the probabilities shift in the other direction, and the value of π(C/A) goes up. I chose a direction just for clarity's sake. Hájek states his argument in terms of Venn diagrams in which the quantity of 'mud' in a region represents the probability of its proposition, and speaks of moving mud in either direction across lines.

Second possibility. A→C is not a Boolean combination of A and A&C. In that case, in the truth table for A and A&C there is at least one line on which A→C may be true and may be false. Either (i) with A&C true, A→C may be true or false; or (ii) with A&¬C true, A→C may be true or false; or (iii) with ¬A true, A→C may be true or false. (If each of those failed, A→C would be a Boolean combination of A and A&C after all.) Let us take these one by one.

(i) A→C takes both truth values within A&C.

That leaves room for P* to differ from P by giving ((A→C) & (A&C)) a lower probability, with a correspondingly higher one for (¬(A→C) & (A&C)). This lowers the probability of A→C, but makes no change in the probability values for A&C or for A, and so it does not alter π(C/A). In this case, then, the conditional probability and the probability of the conditional come apart.

(ii) A→C takes both truth values within A&¬C.

That allows P* to differ from P by giving ((A→C) & (A&¬C)) a lower probability, with a correspondingly higher one for (¬(A→C) & (A&¬C)). As in case i, this lowers the probability of A→C, but does not alter π(C/A). Again the two items equated by the Equation come apart.

(iii) (A→C) takes both truth values in ¬A.

Then P* can differ from P by giving ((A→C) & ¬A) a lower probability, with a correspondingly higher one for (¬(A→C) & ¬A). Yet again, this lowers the probability of A→C, but does not alter π(C/A). So once more the conditional probability comes apart from the probability of the conditional.

It is iii in this part of Hájek's argument that corresponds to the heart of the Carlstrom–Hill argument. He points out (p. 120) that if → is to be a conditional operator, nobody will allow (ii) that A→C can take the value T when A&¬C, and many will deny also (i) that it can have the value F when A&C; but he leaves those cases in, so as to free his argument from any assumption about → except that it is a binary proposition-forming operator on propositions.

29. STALNAKER AGAINST THE EQUATION

Bas van Fraassen (1976) has sought to protect the Equation from Lewis's proof by challenging its assumption—shared by almost everyone—that a single conditional operator is at work throughout. As we shall see in §34 there are reasons for thinking that many indicative conditionals are in a certain way subjective; and van Fraassen appeals to those considerations in support of his view that A→C attributes a triadic relation to A, C, and the speaker's epistemic state. On this basis, he can find fault with Lewis's diachronic proofs, and with the interpersonal proof of Carlstrom and Hill, including Hájek's reinforcement of the latter. These assume that how → relates to its antecedent and consequent remains constant from time to time, and from person to person; but each proof involves a change of time or of person, and so in each the third relatum changes, which means that the arguments fail if van Fraassen is right.

It would be depressing for the study of conditionals generally if he were right about this, and his view has not won much favour, for reasons we shall examine in §37. Still, we should note that van Fraassen's thesis does protect the Equation from the arguments of Lewis, including all the versions of it that others have devised, and from the argument of Carlstrom and Hill, including Hájek's amplified version of that. It was left to Stalnaker to devise an argument that penetrates van Fraassen's defence of the Equation.

Lewis's first triviality proof led Stalnaker into an admirable sequence of actions: he dropped the Equation ('Stalnaker's Hypothesis'), argued against those who tried to defend it against Lewis, and finally (1976) devised a disproof of it that is invulnerable to van Fraassen's manoeuvre. Whereas the disproofs of Lewis, Carlstrom and Hill, and Hájek all concern pairs of probability functions, Stalnaker's disproof shows, as Dorothy Edgington wrote to me, 'that you can't even make the Equation work in a single probability function'. Thus, van Fraassen's thesis has no bearing on it.

Here is my variant on Edgington's adaptation (1995b: 277) of Stalnaker's argument. We start with two propositions A and B, the conditional A→B, and three further propositions constructed from these:

E is ¬A & (A→B)
C is ¬E
D is A&¬B

These conform to this partial truth-table, in which C→D is thrown in for good measure:

	A	B	A→B	C	D	E	C→D
1.	T	T	T	T	F	F	F
2.	T	F	F	T	T	F	T
3.	F		T	F	F	T	F
4.	F		F	T	F	F	F

Note that E is true just at line 3; C is true just at lines 1, 2, and 4; and D is true just at line 2. The values for C→D in this table require comment. Clearly C→D is false on lines 1 and 4, where its antecedent is true and its consequent false. We are to count it as true on line 2 because there its antecedent and consequent are both true (see §47). As for its being false on line 3: that follows from E's being true on that line, given a Lemma which I now prove:

Lemma: C→D is incompatible with E.

C, being the negation of E, is A ∨ ¬(A→B), and so C→D is

(i) (A ∨ ¬(A→B)) → (A&¬B).

This implies

(ii) A→¬B.

Here is how. Because C is true just at lines 1, 2, and 4, it is equivalent to something of the form A ∨ (¬A&G); that is because its truth requires either one of the lines where A is true or a line (4) where A is false and something else (never mind what) is true. So C→D has the form ((A ∨ (¬A&G)) → (A&¬B), which entails this disjunction:

(A → (A&¬B)) ∨ ((¬A&G) → (A&¬B)).

Assuming that ¬A is compatible with G, the second disjunct has no chance of being true, because it has ¬A as a conjunct in the antecedent and A as a conjunct in the consequent. There remains the first disjunct, (A → (A&¬B)), which plainly entails A→¬B, which is ii, QED. But E plainly implies

(iii) A→B.

So C→D entails A→¬B, and E entails A→B, from which follows the Lemma saying that **C→D is incompatible with E**, which settles that C→D is false on line 3 of the table, and thus true just on line 2.

Now let us look at two items that the Equation says are the same, namely π(D/C) and P(C→D)—the probability of D given C, and the probability of *If C, then D*. Let us take the latter proposition, C→D, first. We have seen that it is true just at line 2 of the truth-table, which means that P(C→D) is the probability V of that line's being the whole truth of the matter. Now for the other half of the Equation: π(D/C). By the Ratio Formula this equals P(C&D) ÷ P(C); but P(C&D) also gets its value solely from line 2, so it also equals V. Thus, the Equation implies that V = V ÷ P(C), from which it follows that P(C) = 1, and thus that P(E) = 0. If we allow this, we must conclude that there is no chance at all that E is true, that is, that A is false and A→B is true. It would be absurd to allow that in every probability distribution this is how things stand; and that is a reason to reject the Equation as a clearly vulnerable contributor to this result. This case against the Equation does not bring in relations between different probability functions, whether at different times or for different people.

As well as fending off van Fraassen, Stalnaker's argument against the Equation is also secure against an attack that Blackburn (1986: 221–5) brings against the first Lewis proof and could also have brought against the second. Each of those proofs relies on If-and (§25), but Stalnaker's does not.

30. SOME WAYS OF ESCAPE

In §39 we shall meet reasons for thinking that indicative conditionals cannot be freely embedded in larger propositional structures. If that is right, it provides a way of fending off Lewis's arguments against the Equation. The first of Lewis's proofs implicitly but essentially involves something that appears explicitly in Blackburn's and Edgington's versions of it, namely P(C & (A→C)); the second includes things of the form π((A→C)/Q) and π(Q/(A→C)). We have seen that the Carlstrom–Hill proof performs computations with P(X&¬A) and P(X&A), which embed an indicative conditional if X is our candidate for A→C. Hájek's reinforcement of that argument does the same. Stalnaker's disproof of the Equation also uses compounds in which indicative conditionals are elements. So the Equation is sheltered from this hail of missiles if it is accompanied by a denial that such embeddings of indicative conditionals are legitimate.

Those who want the Equation and do not want to restrict embedding of indicative conditionals might give to van Fraassen's view of → a more tolerant hearing than I have. As for the avoidance of that by Stalnaker's argument: van Fraassen has a basis for dissenting from that too, namely a rejection of some of its logic. For example, the argument in the above version of it assumes at one point that (P ∨ Q) → R entails (P→R) ∨ (Q→R), which van Fraassen denies. I shall not go further into the logical details.

31. HÁJEK AGAINST THE EQUATION

We have seen three suggested escapes for the Equation: restrict embedding, read $\to$ as ternary, prune the logic. I now add that Alan Hájek (1989) claims—justly, so far as I can see—to block all these routes, through an argument that refutes the Equation without embedding any conditionals, using only one probability function, and using no conditional logic except for one wonderfully safe principle, namely §21's Addition Theorem. (This does not occur on Hájek's pages, but that is because he does not, as I shall do, state the rationale for one of his steps.) I shall expound enough of his argument to show what kind of thing it is.

In thinking about idealized belief systems we often casually assume that we are dealing with propositions many of which hold at an infinity of worlds, but for no actual believer is that the case: neither your belief system nor your uncle's distinguishes literally *infinitely* many different complete ways that things might be. So we lose no real scope by theorizing in terms of finite arrays of worlds.

That is what Hájek does in his almost premiss-free argument against the Equation. He sets out the argument with unaccommodating brevity; I shall take it more slowly. Start with a probability distribution—any one you like, with nothing stipulated except that it recognizes only finitely many worlds. Attend to the probabilities that the distribution assigns to those worlds, ignoring its probabilities for various less specific propositions—that is, ones that are true at more than one world. Let the probabilities of the several worlds be $p_1, p_2, \ldots, p_n$ with these taken in never-descending order so that $p_1 \leq p_2 \ldots \leq p_n$. The argument considers two cases separately: where p_n, the highest (or highest-equal) probability assigned to any world, is < 0.5; and where p_n is ≥ 0.5. The general idea of the argument shows clearly enough in the first case, which I shall present.

Consider all the conditional probabilities—as expressed through the Ratio Formula—whose numerator is p_1 and whose denominator is $1 - p_2, 1 - p_3, \ldots$ and so on in order up to $1 - p_n$. This yields a series in which each member is $\leq$ its successor—the denominators are not increasing, so the values of the fractions are not shrinking. This gives us an $(n - 1)$-membered series of conditional probabilities; I shall call it the Hájek series. According to the Equation they have to be matched by $n - 1$ unconditional probabilities.

Because $p_n < 0.5$, it follows that $(1 - p_n) > 0.5$, and so $p_1 \div (1 - p_n) < 2p_1$. That is, the highest conditional probability in the Hájek series is $< 2p_1$. Furthermore, because $p_1 \leq p_2$ it follows that $2p_1 \leq (p_1 + p_2)$. Putting these two results together, we get that $p_1 \div (1 - p_n) < (p_1 + p_2)$.

So the conditional probabilities in the Hájek series all lie *strictly* between p_1 and $(p_1 + p_2)$—that is, they are greater than p_1 and less than $(p_1 + p_2)$. According to the Equation they are matched by unconditional probabilities which must lie within that interval. Where are these matching probabilities to come from?

The only unconditional probabilities that we have mentioned so far are p_1, ..., p_n, which are the probabilities that the person accords to *worlds*, that is, to propositions that are as specific (strong, detailed, rich) as he gets in his thought. Those are not the only probabilities that his belief system involves, however. There are also (finitely) many non-world probabilities, as I shall call them; that is, probabilities of non-world propositions, each of which is equivalent to a disjunction of two or more worlds; and many of those probabilities will not be any of p_1, ..., p_n. Might some of *them* be identified with probabilities in the Hájek series? No, and the next paragraph explains why.

Each world is inconsistent with each other world, and so (by the Addition Theorem) the probability that some disjunction of worlds is true equals the sum of the probabilities of the individual worlds. Therefore, the probability of any non-world proposition is the sum of the probabilities of its constituent worlds— the worlds at which it is true—and so the smallest of these non-worlds probabilities involves the two worlds with the lowest probabilities, namely p_1 and p_2, which means that it $= (p_1 + p_2)$. I repeat: **the smallest non-world probability $= (p_1 + p_2)$**. It follows that no non-world probability can be equated with any of the $n - 1$ conditional probabilities in the Hájek series, because the latter all lie strictly *between* p_1 and $(p_1 + p_2)$. The *smallest* non-world probability is larger than the *largest* probability in the Hájek series.

Therefore, the only non-conditional probabilities that might be equated with the probabilities in the Hájek series are the probabilities of worlds, $p_2, p_3, ..., p_n$— omitting p_1 because it is too small. So our $(n - 1)$-membered non-descending series of conditional probabilities must be matched, one for one, with the $(n - 1)$-membered non-descending series of unconditional world probabilities, which implies that the former series must *be* the latter series: $p_1 \div (1 - p_2) = p_2, ...,$ and so on up to $p_1 \div (1 - p_n) = p_n$. Putting it generally: for $i = 2, 3, ..., n$ we have $p_i = p_1 \div (1 - p_i)$.

From this by simple algebraic moves we get $p_i \times (1 - p_i) = p_1$, whence $p_i^2 - p_i + p_1 = 0$. This is a quadratic equation that leads, by standard moves that any algebra text will explain, to this:

$$p_i = [1 \pm \sqrt{(1 - 4p_1)}] \div 2.$$

That gives two possible values for p_i, but we can set aside one of them, namely $p_i = [1 + \sqrt{(1 - 4p_1)}] \div 2$, because that gives a value for p_i that is > 0.5, whereas we are attending to the case where the highest $p_i < 0.5$. So we are left with the other value:

$$p_i = [1 - \sqrt{(1 - 4p_1)}] \div 2,$$

which is a constant. So p_i has the same value for each value of $i = 2, \ldots, n$, from which it follows that $p_2 = p_3 \ldots = p_n$.

This is wild enough: an *a priori* proof that an arbitrarily selected belief system has at most two distinct world probabilities—p_1 and p_2. But there is more. From the foregoing argument it follows that no unconditional probabilities lie strictly between p_2 and $(p_1 + p_2)$. We have constructed a series in which each member is $\leq$ its successor, right up to $\leq (p_1 + p_2)$, but nothing in what we have done prevents it from being equalities all the way; and our latest result requires us to suppose that that is just what they are.

But there *is* a conditional probability in this interval, namely $p_2 \div (1 - p_1)$. This is obviously greater than p_2, and Hájek easily proves that it is less than $p_1 + p_2$, as follows. In it, add p_1 to both numerator and denominator and you get a fraction with a higher value than the original has; it is the fraction $(p_1 + p_2) \div (p_1 + 1 - p_1)$, which simplifies to $p_1 + p_2$. So $p_2 \div (1 - p)$ is less than something that equals $p_1 + p_2$, so it is itself less than $p_1 + p_2$. It therefore lies strictly between p_2 and $(p_1 + p_2)$, which contradicts our previous result that no unconditional probability lies in that interval. So the hypothesis of the argument—the Equation—must be dropped.

That was for the case where $p_n < 0.5$. For the remaining case, where $p_n \geq 0.5$, the argument is similar in general structure. I shall not take us through it, though the argument needs it. (Still, we should note how weird it would be for p_n to be ≥ 0.5 for any human being. That would involve someone's thinking that a certain conjunction, answering every question he can think of, purporting to delineate reality in as much detail as he has made room for in his mind—saying why Christopher Marlowe was killed, how many fleas there were in Chad last Wednesday, when and how an Aids vaccine will be developed, and so on—*is at least as likely as not to be true*.)

The above argument of Hájek's does not embed any conditionals, or involve two or more probability functions, or employ any disputable conditional logic. It refutes the Equation on the strength of a meagre input of premises, leaving almost no leverage for a defence.

Almost no leverage—but the Equation can be sheltered from this bombardment by a theory that was developed by Ernest Adams and has been espoused by Allan Gibbard, Dorothy Edgington, and others including myself. I shall not defend Adams's theory purely on the grounds that it alone can rescue the

Equation, because such a defence could be run contrapositively. David Lewis called an argument a way of estimating what it would cost to deny the conclusion; if the price of denying Adams's theory is relinquishing the Equation, one might think that to be a bargain! To count the arguments in the present chapter as favouring Adams's theory, we need independent grounds for accepting the Equation. The Ramsey test thesis, stated in terms of 'acceptability', is hard to deny (though I have seen people try); but when it grows into a thesis about the 'probability' of a conditional, doubts might well set in. Such doubts must be allayed if Adams's theory is to recommend itself to us.

I hope to allay them in the next two chapters, thereby firming up the argument from 'Only Adams's theory can rescue the Equation' to 'Adams's theory is true'. These chapters will also provide independent grounds for accepting Adams's theory—grounds that persuaded some philosophers before Lewis ever opened fire on the Equation. Thirdly, they will help to explain *why* Adams is right. However well the first two tasks are carried out, we should not be satisfied without the third.

I should report, finally, that Adams (1998: 198–9) offers an argument that he apparently sees as a variant on Hájek's; see his note on 'Hayek's [*sic*] Triviality Result' on p. 203. Though much simpler than Hájek's, Adams's argument needs a vastly stronger premiss, namely one stating *what* finite number of worlds we are dealing with.

6

The Subjectivity of Indicative Conditionals

32. TRYING TO OBJECTIVIZE THE RAMSEY TEST

Faced with the Ramsey test thesis, which links

> the degree of credence that a given person gives to A→C

with

> that person's probability for C on the supposition of A,

one naturally wants first to filter out the mentions of a person, replacing the thesis by something that links

> the degree of credence that *ought* to be given to A→C

with

> the *objective* probability of C given A.

This offers to free us from the person-relativeness which permeates the Ramsey test thesis—to take us away from subjective and over into objective probability, promising cooler air to breathe, less cluttered ground to tread.

No analyst of indicative conditionals has adopted or even explored this 'objectivized Ramsey' approach (as I shall call it), which indicates that it is not a live option. Still, we need to understand *why* it is dead. I shall devote this section to trying to make it breathe.

This conditional might be a reasonable thing for someone to accept: 'If he sold his shares before last Wednesday, his idea of friendship is different from mine.' (For discussion's sake, pretend the pronouns are replaced by proper names.) Even when that is reasonable, though, no probabilifying relation links this A to this C. For objectivized Ramsey to cover Shares → Friendship, it must link the probability of this conditional with the probability of Friendship given (Shares

& P), where P is some fact not stated in the conditional. We might think of P as including a complex fact about the relations between the two people.

For this to be one of our results, we need objectivized Ramsey to provide a *general* account of what the facts P are such that the probability of A→C is tied to the probability of C given A&P. What account can this be? Well, try this:

OR$_1$: P(A→C) is proportional to the value of $\pi(C/(A\&P))$ for some true P.

This will not do, because it will bestow different probabilities on a single conditional, through different selections of P. Wanting uniqueness, we might try:

OR$_2$: P(A→C) is proportional to the highest value that $\pi(C/(A\&P))$ has for any true P.

Different Ps yield different conditional probabilities, but to get the objective probability of the conditional we take the P that yields the highest probability— thus says OR$_2$. This could look promising only to someone who accepted the following:

> We can consider the probability of C relative to values of P that are increasing in strength (each one containing its predecessors as conjuncts, so to speak); as the Ps get stronger, the probability of C given A&P increases; and the highest such probability reflects the strongest input of fact—which is why we are to think of this as the objective probability of A→C.

This assumes that as the factual input grows so does the probability; but that is wrong, because reasoning with probabilities is not *monotonic*—a term I now explain. In mathematics, a function is monotonic if with increasing arguments (inputs) its values (outputs) either always increase or always decrease. On a loose analogy with that, a system of reasoning is called 'monotonic' if, as the premisses of any argument are strengthened, the set of inferable conclusions either stays the same or increases. That is, *adding* to the premisses never implies *removing* anything from the set of conclusions. No probabilistic system of reasoning is 'monotonic' in this sense, because adding to a body of evidence may detract from the probability of some conclusion. Thus, settling for the highest probability of C given A&P may involve bringing in a sparse factual P, when a richer P would yield a lower probability. So we have no reason to tie the objective probability of A→C to the highest probability C has relative to A&P where P is true; and therefore OR$_2$ has nothing to recommend it.

A third try for uniqueness:

OR$_3$: P(A→C) is proportional to the value of $\pi(C/(A\&P))$ where P is the whole truth.

This fails too, because when A is false, ¬A is part of the whole truth; so that this latest proposal will confer on A→C (when A is false) whatever probability C has given (A&¬A& Q), where Q is the rest of the whole truth. If you want to tell a story about the probability of C given a contradiction, go ahead and tell one. But it will have to assign the same probability (presumably either 0 or 1) to every C in relation to any contradiction; so that OR$_3$ gives the same probability to every indicative conditional whose antecedent is false.

Bad as OR$_3$ is, it points to something more promising:

OR$_4$: P(A→C) is proportional to the value of $\pi(C/(A\&P))$ where P is the strongest portion of the whole truth that is compatible with A.

In this, we must understand 'compatible' to involve causal as well as logical compatibility. The idea will have to be that we get the probability of A→C by taking the whole truth, minimally adjusted (if need be) so as to make the conjunction of it with A logically and causally coherent, and we then investigate the probability of C given this conjunction.

Why causally as well as logically? Well, in a situation where there was no high tide last night, the conditional 'If there was a high tide last night, the beach will be clear of driftwood this morning' may well be highly probable. This requires, according to OR$_4$, that its consequent is probable relative to its antecedent together with a portion of the entire truth; and that fragment must omit not merely *There was no high tide last night* but also the likes of *The driftwood stayed firmly on the sand throughout the night.*

Of the versions of objectivized Ramsey that we have looked at, OR$_4$ is structurally the most similar to the subjective Ramsey test with which we started. Each of them says: take a certain body of propositions, add A to it, adjust the rest in a minimal way so as to give A's high probability a comfortable fit, and then see whether the resultant body of propositions implies a high probability for C. They differ only in the initial body of propositions: for subjective Ramsey, it is *everything the speaker believes*; for OR$_4$ it is *the whole truth.*

33. DAVIS'S THEORY

I shall discuss OR$_4$ by considering Wayne Davis's account of indicative conditionals, which is close to it (1979; see also his 1983). He asks what makes a conditional *true*, rather than what makes it *probable*, but this difference does not matter here. My topic is Davis's attempt to evaluate indicative conditionals *objectively*.

Where the (subjective) Ramsey test has you evaluating A→C by adding A to *your present system of beliefs* . . . etc., Davis says that you should add A to *the*

whole truth about the actual world . . . etc. Both approaches say that after adding
A you make the smallest adjustments you need for the resultant set of propositions to be consistent, and then see whether the resultant set implies C or a high
probability for C. In the Ramseyan approach, there is a subjective element in the
input, and so the resultant judgement on C is subjective also. Davis, on the other
hand, admits no subjectivity anywhere: he aims to give a procedure that will
assign to the conditional an objective truth value. He expresses his theory in the
language of 'worlds': A→C is true just in case the A-worlds most like the actual
world are also C-worlds. (A-worlds are worlds at which A is true, similarly for
C-worlds etc.) I formulate it differently—not to expose Davis to further criticism, but to postpone worlds until I am ready for them.

Consider this:

> If the British did not attack Suez early in 1956, the Israelis rigged the situation
> to make it look as though they had.

Davis will call this *true* because of all the evidence the world contains that the
British did attack Suez. A world-description that does justice to that evidence and
yet includes *The British did not attack Suez early in 1956* will imply—logically or
causally—that there was an Israeli frame-up. This is one half of Davis's ingenious
Y-shaped analysis of indicative and subjunctive conditionals (§4), which I shall
examine in §138. My present topic is the account of indicatives taken on its own.

Jackson thinks that Davis's analysis falls to counterexamples (1987: 72–4). He
adduces 'If I have misremembered the date of the Battle of Hastings, it was not
fought in 1066'. Davis's theory implies that this acceptable conditional is false,
Jackson alleges, concluding that the theory itself is false. Here is the argument,
in my words:

> Suppose that I do not misremember the date of the Battle of Hastings. Then
> there are two ways to adjust the truth about the actual world so that I can con-
> sistently add *I misremember the date of the Battle of Hastings* to it. (1) I can
> delete the truth that the battle was fought in 1066. (2) I can delete the truth
> that I remember the date of the battle as 1066. For Jackson's conditional to be
> true by Davis's standards, the most conservative adjustment must be 1. But by
> any reasonable standard, the most conservative adjustment is 2—changing
> the truth values of a few propositions about a few neurons, rather than the
> facts about the date of an important battle. So our intuition clamorously says
> True, while Davis's theory says False. The theory is wrong, therefore.

Thus Jackson. This argument is slippery. Suppose I entertain 'If Henry has misremembered the date of the Battle of Hastings, it was not fought in 1066'. For

me, the thought of Henry's misremembering the date is the thought of his not remembering it as 1066, because I am sure that this is the correct date; so for me the conditional is unacceptable. Jackson's first-person version trades on my knowing for sure what I remember the date *as*, so that for me the thought of my misremembering the date has to be the thought (not of my remembering it as something other than 1066, but rather) my remembering it as 1066 and being wrong about this. That gives the conditional the truth value Jackson wants it to have, but only by pummelling it into a shape that makes it tantamount to 'If I am wrong in thinking that the Battle of Hastings was fought in 1066, then it was not fought then.' This is boring, logically true, an independent conditional (§§7, 62), and not fit to help in refuting Davis.

Even if Jackson's example were fatal to Davis's analysis, it would not explain its error. If we are to gain understanding, we need a proper diagnosis, enabling us to see why the analysis is wrong and what makes it plausible.

Davis makes indicative conditionals seem to have objective truth values by considering only cases (Oswald and Kennedy, Booth and Lincoln) where much relevant evidence is known to all of us, and it virtually all favours one side. In each case we have the public death of a world-famous figure: the world shouts at us that if Booth didn't kill Lincoln, someone else did. But this is an accident of the examples. Furthermore, even in those cases there could in principle be over-whelming evidence—out there in the world, though not known to us—that goes the other way, making it almost certain that nobody other than Booth killed Lincoln. (I am here following Warmbröd 1983: 250. His way of tackling indicative conditionals through the notion of subjective truth is worth thinking about, though I choose not to discuss it here.)

I now vary the example so as to filter out the distracting fact that Lincoln's death was a world-famous event. Toxic chemicals are found in the creek, and there is strong and widely available evidence that one of two local people dumped it there. In fact, the culprit was a local manufacturer named Capone; the other suspect is a right-wing radical activist named Siegel. The well-informed Speaker One says:

C: If Capone didn't poison the creek, then Siegel did.

You might think this to be objectively true, so that any sufficiently well-informed person will accept it. But now consider Speaker Two: he has all the evidence that Speaker One has, and also has powerful evidence (there is plenty of it lying around) that Siegel did not do the deed. Speaker Two will not accept C, and may put in its place:

If Capone didn't poison the creek, it was poisoned by someone from out of town, or the like; or, if he does not have strong evidence that the creek was poisoned,

If Capone didn't poison the creek, it wasn't poisoned.

The illusion of an objectively true indicative conditional was created by taking one that would be acceptable to someone with a certain distribution of knowledge and ignorance, in a case where that distribution is common property, shared by all concerned. This makes it 'objective' in the sense of inter-subjective: all the relevant 'subjects' have it. But it is still a contingent generalization of something that is basically personal, and thus 'subjective' in the strongest sense.

34. GIBBARDIAN STAND-OFFS

A famous example of Allan Gibbard's (1981b: 231–2) gives us a clearer view of the subjectivity of some conditionals, or at least of their resistance to being objectivized in Davis's way. The example concerns a stand-off—a case where one person is fully entitled to accept A→C while another is fully entitled to accept A→¬C. I stress *fully* entitled; these acceptances are intellectually perfect. Here is the story.

A hand of poker is being played, and everyone but Pete and one other player have folded. Two onlookers leave the room at this point, and a few moments later each sees one player leave the gaming room. Winifred sees Pete without the scowl and the trembling cheek that he always has after calling and losing, and concludes that *if Pete called, he won*; Lora sees Pete's opponent caressing more money than he owned when Lora left the room, and concludes that *if Pete called, he lost*.

As well as changing the names for mnemonic reasons, I have altered each person's basis for her conditional. Here is why I changed Lora's. In Gibbard's example, she judged that *if Pete called, he lost* because she had evidence that Pete had a losing hand. That basis for the conditional also supports:

If Pete were to have called, he would have lost, and
If Pete had called he would have lost,

which are subjunctive conditionals, which almost nobody has thought to be subjective or person-relative—the exceptions being Chisholm (§120) and Lycan (§37). Gibbard's conclusion did not depend on this detail in his example, his handling of which is philosophically flawless. In the subsequent debate about it, however, the pure signal of his argument has sometimes been invaded by noise coming over the wall from the subjunctive domain. I have suppressed that clamour by changing the bases for the two conditionals so as to protect them from being thought of as subjunctives in disguise.

Winifred's and Lora's conditionals cannot both be true, because their being so would conflict with the principle of Conditional Non-Contradiction:

CNC: $\neg((A{\rightarrow}C)\ \&\ (A{\rightarrow}\neg C))$,

which is almost indisputably true. According to the horseshoe analysis, CNC is false, because exactly half of the conjunctions of the form $(A{\supset}C)\ \&\ (A{\supset}\neg C)$ are true, namely those where A is false. But on no other account of indicative conditionals has CNC any chance of coming out false.

It is conspicuously true according to any analysis which, like Davis's, ties the truth of A→C to C's being true at a certain 'world'; because on no viable account of what worlds are can C and ¬C both be true at a single world. CNC is true also according to theories that include the Ramsey test thesis. Suppose CNC is false. Then sometimes A→C and A→¬C are both true, in which case one person could coherently accept both. Such a person would have a belief system such that adding A to it and conservatively adjusting to make room for that leads to a probability > 0.5 for C and to a probability > 0.5 for ¬C. Obviously, it would be irrational to think it more likely than not that C and also more likely than not that ¬C. So the two conditionals could not rationally both be accepted by one person at one time, so they cannot both be true. Nobody has been so bold as to suggest that they may both be true although no rational person could accept both at once.

We can take it as settled, then, that Winifred's and Lora's conditionals are not both true. Then is at least one false? Gibbard says No, because: 'One sincerely asserts something false only when one is mistaken about something germane. In this case, neither [Lora] nor [Winifred] has any relevant false beliefs . . . and indeed both may well suspect the whole relevant truth.' Gibbard must mean that one sincerely asserts something false only if one is mistaken about some relevant *nonconditional* matter of fact. That is plausible, so this argument has force.

The final clause in what I have quoted from Gibbard points to a way of strengthening his argument. Suppose you are on the scene; you trust both speakers not to have hallucinated evidence, or to have been muddled about its significance, and are thus led to conclude that Pete folded, which indeed he did. In this case you take a coherent route from your informants' correct evidence and sound thinking to your true conclusion. Can we believe that this route runs through at least one falsehood? Sometimes one does coherently get from falsehood to truth, but only through luck, and in our present case luck has nothing to do with it.

That tells against either conditional's being false. The stronger thesis that one is true and the other false is also open to a different objection, namely that there is no basis for choosing the culprit. You may think: 'On the contrary: a certain fact favours one conditional over the other, though we may not know what fact it is or, therefore, which conditional should be crowned. The deciding fact concerns whether Pete had a losing hand. If he did, then Lora's conditional wins; if he did not, Winifred's.' I have encountered this in debates about Gibbardian stand-offs; it is to be found in Pendlebury 1989: 182–3; and it is treated with respect in Lycan 2001: 169. The idea must be that if Pete had a losing hand, then Winifred's conditional—however soundly based and sincerely accepted—is doomed by a fact she does not know about the hands.

To see how wrong this is, let us turn to Gibbard's original story (pp. 226–7), in which Winifred watches the game for a while, sees the opponent's (very strong) hand, signals its contents to Pete, and then leaves the room. Standing outside, and reflecting on Pete's competitive nature, Winifred has powerful grounds for thinking 'If Pete called, he won'. Our objector has to say 'Nevertheless, her conditional is doomed by the fact about the hands'; but this looks weaker than ever, because in this version of the story she herself is pretty sure of that fact. Knowing the strength of the opponent's hand, she correctly infers that Pete's hand is a losing one, which leads her to accept that if Pete were to call he would lose. Our objector must say not merely that her confident 'If Pete called, he won' is condemned by the fact about the hands, but further that in accepting it she exhibits a muddle, because she knows better. It is an unlikely tale.

Still, we can avoid the distracting need to deal with such objections, and let the pure signal of Gibbard's point come through, by moving to a new example where subjunctives cannot get under our feet and trip us up:

> Top Gate holds back water in a lake behind a dam; a channel running down from it splits into two distributaries, one (blockable by East Gate) running eastwards and the other (blockable by West Gate) running westwards. The gates are connected as follows: if east lever is down, opening Top Gate will open East Gate so that the water will run eastwards; and if west lever is down, opening Top Gate will open West Gate so that the water will run westwards. On the rare occasions when both levers are down, Top Gate cannot be opened because the machinery cannot move three gates at once.
>
> Just after the lever-pulling specialist has stopped work, Wesla knows that west lever is down, and thinks 'If Top Gate opens, all the water will run westwards'; Esther knows that east lever is down, and thinks 'If Top Gate opens, all the water will run eastwards'.

Each has a sound basis for her conditional. Someone might rightly trust both speakers and soundly infer that Top Gate will not open; and it would be absurd to think there *must* be some asymmetrical fact making one conditional true and the other false. This example contains nothing analogous to the winning-or-losing-hand feature of Gibbard's example, which has misled some students of it.

Objection: 'In your example, both conditionals are wrong. Top Gate *could* not have been opened while both levers were down; each conditional implies that it could have been; so both are false.' This response leads to fatal conclusions. In particular, for any false A whose falsity was causally determined by the antecedent state of the world, *every* instance of A→C will be judged false (except perhaps ones where A entails C). 'If the avalanche that we heard came over the crest into this valley, we shan't get home tonight', 'If there was a specially high tide last night, those logs will have been floated off the beach', 'If she fought off the infection, it will be such a relief'—and so on, a swath of falsity will be cut through the middle of what we had thought were innocent conditionals. This defensive objection leads to disaster.

35. HOW SPECIAL ARE STAND-OFFS?
DOES IT MATTER?

In stand-offs like Gibbard's and mine, we have two conflicting indicative conditionals neither of which is objectively false or objectively true. How special, how unusual, are such pairs? If they are a tiny enough subset of the whole, they may be a misleading guide to the analysis of indicative conditionals generally.

If a 'stand-off' requires two people who actually do accept respectable though conflicting conditionals, such cases may be rare; but that does not answer the question we should be asking. Suppose my Top Gate story is true except that Esther is not on the scene, and nobody actually accepts 'If Top Gate opens, all the water will run eastwards'. The basis for this conditional is there in the concrete situation, but nobody does with it what Esther does in my story. This difference cannot affect the status of Wesla's 'If Top Gate opens, all the water will run westwards'. In the original story, the real obstacle to calling that conditional objectively true, or objectively false, came from the fact that the rival conditional was equally supported by the concrete situation; it did not need someone to have actually accepted it.

Perhaps the noun 'stand-off' is appropriate only when two people accept rival conditionals. If so, reword the question, and ask about the prevalence of *stand-off situations*—by which I mean states of affairs containing adequate bases for two conflicting indicative conditionals.

I shall address this question as it arises for indicative conditionals with false antecedents. When an antecedent is true, the picture changes (§§46–7), and in the meantime I set that aside. Ever so many of our indicative conditionals *do* have false antecedents, and we want to understand how they work—which involves coming to understand how they should be evaluated. So bear patiently with this temporary restriction in the scope of the enquiry.

Without having any statistics, I confidently assert that the vast majority of acceptable F→C conditionals (that is, instances of A→C where A is false) are based upon stand-off situations. Virtually all the ones Davis has in mind are like that (§33). These are conditionals to the effect that if A obtained at some earlier time then so did C, accepted on the strength of evidence that A&¬C did not obtain. But *ex hypothesi* A&C did not obtain either, and the world is probably cluttered with evidence against that conjunction too; in which case someone who noticed it and nothing else would be justified in accepting A→¬C.

This also holds for many conditionals saying that if A comes to obtain in the future then so will C. Such a conditional can be accepted on the strength of present evidence that A&¬C will not come to obtain; and, as before, there may often be equally strong evidence that A&C will not come to obtain either. My Top Gate example is like this.

What about the many Future → Future conditionals that are accepted at a time when the world does not contain strong evidence that A will not come to obtain? When a physician justifiably says 'If you take this drug, you will recover', could a rival conditional be equally justified? Probably not, but we need to grasp *why* not. (I labour this because it took me so long to clear my thoughts about it.) We are confining ourselves to F→C; so we want to evaluate the physician's conditional on the understanding that the patient will not in fact take the drug. Now, if the causes of her not taking it already exist—are lying around in the world so they could in theory be known—then someone might learn of *some* of them as part of an evidential package that does not assure him that the patient won't take the drug, but does assure him that the conjunction (She will take the drug & She will recover) will not come true. This person would be entitled to accept 'If she takes the drug, she will not recover', which would create a stand-off. My Top Gate story illustrates the simplest kind of instance of such a package; if it is all right, then more complex examples are also possible, and they may spread over much of the conditionals territory.

But not over all of it. Presumably in many Future → Future cases where the antecedent will turn out to be false, the present state of the world does not contain sufficient conditions for this falsity; or if it does, they are—as in my doctor–patient example—so remote from anything we can know that it seems perverse to think of them as possible bases for a stand-off. It would be rash to contend, as I did until warned by Dorothy Edgington, that every well-supported F→C belongs to a stand-off situation.

Nevertheless, I do contend that they are all subjective. Whether a given instance of F→C could be party to a stand-off depends entirely upon what the outside world contains, not on the frame of mind of the person who accepts or asserts it. The person's input into the conditional is just what it is for any conditional—a high subjective probability for C given A. The world may be laid out in such a way that the high value for $\pi(C/A)$ is backed up by the causal impossibility of A's becoming true without C's becoming true, or by some high objective relative probability; but that does not affect what the person means by what he says, what kind of semantic item he produces.

Compare two cases in each of which someone accepts 'If Top Gate is opened, the water will flow eastwards'. (1) The one described in my example, where sufficient conditions exist for Top Gate not to open, and . . . etc., yielding the stand-off. (2) It is causally possible for Top Gate to be opened, but impossible for it to be opened without the water flowing eastwards. In 1 there can be a stand-off, in 2 there cannot. But the very same conditional sentence is used in each to express something the speaker accepts. The conditional in 1, we have seen, cannot be understood as objectively true or false; how can we treat the conditional in 2 differently? Notice that for all I have said to the contrary, Esther$_1$ (so to speak) may think she is in 2, and Esther$_2$ may think she is in 1. The difference between 1 and 2 that affects their capacities for stand-offs are entirely external to the Esthers; it should not influence our accounts of what these two people are doing in accepting their conditionals.

Last stand: 'Esther$_2$ might believe she is in 2, and might build this belief into the meaning of her conditional. When she says "If Top Gate is opened, the water will flow eastwards" she means that it is causally possible for Top Gate to open and causally impossible for it to do so without the water's flowing eastwards. Is there anything subjective about what *she* is saying?' No. What she means by her conditional is an objectively true proposition about the world, with no covert reference to her belief system. But this is not a permissible meaning for her conditional to be given; it is not a meaning that it conventionally *has*. In §134 I shall discuss certain related claims attributing to conditionals an array of different meanings, and shall give reasons for dismissing nearly all of them.

36. SUBJECTIVITY THROUGH SELF-DESCRIPTION

Indicative conditionals, I conclude, do not have objective truth values. Well, then, do they have subjective truth values? What could that mean? We could stipulate that if P(A→C) is high for you now we shall say that A→C is 'true for' you now. But this would merely allow the *word* 'true' to come on stage; it wouldn't let it do any work once it got there.

The only way to combine real subjectivity with real truth is to suppose that when someone asserts A→C, the proposition he asserts has a truth value in the normal way, but that *what* proposition it is depends not only upon A and C and the normal meaning of → but also on some unstated fact about himself. Analogously, if I hold up a painting and say 'May Smith painted this', I express a proposition, but *which* one depends not only on the sentence I utter but also on what I am holding up while uttering it. If I say to you 'You have been helpful to me', the proposition I express depends not only on the sentence I utter but on who I am, who you are, and when I speak.

So we have to consider the idea that what someone means by a sentence of the form A→C depends in part upon his overall epistemic state, that is, upon how probabilities are distributed across the propositions on which he has opinions. This opens the door to the possibility that when Winifred asserts Called → Won while Lora asserts Called → Lost, each woman says something true, just as they might if one said 'May Smith painted this' and the other, holding up a McCahon, said 'May Smith didn't paint this'.

This amounts to the proposal that → is not a binary but a ternary operator, involving A, C, and the overall belief state of the speaker. So Winifred's conditional applies a triadic relation to the triple {Called, Won, Winifred's belief system}, while Lora's applies the same relation to the triple {Called, Lost, Lora's belief system}. These do not conflict.

Two versions of this line of thought arise from two ways of referring to one's own belief system. One is (1) through an identifying description such as 'my belief system', the other is (2) through some device—a proper name, perhaps—that does not describe the belief system in question as one's own. Because I found this difference hard to get clear about, and because it is crucial in our present context, I shall stay with it for a few moments.

Here are two semantic myths. (1) Everyone uses the name 'Natus' to mean 'the place where I was born'. (2) Each person uses the name 'Natus' to refer to a particular place; the places vary from person to person; and nothing in the meaning of 'Natus' enables one to read off from someone's use of the name any information about the place to which he refers. These are alike in that in each of them one person's 'The aquifer in Natus is polluted' need not conflict with someone else's 'The aquifer in Natus is not polluted'. But they also differ. In 1 a person who says 'The aquifer in Natus is polluted' says something about himself, namely that he was born in a place with polluted water; whereas in 2 a person who says 'The aquifer in Natus is polluted' does not refer to himself at all. He asserts of a particular place that it has polluted water; but no information about the place can be read off from what he says. Let us first look into the 1-like or self-describing version of this story.

We are to suppose that Winifred differs from Lora in the way that someone who says 'I am hungry' differs from someone else who says 'I am not hungry'. When you assert an indicative conditional (on this view) you talk about yourself; when you say A→C you are reporting that your value of $\pi(C/A)$ is high. This brings in subjectivity through the reference to yourself, yet what you express is a normal proposition with a truth value.

This account of indicative conditionals has virtues. Sheer information about people's conditional probabilities can be useful: in the poker game example, if Winifred tells me that her probability for *Pete won* given *Pete called* is high, and Lora tells me that hers is low, I learn things giving me evidence that Pete folded. Similarly with the Top Gate example.

But this is not what indicative conditionals mean. Winifred tells me 'If Pete called, he won', and I say 'Are you sure?' She replies 'Yes, I am pretty sure I'm right.' If she had meant that her value for the conditional probability is high, then her reassurance to me would have meant that she is pretty sure it *is* indeed high. But confidence in a conditional is not like that. Common sense and the Ramsey test both clamour that Winifred is not assuring me that her value for a certain conditional probability is high, but is assuring me of that high value. She has not asked herself 'How sure am I about the conditional probability?' but rather 'How high is the conditional probability?' She aims to convince me of that probability, not the proposition *that* it is her probability. Also, if her probability for Won given Called is only a little above 0.5, she may be utterly certain that that's what it is, yet only mildly inclined to accept Called→Won. None of this could be right if she and I took her to be simply reporting a fact about her belief system.

It is not useful to appeal to the theoretical hunches of folk who have not confronted the problems and wrestled with the difficulties; so one should not object to the 'self-description' understanding of indicative conditionals on the grounds that the plain person would wrinkle his nose at it. I am not doing that. I appeal not to common opinion but to common usage, contending that the 'self-description' account of indicative conditionals contradicts how they fit into our lives, the role they play in our thought and talk. So failure meets this attempt to show how indicative conditionals can have truth values yet be subjective in the way they are shown to be by the Gibbardian stand-off.

37. SUBJECTIVITY WITHOUT SELF-DESCRIPTION

If → is to be ternary, therefore, the belief system in question must be referred to other than through the description 'my belief system', which pretty clearly implies that it must be referred to without use of any description. On this view, what Winifred asserts is not what Lora denies, but neither woman talks about herself. It is as though Winifred said that R₃(Called, Won, Henry) and Lora said that R₃(Called, Lost, James), with their names for their belief states not being replaceable by definite descriptions, and in particular not being replaceable by 'my belief state'. This still makes indicative conditionals subjective, in that what is said by any instance of A→C depends in part upon who says it, but it also gives what is said on each occasion a solid old-fashioned truth value.

The price is too high. I have learned about the difficulties from Gibbard (1981*b*: 231–4) and Stalnaker (1984: 110–11). They present them in the context of a theory according to which A→C says that C obtains at a certain A-world. In this context subjectivity comes in through the proposal that what A-world a speaker of A→C selects depends in part on her belief system; so Winifred and Lora refer to different A-worlds in their seemingly but not really conflicting conditionals. In one version of this approach, each means 'the A-world that relates thus and so to my belief system'; but that is the self-description account, which we have seen to be false. In the other version—our present topic—each means something more like 'the A-world that relates thus and so to Henry', where 'Henry' picks out a belief system, or a part of one, without describing it. The fatal flaws in this attempt at subjectivity, however, can be brought out well enough without mentioning worlds.

The account of the subjectivity of indicative conditionals that we are now considering has bizarre consequences for communication. I ask both Winifred and Lora 'If Pete called, did he win?' Winifred says 'Yes' and Lora says 'No', and both are right. Now four results emerge, in a crescendo of strangeness. They are not answering a single question. There is no single conditional question that I could have put to both. There is not even a coherent conditional question that I could put to either; for there is no privileged belief system for someone who has no probability for A→C and is merely asking about it. And even if there were, I could have no way of putting to either of them the very question that she would answer. This is all too much to swallow, say Gibbard and Stalnaker, and who could disagree?

This speaker-relative view might seem to be strengthened—to gain innocence by association—from the existence of indexicals. But the latter, as Alan Hájek has pointed out to me, count against rather than for the view. When someone speaks using 'I', 'you', 'here', 'now', or 'this', we are not left floundering to know what he or she is talking about. All we need is to know who is talking, or to whom, or where, or when, or indicating what. No such apparatus comes to our aid in understanding indicative conditionals on the view of them we are now considering.

The comparison with indexicals fails in another way. When someone uses 'I' to express a proposition, Stalnaker points out, we can re-express it in other ways; when Miles tells me 'I am hungry' I can report that Miles is hungry; and similarly with 'you', 'here', and the rest. But if someone asserting A→C expresses a proposition that is determined by her beliefs but is not *about* them, there can be no speaker-neutral way to express it. When you assert A→C to me, I literally cannot say what you have told me.

William Lycan (2001) offers an ingenious account of conditionals through which he aims to give a unified treatment of indicatives and subjunctives, allowing conditionals of each kind to have truth values. I shall comment on the second part at the end of §84. The first part—the attempt to cover indicatives—requires Lycan to put something subjective into the truth-conditions for such conditionals; which he does. According to his analysis, the truth of A→C depends upon whether C obtains in a certain class of states of affairs in which A obtains, the class being partly defined by their being states of affairs that *the speaker* regards as real possibilities in a certain sense. This theory evaluates indicative conditionals subjectively, then, and from time to time Lycan does speak of some conditional as 'true for' this or that person. What brings his theory down in ruins, I believe, is his failure to address the issue I have discussed in these two sections. Lycan builds something speaker-relative into what he calls the *truth* conditions of indicative conditionals; but he does not even ask whether speakers of such conditionals are always talking about themselves, or whether . . . and so on.

Objection: 'You have jumped across something. Go back to your "Natus" stories. In one, (1) everyone uses "Natus" to mean "the place where I was born"; in the other, (3) everyone uses "Natus" as the proper name of some place, the places being different for different speakers. You have neglected to consider the intermediate story that (2) everyone uses "Natus" as the proper name of the place where he was born. Analogous to this is the possibility that Winifred means by her conditional something of the form R_3(Called, Won, Henry), where "Henry" is a proper name for her belief system, and everyone knows that that's what it names. According to 2, communication succeeds because we all know that when someone accepts an indicative conditional of the kind here in question, she does so on the basis of a relation between A, C, and her present system of beliefs; but in asserting the conditional the speaker does not speak about herself, because she implicitly refers to the relevant belief system not as "mine" but through a proper name.'

Plausible as this is, I think it is wrong. If the information (P) that *the relevant belief system is the speaker's own* is something the hearer must know if he is to understand what the speaker says, does not that make P a part of what the speaker means by what she says?

Even if this were not so, the proposed account of indicative conditionals still mislocates their point, purpose, and interest. On this latest account, if we allow it to survive, someone who says A→C is giving news about a triadic relation holding amongst A, C, and a certain belief system. It follows that a hearer who says 'You have convinced me' or 'I'm sure you are right' or the like is not saying or even hinting that his own probability for C given A is high; he is merely agreeing that C is high given A within the belief system to which the speaker has somehow referred.

7

Indicative Conditionals
Lack Truth Values

38. NTV

We have found good reason for denying each of these bottom-line accounts of the conflicting conditionals in a Gibbardian stand-off:

Both are false,
One is true and one false,
Both are true.

The first of these belies how smoothly a truth can be inferred from the conjunction of the two; it also implies that countless conditionals that would ordinarily be thought to be acceptable are actually false because in the circumstances their antecedents could not have been true. The second alleges an asymmetry where there is none. The third runs into the difficulties of self-reference (§36) or failure of communication (§37). There remains only this:

Neither is true and neither is false.

This is part of the more general view that indicative conditionals are not propositions, and do not have truth values. Following Lycan, I shall call this 'NTV' for short.

NTV has been advocated and richly developed by Adams (1975: 1–42; 1981*b*; and elsewhere), whose work has convinced others—including Gibbard, Edgington, McDermott, and myself—that he is right.

Adams agrees with Jackson that A→C has Ramseyan conditions for something other than truth, and that the conventional meaning of the indicative 'if' explains this; and Jackson, despite retaining the word 'assertibility', agrees with Adams that the value in question is acceptability. But where Jackson takes this Ramseyan element to be added to a truth condition for indicative conditionals, Adams sees it as the whole story about them. He has no prefatory chapter about what makes these conditionals true or false, because he holds that they are neither.

Before exploring further reasons for accepting NTV, I need to spend two sections on one of its consequences.

39. EMBEDDING INDICATIVE CONDITIONALS

Items with truth values can be freely embedded in larger truth-functional constructions; however complex these are, you can keep your bearings with them, moving sure-footedly with the relevant truth tables as your guide. But when you want to embed something that lacks a truth value, this guide is not available and you cannot move an inch without special help. This is evident with questions and injunctions: 'It's the anniversary of the Pearl Harbour attack today or shut the door!'; 'Are you going anywhere amusing for Christmas? unless air fares have gone up horribly.'

So if A→C were a proposition, it could be embedded in larger propositional structures quite freely. We could negate, disjoin, and conditionalize on indicative conditionals, always having their truth-tables to guide us so that we would always know what we were saying. Adams's theory undermines this procedure. It does not imply that indicative conditionals cannot be embedded, but it cancels the all-season embedding licence, and says that each proposed form of embedding should be judged separately, on its own merits (Adams 1975: 31–7).

Some of Adams's followers have urged this as a merit in his position—as part of the case *for* it—pointing to intuitive evidence that indicative conditionals are indeed not freely embeddable. (See Levi 1988, Edgington 1995b: 280–4, and Gibbard, below.) Even his critic Jackson pays tribute to this evidence. He started (1979: 124) by allowing embedding with no mention of restrictions on it; Appiah (1984: 80) pointed to difficulties; and Jackson has since become more cautious. According to his horseshoe analysis, A→C is logically equivalent to A⊃C, making it unrestrictedly embeddable so far as truth conditions are concerned. But the extra bit—the Ramseyan condition that Jackson ties on through conventional implicature—may not survive embedding, he says (1987: 129): when an indicative conditional occurs as an element in something more complex, the latter's sense cannot be automatically read off from Jackson's account of A→C when it stands alone. Indeed, he acknowledges, his account does not imply that any grammatical embedding of an indicative conditional must generate 'a meaningful sentence'. This is a prudent response to the intuitive evidence that indicative conditionals do not freely embed. (It is also a sixth respect—to be added to the five of §16—in which the Ramseyan feature of → differs from all of Jackson's other examples of conventional implicature.)

Gibbard, who accepts Adams's view that indicative conditionals are 'not propositions', meaning that they lack truth values, hammers at the issue about embedding:

That a non-propositional theory of indicative conditionals fails to account for some embeddings . . . may be a strength. Many embeddings of indicative conditionals, after all, seem not to make sense. Suppose I tell you, of a conference you don't know much about, 'If Kripke was there if Strawson was, then Anscombe was there.' Do you know what you have been told? (Gibbard 1981b: 235)

Some embeddings of conditionals 'do seem to be assertable', says Gibbard, but only because they are read in special ways that do not come straight from the conventional meanings of the sentences. He introduces the example of someone who knows that a cup was being held about twelve inches above a carpeted floor, and asserts:

Cup: If the cup broke if it was dropped, it was fragile,

which seems like a permissible thing to say. There is much to learn from Gibbard's elegant discussion of this. Note first that this example brings no comfort to the horseshoe analysis. Suppose the cup was not dropped, did not break, and is not fragile. In that case the material conditional:

Matcup: (The cup was dropped ⊃ The cup broke) ⊃ The cup is fragile

is false, since it has a true antecedent and a false consequent, though Cup still sounds all right. Someone who thinks that Cup is equivalent to Matcup because → is ⊃ must explain why Cup is assertible when it is false. Conversational implicature will not help, Gibbard points out (p. 236): it explains unassertible truths, not assertible falsehoods. The same holds for Jackson's use of conventional implicature.

Still, Cup does seem all right, and does seem to embed an indicative conditional, and an Adams theorist must explain this. Well, Gibbard suggests, perhaps it strikes us as assertible because its antecedent, 'The cup broke if it was dropped', could be asserted on the grounds that the cup is disposed to break upon being dropped (call this proposition 'Basis'), and in a given context we might find Cup acceptable because we understand it not as meaning

(The cup was dropped → The cup broke) → The cup is fragile,

but rather as meaning

Basis → The cup is fragile,

which does not embed an indicative conditional.

This (mis)understanding of 'The cup broke if it was dropped' depends on its being thought to rest upon Basis. In another situation it might be accepted for a quite different reason. For example, I instruct my assistant 'If the cup is dropped and does not break, come and tell me; otherwise I do not want to be disturbed', and I hear nothing from her all day; I can then say 'I suppose that *if the cup was dropped, it broke*'; and I shall not be tempted to think it makes sense to treat this as the antecedent of a larger conditional such as Cup.

In logical systems, conditionals are and must be unrestrictedly embeddable. I account for this by saying that those are indeed material conditionals, ⊃ being just what one needs for logic and mathematics. The 'if' of most plain English is not the 'if' that is used when logical formulae are expressed in words—except when we are doing specifically the logic of ordinary indicative conditionals (Chapter 9).

This section barely scratches the surface of what is evidently a highly complex business. Max Kölbel (2000) presents some other embeddings of conditionals, and shows how an Adams theorist might deal with them, but then he comes to existentially quantified conditional statements such as 'There is a boy in my class who will get angry if I criticize him', which he says presents for the Adams theory a problem that he (Kölbel) does not know how to solve. Edgington (2000) responds that this example, although it presents difficulties, does not tell against Adams's theory. For this she has particular reasons, arising from treatments that she suggests for the example, and also a more general, counter-attacking reason:

Compounds of conditionals are hard: much harder than one would expect if conditionals have truth conditions. David Lewis wrote 'We think we know how the truth conditions of sentences of various kinds are determined by the truth conditions of constituent subsentences, but this knowledge would be useless if any of those subsentences lacked truth conditions' (1976: 141–2). Now this knowledge *is* useless (or at least far from sufficient) when we try to figure out how conditionals function as subsentences. If conditionals had truth conditions, it would not be. So reflections about compounds support the conclusion that conditionals don't have truth conditions. (Edgington 2000: 115)

McGee (1989) has offered some theory that would allow for embeddings of indicative conditionals, starting with the assigning of a probability to (A→B) & (C→D) and building from there. Plausible counterexamples to his account have been offered by Lance (1991). For some general comments on all this, see Edgington 1995*b*: 308–11.

Lycan sees it as a problem for NTV that 'Indicative conditionals embed in longer sentences' (2001: 77). I do not well understand two specific problems he presents concerning this, but I do understand him when he writes that NTV must confront such sentences as

S: Marsha believes that John will leave if she does, and Sharon dislikes John so much that if she concurs, she will try to persuade Marsha to leave.

While declining Lycan's invitation to bring this under 'rules for projecting assertibility values' etc., or under a three-valued logic, I offer an informal account of what should be going on when someone asserts S. In affirming S, the speaker asserts two propositions: (*a*) that Marsha gives a high probability to *John will leave* conditional on *Marsha will leave*; and (*b*) that Sharon greatly dislikes John. The speaker also (*c*) expresses his own high probability for *Sharon will try to persuade Marsha to leave* conditional on *Sharon will concur*, and (*d*) offers his acceptance of *b* as a salient reason for this high conditional probability. I am not sure whether to classify *d* as a matter of asserting or of merely expressing, but I cannot see that it matters much. As for the mingling of a truth valued assertion with something non-truth valued that is based upon it, there is nothing exotic about that. Compare: 'She hit him so hard that it wasn't funny', 'It was too like Boucher to be beautiful'.

If you are puzzled over *what* Sharon is being thought to 'concur' in, don't hold that against my account. It comes from Lycan's example, and puzzles me too.

40. A SPECIAL CASE: A → (B→C)

An embedding that has received much deserved attention is A → (B→C). It is natural to think of this as somehow linked to (A&B) → C. When you are told

If Kripke was there, then if Strawson was there Anscombe was there,

you will find it natural to equate this with

If Kripke and Strawson were there, Anscombe was there.

Equating these is tantamount to accepting the thesis I called If-and in §25, namely

$$\pi(Q{\to}R)/A) = \pi(R/(Q\&A), \text{ when } P(Q\&A) > 0.$$

I agree with Gibbard (1981*b*: 237) and others that we can naturally hear A → (B→C) as meaning the same as (A&B) → C, and this seems to be because they are strictly equivalent. In §25 we saw an argument of Hájek's for this, but there are other considerations as well.

Ask yourself what you *could* mean by the nested conditional other than what is meant by the other. What could conceivably count against either but not the other? To confirm the linking of those two, apply the Ramsey test to A → (B→C): suppose the addition of A to your system of beliefs, allow it to ramify conservatively through the system, and see what probability for B→C results. The latter probability depends on a second application of the Ramsey test. Here are the two in tandem: suppose the addition of A to your belief system S_1, letting it ramify to produce system S_2; suppose the addition of B to S_2 and allow it to ramify, yielding system S_3; now see what value P(C) has in S_3. This coherent two-step procedure gives a kind of legitimacy to A → (B→C). However, those two Ramsey-test steps are, just precisely, the two halves of the procedure needed to get the probability of the unproblematic (A&B) → C. For this reason, I accept If-and, which I am now understanding as the thesis that A → (B→C) is logically equivalent to (A&B) → C.

It might be objected that the upshot of adding A and letting it ramify, *then* adding B to the result and letting that ramify, could differ from the upshot of adding A&B and letting it ramify. This objection is wrong, but the thought that generates it is worth examining. In this matter I have been greatly helped by Lance and Stalnaker. Here is an example of the generating thought:

We have two urns with balls in them. Urn 1 has 90 red iron balls and 10 green copper ones. Urn 2 has 90 green iron balls, and 10 red copper ones. Agnes has picked an urn at random, and then drawn a ball out of it at random. After noting its colour and composition, she replaced it and then drew a second ball at random from the same urn. We know all this. In discussing this, let

R = the first ball she picked was red.
G = the second ball she picked was green.
C = the second ball she picked was copper.

Our probability for (R&G) → C should be 0.1. Why? Because the supposition of R&G does not make either urn likelier than the other to be the one Agnes picked; and with regard to the two urns taken together, the probability of C is 0.1 because one tenth of all the balls in the two urns are made of copper.

But now consider R → (G→C). When we add R hypothetically to our stock of beliefs, the probability that she picked urn 1 goes to 0.9. And under the assumption that she picked urn 1, the probability of G→C goes to 1, because in that urn all the green balls are made of copper. On the assumption that Agnes picked urn 2, the probability of G→C goes to 0, because there are no green copper balls in that urn. So the probability of G→C conditional on R is $0.9 \times 1 + 0.1 \times 0 = 0.9$. So our probability for R → (G→C) should be 0.9.

This claims to show that the two Ramsey procedures can yield different results—which would kill my argument and provide a counterexample to If-and. Do not dismiss the example as too artificial to be interesting; balls and urns are just a device to make clear the shape of the thought. Once you have this clear, you will find you can devise meatier and humanly more interesting examples.

However, the example reaches its damaging conclusion by relying on a wrong account of the probability we should assign to R → (G→C). When you conduct the first Ramsey-test step, supposing that P(R) = 1, what is your total belief state? Well, it includes R, and also includes a 0.9 level of credence that Agnes drew from urn 1. Into that frame of mind, introduce the supposition that P(G) = 1, and many further changes may ensue—for example an extinction of your previous belief that Agnes has never held anything green in her hand. *One of the changes will be a lowering of your probability for Agnes's having picked urn 1.* The supposition of R made that proposition highly likely, but the further supposition of G makes it much less so. In fact, it ought to reduce your probability for it to 0.5, meaning that you are neutral as between the two urns; and this, given the rest of what you believe, will lead you to P(C) = 0.1. Thus, by Ramseying first on R and then on G, you reach the same state as you would have by Ramseying on R&G. In conducting the Ramsey procedure for evaluating R → (G→C) you must freeze P(R), holding it steady at the value 1; but you are not required to freeze every credence level that results from P(R) = 1; all of those are revisable in any further Ramseyan steps we take.

I am not saying this:

> Although strictly speaking A → (B→C) is meaningless, it does no harm for us to 'hear' it as meaning what (A&B) → C does, this being a useful bit of semantic opportunism.

On the contrary, I welcome A → (B→C) as a perfectly good indicative conditional which is logically equivalent to (A&B) → C. As we have seen, we can apply the Ramsey test to it: the input is A, the output a high probability for B→C. Contrast this innocent procedure with trying to conduct the Ramsey test on (A→B) → C. You cannot just start with a hypothetical input of a high probability for A→B; such a probability must be the upshot of many other parts of a belief system, and there might be many different ways in which it could be produced. Take some one of them as input for the Ramsey test and you are dealing not with (A→B) → C but rather with P→C where P is a basis for A→B. If on the other hand you take A→B itself as your input for the Ramsey test, it is too indeterminate for the test to be conducted. This difference explains the intuitive difference in how the two complex conditionals sound to us—one natural, the other weird.

The natural A → (B→C) has historical interest. In his famous 'barber-shop paradox', Lewis Carroll (1894) tells this tale. (1) Three barbers—Allan, Brown, and Carr—never leave the shop empty during the day. Also, (2) Brown has a nervous disability rendering him invincibly unwilling ever to go out except in Carr's company. From 1 Carroll infers

If Allan is out, then if Brown is out then Carr is in; A → (B→¬C).

From 2 he infers:

If Brown is out, then Carr is out; B→C.

The 'paradox' is that the supposition (A) of Allan's being out yields a conditional (B→¬C) that is contradicted by another conditional (B→C) which is established. This seems to entail that (¬A) Allan is in. Yet 1 and 2 patently do not entail ¬A, for they are satisfied when Allan is out and Brown is in. What, then, has gone wrong? I answer that A → (B→¬C) means the same as (A&B) → ¬C; but 1 and 2 jointly entail that Allan and Brown are never out at the same time, so we should dismiss this conditional because we accord a probability of zero to its antecedent.

A → (B→C) is also involved in a supposed counterexample to Modus Ponens, which I shall discuss in §61.

Finally, let us consider the special case where A = C. If-and implies that C → (B→C) is equivalent to (C&B) → C; the latter is necessary; and from that two troubles have been thought to arise. I shall consider one in §53, when we are ready for it. The other can be dealt with now.

From If-and it seems to follow that C → (B→C) should be endorsed in all its instances, even ones where B is inconsistent with C. Gibbard (1981b: 234) has bitten the bullet on this, contending that C → (B→C) is indeed a logical truth that would be 'accepted even by someone for whom C is assertible and B→C is not' (246 n. 17). Perforce, he accepts 'If Andrew Jackson was President in 1836, then even if he died in 1835, he was President in 1836', as a logical truth.

Happily, we need not swallow that pill. Whether or not A = C, when A is incompatible with B, no probability should be assigned to A&B → C, because of zero-intolerance. Therefore (by If-and) no probability should be assigned to A → (B→C) either. And if we set If-and aside, and consider A → (B→C) on its own by examining its Ramseyan credentials, we again find that it can have no probability when A is inconsistent with B. To evaluate it in the Ramseyan manner, we must first suppose P(A) = 1 and then, holding that steady, we must further suppose P(B) = 1; but this cannot be done when A is incompatible with B.

So If-and is safe. It means that the probability of A → (B→C) always equals the probability of A&B → C for the same values of A, B, and C. It is silent about the case where A is incompatible with B, for there neither conditional has any probability. Near the start of this section I formulated If-and in a way that explicitly covers it against this supposed difficulty.

41. FOUR ROUTES TO NTV

I know of four bases upon which one might accept NTV. One I went through in Chapter 6: many indicative conditionals have a subjective element to them, yet they are not devices whereby the speaker reports some fact about himself. The only other way to accommodate this subjectivity is to suppose that in an indicative conditional the speaker *expresses* but does not *report* a fact about his own state of mind. In the absence of anything else he could be reporting, the conclusion is that indicative conditionals are not reports at all; that is, they are not propositions with truth values.

Secondly, there are short, direct arguments for NTV. Edgington 1986 gives one, and an even sharper and more stripped-down argument occurs in her 1995*b*: 278–80 (see also Adams 1983: 290–1). It has two premisses:

(1) Being certain that A∨C, without being certain that A, is sufficient for being certain that ¬A→C.

(2) It is not necessarily irrational to disbelieve A yet also disbelieve that A→C.

1 concerns a special case of the or-to-if inference (§18), namely the inference from perfect confidence in the disjunction to perfect confidence in the conditional. 2 contrasts → with ⊃, for it *is* irrational to disbelieve A and also disbelieve A⊃C.

Now, adopt the hypothesis that A→C is a proposition, which always has a truth value. Because of premiss 2, it must be possible for A→C to be false while A is false, and thus while A⊃C is true. It follows trivially that ¬A→C could be false while ¬A⊃C is true, that is, while A∨C is true. In that case, being perfectly certain that A∨C would not entitle one to be perfectly certain that ¬A→C, and so premiss 1 would fail.

In short, 1 requires → to be stronger than ⊃, while 2 requires it not to be. So the hypothesis is false; A→C is not a proposition.

The Adams form of NTV lets us satisfy both premisses at once. Premiss 1 is true because having a probability of 1 for A∨C involves having a probability of 0 for ¬A&¬C, which involves having a belief system such that: if you add ¬A to it and conservatively adjust the rest to make room for it, the result is a probability of 1 for C. This is just to say that P(¬A→C) = 1. And premiss 2 is true because one can have a low probability for A and also a low probability for C given A.

Handle both premises in terms of probabilities, and all goes well; handle them in terms of truth values, and they conflict.

At the end of §31 I mentioned a third route to NTV, namely the argument based on its unique power to protect the Equation from the 'triviality' proofs of Lewis and others. Let us now look into this.

The mere denial that A→C is a proposition, which always has a truth value, does not on its own extricate Adams from Lewis's triviality proofs. Thus Lewis:

> Merely to deny that probabilities of conditionals are probabilities of truth, while retaining all the standard laws of probability . . ., would not yet make it safe to revive the thesis that probabilities of conditionals are conditional probabilities. It was not the connection between truth and probability that led to my triviality results, but only the application of standard probability theory to the probabilities of conditionals . . . Whoever still wants to say that probabilities of conditionals are conditional probabilities had better also employ a non-standard calculus of 'probabilities'. . . But if it be granted that the 'probabilities' of conditionals do not obey the standard laws, I do not see what is to be gained by insisting on calling them 'probabilities'. (Lewis 1976: 141)

I have not found Adams suggesting that the Equation can be rescued from Lewis's triviality results just by the denial that A→C always has a truth value, though others have made that mistake. Of the two escapes from the Lewis result that Adams *does* offer (1975: 7, 35), I find the second more helpful. It depends upon the fact that his theory sets limits on how freely indicative conditionals can be embedded in larger propositional compounds. The Lewis argument assumes—Adams writes—that 'probabilities attach to truth-conditional compounds (in particular conjunctions) of conditionals in such a way as to satisfy the [standard] axioms', and Adams denies that they do. And he has met Lewis's challenge 'Then why call the concept you are working with *probability?*' by saying that what he calls the probability of A→C is, roughly speaking, a measure of the 'desirability of believing' A→C, and that this—as he wrote to me—makes it 'appropriate to call [the items in question] *probabilities*, whatever laws they satisfy'.

In fact, the concept of what Adams calls 'probability' deserves that name because it *does* satisfy the standard axioms. Where he parts company from the Lewis proofs is not in the axioms, but rather in his view about what expressions can be substituted for the sentential letters in them. A fully axiomatized logic of probability will contain a rule of inference permitting the substitution of any well-formed sentential formula for any single sentential letter in any axiom or theorem; and that is what Adams rejects.

Sometimes a statement that seems to embed an indicative conditional may be all right because it admits of a saving interpretation. For example, we can understand the assertion of (A→C) & (B→D) as the assertion of A→C followed by the assertion of B→D, which is unproblematic (Adams 1975: 32–3). Presumably, then, Adams could also make sense of the assertion of A & (A→C), equating it with a pair of assertions, one of A and one of A→C. What the various disproofs of the Equation need, however, is not the mere *assertion* of such a conjunction but the *assignment of a probability* to it; and Adams's scheme confers no sense on that.

Lewis remarked in passing that his triviality results might be evaded by restrictions on embedding, calling such restrictions a high price to pay, and offering this as 'an inconclusive objection' to the thesis that indicative conditionals do not have truth values (1976: 85). Against this, I submit that the intuitive linguistic data assembled by Gibbard and others (§§39–40) show this to be not a drawback but a merit in the Adams theory.

The ban on embedding protects the Equation from Lewis's original proofs, and from Edgington's and Blackburn's versions of the first of them (§25); also from the proof of Carlstrom and Hill and its generalization by Hájek 1994 (§§27–8), and from Stalnaker's proof (§29). Look back at each of those and you will see indicative conditionals occurring in compounds that are suspect from the point of view of Adams's theory.

This line of defence fails against Hájek's extraordinary 1989 disproof of the Equation, which does not embed. But it conflicts with NTV in a different way, which offers a different line of defence. Hájek's argument requires A→C to be a free-standing proposition that can be assigned a probability that is to be *matched* by a certain conditional probability, namely $\pi(C/A)$. The proof shows that there cannot be enough conditional probabilities to provide the needed matches. In Adams's theory, the Equation does not assert an equality; rather, it *defines* $P(A→C)$ as $\pi(C/A)$, telling us what a conditional probability is. This does not make it trivial. Although the Equation, on this account of it, does not embody a substantive claim, it does clarify the notion of the probability of an indicative conditional; and to this Adams adds the substantive thesis that there is no more fundamental fact about $P(A→C)$ than this; and, in particular, that $P(A→C)$ is *not* the probability of truth for a proposition A→C.

Adams was proposing that indicative conditionals do not have truth values long before Lewis's triviality results were achieved. (See Adams 1965: 170; 1966: 265–6. I found these references in Edgington 1995a: 70.) But Lewis's results and their successors strengthen the case for his view. It is hard to avoid the idea that any sound understanding of indicative conditionals will have at its heart the Equation, which seems to be tenable only on the basis of Adams's theory.

The fourth of the routes to NTV that I mentioned at the start of this section is an argument of Richard Bradley's (2000). Its author presents this in a forbiddingly compressed form. I shall expound it with help from Dorothy Edgington's defence of it against my initial conviction that the argument rests on a simple error.

Premiss 1 is that for any three propositions Q, R, and S such that neither Q nor R entails S, it can be that P(Q) > 0, P(R) > 0, and P(S) = 0. I thought at first that this fails when Q&R entails S, but that was a blunder on my part. A theologian might give some credence to 'All men are mortal' and some to 'Jesus is a man', while regarding it as utterly ruled out that Jesus is mortal. To see through my error more clearly, inspect Fig. 1, a Venn diagram, for the case where S is entailed by Q&R but not by either Q or R. You can see that if P(S) = 0 then P(Q&R) = 0; every chance of S's being false is a chance of (Q&R)'s being false; that's what it is for the conjunction to entail S. But even if *that* part—the shared part—of Q's and R's territory has a probability of zero, Q and R as such can have probabilities higher than that. For a proof in terms of Boolean algebras, see Bradley 2000: 220–1.

Premiss 2 says that it is always wrong to assign probability > 0 to A and to A→C while holding that P(C) = 0. To use one of Bradley's examples: it would be absurd to say that we may go down to the beach, and it may be that if we go to the beach we shall swim, but there is no chance at all that we shall swim.

Clearly 1 is on a collision course with 2; and the most plausible escape is to keep A→C outside the scope of 1 by denying that it is a proposition.

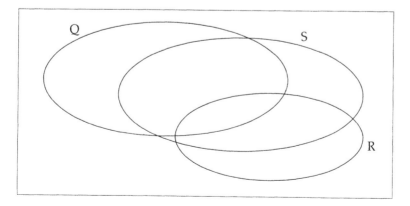

FIG. 1

42. NTV AND MORAL EXPRESSIVISM

Let us pause to compare indicative conditionals according to Adams with moral judgements according to *expressivism* about them—that is, the thesis that such judgements lack objective truth values and serve only to express certain of our attitudes (see e.g. Hare 1952, 1963, 1981, and Gibbard 1990). I shall continue to use 'NTV' to name only the thesis that indicative conditionals lack truth values; it could be used to name moral expressivism as well, but I do not so use it.

NTV and moral expressivism are both theses in semantics, but they differ. Most adherents of expressivism see it as semantics in the service of the metaphysical thesis that there are no objective moral facts or properties, that good and bad or right and wrong are not features of reality. The semantics is not required for the metaphysics. If expressivism is mistaken, our moral judgements do entail the existence of objective moral facts and properties; but one may still deny that there actually are any. Thus Mackie (1977: 35), who rejected expressivism and condemned all our moral judgements as false because they entail a false metaphysic. Nor does the semantics entail the metaphysics, though it exerts pressure in that direction. An expressivist is unlikely to regard the metaphysical question as interestingly open. If his semantics is right, then none of our actual moral judgements entails that there are objective moral facts or properties; and the metaphysical question—are there such facts and properties, though we never say anything about them?—will starve to death.

This contrasts strongly with NTV, a thesis whose interest lies wholly within semantics rather than being offered as a step towards a metaphysical conclusion. Still, we can usefully compare these two semantic theses, considered just in themselves.

The expressivist holds that the thrust of a moral judgement comes purely from the speaker's attitudes; seeing that such judgements do not report the speaker's attitudes, he concludes that they express those attitudes without actually saying what they are. Analogously, the Adams theorist holds that the conditional nature of an indicative conditional comes from a relation between two of the speaker's subjective probabilities; he sees that such conditionals are not reports on one's subjective probabilities; so he opts for NTV, the view that in asserting A→C a person expresses his high probability for C given A, without actually saying that this probability is high.

Statements of the two kinds are alike in how they can be useful to others. If you tell me that a certain kind of action is wrong, I learn something about your attitude to it; and I would have learned this if instead of expressing the attitude you had told me that you have it. Similarly with your asserting A→C: from your expressing your high probability for C given A, I learn what I would also have learned if you had told me that for you this probability is high.

However, the two kinds of statement differ in what is involved in believing or accepting them. If your moral judgement or your conditional had been a self-report, my believing it would merely be my believing in your sincerity. We have room for an acceptance that goes far beyond mere trust in the speaker's sincerity. When you convince me that the elimination of all pain would be bad, you let me know of your adverse attitude to the idea of eliminating all pain and you bring me to share it. When you convince me that A→C, you let me know that you have a high probability for C given A and you bring me to share it.

I have been told that only items with truth values can properly be said to be 'asserted' and 'believed'. If this were so—and I know of no evidence for it—we could easily speak of indicative conditionals as being *affirmed* and *accepted*, and expressivists could adopt those terms in relation to moral judgements. Nothing substantive turns on this choice of terminology, so far as I can see.

Lycan has marshalled ten arguments (2001: 73–81) against NTV, of which the first alleges that it is 'peculiar to say the least' to suppose that 'alone among English declarative sentences, *indicative conditionals* by their nature lack truth values'. In fact, indicative conditionals are merely one species in the genus of declarative sentence whose members do not have truth values. A given sentence S gets into the genus by having these two features: (1) Someone who uses S declaratively in an assertion is in the last resort answerable only to his own state of mind; (2) We do not standardly treat such a person as thereby saying what his state of mind is. The 1–2 combination makes it reasonable to say that S express-es the speaker's state of mind but does not say that P, for any P; which implies that S does not have a truth value. Typical members of the genus are: 'This story is disgusting.' 'That joke is not funny!' 'What he did was wrong.' 'Miss Morgan is so uninteresting' (to which Mary Garth, making my point, replied: 'She is interesting to herself, I suppose' (*Middlemarch*, ch. 12)). The moral example is controversial, but the fact that some philosophers of repute accept 'expressivism' about moral judgements—and are taken seriously by Lycan on his p. 80—makes his 'peculiarity' objection look peculiar.

We can turn on its head a criticism that Jackson levels against NTV (1987: 57), namely that it makes indicative conditionals *special*—Jackson's italics. Well, not so very special, as we have just seen. Jackson, on the other hand, tries to keep spe-cialness at bay by implying that what he attributes to indicative conditionals is routine conventional implicature; but we have seen that his good account of the latter, and his examples of it, have almost no fit with indicative conditionals on his own account of those (§16). If they did conventionally implicate that they satisfy the Ramsey test, that *would* be special!

Jackson also defends himself against Appiah, who wrote that Adams and NTV cover the ground, so that we need not 'tack on' truth conditions as well. Jackson protests: 'To have assertibility conditions best explained by certain truth-conditions *is* to have those truth-conditions. You do not need to "tack" something extra on!' (1987: 58). I think that Appiah had the wrong metaphor: rather than being 'tacked on' as an arbitrary appendix to Jackson's story, his horseshoe analysis is an idle first chapter.

43. THE SALUTARY LIMITS OF NTV

To understand NTV properly, one must grasp why the self-descriptive account of indicative conditionals (§36) is not right. When you assert A→C, I do take some information away from this, namely that your probability for C given A is high. I can then make use of this as I see fit. What I get from your telling me that A→C is exactly what I would have got if you had instead told me your value for $\pi(C/A)$. What primarily interests me is (in most cases) what probability I should assign to C on the supposition of A; but if your saying A→C gives me any help with that, it is exactly the help I could have got from your reporting to me that for you C is highly probable given A. Either way, I get *information* about your epistemic state, which I use in the light of my estimate of your cognitive abilities. I get nothing else.

Friendly proposal: 'Having gone so far, why not take the further step of allowing that my assertion of A→C *is* my report on my conditional probability for C given A? This would free you from the unpopular denial of a truth value to my conditional—a large reward in return for a non-existent risk.'

On the contrary, it would be a 'large reward' in return for a lie. Your assertion of A→C was not a report on your state of mind because neither you nor I treated it in that manner. I sketched this point in §36, but need to re-emphasize it now. When I asked 'Are you sure?' and you said 'Yes, fairly sure', you were not assuring me that your probability for C given A was high; rather, you were expressing confidence in that high conditional probability. There is abundant linguistic evidence that the spectrum of notions relating to confidence—doubt, indecision, certainty, and so on—when applied to indicative conditionals *all always* relate to the height of the person's conditional probability for C given A, and *never* to the person's confidence about what his or her probability for C given A is.

Something similar holds for other kinds of utterance through which we express rather than report states of mind—ones in which we express moral disapproval, general disgust, admiration, amusement, and so on. Suppose we were to forgo 'That is funny' and its like, and to settle instead for self-reports such as 'That amuses me'. This shift would not dramatically alter our thought or speech, but it would make some difference. In place of the likes of this:

> I say 'That is funny',
> You say 'No it's not', and
> I respond by trying to get you to be amused by the item as I am,

we would have the likes of this:

> I say 'That amuses me',
> You say 'It doesn't amuse me', and
> I respond by trying to get you to be amused by the item as I am.

Though not a large difference in the substance of what is going on, this is a significant difference in the language used.

Similarly for the others. In the case of moral judgements, there would be a larger difference, because so many people think that such judgements are truth valued reports on facts that are not subjective. To those people, things would seem enormously different if we traded in 'That is evil' for a suitably strong statement about one's opposition to the item in question, because *they* would think that we were trading in metaphysically grounded morality for mere self-reporting. But this supposed difference has nothing to do with my topic, which is the difference between expressing a state of one's mind and reporting it.

Some philosophers have contended that NTV clashes with deflationism about truth (or about 'true'). According to this, calling something 'true' is equivalent to repeating or endorsing it; one can repeat or endorse an indicative conditional; so the deflationist should say that such conditionals can rightly be said to be true. Lycan—himself no deflationist—thinks that deflationists about 'true' who are expressivists about moral judgements are caught in 'either a flat contradiction or as near to one as matters' (2001: 80 n. 9); and he implies a similar judgement on any deflationist who accepts NTV (about indicative conditionals). This is a misunderstanding. Whatever exactly deflationism is, it is a doctrine about *all* uses of 'true'; it aims to contribute to the consideration of meaning and truth *in general*, and to be applicable equally to 'That is funny' and 'That amuses me', to A→C and to A. Whatever the grounds for it, they cannot conflict with NTV, which is *essentially* a limited doctrine, applying to some sentences and not others, because of differences in our handlings of the two sorts. The crucial fact is that when someone asserts a sentence of this kind, he expresses but does not report a fact about his state of mind; and we can contrast this with a different sentence that would report such a fact, and *that we would call true or false*.

How can global deflationism be stated so as to avoid riding roughshod over local doctrines such as NTV? Hartry Field has satisfied me that this is a deep and complex matter (see Field 1994); I am neither equipped nor willing to swim in those deep waters; but I think that for my purposes something shallow will suffice. I suggest: *for every sentence S that can properly be said to be true*, saying that S is true is equivalent to affirming S. Something like that. It would be mere incompetence to express deflationism in such a way as to smudge the line between sentences that can and ones that cannot properly called true.

44. MEANING AND EXPRESSING

Jackson and Pettit (1998) presented 'a problem for [moral] expressivism' which is, as Jackson has written to me, equally a problem for NTV. I shall present the Jackson–Pettit position directly in relation to NTV (about indicative conditionals); if I can defang that, it will be a relatively simple task to solve it for moral expressivism as well.

The challenge from Jackson and Pettit says that the friends of NTV assert two things that they cannot reconcile: that A→C *does express* a subjective conditional probability, and that A→C *does not report the existence of* such a probability. We have the two turns of phrase, and we can relate them differently to 'true' and the rest, but can we explain, using a solid, basic, realistic theory of meaning, what it is to use a sentence to express a state of your mind without outright reporting that you have it? Jackson and Pettit hold that we cannot.

The expressing/reporting distinction is not itself under challenge. It is safe to say that *Wow!* and *Ugh!* and their like express states of mind that they do not report. But they are blocked from being reports by their lack of semantic structure. Our way of drawing the expressing/reporting line for them does not—as Jackson and Pettit point out—help us with moral judgements or indicative conditionals.

In meeting their challenge, I take my stand on something on which they also rely, namely the view—shared with Locke, Leibniz, and Grice—that the entry level into the concept of meaning, and into the basic varieties of meanings, is that of communication between speaker and hearer. Some semantic happenings are not tied to utterer-recipient relations, but we can understand them only *through* our grasp of the entry level.

At that absolutely basic level of analysis, the way to understand

When he uttered S, what he meant was . . .

is through its involving

> When he uttered S, he intended to bring it about that . . .

The mode of involvement is complex, and philosophers still disagree about what it is. I hold that H. P. Grice presented the true core of it, in work (§4) that connects only loosely with the ideas of his discussed in Chapter 2 above; and I explain and defend it in my *Linguistic Behaviour* (1976). But none of that need detain us now. The bare notion of uttering S intending to bring it about that Q is always part of the fundamental story about linguistic meaning, and the question of *what* someone means by an utterance depends upon *what* he intends to bring about by making it. The Gricean complexities have to do with what else must be the case for a given uttering-and-thereby-intending to count as meaningful at all; but that is the same story across the board, whereas we are concerned with how some meanings differ from others.

The operative intention is always to produce some change in a hearer. In an injunction, you intend to get the hearer (me) to do something; in an assertion, to get me to believe something. Neither intention will succeed, however, unless you get me to believe something *about you*: saying 'The door is closed' won't get me to believe it is unless I think that *you believe it is*; and saying 'Close the door' won't get me to close the door unless I think that *you want me to close it*. (None of this holds without exception; but let us blink away the distracting drizzle of marginal counterexamples, in order to see the central truth of the matter.)

Why, then, do we not understand 'The door is closed' as reporting that the speaker thinks the door is closed? and 'Close the door' as including a report that the speaker wants the door to be closed? If those two bits of information about the speaker's frame of mind are needed for the further intention to be realized, why do we not allow them to help dictate the meaning of what is said?

It is because we take the utterance's meaning to be determined by the speaker's *telos* or end or ultimate aim. He wants to get the hearer to believe things about what he, the speaker, thinks or wants; but those are wanted only as means to the *telos*, and so they are excluded from the meaning.

In individual cases a speaker may be interested in less. You may say 'The door is open' solely because you want me to believe that *you* think the door is open, with no interest in whether I come to think so too; or you may say 'Close the door, please' only because you want me to think that you want the door to be closed, with no interest in my closing it.

Or a speaker may be hunting for bigger game. He may aim to get the hearer to think the door is open and thence to conclude that James (who said it is closed) is a liar; or to close the door thereby preventing a quarrel from being overheard.

But those are idiosyncrasies. The two utterance-types are *generally* associated with aims that go as far as the hearer's coming to think that the door is open (in one case) or his closing the door (in the other); and there is no further-out aim with which they are *generally* associated. This seems to be what sets the limits to our ideas about 'what he actually said' as distinct from what he suggested, indicated, enabled hearers to infer, or was otherwise 'up to'. Among other things, it fixes what counts as *success* with utterances of either kind: we succeed with an assertion when the hearer believes it; we succeed with an injunction when a hearer obeys it.

As well as *success* there is *support*. What supports the assertion is evidence that the door is open (not that the speaker thinks so). The injunction gets support from reasons for closing the door, or inducements to close it; and, while these may include evidence that the speaker wants the hearer to close the door, they can include much else as well—facts about eavesdroppers, draughts, the law, and so on.

This can all be reapplied to the view that a moral judgement expresses the speaker's attitudes without reporting on them; but that application is complicated, and I shall not go into it here. Rather, I return to the challenge that Jackson and Pettit present to the expressivist or NTV element in the Adams position on indicative conditionals.

When I tell you that A→C, my chief concern is ordinarily not to convince you of a fact about my belief system, but rather to make it a fact about yours; not to convince you that my value for $\pi(C/A)$ is high but to get yours to be high. This goes hand in hand with the facts about support. I do not support my assertion of A→C with evidence about my state of mind; but rather with assertions that will, if you believe them, tend to raise your value for $\pi(C/A)$.

Thus, while it is true that from my asserting A→C you can infer something about my beliefs, the facts about *success* and *support* show that my ultimate meaning-conferring aim is not to give you beliefs about my beliefs, but rather to influence one of your subjective probabilities.

Jackson and Pettit did us a service here. Without a challenge like theirs, and an adequate response to it, NTV might be left as a rather abstract doctrine that we did not fully grasp even though we knew we had to accept it. If we are utterly convinced of the Equation, and wholly persuaded of the soundness of Hájek's 1989 proof (§31), we can escape from contradiction only by denying that there is a truth valued proposition A→C—and thus accepting NTV (for indicative conditionals). But it would be dismal if we had to leave it at that. It is one thing to be convinced of NTV's truth, and a wholly other thing to grasp what its truth amounts to, what facts about our uses of indicative conditionals deprives them of truth values. That is what, in effect, Jackson and Pettit were demanding.

45. 'IF' AND 'WHEN'

I have parried three of Lycan's thrusts at NTV—about indicative conditionals 'alone among English sentences', about deflationism, and about embedding. Others will be dealt with in appropriate places, but one more can be discussed here. Lycan writes: 'The claim that ordinary conditional sentences lack truth values is grossly implausible on linguistic grounds' (2001: 74). The phrase 'grossly implausible' sets the tone for a page that also uses 'bizarre', 'amazing', 'crass', and 'crazy'. Lycan bases his scorn on a pair of points about how 'if' relates to 'when'. The first is that the defenders of NTV have the problem of explaining how 'those two words could have virtually the same syntax but differ so drastically in their semantic treatment'.

The semantics of 'if' and 'when' differ greatly because, along with their syntactic alikeness, 'if' ranges across possibilities whereas 'when' does not. That is what makes it all right to say 'I don't know whether the bud will open, but if it does . . .' and all wrong to say 'I don't know whether the bud will open, but when it does . . .'. A speaker's epistemic state determines the range of possibilities that he encompasses in a dependent indicative conditional; but he is not speaking about that state; and so we say that he is expressing it without asserting anything true or false. Nothing like that holds for 'when'.

Consider how 'That is grammatical' differs from 'That is funny'. Does not that show that a humble difference in word-meaning can, despite sameness of syntax, make the difference between objective factuality and truth valueless expression of a state of mind?

Lycan's second point about linguistic implausibility is that 'if' and 'when' are—as he has argued in his first two chapters—also semantically greatly alike; so much so as to make it incredible that 'I will leave when you leave' has a truth value while 'I will leave if you leave' does not. He rubs this in by pointing to the 'if and when' locution: 'If and when she submits a paper, we'll read it within a month'—Lycan challenges the friends of NTV to say whether that has a truth value or not. I answer that it does not. It means 'If she submits a paper, we'll read it within a month of the time when she submits it'. All other decent 'if and when' statements can be treated similarly, putting 'when' into the consequent. 'If and when you leave, I'll leave' means 'If you leave, I'll leave at the time when you do'.

8

Uses of Indicative Conditionals

46. TRUE → FALSE IS FALSE

Up to here, I have taken NTV to be the view that no indicative conditional has a truth value. In fact, Adams and most of his followers have allowed that whenever A is true and C false, A→C is false. This means *objectively* false: we can judge True → False to be false without reference to who is supposed to be asserting or accepting it. A conditional with a true antecedent and false consequent is a defective intellectual possession for anyone at any time: it is ripe for use in Modus Ponens because A is true, and if so used will lead to error because C is false. (Modus Ponens is not the only use for indicative conditionals, but it is one important one—though see §61.) It does no harm to call a True → False conditional 'false', meaning this in a sternly objective way, so long as we remember that unfalse conditionals need not be true. (For a different view about which indicative conditionals are false, and why, see Warmbröd 1983: 252–3, 258.)

Something else must also be borne in mind. When we deny a truth value to A→C, we are mainly refusing to construe it as a report on the speaker's belief system. As I have already perhaps over-emphasized, NTV concerns two ways in which someone's state of mind can be involved in something he says—as reported, and as merely expressed. But when we allow that T→F can be called 'false', we are not treating it as a report on the speaker's state of mind: if it were such a report, it might well be true! In calling it 'false' we do not pass judgement upon it as a report; rather, we pass judgement on the state of mind expressed by the conditional.

Perhaps that is why Adams regards this as an 'auxiliary' and 'technical' use of the term 'false' (1965: 187; 1981a: n. 5). I see his point, but on balance I agree with McDermott (1996: 24) that it is ordinary, objective falsehood in the normal sense of 'false'.

The thesis that True → False is always false provides a neat way of explaining conditionals like 'If Bennett is a logician, I'm a monkey's uncle'. An audience for this will know, and know that the speaker knows (and knows that they know) that the consequent is false. So it is mutually known that the conditional is false unless its antecedent is false, i.e. unless Bennett is not a logician; and this is all so obvious that everyone takes it that this is what the speaker meant to convey. This little result does not, however, count strongly for the thesis that True → False is always false; for we could dispense with that and explain in probabilistic terms how 'monkey's uncle' conditionals work.

I shall use 'Adams*' to name the thesis that True → False is always outright false and that no *other* indicative conditional has a truth value. Moving from 'No indicative conditional ever has a truth value' to Adams* reduces the distance from Jackson's position. The gap could then be closed entirely if Jackson took a certain step the other way. On his account, the mere news that A→C is true tells us so little—goes such a tiny distance towards the conditional's being acceptable—that it is misleading to apply the word 'true' to it. We see evidence for this in the energy he must throw into showing why so many putatively true conditionals are absurd, ridiculous, and so on. If he replaced the misleading accolade 'true' by the milder epithet 'not false', then he would be dividing indicative conditionals into the false and the not-false, with the former all being of the type True → False and the latter being evaluated purely through the Ramsey test. This position—call it Jackson*—is identical with Adams* at the bottom line.

This irenic proposal demands more from Jackson than he will yield, no doubt, because to adopt Jackson* he would have to give up the horseshoe analysis; and then he would need a new account of how the Ramsey test comes to be valid for indicative conditionals.

It is a lot to ask, but I think Jackson should accede to it. His joining of a clamorous assertibility (or 'assentability') condition to an almost inaudible truth condition, and the failures of fit between this supposed instance of conventional implicature and all the others he gives—what a relief it should be to drop this and instead adopt Adams*!

Jackson acknowledges that in using indicative conditionals one needs only to be guided by their Ramsey-test assertibility conditions (as he calls them); which amounts to admitting that Adams's account fits all the facts about usage as well as his own does. 'But this is consistent'—he adds—'with insisting that one who does not know that A→C is true if and only if A⊃C lacks something in the way of *philosophical* understanding' (Jackson 1987: 58). He has to be referring to the 'understanding' offered by his thesis about *how* the Ramseyan feature of A→C attaches to it, namely through a convention whose rationale is that it helps the speaker to communicate his central message, which is A⊃C. I have argued that this thesis does not increase our understanding, because it is false.

47. IS TRUE → TRUE TRUE?

The optimistically proposed *rapprochement* with Jackson would be even harder to resist if on the Adams side we adopted Adams**, that being my name for the result of according truth to True → True, as well as falsity to True → False, while holding that no other indicative conditional has a truth value. The idea that T→C always has the same truth value as C has attracted several philosophers, including Mackie (1973: 106–8), who argued for it against a background of views different from any discussed here.

We can accept that T→T = T without crashing into any of the rocks that we have so far charted. In particular, accepting that T→T = T does not make trouble for the Gibbardian stand-offs, for in them the conflicting conditionals always have a false antecedent.

Before looking into reasons for agreeing that True → True is always true, let us dispose of two bad reasons against it.

If we adopt Adams**, we shall have to call 'true' many conditionals that would be stupid things to say, such as: 'If Michelangelo painted the Sistine ceiling, Bellini composed *I Puritani*.' Well, in most circumstances it would be stupid to say this, but not more so than asserting such acknowledged truths as 'Either Michelangelo painted the Sistine ceiling or Bellini composed *I Puritani*'. Gricean theory can handle this matter.

Secondly, suppose I affirm A→C because for me C is highly probable given A, and it turns out that A&C but for reasons having nothing to do with the ones I had in mind. Should not this count against my having said something true? I examine the deserted campsite and announce 'If the Cherokee weren't here, then the Apache were'; in fact, Cherokee haven't been here and Apache have; but I have read the evidence wrongly—all the supposed signs of possible Apache presence came from Iroquois who had used the site after the Apache left. Will we call my conditional true, just because its antecedent and consequent are both true? A defender of Adams** can say: 'Yes, it was true, though you get no credit for that. If you had left the Cherokee out of it and just said "The Apache were here", that too would have been true by dumb luck.'

As well as giving this answer to the second objection, Dorothy Edgington positively supports the thesis that T→T is always true and T→F always false, while still maintaining that F→C has no truth value. She relies on an account of what one does in asserting A→C. One does not assert a conditional proposition, because there is no such thing; rather, one makes a conditional assertion (§51). It is, she writes, 'an assertion of C when A is true, and an assertion of nothing when

A is false.' She continues: 'It is natural, then, to say my conditional assertion is true if A and C are both true, and false if A is true and C is not, and has no truth value when A is false' (1995b: 290). It may be natural, but it does not quite follow. Granted that when A is true I make an assertion that is true or false depending on whether C is true or false, that falls short of calling my entire conditional true or false in such a case.

It might be good to call A→C 'true' when A and C are both true; but I am not yet convinced of this. Edgington warns us that if we do take this line we must distinguish believing A→C from believing it to be true. As it is true (according to Adams**) only if both A and C are true, believing it to be true is believing that A&C; but one can believe or accept A→C without believing A&C. This points to an underlying source of worry about Adams**, namely that its basis for applying 'true' has not enough to do with the home ground of indicative conditionals, namely conditional subjective probabilities. The Adams* thesis that T→F is always false, though stated purely in terms of the truth values of A and C, can be connected with the home ground. Given any serious reason for interest in which conditionals to accept, when A is true and C false it is objectively, interpersonally, *bad* to accept A→C or to give a high value to C given A. You may say that it is objectively, interpersonally, *good* to accept A→C or to give a high value to $\pi(C/A)$ when A and C are both true; but there the case is different. The attempt to arrive at the most probable conditionals one can find is, in effect, an attempt to get as far as one can from accepting A→C when A is true and C false. It is not in a comparable way an attempt to get as near as one can to accepting A→C when A and C are both true. Accepting Adams*, I reserve judgement on Adams**, though I am sure the issue is not a weighty one. For further arguments in favour of Adams**, as well as other good things, see McDermott 1996.

In these two sections, my topic has been indicative conditionals whose antecedent is true and that are *dependent*, in the §7 sense of the term. When C can be extracted from A by logic alone, or by logic and causal laws, the frame of mind of anyone who accords a low probability to A→C is open to criticism; there is nothing subjective about this, because different states of information about matters of particular fact are irrelevant to it. So we have a good reason to call A→C true when A entails or causally implies C, whether A is true or false. The same holds when A implies C through general moral principles alone, unless moral expressivism is correct. In the latter case, independent moral conditionals lack truth values after all—but that is because they are moral, not because they are indicative conditionals. Or so I maintain. For a defence of the dissenting view that A→C lacks a truth value when A is false, even if A entails C, see McDermott 1996: 15–17.

The question about the status of A→C when A causally implies C is 'one in the eye for' NTV, writes Lycan (2001: 71; see also 78–9). Well, it would discomfit a version of NTV that denied truth values to all indicative conditionals; but not the version that denies a truth value to A→C only when *A is false and does not logically, causally, or morally imply* C. Lycan seems not to entertain the thought of such a qualified version of NTV, and I wonder why. Critics may find it suspect because it has a funny shape, resulting from ad hoc trimming back of unrestricted NTV. I reply that the trimmings are indeed ad hoc: each responds to a threat of falsity in the way sensible people *do* meet such threats, by not saying the thing that was going to turn out false.

48. INFERENCE TICKETS

The non-propositional view of indicative conditionals was adumbrated long before Adams, in Gilbert Ryle's view that conditionals are not propositions but 'inference-tickets' (1949: 116–25); though he wrongly said this of subjunctive conditionals, exposing himself to Geach's jibe (1957: 7) that Ryle thought 'The rubber has begun to lose its elasticity' reports 'the incipient expiry of an inference-ticket'.

With conditionals like the Thomason examples (§12), the notion of an inference ticket must be handled warily. When I accept 'If my business partner is cheating me, I will never realize it', I am not setting myself up to infer, in a situation where I come to think my partner is cheating me, that I will never realize that he is doing so. Still, if I assure you of this conditional and you trust my ability to estimate such things, *you* may accept it for use as an inference ticket. Quite generally, A→C is an inference ticket that may be used by anyone who accepts the conditional, unless C entails someone's not knowing or believing A; and even then the ticket can be used by anyone except that person.

Do not let the phrase 'inference ticket' lessen your sense of the worth and dignity of indicative conditionals. They are important devices for moving from beliefs to other beliefs. Is your acceptance of A→C itself a belief? It does no harm to call it that. As Adams points out, the conditional probabilities that indicative conditionals express fit into our cognitive scheme of things along with our non-conditional beliefs; they arise from some beliefs and give rise to new ones in their turn; they are answerable to empirical evidence; they are subject to a rigorous logic (Chapter 9). One naturally thinks of beliefs as always aiming at truth, and we cannot maintain this for beliefs in indicative conditionals. But they can have other virtues that are proper objects of our cognitive endeavours; so we have plenty to aim at, even if truth is not our target.

According to NTV, an indicative conditional can also be communicated. To communicate A→C is to express one's assigning a high probability to C given A; not to report that one has that conditional credence level, but deliberately to show that one has it. Gibbard deals with this neatly. Having shown how indicative conditionals can be communicated, acquired from someone one trusts, and so on, he continues: 'Conditional beliefs—states of high conditional credence—are just as much states of mind as are unconditional beliefs. There is no reason in what has been said here to suppose that a conditional belief constitutes an unconditional belief in a conditional proposition' (Gibbard 1981*b*: 230).

49. ROBUSTNESS₁ AND ROBUSTNESS₂

In §12 above, I distinguished these two forms of statement:

(1) For you at this moment, the probability of C on the supposition of A is high.

(2) As you are now constituted, if you came to be fairly sure of A you would also be or become nearly as sure of C.

To show how 1 might be true even though 2 was false, I gave an example about cancer and religious faith. Here is another. Someone spitefully asks the Marquis whether his wife has a lover. He replies coolly and truthfully that he thinks not, adding that *if the Marquise has been unfaithful to him, that is a secret known only to her, her maidservant, and her lover.* This could pass the Ramsey test. Putting together everything else the Marquis believes about the circles in which he moves—who would blab and to whom, and so on—the supposition of (A) his wife's infidelity generates the conclusion that (C) there has been this three-person secret. So for him C is in Jackson's sense *robust* relative to A. But if the Marquis actually came to believe his wife to be unfaithful, this would unhinge him, driving him into wild conspiracy fantasies involving half of France and banishing any thought of a tight little triangular plot. So it is not the case that if he came to believe A, he would also come to believe C.

In Jackson's terminology, statement 1 of my displayed pair says that for you C is robust with respect to A; but I shall now follow Lewis in using 'robust₁' for this, and 'robust₂' for statements like 2. Thus, in my example, the proposition that only three people know about the Marquise's infidelity is, for the Marquis, robust₁ but not robust₂ with respect to the proposition that she is unfaithful. (I continue to ignore the restriction, sometimes found in Jackson and Lewis, to cases where the person accords a high probability to the consequent. It explains the choice of the word 'robust', but has had no other significant role.)

To the extent that I am rational, won't the two kinds of robustness coincide? Rationality involves aiming to align the causal links amongst one's beliefs with the logical, evidential relations amongst them. So robustness$_1$ implies robustness$_2$ for a person who is secure against irrational disturbances such as occur in my two examples.

Several writers have implied that this is not right, and that robustness$_1$ can exist without robustness$_2$ even for a person who is durably reasonable. This is because of the Thomason examples. Let A be 'The Dean of my College sells drugs' and C be 'I will never think that the Dean of my College sells drugs'. For me now, C is robust$_1$ relative to A, as can be seen through the Ramsey procedure: when I add the Dean's being a drug-runner to the rest of my system of beliefs, and allow it to radiate its effects through the system, the resultant belief scheme includes a high probability for my never thinking he sells drugs. To suppose that he does so requires me—given the rest of what I think—to suppose that he has been skilfully secret about this activity, which for me implies that he will continue to be secret so that I shall never suspect.

On the other hand (so the argument goes) for me C is not robust$_2$ relative to A: if I learned that the Dean sells drugs I would not be led to believe that I would never think he does—quite the contrary! In this case, robustness$_1$ differs from robustness$_2$ for a reason not involving irrationality (thus Jackson 1987: 12).

Stalnaker uses robustness$_2$ to define conditional belief, and seeks to align it with robustness$_1$ through a general stipulation of rationality (1984: 104–5). So he needs to neutralize the Thomason examples, and he does. Robustness$_2$ when properly understood, Stalnaker says, involves the notion of the probability one would assign to C if one came to accept A *while not acquiring other new beliefs as well*. Consider these:

(A)   The Dean sells drugs.

(A*) I believe that the Dean sells drugs.

These are distinct propositions; neither entails the other; I disbelieve both. But any input from the world that added A to my belief system would add A* as well—not as inferred from A but as accompanying it, a further new datum acquired at the same moment. Stalnaker concludes that in this case (C) 'I do not believe that the Dean sells drugs' really is (for me) robust$_2$ relative to (A) 'The Dean sells drugs'. One might instead call the question empty, because the event whose outcome would determine whether C is (for me) robust$_2$ relative to A cannot occur.

So a general rubric about rationality may be enough to close the gap between robustness$_1$ and robustness$_2$.

This would be denied by Vann McGee (2000), who has offered an example, involving neither irrationality nor the Thomason wrinkle, in which robustness$_1$ is not accompanied by robustness$_2$. The example challenges the premiss Jeffrey used in deriving his principle of Generalized Conditionalization (§26), namely that your value for C given A should be the same after you become sure of A as it was before.

McGee points out that this seems to be wrong in one special kind of case—namely, one where you accept A→C because of your trust in the judgement of someone who accords a high probability to A→C and a low one to A. Because you trust this expert, you take on board his high probability for A→C; but when you become sure of the truth of A, which he thought improbable, your faith in him weakens, your credence for A→C goes down accordingly, and you are left reluctant to infer C. This iconoclastic point threatens not only Jeffrey's premiss, but also Modus Ponens for →, and the Ramsey test thesis.

It is, however, a restricted and marginal affair. In most cases, a rational person's probability for A *is* independent of his probability for A→C; indeed, they are bound to be independent if the person is thinking for himself. The McGee phenomenon—in which your value for $P(A→C)$ varies because your value for $P(A)$ does—can occur only when you (1) hand your mind over to an authority regarding A→C, but (2) remain willing to think for yourself regarding A, and (3) will lose faith in the authority if he is (in your opinion) wrong about A. In face of this almost pathological mixture of self-sufficiency and servility, the three doctrinal items I have mentioned must give way; but that is not much of a defeat.

Let us return to the question of what gaps there are between the two kinds of robustness. 'What really matters', said Lewis, 'is robustness$_2$' (1986e: 155–6). We associate indicative conditionals with robustness$_1$, he suggested, because it is relatively accessible and usually serves as 'a reasonable guide' to robustness$_2$, which we cannot easily learn about directly. He was assuming, I suppose, that indicative conditionals are primarily meant for use in Modus Ponens; that is why the Ramsey test is valid for them, and why we scorn conditionals that are accepted purely because their antecedents are false. This seems to imply that for us what matters most is robustness$_2$, for you cannot actually use A→C in Modus Ponens except by actually believing A and still giving a high probability to C.

I am not convinced. One's acceptance of A→C can have various kinds of significance even if one never comes to believe A. My acceptance of 'Even if I have terminal cancer, God does not exist' expresses a part of my way of looking at things and connecting or disconnecting them; it may matter to me to be clear that this is where I stand; it might even matter to you.

I have discussed robustness without mentioning 'dispositions'. Most of us down the years have taken 'x is disposed to ϕ upon ψing' to mean something like

(i) if x were to ψ it would ϕ.

This would make it wrong to equate accepting A→C with being disposed to believe C upon coming to believe A, because of cases like that of the Marquis, who accepts the indicative conditional but of whom the corresponding subjunctive is false. So I thought, until David Lewis pointed me to work by C. B. Martin (1994) which argues that 'x is disposed to ϕ upon ψing' should mean something more like

(ii) x has an intrinsic property F such that if x were to ψ *while retaining F*, it would ϕ.

Lewis rightly warned me that 'Martin wouldn't defend analysis ii'. But I cannot see that Martin makes any *case* against ii. That is one reason for disputing his conclusion (1994: 7) that 'there is no hope for' the project of explaining dispositions through subjunctive conditionals.

Most dispositions fit i as well as ii, but some—known to their aficionados as 'finkish dispositions'—do not. An example would be a crystal whose structure causally suffices for its breaking when struck, except that the immediate effect of its being struck would be to change the crystalline structure to something sturdier. (For a full discussion, see Lewis 1997.)

So we can say that the Marquis has indeed a disposition, upon learning that his wife has a lover, to believe that this has been known only to . . . etc. His having it will not show up in the truth of the corresponding subjunctive conditional, because it is a finkish disposition—one based on an intrinsic property that would be lost if the antecedent of the relevant conditional came true. (Thus Mellor 1993: 241 n. 24.) What intrinsic property would it be? Presumably the property of having a belief system satisfying the Ramsey Test for A→C. If so, then for you to be (post-Martin) disposed to believe C upon coming to believe A is for C to be, for you, robust₁ with respect to A; and for it to be robust₂ with respect to A is for it to be true that if you did come to believe A you would come to believe C— which we used (pre-Martin) to call having a disposition to believe C on coming to believe A. However, I shall continue to move around in these regions without using 'disposition' or its cognates at all.

50. NON-INTERFERENCE INDICATIVE CONDITIONALS

Sometimes my Ramsey test of A→C leads to a high probability for C, not because A's probability hoisted C's but because I was already pretty sure of C and the supposition of A did not alter this. I add to my actual present belief system the supposition that it is now snowing in Auckland, make conservative adjustments to make room for this, and find that the resultant belief system *still* accords a high probability to the proposition that ripe bananas are usually yellow.

If the Ramsey test seals the fate of any indicative conditional, then what are we to make of the above example? We must either admit (1) that the Ramsey test thesis is after all false, or conclude (2) that the Ramsey test, properly understood, is not the procedure I have described with Auckland and bananas, or contend (3) that I should accept the conditional 'If it is snowing in Auckland now, ripe bananas are usually yellow'. I choose 3.

Lycan (2001: 89–90) gives a similar example and says scornfully that in this case A→C would not be given much credence by anyone who was not 'infected . . . by discussions of conditionals couched from the beginning in probability theory'. He offers no discussion in support of that slap, instead bustling along to offer a general reason for 'deploring the custom of approaching the semantics of conditionals from the direction of probability theory'. Let us back up a little, and look.

Auckland → Bananas and Lycan's example are acceptable *non-interference conditionals*. I take the label 'non-interference' from Reichenbach (1976: ch. 7), who used it for similar subjunctive conditionals. The latter, which have also misled some philosophers, will be my topic in §91.

When you perform the Ramsey test on a non-interference indicative conditional, C comes out with a high probability because you gave it one already, and that was not affected by the supposition of A. Such a conditional can be a perfectly sensible thing not only to accept but to say. I fume 'If George told them about our plan, he broke a promise to me', and you coolly reply 'If he *didn't* tell them about our plan, he broke a promise to you'; you say this because you are sure enough that George has broken some other promise to me, but you express it as a conditional so as to echo my conditional. Your choice between 'If he didn't tell . . . etc.' and 'Whether or not he told . . . etc.' is stylistic, rhetorical. The two sentences are far from equivalent, but *in this context* either would serve your purpose. Another example: I express a fear that the refrigerator will explode if you open its door, and you assure me that if I open the door it won't explode. You base this on your belief that the door-opening and the non-explosion are irrelevant to one another, and you put it in a conditional form because *I* think they are connected. This second example is a favourite of Lycan's; he calls it and its ilk 'weak conditionals', and theorizes about them at length—but not when he is drawing a bead on the Ramsey test, because then they would spoil his aim.

Now, Auckland → Bananas and Lycan's comparable example are hard to provide normalizing contexts for. In any context I can think of, each would be an idiotic thing to say. So would 'Mt Everest is more than seven times as large as the average hamster', 'Either Io is volcanic or the speed limit on Bowen Island is 1,000 kph', and 'At least two people have been born in the past millennium'. They are all true nonetheless.

Lycan wants his semantic theory of conditionals to enable him to pick out the stupid-to-say non-interference conditionals and declare them to be not even acceptable. I shall argue at the end of §84 that the attempt fails. It is in any case not worth trying. The facts can be explained through a general distinction, which we certainly do have, between acceptable-and-reasonable-to-say and acceptable-and-stupid-to-say. It is extravagant to equip a theory of conditionals with extra machinery to plough that field again.

As a final aid to intuition, think about the 'whether or not' cousins of non-interference conditionals. You would not want to reject 'Whether or not it is snowing in Auckland now, ripe bananas are usually yellow', even when you could see no point in saying this. Well, if 'Whether or not A, C' is acceptable, then so are A→C and ¬A→C.

51. INDICATIVE CONDITIONALS AND SPEECH ACTS

Dorothy Edgington has a persuasive view about what it is to *say* or *affirm* an indicative conditional. We have seen her using it in support of (Adams**) the thesis that T→T is always true, but its power goes far beyond that. I especially like her extension of it to other kinds of speech act. 'It is overwhelmingly plausible', she writes, 'that the clause "if he phones" does the same job in conditional statements, commands, questions, promises, expressions of wish, etc.; and hence that a theory of conditionals should be applicable to more than conditional statements' (1995b: 288). She develops this idea in detail in connection only with injunctions, first asking what can be meant by 'If you write the article, submit it to *Mind*', and arguing that it does not mean 'Bring it about that (You write the article ⊃ You submit it to *Mind*)', that is, 'Either don't write the article, or submit it to *Mind*'. Edgington's best reason for rejecting that interpretation aligns injunctions with expressions of desire: she points out that the Write → Submit injunction expresses only a preference for Write & Submit over Write & ¬Submit, and remains perfectly silent about any preference for ¬Write over Write & ¬Submit. This supports the view that a conditional with an imperative consequent is a conditional injunction—it commands the hearer to make-true the consequent on condition that the antecedent comes true, and commands nothing otherwise. This is analogous to the thesis that affirming an indicative conditional is asserting C conditional on A's being true, and asserting nothing in the event of that condition's not being fulfilled.

Asserting nothing, not *doing* nothing. The affirming of a conditional, or the issuing of a conditional injunction, can have effects in the world even if its antecedent is false, as when I say to you 'If you write a favourable letter of reference for [name], then all my professional mentoring of you has been in vain': this might be extremely informative to you, influencing your conduct, even if— perhaps *especially* if—you do not write the letter. Another example: I say to you 'If I have hurt your feelings, I apologize'; in fact your feelings are not hurt; so I have not apologized, but I have done something significant.

Try out these ideas of Edgington's for yourself on some other speech-acts, such as optatives and promises. Think, for example, about the difference between keeping a conditional promise and not breaking it. I shall briefly apply them to just one more—questions. Some if-questions unconditionally ask whether a certain conditional is highly probable: 'If John is over 60, is he entitled to a rail card?' (McDermott 1996: 29; Woods 1997: 76). But they are in the minority. More typical is 'If Mödl sang, could you hear that she had a cold?', which does not ask for the truth value of 'Mödl sang ⊃ You could hear that she had a cold'. 'She didn't sing' does not answer your question, but tells you why it does not arise. In short, you have asked a conditional question—something that asks 'Could you hear that she had a cold?' on the condition that she sang, and does not ask anything otherwise.

The whole speech-act story looks good, with its different parts supporting one another.

52. BISCUIT CONDITIONALS

DeRose and Grandy (1999) applaud Edgington's view that affirming an indicative conditional is making a conditional assertion, add further arguments for it, and use it to explain an odd sort of conditional sometimes dubbed a 'biscuit conditional'. This commemorates an example of J. L. Austin's: 'There are biscuits on the sideboard, if you want them.' Another example: 'PBS will broadcast *Die Walküre* tonight, if you like Wagner.' These *could* be ordinary conditionals: biscuits have been put on the sideboards of all the guests who want them; PBS's programming is guided by your likes and dislikes. But normally they are not ordinary, as can be seen from the fact that if one responded 'And if I don't want them . . .?' or 'And if I don't like Wagner . . .?' this would be seen as a joke.

Biscuit conditionals are a jejune topic, but the question of how far off the main road they lie is of some interest. Dudman (1984*b*: 148) holds that in them '"if" is *misused*'; at the other extreme, DeRose and Grandy offer to provide a unified account of them and ordinary indicative conditionals. Affirming A→C, they say, is asserting C conditionally on A's being true. Why would you do this rather than asserting C unconditionally? For ordinary conditionals: you are not sure that C is true. For biscuit conditionals: you are not sure that C is relevant to the hearer's interests. These are different reasons for making your assertion of C conditional on something; but the underlying idea of a conditional assertion is the same.

Suppose I say to you 'There are biscuits on the sideboard if you want some', and you don't want any, and there aren't any. DeRose and Grandy must say that in this case I have not outright asserted a falsehood: my antecedent was false, so I have asserted nothing. Biting the bullet, they accept this commitment (pp. 414–15), arguing that in such a case I do not assert but merely *conversationally implicate* a falsehood (in Grice's sense; see §10). This is their least persuasive offering in this paper.

Their account of biscuit conditionals, even at best, does not deeply unify them with ordinary ones. It unifies them at the level of the thesis that 'indicative conditionals are devices of conditional assertion' (p. 407); but the core truth about such conditionals is not this but its *source* in the view that indicative conditionals express subjective conditional probabilities.

Geis and Lycan (1993) discuss biscuit conditionals at length, calling attention to a much larger class of what they call 'nonconditional conditionals'—sentences of the form 'If P, Q' which nevertheless seem to lack all the serious marks of conditionality. Examples: 'If I may remind you, I have been working here for seventeen years'; 'I've been out buying David's present, if you care', 'It was a great article, if I do say so myself'. In a postscript to that (2001: 206–10) Lycan switches to the view that all of these are, after all, genuine conditionals. He likens them to ordinary non-interference conditionals (§50), and says that some apparent differences can be explained pragmatically.

9
The Logic of Indicative Conditionals

53. PROBABILISTIC VALIDITY

Here is a valid argument form:

The first thing he did was F.
The first thing he did was to introduce himself.
∴ His introduction of himself was F.

As long as there is no malpractice with tenses or with 'he', the premisses of any instance of this cannot be true while the conclusion is false. What if F = funny? When you say things of the form 'x is funny', you do not attribute a property, funniness, to the subject; there is no such property. What you do rather is to *express* your own amusement, thereby saying something that lacks a truth value (§42). Yet the validity of the above argument form guarantees the virtue of this argument:

The first thing he did was funny.
The first thing he did was to introduce himself.
∴ His introduction of himself was funny.

Its virtue is not classical or truth-conditional validity; it does not consist in the fact that the premisses cannot be true when the conclusion is false. Rather, it consists in the fact that someone who believes the second premiss and has a frame of mind apt for asserting the first also has a frame of mind apt for asserting the conclusion.

Thus, some sentences that lack truth values can enter into logical arguments just as though they had them. These are sentences that are deprived of truth values by their use of a predicate such as 'is funny', 'is wrong', 'is disgusting', or the like. Some of their logic is just that of any predicating sentences, and the lack of truth values does not affect it.

Where indicative conditionals are concerned, however, the case changes. They are deprived of truth values by their form, not by their mere inclusion of some special word. The only wider class of sentences on whose logical back they can ride are ones occurring in the propositional calculus. This, for example, is universally valid:

Q&R ∴ Q,

and instances of it where Q or R is an indicative conditional are all right. Much of the propositional calculus cannot be applied to indicative conditionals because there are limits to how far they can be embedded in larger propositional structures (§39); but when the embedding is all right, so are the classically valid inferences. The validity of the above argument form, for instance, ensures that a frame of mind apt for asserting 'The economy is slumping and if X is as stupid as he seems then we are in trouble' is apt for asserting 'If X is as stupid as he seems then we are in trouble'.

That is plain sailing. But a problem arises when we try to evaluate an argument *using* an indicative conditional. I mean by this that the conditional's form contributes to the workings of the argument, rather than the conditional's occurring as a mere substitution instance of a propositional variable. Consider:

If X is as stupid as he seems, then we are in trouble.
X is as stupid as he seems.
∴ We are in trouble.

There is nothing on whose back this can ride. Nor can we ask whether it is classically (truth-conditionally) valid, for that requires being such that when its premisses are true so is its conclusion, whereas the first premiss of this cannot be true (or false). Well, according to Adams** (§47), the first premiss can be true if the second is, and in just that case the conclusion is true; so that Adams** endorses Modus Ponens, and thus the above argument, as *classically* valid! But that is an isolated, opportunistic application of classical notions to inferences using indicative conditionals, and it holds only on the basis of something that is not universally accepted. The general question about how arguments using indicative conditionals can be valid still stands.

A variant of this question is: Given that indicative conditionals lack truth values, how can there be truths about what they logically entail and are entailed by? Consider this threesome:

(1) A logically entails C
(2) A→C
(3) A⊃C

One naturally thinks that they are in descending order of strength, so that 1 entails 2, which entails 3. That 1 entails 3 (we can explain) comes from the absolute impossibility that 1 should be true and 3 false. But $(A{\rightarrow}C)$'s lack of truth value debars us from explaining in that kind of way either 1's entailing 2 or 2's entailing 3. How then can we explain these entailments? And what justifies my assumption, when presenting of the 'inferential exception' to the zero-intolerance of indicative conditionals (§23), that the move from 'If anyone admires the Rolling Stones, he (or she) will never be Pope' to 'If any member of the Curia admires the Rolling Stones, he will never be Pope' is valid?

The present chapter will outline Adams's solution to this problem, relying mainly on his 1975 book. He has extended and refined this work in his 1996, and further still in his impressive *Primer of Probability Logic* (1998). Aiming to give readers the kind of help I needed when I first encountered Adams's work, I shall—greatly aided by Dorothy Edgington—spell things out quite slowly.

The main insight that Adams brought to this matter is best stated with help from 'uncertainty'—a technical term used in probability studies. A proposition's uncertainty is its improbability, which equals 1 minus its probability. In symbols: $U(Q) = P(\neg Q) = 1 - P(Q)$. Although uncertainty can be simply reduced to probability through this equation, we sometimes find it helpful to invoke it separately—as in the present topic.

Now make the acquaintance of the notion of *probabilistic validity*. To get a feel for it, reflect that no instance of a classically valid argument form allows *falsity* to enter along the way from premises to conclusion. Then think of a probabilistically valid form as one no instance of which allows *improbability* to enter along the way. In other words, it is true by definition that in a probabilistically valid argument *the uncertainty of the conclusion cannot exceed the sum of the uncertainties of the premises*. (Adams 1975: 1–2 is misleading about this; treat those pages with caution.)

It is worthwhile to note that an argument can be probabilistically valid even though each premiss is highly probable and its conclusion utterly improbable. The so-called lottery paradox shows this. A million people have entered an unrigged lottery whose rules guarantee that someone will win. Now we conduct an inference with a million premises of the form

Entrant e_i will not win the lottery,

for every value of i from 1 through 1,000,000, together with one further premiss:

The lottery will be won ⊃ It will be won by one of $e_1, \ldots, e_{1,000,000}$.

From this it follows by classically valid logic that

The lottery will not be won.

This conclusion is false; but so is one premiss, so classical validity is not infringed. What about probabilistic validity? Well, each premiss is enormously probable, while the conclusion has a probability = 0; but the argument is probabilistically valid, because the uncertainty of the conclusion is not greater than—and happens to be equal to—the *sum* of the uncertainties of the premises. One million one-millionths equals 1, which is the uncertainty of the conclusion. No extra improbability has filtered into the argument along the way. What enabled us to get from premises that are severally probable to an improbable conclusion was the sheer number of the premises.

Now, probabilistic validity is something an argument can have even if it uses indicative conditionals in premises or conclusion. Although these cannot be relied upon to have truth values, they can always have probabilities; and we can ask of a given argument form whether in any instance of it the conclusion could have a level of uncertainty (for a given person at a given time) that exceeded the sum of the uncertainties (for that person at that time) of the several premises. With this concept at our disposal, we can evaluate logical arguments using indicative conditionals, despite their lack of truth values and despite there being no more general logic upon whose back these arguments can ride.

Before going along that path, let us see how probabilistic validity behaves in arguments that are candidates also for classical validity because all the sentences in them have truth values. We start with the theorem labelled 10 in §21 above:

If Q entails R, then $P(Q) \leq P(R)$.

We proved this from the axioms of probability logic, and from it we can derive the important theorem that among arguments from a single premiss, whatever is classically is also probabilistically valid:

First result: If Q entails R, $U(R) \leq U(Q)$.

In one-premiss arguments, therefore, probabilistic validity will take care of itself, tagging along safely on the heels of classical validity. What about reasoning from more than one premiss? An argument of the form Q, S ∴ R can be expressed as one of the form Q&S ∴ R, and then our previous result holds: if the argument is classically valid then it is also probabilistically so—$U(R) \leq U(Q\&S)$. In real life, however, we often move to conclusions from premises that are accorded subjective probabilities separately rather than in a single conjunctive lump. In studies of classical validity, 'Each premiss is true' stands or falls with

'The conjunction of all the premises is true'. Replace 'true' by 'probable' and the equivalence no longer holds. So we need to be able to relate the uncertainty of the conclusion of a classically valid argument to the uncertainties (plural) of its premisses taken separately.

We do this with the aid of:

Second result: $U(Q \& S) \leq U(Q) + U(S)$,

that is, the uncertainty of a conjunction never exceeds the sum of the uncertainties of its conjuncts. To see why, bear in mind that just now we are attending only to propositions that can be true; and the probability of such a proposition is its probability of being true, its uncertainty the probability of its being false. Now, the probability that Q&S is false obviously comes from the probability that Q is false and the probability that S is false. It cannot exceed the sum of those two probabilities, because if it did there would be a chance for Q&S to be false although Q and S were each true. This leads to the 'second result', given above. We cannot strengthen it to the equality $U(Q\&S) = U(Q) + U(S)$, because there can be overlap between the chances of Q's being false and the chances of S's being false, and a mere summing of the separate uncertainties would double count the ones in the overlap. It can easily happen, indeed, that $U(Q) + U(S) > 1$, but it cannot be that $U(R) > 1$. For me, U(I shall live to be 90) ≈ 0.95 and U(I shall write a book on Hegel) ≈ 0.99; but it cannot be that for me U(I shall live to be 90 and write a book on Hegel) ≈ 1.94. Thus, the sum of the uncertainties of the conjuncts need not equal the uncertainty of the conjunction, but sets an upper bound to it.

Put together the first and second results displayed above, and we get:

Third result: If Q, S entail R, then $U(R) \leq U(Q) + U(S)$.

We can easily generalize this to something holding for any number of premises:

If Q, S, . . . , X entail R, then $U(R) \leq U(Q) + U(S) + . . . U(X)$.

So we have the important general result that *in a classically valid argument the uncertainty of the conclusion cannot exceed the sum of the uncertainties of the premisses.* This means that any classically valid argument is also probabilistically valid.

What Adams found, then, is that any argument that is classically or truth-conditionally valid also has *another* virtue, probabilistic validity. An argument using indicative conditionals cannot have the former of these virtues, but it can have the latter, and that is a basis upon which we can evaluate it, as I shall often do in the present chapter.

As a preliminary exercise, let us consider an argument which I have held over from §40, concerning the thesis If-and:

A → (B→C) is logically equivalent to (A&B) → C.

Adams (1975: 33) can be read as objecting to this on the following grounds. If If-and is universally correct, then it holds when A = C. That equates C → (B→C) with (C&B) → C. But the latter of these is necessary; so according to If-and the former is necessary also, in which case the 'argument from the consequent'—

C ∴ B→C

- is valid, and Adams is rightly sure that it is not. For many values of B and C, a rational person can be much more uncertain of B→C than of C.

Does that imply that C → (B→C) is not necessary? If it does, then we must deny that C&B → C is necessary or else deny the equivalence of the two—that is, deny If-and. The threat of losing If-and is fairly dire, given how well it stands up to philosophical probing, and given Stalnaker's and Hájek's formal arguments for it.

Well, as a start on clearing up this mess, I argue that C → (B→C) *is* necessary, which nips in the bud the threat to If-and. Because this is an indicative conditional, its necessity cannot consist in its being true at all worlds; rather, it must consist in a rational requirement that every instance of it be accorded probability = 1. The way to test this is through the Ramsey procedure: to a rational belief system, add P(C) = 1 for some C, adjust minimally to make room for that, and then see what the value is of P(B→C) in the resultant system of beliefs. Well, any system in which P(C) = 1 had better be one in which P(B→C) = 1 also. If not, then someone could rationally give C some chance of being false if B is true, while giving it no chance at all of being false. This is incoherent. Another way to see this is through the ratio formula which equates P(B→C) with P(B&C) ÷ P(B). Because P(C) = 1, P(B&C) = P(B), and so our value for P(B→C) simplifies to P(B) ÷ P(B), which = 1.

So we have excellent reason to regard C → (B→C) as probabilistically necessary, to coin a phrase; as of course is B&C → C also. Where (what seems to be) Adams's argument goes astray is in its final move from the necessity of C → (B→C) to the validity of C ∴ B→C. It is valid to go from the (truth-conditional) necessity of a *material* conditional to the (truth-conditional) validity of the corresponding argument form; but there is a definite mistake involved in going from the (probabilistic) necessity of an indicative conditional to the probabilistic validity of the corresponding argument form. Probabilistic necessity has to be understood through the Ramsey procedure, which always starts by supposing the antecedent to have probability 1. Probabilistic validity, on the other hand, is defined in terms of a relation of probabilities across the whole range; it does not just ask how B→C fares when P(C) = 1. It also asks whether P(B→C) could be lower than P(C) when the latter has values other than 1. Clearly it could; but when P(C) = 1 the picture changes, and P(B→C) is locked at 1 also.

54. A→C AND MODUS PONENS

Probabilistic validity is not everything. The form of argument A, A⊃C ∴ C is probabilistically valid; it has to be, because it is classically valid. Still, A⊃C is unsatisfactory for use in Modus Ponens, because one may accept it for a reason that will vanish if one comes to accept A. In so far as the *point* of indicative conditionals is their use in Modus Ponens, they must have a built-in guarantee that they can safely be thus used. We know what provides it. In Jackson's terminology, it is the fact that when you accept A→C the consequent C is, for you, robust with respect to A. If that is the whole essence of A→C—something that cannot be dispensed with but need not be added to—we get the result that P(A→C) = π(C/A), which then leads by a winding road to Adams's view that indicative conditionals are inference tickets rather than propositions. But I repeat myself.

What spoils A⊃C for use in Modus Ponens is that it can be accepted because A is rejected. Its big defect will therefore be visible only when P(A) is low—and not always then. This is an informal way of putting something that Adams presents more technically in his thesis that *the uncertainty of an indicative conditional equals the uncertainty of the corresponding material conditional divided by the probability of its antecedent* (1975: 3–4). Let us trace out the proof of this important theorem. We start with a certain quantity:

U(A→C).

By the interrelations of U and P this is equivalent to

P(A→¬C)

which by the Ratio Formula is equivalent to

P(A&¬C) ÷ P(A)

which, by the interrelation of U and P, is equivalent to

U¬(A&¬C) ÷ P(A)

which, by the definition of ⊃, is equivalent to

U(A⊃C) ÷ P(A).

Go in a jump from top to bottom and you get:

Fourth result: $U(A{\rightarrow}C) = U(A{\supset}C) + P(A)$,

QED. Thus, the higher the value of $P(A)$ the nearer the two probabilities—of the indicative and the material conditional—are to being equal. That is why it is only when $P(A)$ is low that $A{\supset}C$ comes to grief when used in Modus Ponens. We shall soon see Adams putting this powerfully to use.

The move from the first to the second line in the above argument assumes that $A{\rightarrow}\neg C$ is the contradictory of $A{\rightarrow}C$. So indeed it is, because, for given values of A and C and a given rational person at a time, the probabilities of the two add up to 1. Using the Equation and the Ratio Formula, it is easy to prove arithmetically that $P(A{\rightarrow}C) + P(A{\rightarrow}\neg C) = 1$. It is also intuitively evident that it is right.

55. ADAMS'S USE OF VENN DIAGRAMS

Adams ingeniously adapts Venn diagrams to say things about the probabilistic validity of inference forms. Venn diagrams are standardly used to handle truth-conditional validity only, and their basic features are topological. We represent propositions by ovals within a rectangle (the latter representing the limits on what is possible, or representing the necessary proposition). Then we can represent 'P entails Q' by putting P's oval entirely within Q's; 'P rules out Q' by putting their ovals outside one another, not touching; 'P neither entails nor rules out Q' by giving their ovals a common portion that does not exhaust either oval; and so on.

Think of each point on the rectangle as representing one possible world. Then each perimeter encloses a class of possible worlds and thus represents the proposition that is true at exactly those worlds. Thus, if ovals P and Q have some overlap though neither contains the other, this means that there are worlds at which P&Q is true, worlds at which P&¬Q is true, and worlds at which ¬P&Q is true. If some of the containing region ('the rectangle') lies outside both ovals, then at some worlds ¬P&¬Q is true.

Although this is all purely topological, having only to do with what is inside or outside what, it has some metrical side-effects. The main one is the fact that if Q entails R and not vice versa, Q's oval is smaller than R's, as in Fig. 2. Venn diagrams give no significance to *how much* bigger one oval is than another. Adams adapts them by adding further significance to metrical features of the drawings: he lets the size of a proposition's oval represent how probable it is in the belief scheme of the person in question (1975: 9–10).

For example, 'Q rules out R and is more probable than it (but is not certain)' will be represented by Adams through something like Fig. 3. He attaches the same significance to the size of the region outside an oval: an oval and the remainder of the rectangle add up to the rectangle, just as $P(Q) + P(\neg Q) = 1$.

In a diagram of the sort Adams highlights, $P(A{\rightarrow}C)$ is represented by what proportion of the A oval overlaps the C oval. This can be derived from our two equations—$P(A{\rightarrow}C) = \pi(C/A) = P(A\&C) \div P(A)$—but I shall come at it informally, without relying on the Ratio Formula. The probability of $A{\rightarrow}C$ is high for someone if he thinks that most chances of A's being true are also chances of C's being true. Thus, the diagram of his thought puts only a little of the A oval outside the C oval, putting most of it inside. So the value of his probability for $A{\rightarrow}C$ equals the proportion of the A oval lying within the C oval.

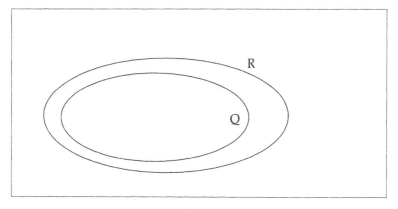

FIG. 2

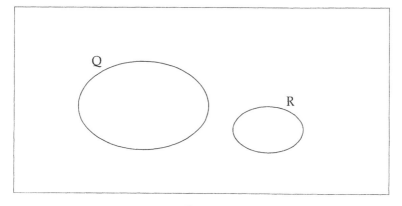

FIG. 3

This fits what we independently know about probabilities of conditionals. For example, that $P(A \rightarrow C) + P(A \rightarrow \neg C) = 1$; the part of the A region lying inside C together with the part lying inside $\neg C$ add up to the whole of the A region. This holds, no matter what the size is of the A and C ovals.

Another result illustrated by Adams's diagrams is that if $P(C) = 1$ then $P(A \rightarrow C) = 1$. This is certainly correct so far as the diagrams go: if $P(C) = 1$ then C is represented by the entire rectangle, and thus no part of A's region can lie outside it. As I showed in §40, the Ramsey procedure endorses this. I am perfectly certain of C, and want to consider whether $A \rightarrow C$; I pretend to be sure of A, and then adjust the rest of my beliefs so as to restore harmony within the whole. If my most conservative way of doing this lowers $P(C)$, then I was not perfectly certain of C's truth after all, because it turns out that a discovery that I might make would make me less than perfectly certain of C. Accepting $A \rightarrow C$ on the ground that $P(C) = 1$ is accepting it as a special sort of non-interference conditional (§50).

It is also satisfactory that Adams's diagrams cannot represent $P(A \rightarrow C)$ when $P(A) = 0$. If $P(A) = 0$, then A has no area, so it cannot be diagrammed. This is just what we want.

As well as fitting the facts about how the probabilities of conditionals relate to other probabilities, Adams's diagrams also highlight certain structural features of his theory about indicative conditionals. I shall present two.

(1) The diagrams dramatize the idea that indicative conditionals, because they do not always have truth values, are not propositions and do not correspond to sets of possible worlds. Like Venn's original diagrams, Adams's adaptation of them represents a proposition by a region within the rectangle; but it does not represent an indicative conditional in this way *or in any other*. If we demand 'Show us which parts or features of a diagram of Adams's represent $A \rightarrow C$', there is no answer; all that is represented is something of the form $P(A \rightarrow C) = n$. This reflects the fact that Adams's theory tells us what indicative conditionals are *by* telling us what it is to accord probabilities to them. The fundamental reality is not $A \rightarrow C$ but rather $P(A \rightarrow C)$, and Adams represents this by a *feature* of the diagram, not by a *part* of it.

Two people can differ in how likely they take a single indicative conditional to be, which suggests that there is a detachable item—the conditional—for them to disagree about. But the suggestion is false. If you attach a higher probability to $A \rightarrow C$ than I do, this means that you and I differ in the values we assign to $\pi(C/A)$, which is a ratio between two probabilities. The reality underlying our talk about our different attitudes to 'the same conditional' is a difference in our levels of belief in one or both of two genuine propositions, A&C and A. The ratio between your probabilities for those differs from the ratio between mine; and that is the whole story. It concerns those two propositions, not any item that can be called the conditional A→C. (If the Ratio Formula is wrong, so is what I have just said; but I could replace 'ratio between two probabilities' by 'relation between two probabilities', the relation being defined by the Ramsey test; and the basic story would be the same.)

(2) Adams's diagrams cannot represent compounds in which conditionals are embedded. They can represent A and C and B, and they can bring A→C into the picture indirectly, by representing its probability; but they cannot represent B & (A→C), because they cannot represent A→C.

It might be thought unsatisfactory that Adams's theory and his diagrams forbid even so simple a construction as ¬(A→C), but really it is not a loss. The theory does let us say what a person accepts in rejecting A→C, namely A→¬C.

56. ADAMS AND VENN: COMPARISONS AND CONTRASTS

The representation of probability by region size in Adams's diagrams accords with the slight metrical significance of Venn diagrams. If Q entails R but not vice versa, then in a Venn diagram Q's oval coincides with or lies inside R's, and is therefore not larger than the latter. In such a case, a logically idealized thinker will accord to Q a probability no larger than $P(R)$—this is because of §21's theorem 10:

If Q entails R, then $P(Q) \le P(R)$,

with which we are now familiar. So we have $P(Q) \le P(R)$; and a diagram of Adams's sort represents this by making Q's region no larger than R's.

Again, if Q entails R then all of Q's region overlaps R's in both diagrams. According to Adams's reading of his diagram, this says that $P(Q \to R) = 1$; which is right if that entailment holds. In this case, Q→R is an *independent* conditional—that is, one in which the consequent logically or causally follows from the antecedent alone (§7)—and for that reason I keep it at arm's length. Still, this point of Adams's is sound: it does no harm to apply probability logic to conditionals that are secured by logic alone, saying for example that when A entails C the probability of A→C is 1. You can easily derive that from the Ratio Formula.

Adams's diagrams do not merely add to Venn ones—they alter them in one respect. In Venn diagrams the containing rectangle represents the necessary proposition, or the set of all possible worlds, and regions within it represent contingent propositions, ones that conflict with some possibilities. In Adams's diagrams, on the other hand, the rectangle represents any proposition to which the person accords probability 1, and regions within it represent propositions of whose truth the person is less than certain—propositions that conflict with something that is, for him, epistemically possible. According to Regularity (§26), an ideally rational believer assigns probability = 1 only to absolutely necessary propositions; in which case the two sorts of diagram do after all attach the same significance to the rectangle. If Regularity is wrong, however, we have here a difference.

It is an intelligible and inoffensive one, however: what the whole rectangle means in the Venn diagram is at least isomorphic with what it means in the Adams adaptation. Here are two examples of this. (1) Venn: If Q_1 and Q_2 are both necessary, they can be substituted for one another *salva veritate* in any statement about entailment, necessity or possibility. Adams: If $P(Q_1) = P(Q_2) = 1$, those two propositions can be substituted for one another in any statement about that person's absolute or conditional probabilities; for example, it follows that $\pi(R/Q_1) = \pi(R/Q_2)$, that $P(R\&Q_1) = P(R\&Q_2)$, and so on. (2) Venn: In many contexts a necessary proposition can be dropped—because if N is necessary then N&Q is equivalent to Q, so is N⊃Q, and so on. Adams: If $P(N) = 1$, then N can be dropped from various compounds without affecting the person's credence levels: if for him $P(N) = 1$, then for him $P(N\&Q) = P(Q)$, and so does $P(N\supset Q)$, and so on.

Venn diagrams can naturally be interpreted in terms of worlds, as I did recently: if Q entails R and not vice versa, then every Q-world is an R-world and not vice versa, and this is represented by a diagram in which Q's oval lies inside R's. Let us see whether we can extend this idea to Adams's diagrams and to the associated notion of probability. To do so, it seems, we must associate the size of a region in one of Adams's diagrams with *how many* worlds it represents; which raises a difficulty if there are infinitely many possible worlds. We might deal with this by finding some way of dividing an infinity of worlds into a finite set of clumps, and then counting those (§101). Alternatively, we can contend that in any realistic treatment of subjective probability we have only finitely many worlds to deal with. We have seen Hájek take this line in his 1989 argument against the Equation (§31).

57. FOUR PROBABILISTICALLY INVALID ARGUMENT FORMS

With illustrative help from his diagrams, Adams defends various theses about the logic of indicative conditionals. So far, I have mentioned only a feature shared by A→C and A⊃C, namely supporting Modus Ponens (though see §61); but Adams's theory commits him to several logical differences between those two. Above all, these two forms of argument:

¬A ∴ A→C
C ∴ A→C

which would both be classically valid if → were ⊃, are not probabilistically valid and so are not endorsed in Adams's theory. The latter does imply that when my value for P(A) = 0, I should have no value for P(A→C); and that when my value for P(C) = 1, my value for P(A→C) should be 1. But nothing follows about the value for P(A→C) when P(A) is low but > 0, or when P(C) is high but < 1. Edgington (1995a: 71) has a helpful discussion of the probabilistic failure of those two forms of argument, which she acknowledges having learned about from Ellis 1973. See also Adams 1975: 11–12.

Those two 'paradoxes of material implication' are unpopular anyway, frequently being adduced as refuting the horseshoe analysis. Adams's theory rejects some other proposed argument forms as well, however, and since these are not as obviously absurd as are the notorious two, his denial of them is not so obviously a merit in his theory. Here are the four main ones:

1. A∨C ∴ ¬A→C   (Or-to-if)
2. A→C ∴ ¬C→¬A   (Contraposition)
3. (A→B), (B→C) ∴ A→C   (Transitivity)
4. A→C ∴ (A&B) → C   (Antecedent Strengthening)

Each would be classically valid if → were replaced throughout by ⊃. Indeed, as we saw in §18, by attributing truth values to indicative conditionals and accepting argument form 1, we would commit ourselves to the horseshoe analysis of →. This is not true of any of the other three, for they are classically valid for → = entailment as well as for → = ⊃. Adams says, however, that if any of the four is added to his logic for probabilistic validity, the latter will collapse into the truth-conditional propositional calculus, and that 'the reader can easily [sic] verify' that this is so (1966: 311–12). I needed his personal help to see how to verify this, and shall here give just one part of the story, namely the use of (4) Antecedent Strengthening to derive (1) Or-to-if. The derivation also uses Limited Transitivity, that is, the inference form

A→B, (A&B) → C ∴ A→C.

This is weaker than Transitivity, and is a theorem in Adams's conditional logic. In the derivation, T is any tautology.

(i) A∨C (given)

(ii) T → (A∨C) (follows from i)

(iii) (T&¬A) → (A∨C) (from ii by Antecedent Strengthening)

(iv) ((T &¬A) & (A∨C)) → C (logical truth, because the antecedent entails C)

(v) (T&¬A) → C (from iii and iv by Limited Transitivity)

(vi) ¬A→C (equivalent to v).

Thus, from A∨C we get ¬A→C; which is to say that we have Or-to-if, which implies that → is merely ⊃. Principles 2 and 3 can also be shown each to have this same dire effect when added to Adams's logic.

The four argument forms have struck many people as intuitively acceptable, Adams says, going so far as to call them 'intuitively rational'. He accepts an onus to explain this. Presumably, nobody will get the impression that a given argument form is valid *just* because it has many valid instances, for that is true of almost every argument form—for example, the form P, Q ∴ R. Adams, however, marks off a determinate, probabilistically valid subset of instances of the four forms, and suggests reasons why people using the forms tend to produce instances belonging to this subset (1975: 18–19). One detail in his reasoning is left obscure, but it comes clear—though still not simple—in Edgington's version (1995b: 285), which I shall follow.

Consider any classically valid argument whose conclusion is a material conditional—express it as 'A⊃C' for short. Being classically valid, the argument must also be probabilistically valid, which means that:

(1) U(A⊃C) ≤ the sum of the uncertainties of the premisses.

(This is the 'second result' in §53 above.) If the premisses include material conditionals, we can—as long as they are not embedded—replace them by indicative conditionals. The result of doing this will be the set of →-premisses, as distinct from the ⊃-premisses with which we began. Now, we saw in §54 above that the uncertainty of A⊃C cannot be higher than that of A→C for the same A and C. So we know that

(2) The sum of the uncertainties of the ⊃-premisses ≤ the sum of the uncertainties of the →-premisses.

Putting together 1 and 2, we get:

(3) U(A⊃C) ≤ the sum of the uncertainties of the →-premisses.

In short, we have taken a classically valid argument, replaced the unembedded material conditionals among its premisses by the corresponding indicative conditionals, and the result is still probabilistically valid.

Now, suppose we replace ⊃ by → in the conclusion. This takes us from a weak conditional to one that may be stronger; so it may be a move from a lesser to a greater uncertainty; so the probabilistic validity of this new argument is no longer guaranteed. Thus, we cannot say:

U(A→C) ≤ the sum of the uncertainties of the →-premises.

But now let us recall our 'fourth result' in §54 above, namely that U(A→C) = U(A⊃C) ÷ P(A), which means that the greater P(A) is, the nearer P(A→C) is to P(A⊃C). From this something important follows, namely: if X is a probabilistically valid argument for A⊃C, then *to the extent that P(A) is high* X is also a probabilistically secure agument for A→C. So Adams can infer this remarkable result (the name and this wording are mine):

> Security Thesis: If X is an argument whose conclusion is an indicative conditional A→C, and if what results from replacing → by ⊃ throughout X is a classically valid inference, then X is probabilistically secure to the extent that P(A) is high.

Probabilistic security is a matter of degree; *how* probabilistically secure an argument is depends, by definition, on *how little* the uncertainty of its conclusion can exceed the sum of the uncertainties of the premises. (There is no concept of 'classical security' related in the analogous way to classical validity. That is because, whereas probabilistic validity depends on a quantitative notion, classical validity does not.)

Adams applies this to the four challenged argument forms, each of which is probabilistically secure to the extent that the antecedent of the conclusion is probable. The counterexamples to them—applications in which the premises are probable for someone for whom the conclusion is not—all involve conclusions with improbable antecedents. This leads him to the following:

> Plausible hypothesis: Recognition that a conclusion's antecedent is not too improbable is a 'tacit premise' in much real life reasoning which appears to be of a pattern which is not universally probabilistically [valid]. (1975: 19)

This would help to explain why the four challenged argument forms are probabilistically secure in 'much real life reasoning'. In attending to them individually, we shall find that the Security Thesis fits every case, so that the 'plausible hypothesis' could explain why each form of argument feels good to most people most of the time. We shall find that it can usually be explained in other ways as well.

58. OR-TO-IF

The Or-to-if pattern of argument is not generally valid. I might assign a high probability to AvC because I am fairly sure of A, in which case the disjunction gives me no reason to assign a high probability to C given ¬A. I think it fairly likely that (The North Koreans started the Korean war v Some Martians started the American civil war); but this is only because I am pretty sure the North Koreans started their war. This does not incline me to think that if they didn't then some Martians fired on Fort Sumter. Fig. 4 shows a diagram of Adams's sort illustrating a case where P(AvC) is high only because P(A) is high, and where P(¬A→C) is low. It is easy to show through the Ratio Formula that AvC can be more probable than ¬A→C. You will find, as the diagram suggests, that counterexamples will be ones where ¬A—the antecedent of the argument's conclusion—is not highly probable.

This fits Adams's Security Thesis, but in explaining the apparent acceptability of Or-to-if (1975: 19–21) he does not directly rely on the 'plausible hypothesis', appealing instead to Gricean conversational implicature, in the manner of §18, to explain the illusion that AvC ∴ ¬A→C is probabilistically valid.

Adams offers a counterexample to Or-to-if (1975: 11–12). Here is one that I like better. Let A = 'There will be snow in Buffalo in 2009' and let C = 'A woman will be elected President of the USA in 2008'. I give a high probability to AvC, and a low one to ¬A→C. Notice that again the Security Thesis is confirmed.

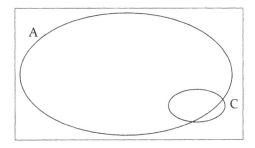

FIG. 4

59. CONTRAPOSITION

Contraposition—the argument form

A→C ∴ ¬C→¬A

—is not virtuous in any theory giving primacy to the Ramsey test, as Adams's does. The fact that for me C is highly probable given A does not guarantee that ¬A is highly probable for me given ¬C.

Appiah presents a nice clean example of the failure of Contraposition, but it too easily admits of being read as involving subjunctive conditionals, which makes it un-ideal for its announced purpose (1985: 171–2). Adams (1988) offers counterexamples like the following, which Jackson has also used. It may be reasonable for me to say (1) 'If he does not live in Paris, he lives somewhere in France', whereas it would be absurd to say (2) 'If he does not live anywhere in France, he lives in Paris', which is 1's contrapositive. One may object to such examples:

> 1 really means 'If he does not live in Paris, he lives *elsewhere* in France', meaning '. . . in France outside Paris'; and the contrapositive of that is all right. It says: 'If he does not live in France outside Paris, he lives in Paris.'

This is not conclusive. It offers a reasonable expansion of 1, but does not show what is wrong with accepting 1 just as it stands.

Still, the proposed counterexample is suspect, because in it P(A→C) is high and P(¬C→¬A) = 0. If Contraposition as such is not probabilistically valid, there ought to be cases where one probability is high and the other is *low but not zero*. If the only apparent counterexamples we could find assigned 0 to the contrapositive, this would look like a discovery not about Contraposition but rather about this class of examples. I say the same about Adams's diagram 3 and verbal example at 1975: 13–14.

Better counterexamples to Contraposition are easy to devise. To get a sense of how to construct them, consider Fig. 4 illustrating the failure of Or-to-if. It also diagrams the case where P(A→¬C) is high and P(C→¬A) low.

Suppose a textual scholar's researches into the newly discovered play *Hate's Labour's Won* leads her to the following position:

> Probably Beaumont wrote it alone; some slight but not quite negligible evidence points to Fletcher's having a hand in it also; there is almost no chance that Fletcher contributed while Beaumont did not. The slight Fletcherian indications in the work nearly all suggest the kind of work Fletcher did with Beaumont at his elbow; it is hardly thinkable that Fletcher should have written this on his own.

This scholar, then, has a high probability for Beaumont → Not-Fletcher and a low one (but not zero) for Fletcher → Not-Beaumont. In applying Fig. 4 to this, A be 'Beaumont had a hand in the work' and C be 'Fletcher had a hand in it'.

You may notice that in the invalid inference from Beaumont → Not-Fletcher to Fletcher → Not-Beaumont the antecedent of the conclusion—namely 'Fletcher had a hand in the work'—has a low probability. This is illustrated by the diagram, and predicted by Adams's Security Thesis.

In this case the protagonist gives high credence to 'If Beaumont was involved in this work, then Fletcher wasn't' and to 'If Beaumont was not involved in the work, Fletcher wasn't'. This lets us refute Contraposition in a dramatic way. The person rationally accepts $A \rightarrow \neg C$ and $\neg A \rightarrow \neg C$, giving a high credence to each; if Contraposition were valid, the person should accept both $C \rightarrow \neg A$ and $C \rightarrow A$—which is contradictory.

If our literary scholar is pretty confident that Fletcher was not involved in the writing of *Hate's Labour's Won*, why should she bother with conditionals on this topic? Here is one of several possible answers. The scholar announces that she doubts that Fletcher was involved, a colleague says: 'Well, if Beaumont had no hand in it, I can see the case for thinking that Fletcher hadn't either; but if Beaumont was involved . . . ' and she breaks in: 'Even if Beaumont *was* involved in the writing of *Hate's Labour's Won*, Fletcher wasn't.'

We have seen Contraposition fail through counterexamples and through Adams's diagrams. It can also be shown to fail using the Ratio Formula and the Equation; you may enjoy devising these proofs for yourself.

Why do people tend to think that Contraposition is all right? Well, the Security Thesis tells us that $A \rightarrow \neg C \therefore C \rightarrow \neg A$ is secure to the extent that $P(C)$ is not low; so what we need to explain is why people are apt to think of $A \rightarrow \neg C$ as asserted only when $P(C)$ is not low, that is, when $P(\neg C)$ is low. The best explanation is Gricean: there will usually be no point in asserting $A \rightarrow \neg C$ where $P(\neg C)$ is high, because the stronger $\neg C$ can be asserted without much loss of confidence. That is why in my Beaumont example I supposed a conversation in which a second person invited the protagonist to assert $A \rightarrow C$, thereby making it pointful for her to counter-assert $A \rightarrow \neg C$.

Adams explains the phenomenon differently. When someone asserts 'If A, $\neg C$', it is natural for hearers to think that $P(\neg C)$ is not high for her, he argues, because if it were high she would more naturally say 'Even if A, $\neg C$'. That would indeed be more natural, as witness my own '*Even* if Beaumont was involved. . .'. This does not explain much, however; and Adams's handling of it seems to assume that 'If A, C' and 'Even if A, C' differ from one another more than they really do. I shall defend a view about how they differ in Chapter 17. Gricean pragmatics play a large role in Adams's discussion of these matters in his 1983: 293–4.

60. TRANSITIVITY AND ANTECEDENT STRENGTHENING

The literature is full of examples purporting to show that Transitivity fails for indicative conditionals, but most come from the borderline territory where indicative conditionals are apt to be thought of as though they were subjunctives. That Transitivity fails for the latter is, as will appear in §65, easy to see and to understand. It is trickier to devise good examples showing Transitivity to fail for indicative conditionals that do not risk being thought of as subjunctives; but it can be done. A farmer, thinking about the state of things on his farm, believes—though not with complete certainty—that the gate into the turnip field is closed and that his cows have not entered that field. He accepts the conditional:

If (A) the cows are in the turnip field, (B) the gate has been left open,

because the least adjustment to his belief system that will admit 'The cows are among the turnips' into it is the dropping of his belief that the gate was closed. Other adjustments would also do the job—lowering his trust in the gate not to fall down, in the cows not to push it down, and so on—but they are more radical than this one. This farmer also accepts:

If (B) the gate to the turnip field has been left open, (C) the cows have not noticed the gate's condition.

He accepts that consequent given that antecedent, because he thinks that the cows are not in the turnip field. Apply Transitivity to those two indicative conditionals—each accepted by one person at one time—and you get:

If (A) the cows are in the turnip field, (C) they have not noticed the gate's condition,

which it would be stupid for the farmer to accept.

It is a fairly straightforward task to establish mathematically—using the Equation and the Ratio Formula—that Transitivity is not probabilistically valid. It is also an interesting exercise to devise a diagram of Adams's sort illustrating the failure of Transitivity. Fig 5 does this, showing a case where $P(A{\rightarrow}B)$ and $P(B{\rightarrow}C)$ are high while $P(A{\rightarrow}C)$ is low. I prefer it to Adams's diagram for this purpose (1975: 16), because in his $P(A{\rightarrow}B) = 1$, and $P(A{\rightarrow}C) = 0$. Mine, allowing that the cows might have inattentively drifted through the open gate, gives a probability < 1 and > 0 to each of the three conditionals.

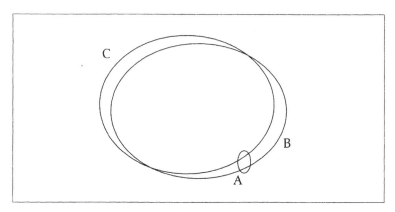

FIG. 5

To explain why Transitivity seems valid, Adams suggests that in inferences that seem to have the form

A→B, B→C ∴ A→C

this is really an ellipsis, and what the speaker or writer means is

A→B, (B&A) → C ∴ A→C

This is probabilistically valid, Adams argues, and so inferences that sound like transitivity of → really are all right but have the form not of Transitivity but of something weaker (1975: 22). Why should speakers tend to say A→C when they mean (B&A) → C? Adams could answer this in Gricean terms: someone who asserts a conditional, thereby inviting us to think about B *given A*, is behaving badly if he goes straight on to say other things about B while silently cancelling the supposition of A.

Adams has shown me that Antecedent Strengthening entails Transitivity, and vice versa; so it is not surprising that the failures of these two principles are similar. The parallel can be seen by adapting the counterexample I brought against one so that it counts also against the other. The farmer accepts 'If the gate to the turnip field has been left open, the cows have been inattentive to the gate's condition', but he does not accept 'If the gate to the turnip field has been left open *and the cows have got in*, they have been inattentive' etc.

Here, as with Transitivity, it is easy to work out arithmetically why Antecedent Strengthening fails. The diagram for such failures is also straightforward. Try it for yourself: all you need is for a large portion of A's oval to overlap C's and a small proportion of (A&B)'s region to overlap C's.

Of the four principles selected for discussion, Antecedent Strengthening is the most richly endowed with obvious counterexamples. Think of any indicative conditional that you accept and regard as contingent, and you will quickly see how to strengthen its antecedent so that the result is no longer acceptable. Take our old friend 'If Booth didn't kill Lincoln, someone else did [kill Lincoln]' (§1), and strengthen its antecedent to yield this: 'If Booth didn't kill Lincoln, the person he killed being not Lincoln but a double, then someone else did kill Lincoln.' There are so many clear counterexamples to Antecedent Strengthening that we do not have to explain why it usually seems valid—it doesn't! Still, things can be said about circumstances under which the acceptability of A→C is evidence for the acceptability of (A&B) → C, and at his 1975: 25–8 Adams says them.

Stalnaker (1984: 123–4) has offered a direct argument against Antecedent Strengthening and thus against Transitivity, which entails it. Counterexamples have value, but ultimately this direct argument should suffice. If Antecedent Strengthening is valid, Stalnaker points out, then we get this special case:

A→C ∴ (A&¬C) → C

as long as A does not entail C. Stalnaker argues that this cannot be right because (A&¬C) → C is intolerable: any conditional whose antecedent is inconsistent with its consequent must be false, except perhaps in the special case where the antecedent is itself impossible. So Antecedent Strengthening implies that every contingent indicative conditional—every one in which A does not entail C—is false because it entails something false. This seems to be decisive.

The failure of Antecedent Strengthening for indicative conditionals is one symptom of the non-monotonic nature of any reasoning where probability is involved (§32).

61. MODUS PONENS

Although I have written throughout as though Modus Ponens were plainly valid for indicative conditionals, this has been challenged by McGee and Lycan, and perhaps by others. I shall discuss three of their reasons.

One of Lycan's objections to Modus Ponens rests on the undisputed fact that Antecedent Strengthening fails for indicative conditionals, so that P(A→C) may be very high for a person for whom, at the same time, P((A&B) → C) is low. Or, in Lycan's terms, A→C can be true for someone for whom (A&B) → C is false. Because of this, unrestricted Modus Ponens does fail for →; that is, the form of Modus Ponens that says that from A→C and *anything that entails A* it is legitimate to infer C.

Putting flesh on those bones: while I have a high probability for A→C, I am in a condition where it is rational for me, if I come to accept P(A) = 1 without any other change in my belief system except ones that follow from that, to attach a high probability to C. (Understand this to be silently qualified to allow for the Thomason examples (§12).) But it may not be rational for me to make P(C) high conditional on adding to my belief system not only A but also some further item B that I have not inferred from the addition of A.

It is good to be reminded that when → is in question, the only legitimate form of Modus Ponens is the *restricted* one in which the second premiss is just exactly the antecedent of the conditional, and not any old thing that entails it. Objection: 'This is not a form of Modus Ponens, but something else. In so describing it you are just refusing to face a refutation.' I shall not argue about the label. What matters is that indicative conditionals are of service largely as inference tickets, and that this involves their being legitimately usable in the manner I have described. The thesis that Modus Ponens fails for them does not interfere with *that*. It merely reminds us that the ticket is not valid if you bring carry-on luggage. I shall continue to use the terminology of '(un)restricted Modus Ponens' for (in)valid forms of this inference pattern.

Lycan rejects even restricted Modus Ponens. He holds that indicative conditionals have truth values, and that someone who accepts A→C accepts something true if C obtains in every relevant A-situation that she *can* envisage. So it could happen that in accepting A→C she accepts something true although A is true and C false, the latter in an A-situation she could not have envisaged; in which case Modus Ponens would lead her from truth to falsity (Lycan 1993: 417–18).

Lycan's exposition of his view is not ideally clear, and some of its features suggest that he is backing off from the bold thesis that T→F can be true. But I think it is there, as it seems to be also—though again in a somewhat muffled form— when he revisits this territory in his 2001: 48–72.

To be swayed by this, I would have to retract large portions of my Chapters 3–8, and I am not about to do that.

A third objection to Modus Ponens—again to the restricted form of it—is an argument that was mentioned in Adams 1975: 33, taken up and endorsed by McGee 1985, and heralded by Lycan as furnishing a 'triumph for my semantics . . . the greater for being entirely unanticipated' (1993: 425). During the 1980 Presidential campaign, in which Reagan was leading Carter, with Republican Anderson a distant third, it was highly reasonable, McGee says, to accept

(1) If a Republican wins the election, then if it's not Reagan who wins it will be Anderson,

and it was correct to predict

(2) A Republican will win.

McGee and Lycan contend that from these by Modus Ponens one gets

(3) If it's not Reagan who wins, it will be Anderson,

which would have been an absurd thing to accept.

I deny that it was reasonable to accept 1. Any informed person back then, faced with 1, would have replied: 'Look, if a Republican wins, it *will* be Reagan.' Every such person had a belief system such that, if 'A Republican will win' was fed into it and minimal adjustments made, the resulting belief state accorded no probability at all to any conditional starting 'If Reagan doesn't win ...' except for independently true bores such as 'If Reagan doesn't win, then somebody won't win'.

Certain known facts about the election process, conjoined with 'A Republican will win' and 'Reagan will not win', *entail* 'Anderson will win'. But this merely illustrates how far logical entailment is from ordinary indicative conditionals.

There is also a shorter route to the same conclusion about McGee's argument. Relying on If-and (§40), we can maintain that 1 is equivalent to 'If a Republican wins the election and it's not Reagan who wins, it will be Anderson', which should be rejected because of zero-intolerance.

In rejecting this argument of McGee's, I do not want to demean his substantial project (1989) of extending Adams's work to cover a range of embeddings of conditionals. I do not report on this, because I have not mastered it; but it does not look negligible.

62. INDEPENDENT INDICATIVES

Having completed my main account of indicative conditionals, I can discuss how dependent conditionals relate to independent ones within the indicative group (§7). I shall confine myself to logically true independent conditionals. For causal and moral ones, the main outlines of the story are the same, but with tedious complications of detail.

I have been building on Ramsey's bedrock idea about what goes into someone's finding A→C to be more or less probable, namely, letting P(A) = 1 interact with the rest of his belief system, and seeing what the effect this has on the latter's probability for C. Where he accepts A→C as a logical truth, identity does not interact with the rest of his belief system: he gets C out of A purely through logical principles. In this case there is no source for subjectivity (except in so far as people may have different opinions about what is logically true), nor is there anything to block Antecedent Strengthening, Transitivity, and the rest from being valid. Furthermore, with logically true conditionals—as handled by a logically idealized person, for whom $P(A) = 1$ if A is necessary—the concept of probability is flattened. The person's probability for the conditional itself will always be 1, and the equation $P(A) \leq P(C)$ will always hold. There will be no use for probabilities other than 0 and 1.

These facts are plain enough, and beyond dispute. Still, a non-trivial question arises about how to handle them theoretically. In the following, I shall assume that when we are dealing with a logically true conditional, we are considering its behaviour in the hands of someone—call him 'Bright'—who knows for sure that it is logically true. Now, compare two things said or thought by Bright:

(1) If she reports that payment to the income tax authorities, I shall be in trouble.

(2) If that man is a cannibal, he is not a vegetarian.

Our best account of 1 is that Bright means it as an expression of his high probability for *I shall be in trouble* given the truth of *She will report . . . etc.* But what about 2? One is tempted to say that although he uses the form A→C, he really means that the man's being a cannibal *logically entails* his not being a vegetarian. The disunity this would bring into our account of indicative conditionals should give us pause, however; and there is a definite obstacle to going this way. It is that a stupid anthropologist—call him 'Dim'—might accept 2 without realizing that the meaning of 'cannibal' secures its truth. Dim bases 2 on data he has about cannibals who were not vegetarians, the lack of evidence of any who were, beliefs about the value of the sampling he has done, and so on. He certainly does not mean 2 as an entailment statement; but if he doesn't and Bright does, then 2 is radically ambiguous; and in analytic philosophy the 'ambiguity' diagnosis is usually wrong.

We shall do better to suppose that each person means 2 to express his high value for $P(C)$ given A, this being the outcome of the relevant Ramsey test. It happens that in Bright's mind the Ramsey test for 2 is a peculiarly simple affair, and Bright knows this; whereas for Dim the test has the usual complexities. Thus we can capture the real difference between the two without descending to the idea that 2 is ambiguous.

This explains why independent indicatives can be zero-tolerant (§23). The zero-intolerance of dependent indicative conditionals comes from the fact that if I am utterly sure that not-A, I have no disciplined way of adjusting my other particular beliefs to make room for $P(A) = 1$. In performing the Ramsey test, it is understood that one's most general principles are held steady without adjustment, and one's beliefs about particular matters of fact (and perhaps about less general matters of fact) are adjusted; the pressure for adjustment comes from the high value for $P(A)$, and the most general principles are the conduits along which the pressure is transmitted. With an independent conditional, the added $P(A) = 1$ sends pressure straight through the logical conduits to generate $P(C) = 1$; no adjustment of other beliefs comes into it; so there is nothing to make zero-intolerance kick in.

'In a context where it is understood to be logic all the way, isn't it irresistibly tempting to understand indicative conditionals as entailment statements?' If you find it so, give in; but not by postulating sentence ambiguity as something we *must* allow, and—connected with that—not presenting this diagnosis as a primary bearer of theoretical load. The Ramsey-based account that Adams gives carries all the weight; but in a special kind of case where the story flattens itself into something simpler, and this fact is clear to all concerned, then it *does no harm* to suppose that this shared understanding enters into what the person's conditional sentences mean in this context.

10

Subjunctive Conditionals—
First Steps

63. WORLDS: EXTREME REALISM

For the analysis of subjunctive conditionals there have been two approaches—or three, if you count Anscombe's 1975 'try-on' of the idea that such conditionals are truth-functional. Of the two considerable approaches, one was presented first (so far as I know) by William Todd (1964), then developed more fully by Robert Stalnaker (1968) and—independently, Stalnaker tells me—at the same time by David Lewis (1973*b*). Many others have followed these pioneers. Their approach aims to elucidate these conditionals with help from the concept of a *possible world*. The other approach that matters, launched initially in a 1947 paper by Nelson Goodman, does not rely on the world concept. Some writers in the Goodman camp use the language of 'possible world', but merely as an aid to exposition, not to carry any theoretical load. I shall explore Goodman's work in Chapter 20, and in Chapter 21 I shall arbitrate between it and the 'worlds' approach. The latter will be my topic, or my framework, through ten chapters, starting now.

You might think we need a firm, detailed analysis of the world concept before we can make theoretical uses of it. Against this, I agree with Stalnaker:

The notion will get its content, not from any direct answer to the question, what is a possible world? or from any reduction of that notion to something more basic and familiar, but from its role in the explanations of such a theory [of rational activity]. Thus it may be that the best philosophical defence that one can give for possible worlds is to use them in the development of substantive theory. (Stalnaker 1975: 141)

Still, one issue about the world concept should be faced right away. Stalnaker adopts one side in it when he writes of 'the notion of an alternative way that things may be or might have been (which is all that a possible world is)'; but there is another side.

David Lewis accepted something that has been called 'extreme realism' about worlds. Some writers use the label dyslogistically. I use it as literally accurate: on any spectrum of views about what sort or degree of reality possible worlds have, Lewis's would be at one end, and is in that sense 'extreme'. It starts with the idea that the actual world is a concrete reality—a great cosmos made up of atoms and radiation and space and so on—and that all the possible worlds are metaphysically on a par with it. On this view, the actual world is in no way metaphysically special. When I say:

In the actual world no diamond weighs a million tons,

all I am entitled to mean is:

In the world in which I live no diamond weighs a million tons.

Some worlds contain such a diamond, and if an inhabitant of such a world meant by his words what we mean by ours he could truly say:

In the actual world there is a diamond weighing a million tons.

He would use 'the actual world' to designate the world he inhabits, which is why his statement would be true. Analogously, one person says 'It is raining here' while another says 'It is not raining here', and each speaks truly because they are in different places. See Lewis 1970 and 1973b: 84–91. Lewis developed this line of thought most fully in his 1986a. The only other extreme realist about worlds that I know of is Richard B. Miller (1992).

Like most philosophers, I cannot believe that corresponding to each different position my right foot could have at this moment there are countless worlds, each of them a real cosmos; though I admit to having no *basis* for my incredulity.

I do have a basis for an epistemological objection to extreme realism about worlds. If possible worlds are what Lewis said they are, how can we be informed about them? Lewis might respond: 'You can answer your own question by appealing to your favourite epistemology for modal truths. You can learn that it is possible (not absolutely impossible) that P through thought experiments, consistency proofs and the like. Well, this is also how you learn about other worlds; for discovering modal truths *is* finding out about them.' But if I believed that modal truths were about what transpires at other real worlds, this should—and I hope it would—undermine my confidence that thought experiments, consistency proofs etc. *are* reliable guides to them. Lewis's actual treatment of the epistemic question (1986a: 108–15) differs a little from that, but is vulnerable in nearly the same way.

I am also swayed by a moral objection that Robert Adams (1974: 215–16) levelled against extreme realism. (I shall refer to him again in §76. Everywhere else in this book 'Adams' refers to Ernest W. Adams.) I see a child about to wander onto a busy street where she risks being hurt or killed. If I can save her, I should; I am morally required to. However, while I can affect what happens to this girl, I cannot influence the range of what is *possible* for her: the possibilities are laid out rigidly and immovably, and I can only affect which of them is actual. For most of us, that generates a moral imperative: making some possible harm non-actual—that is clearly worth doing! But it seems less so in the context of Lewis's extreme realism, according to which every possibility is real. By saving this child from being hurt, I do nothing to reduce the total amount of pain suffered; the pain the child *could* have suffered *is* suffered by some child at some world. I merely ensure that the sufferer is not at my world, the one you and I call 'actual'.

Lewis responded that the aim of reducing the total amount of suffering is not a part of common moral sense, belonging only to 'utilitarians of an especially pure sort' whom he evidently did not mind offending (1986a: 127). I think the following fairly expands Lewis's remarks on this topic:

Our deepest moral attitudes concern what goes on at our world; the *basis* of our moral thinking and feeling is a special kind of NIMBY attitude—not in my back yard, not at the world at which I exist. Most of us regard as morally permissible a certain bias in favour of oneself, one's immediate family, one's extended family, one's friends, one's compatriots, one's fellow humans; and extreme realism about worlds teaches us that we are also governed by a bias in favour of *whatever exists at the world one calls 'actual'.*

Most of us accept a morality in which the first six biases are permitted; but we believe that each needs to be defended, and to be constrained. We would be offended by the attitude that a small advantage for my family outweighs any amount of suffering for yours. If Lewis was right, however, the seventh bias is basic, absolute, and unconstrained. It differs in kind from the other six.

The difference makes itself felt when we consider rejecting the biases. If someone had no bias towards his family, we might find this repellently cool and strange; but if his even-handedness took an egalitarian form, in which he was open to appeals for help, but not more to his mother's appeals than to a stranger's, we would still recognize him as a moral agent, though a deformed one. Someone who lacked the seventh bias, on the other hand, would be indiscernible from the most vicious or indifferent amoralist we can conceive of.

When I put this to Lewis, he replied by distinguishing (1) moral thinking, (2) moral feeling, and (3) moral choices. In 1 we should not distinguish between friends and strangers, or between world-mates and occupants of other possible worlds: 'One should judge good and evil accurately for what they are, wherever in space or in time or in the pluriverse they may be located.' In 2 we should make distinctions of the kinds in question: 'The more remote the goods or evils are, and the less we could possibly do about them, the less we ought to heed them and the less we ought to respond emotionally to them.' In 3, a moderate amount of bias, for example in favour of friends and family, is permissible; but 3 is governed by the limits on what we can do to affect the welfare of others: 'Just as one never has the opportunity to benefit past people at the expense of present people . . . so likewise one never has the opportunity to benefit people in one world at the expense of those in another (though one often has the opportunity to affect which are actual and which not).' This is worth pondering, but it does not win me over. I have feelings—sometimes intensely troubled mixtures of horror and pity—for some people who have suffered in the past; but if it fell to me to save someone from torture, my glad triumph would not be clouded by pity for the non-actual person who came under the knife. The actual past and the non-actual present are equally unreachable by me now, but I relate to them emotionally in very different ways. These feelings of mine are not pathological, I submit; but if Lewis was right, they are at bottom unreasonable. Well, perhaps they are. I do not offer this moral argument as conclusive.

64. WORLDS: ABSTRACT REALISM

Many philosophers today theorize in terms of 'worlds', though few agree with Lewis about what worlds are. Two broad ways for having 'worlds' without extreme realism have been proposed: fictionalism and representationalism.

The former, devised by Gideon Rosen, has received a stamp of non-disapproval from Lewis, who wrote to me: 'If you can't resist writing as if extreme modal realism were true, while believing it isn't, may I commend Gideon Rosen's [1990]? There's been some flak over whether this view works on its own terms, but I think that's been satisfactorily sorted out: Rosen [1995].'

Rosen suggests that we understand every statement about worlds as meaning something of the form 'According to extreme modal realism . . .'. For example, 'There could be blue swans' means, for Lewis, that some world contains blue swans; and it means, for Rosen, that according to Lewis's theory some world contains blue swans. Given this approach, Rosen can say 'Some world contains blue swans', but he will mean only that according to extreme modal realism there is such a world.

Rosen candidly exhibits some difficulties about this view (see his 1995 for references to the literature pro and con), but I think he under-emphasizes the biggest drawback in fictionalism, namely its parasitic dependence on extreme realism. If I cannot believe there is a world containing blue swans and talking donkeys, though I believe there could be such animals, what do I *gain* by the thought that the extreme realist who shares my modal opinion will express it by saying that there are worlds containing blue swans and talking donkeys?

Even if fictionalism can be 'fixed', with all its 'i's dotted and 't's crossed, I see no advantages to it. It shows me a way of retaining the language of 'worlds' without the extreme realist ontology, but if I avail myself of it I shall be merely parroting something in which I do not believe. I prefer to put my money on the representationalist approach to possible worlds. At best I shall come up with a somewhat rickety structure, but it will be planted directly on the ground, rather than sitting on the shoulders of a theory that I reject.

According to representationalist theories of worlds, a world is not a concrete thing—a chunk of space and rock—but rather an item that may be *about* such a concrete reality. Such a world, then, must be fit to *represent* a concrete reality, though only one of them actually does so. Lewis asked how this representing is to be done, and canvassed three answers: worlds represent (1) as sentences do, or (2) as pictures do, or (3) 'magically'. He discussed 2 for the sake of completeness, but for 1 and 3 he had particular philosophers in mind. I shall pass by his attacks on 1 and 2, but I need to say a little about 3 because it includes the approach I shall take in this book.

Lewis's target in 3 was the view that a world is a proposition or state of affairs—an abstract entity of the kind Frege assigned to a 'third realm' in addition to the mental and material realms in which he believed. More specifically, a possible world is a *consistent* proposition P that is *maximal*, meaning that every proposition is either entailed by P or inconsistent with it. Or, in yet other words, it is a *total way things might be*.

Lewis objected that this essentially involves the modal notions of consistency and maximalness, yet has no analytic account of modality. He did have such an account: for him, a proposition is a set of worlds, a consistent proposition is a non-empty set of worlds, a maximal consistent proposition is a set containing exactly one world. None of those explanations will serve the turn of someone who, like Lewis's opponents in 3, explains 'world' with help from 'consistent'.

This scores a palpable hit, but it does not persuade me to give up my adherence to (3) the view of worlds as abstract entities, like propositions. There are many concepts of which I want but lack an analytic account; I have, in the company of Descartes, Frege, Wittgenstein, and others, struggled with the modal notions all my adult life (Bennett 1961, 1994, 2000), and I remain unsure what to think about them. But my *horror vacui* is not strong enough to make extreme realism about worlds flow in to fill the explanatory gap.

Lewis's other main point against 3 explains his label for it (1986a: 174–91). Adherents of this kind of position, he charges, have no account of *how* their supposed abstract 'worlds' can represent concrete realities; so that they should be reduced to confessing that this representation is done by 'magic'. The difficulty he saw here can be illustrated well enough by a proposition that is not maximal—for example, *Some monkey holds a bunch of nine bananas*. At a certain time that is false; then it becomes true; and Lewis asked what sort of connection there can be between the truth-maker—namely the monkey that picks up a nine-banana bunch—and the abstract proposition. The truth-maker is one thing, the proposition it makes true is another; how can they be related? Not causally; not by any of the relations that can obtain between (1) sentences and their truth-makers, or between (2) pictures and their veridicality-makers; and there seem to be no other candidates. Lewis also counter-attacked, arguing that there cannot be an answer to this question, because 3 holds that the truth-maker's existence *necessitates* the proposition's truth; but the truth-maker is one thing and the proposition another, and Lewis adhered to the 'Humean' view that 'necessary connections between distinct existences' are to be ruled out (1986a: 181). I am also drawn to a 'Humean' view along those lines; but the only case for it that I know—namely, Hume's own—does not apply to 'existences' such as propositions.

There is much more to be said, but this is not the place for it. I recommend those pages of Lewis to you, and also van Inwagen 1980 and 1986, the latter of which is a pretty satisfying reply to this last argument of Lewis's.

I shall use 'abstract realism' to name the view that worlds are propositions, states of affairs, or ways-things-could-be—abstract objects of some kind. Lewis once remarked to me that the abstract realist might say that 'P is true at w' really means 'P is true **a**ccording **t**o w', so that in these contexts 'at' is an acronym! Whether or not abstract realism succeeds, and even if Lewis was right that it cannot be made deeply secure, it has been the working assumption of most 'worlds' analysts of subjunctive conditionals. I shall go along with that.

As abstract realists we must hold, as Lewis did, that all possible worlds—the actual one and the others—are of the same metaphysical sort. If we took one world to be a big chunk of space, rock etc. and all the others to be states of affairs, we could not usefully compare it with them. But, whereas Lewis thought they are all chunks of rock (to speak), we abstract realists hold that none of them are. In this context we must use 'the actual world' to refer not to this great, expanding, knobbly, wave-saturated thing, but rather to the totality of actual states of affairs; not to something physically containing you, but to something logically containing the whole truth about you. Worlds thus construed can still be compared with one another. In the exchange 'He ought to have shown the contract to his lawyer before signing it', 'Oh, it would not have made much difference', the reply compares a possible state of affairs with the one that actually obtained.

With 'world' thus understood, we do not know which world we exist at. We can truthfully say we live *here*; but that identifies a chunk of space and rock, not a 'world' in the abstract sense. The whole reality of an abstract world is that of a certain *maximal* proposition. To know which such world is actual, then, would involve knowing which maximal proposition is actually true, which would be knowing the whole contingent truth.

A Lewis world (so to call it) is a vast *thing* that lasts through time and undergoes vicissitudes, containing fewer stars and more black holes at one time than at another. An abstract world does not last through time: it conjoins propositions about how things are at various times, propositions *about* alterations, but it does not itself alter. Yet I find it hard to avoid writing as though worlds had histories, and were the scenes of events and subjects of alterations. When I want to contrast

> two worlds that are exactly alike in respect of what they entail about how things are at all times before T, and differ in respect of what they entail about what is the case at T,

I find it easier to express this as a contrast between

> two worlds that are exactly alike at all times before T and become unalike at T.

The advantages are too great to forgo. I shall regularly write as though the worlds in question *had* histories, whereas strictly speaking they *are* histories. This convenient shorthand should not open a crack through which philosophical error will seep in. Everything I say in it could be expressed more correctly.

Wanting to limit my licentiousness, I shall never write of worlds *where* . . . but always of worlds *at which* . . . Whether or not you take this to be short for 'according to which', it at least spares you the 'where', which too easily suggests that worlds are chunks of space and rock.

I follow the conventions whereby 'α' names the actual world, 'A-world' means 'world at which it is the case that A', 'AB-world' means 'A-world that is also a B-world', and 'A$\bar{\text{B}}$-world' means 'A-world that is not a B-world'. I shall occasionally stretch this notation in ways whose meanings will be apparent from context.

In relating propositions to worlds, I shall write that P 'is true' at w, or that it 'obtains' at w, or that it is 'the case' at w. These mean the same; they merely bring a little variety to the prose.

65. TWO FALSE LOGICAL PRINCIPLES

With indicative conditionals I saved up the logic until near the end; with sub-junctives I shall start in a logical vein. The logics are similar, as has often been noted, but I shall make nothing of this until §69, in the meantime treating the logic of subjunctive conditionals considered on its own. Further logical principles will come up for discussion in §72 and §131, when we are ready for them.

Along with the logic—or, rather, *through* it—this chapter and the next will also move some distance into the semantic analysis of our conditionals. When a logical principle involving them strikes us as clearly right, we want, at a minimum, an analysis that is consistent with it. Better would be an analysis that entails the principle, showing why it is valid; and that is what the 'worlds' analysis of subjunctive conditionals can do for us.

Consider the following three conditional relations:

entailment: To say that A entails C is to say that A leads to C by sheer unaided logic; or that it is absolutely impossible that A&¬C; or that every A-world is a C-world.

causal implication: I use 'A causally implies C' to mean that A leads to C by logic conjoined with causal laws; or that it is causally impossible that A&¬C; or that every causally possible A-world is a C-world. (A causally possible world is one that conforms to the causal laws of the actual world.)

material implication: To say that A⊃C is to say that it is not the case that A&¬C; or—though it seems a funny thing to say—that every actual A-world is a C-world.

Lewis called these 'strict conditionals', meaning that each can be defined in terms of the truth of the material conditional throughout a class of worlds. In the case of the third, the class is the singleton of α (the class whose only member is α). Entailment is stronger than causal implication, which is stronger than material implication; this is intuitively evident, and you can easily establish it by thinking of what it means about relations between classes of worlds. My discussion of these relations derives mostly from Lewis 1973b: 4–13, but I shall say it in my own way.

Every strict conditional obeys *Antecedent Strengthening*; none can go from true to false by the replacement of A by A&B as antecedent. The reason is obvious. To say that A⊃C is true throughout a class of worlds is to say that C is true at every A-world in the class; from this it follows that C is true at every

AB-world in the class, since those are a subset of the A-worlds; and to say that C is true at every AB-world in the class is to say that (A&B) ⊃ C holds throughout the class.

Subjunctive conditionals do not obey Antecedent Strengthening. In circumstances where it would be true to say

If you had walked on the ice, it would have broken,

it may be plainly false to say

If you had walked on the ice while leaning heavily on the extended arm of someone standing on the shore, the ice would have broken.

When someone asserts A>C and would generally be taken to have said something true or at least plausible, if A does not outright entail or causally imply C there will be some B such that (A&B) > C will strike us as false. When A *does* entail or causally imply C, A>C is one of those independent conditionals that I undertook in §7 to keep out of the picture.

Transitivity entails Antecedent Strengthening, as I now show. Start with Transitivity:

A>B, B>C ∴ A>C.

If this is valid, then so is every special case of it, including the one we get by substituting A&B for A. This gives us:

(A&B) > B, B>C ∴ (A&B) > C.

This has the form

[Necessary truth], B>C ∴ (A&B) > C,

which means that it is strictly equivalent to

B>C ∴ (A&B) > C

which is Antecedent Strengthening. QED. That is why examples that refute Antecedent Strengthening can also be made to refute Transitivity. For example: if you had walked on the ice it would have broken; if you had walked on the ice leaning on someone's arm etc. you would have walked on the ice; but we do not apply Transitivity and conclude that if you had walked on the ice leaning on someone's arm etc. it would have broken. (That example, like the proof that precedes it, employs an independent conditional, but this does not disqualify it. Such conditionals, though risky to use as intuitive examples, have a secure place in the abstract logic of conditionals.)

Examples devised by Lewis to show the failure of Transitivity and Antecedent Strengthening have been criticized by Crispin Wright, who counters with examples of his own in which Transitivity seems all right. See Wright 1983: 139–40. See also Lowe 1984, Wright 1984, Lowe 1985, Mackie 1980, and Edgington 1995: 253–4.

Wright's examples are best understood, I contend, as ones in which we naturally 'hear' (A>B) & (B>C) as conjoining A>B with (A&B) > C from which conjunction A>C does follow. It is easy to see why an assertion of B>C, following hard on the heels of an assertion of A>B, would be heard as meaning (A&B) > C; it is for the reason that I sketched in §60 for the corresponding fact about indicative conditionals. Gricean orderliness requires that someone who has asserted A>B ought not to go straight on to take B as an antecedent unless he either means it as B-as-a-consequence-of-A or else warns us that he does not. If Wright's examples are valid when understood in this way, they must rely on the principle of Limited Transitivity:

A>B, (A&B) > C entail A>C.

The validity of this will be a topic of §118.

66. ATTEMPTS TO PRESERVE THE PRINCIPLES

Two can play at that game! If opponents of Transitivity can explain away its apparent virtues by distinguishing what people say from what they are naturally understood to mean, perhaps its friends could turn the tables by invoking the same distinction to explain away the apparent counterexamples to it. This would be in the spirit of Grice's attempt to draw the sting of the apparent counterexamples to his thesis that → is ⊃. This attempt to rescue the two logical principles cannot succeed; but I shall examine it at length because we can learn from its failure. I shall focus on Antecedent Strengthening; you will see how to reapply the discussion to Transitivity.

The problem is to reconcile Antecedent Strengthening, namely the thesis:

A>C entails (A&B) > C

with a range of facts of which the following is typical. Sometimes a speaker would be taken to say something true if she said:

(1) If you had walked on the ice, it would have broken,

and false if she said:

(2) If you had walked on the ice while being supported from the shore, the ice would have broken.

The rescue attempt that we are to consider says that subjunctive conditionals are usually *understated*, and that someone who asserted 1 would normally mean something with a stronger antecedent—and thus a weaker overall meaning—than the conventional meaning of 1 supplies. Thus when the speaker asserts 1, she means and is understood to mean something of the form:

(1*) If you had walked on the ice and Q had been the case, it would have broken,

for a value of Q such that it is *not* the case that if she asserted 2 she would mean and be understood to mean:

(2*) If you had walked on the ice while being supported from the shore, and Q had been the case, the ice would have broken.

In short, Q is a conjunct in what she means by 1 *but not a conjunct in what she means by 2*; and so the intended contents of those two assertions—as distinct from the conventional meanings of the sentences—are not related as A>C relates to (A&B) > C. Rather, they are related as (A&Q) > C relates to (A&B) > C; one is true and the other false, but Antecedent Strengthening is untouched. Thus the rescue attempt.

But 2 is merely one among thousands of false conditionals that result from 1 by Antecedent Strengthening. The rescue attempt requires the antecedent of 1 to be 'heard' as silently conjoining material that is inconsistent with each of the myriad of strengthenings, so that someone who asserts 1 is taken to mean something of the sort:

If you had walked on the ice and had not leaned heavily on the arm of someone who was standing on the shore, and had not had ten large helium balloons tied to you, and had not had most of your weight taken by a giant magnet hovering above you, and the ice had not been two feet thick, and . . . , the ice would have broken,

with a few thousand other clauses in place of the ellipses. This is hopeless. The materials needing to be crammed into the meaning of 1's antecedent are too numerous and various for the speaker to have meant them all, even if she knew them all. To cover them all in a general formula we would have to suppose that 1 means:

If you had walked on the ice and nothing had been the case that would stop it from breaking, it would have broken.

This rescues Antecedent Strengthening, but only at the price of making 1 trivial. In this paragraph I have been following the elegant Lycan 1993: 420 and 2001: 61.

Lewis (1973b: 13) also looked into the attempt to rescue Antecedent Strengthening by supposing that antecedents are understated. However, he handled this purely in terms of vagueness, taking it as the idea that 1 as stated is vague and that something in the context enables the speaker to mean and be understood to mean something more precise. Understating can indeed occur against a background of vagueness: she says 'He is bald', and succeeds in conveying that the person has no hair at all on his head; she says 'The party was too crowded', communicating her intended message that the party had just a few too many people for comfort—which is still vague, but less so than the conventional meaning of what she said. Plenty of understating, however, is not like this. You say: 'How did your visit to the studio go?' I reply: 'It was a zero. I didn't get to talk to anyone.' In fact I spoke to the guard at the gate when he asked for my credentials, so what I have said to you is false. But I meant, and you understood me to mean, that I had not been able to talk to anyone who might help me to succeed as a writer of screenplays; which is true. My meaning goes beyond what my sentence conventionally means, but not by a move away from vagueness. Taken in its conventional meaning, what I said was not *vague* but *false*. This pattern of understating—the one that does not depend on vagueness—is what a Q-inserting defence of Antecedent Strengthening needs to appeal to.

Lewis and I differ also in some details of our versions of the proposed defence of Antecedent Strengthening, and in our reasons for rejecting it. I shall not go into this. We have in any case found good reasons to think that Antecedent Strengthening fails for subjunctive conditionals, which implies that Transitivity fails too.

Late in §60 I reported an argument of Stalnaker's against Antecedent Strengthening and thus against Transitivity for indicative conditionals. He really stated it as an argument against those two for *any* conditionals, and it does indeed hold equally strongly for subjunctives. Try it for yourself and you will see.

Stalnaker's argument does no harm to our three kinds of strict conditional. Entailment: there are no true contingent entailment statements, so the argument does not apply to them. Causal implication: If A causally implies C, then A&¬C is causally impossible, and it seems reasonable to suppose that causal impossibilities causally imply anything (§87). Material implication: it is famously and boringly true that if A⊃C then (A&¬C) ⊃ C.

67. VARIABLY STRICT CONDITIONALS

A certain analysis of P *entails* Q equates it with A⊃C *is true at every possible world*; and we have seen that this analysis can explain why P *entails* Q entails

(P&R) entails Q. This reminds us of how analyses can explain logical truths. We need an analysis of subjunctive conditionals that will explain why A>C does not entail (A&B) > C. So far, we know only that subjunctive conditionals do not obey Antecedent Strengthening, which implies that they are not 'strict conditionals' in the sense explained above. That is, there is no set of worlds W such that, for any A and C, A>C means that *A ⊃ C is true throughout W*. Now we should look for a positive analysis of these conditionals, from which the failure of Antecedent Strengthening follows.

An idea that stops short of completely analysing A>C is a promising start on an analysis, and all by its own it explains why Antecedent Strengthening fails for >. It is the thesis that subjunctive conditionals are, in Lewis's phrase, 'variably strict'. For a strict conditional operator O, the following holds:

> There is a class W of worlds such that, for every value of A and C, $O(A,C)$ entails *Every A-world in W is a C-world*.

This yields Antecedent Strengthening, so we cannot have it for A>C. But we can safely have this:

> For every value of A, there is a class W of worlds such that *A>C* entails *Every A-world in W is a C-world*.

We do not have one subset of worlds for all subjunctive conditionals, but for each such conditional there is a relevant subset of worlds. That makes these conditionals variably strict:

> *Each is strict*: it means that A ⊃ C holds through a certain set of worlds, or that every A-world belonging to a certain set is also a C-world.

> *They can vary in a certain way*: what the relevant set of worlds is varies with different conditionals.

This variability blocks the proofs of Transitivity and Antecedent Strengthening that can easily be provided for any unvariably strict conditional. Even if A ⊃ C is true through the class of worlds that determines the truth value of A>C, it does not follow that (A&B) ⊃ C will be true through the *possibly different* class of worlds that determines the truth value of (A&B) > C.

This dizzyingly abstract story says only that when evaluating A>C by considering whether A ⊃ C is true throughout a certain class of worlds, what the relevant class is will depend upon what A and C are. About the nature of this dependence I have said nothing.

As a way into it, recall that I started this book with two questions that an analysis of subjunctive conditionals should answer. How can subjunctive conditionals be contingent? How can they be answerable to empirical evidence? When applied to conditionals whose antecedents are false, these questions press hard: how can what *is* the case bear upon what *would* have been the case if things had been otherwise? Within the possible-worlds framework, the pressure mounts: how can facts about the actual world throw light on how things stand throughout a class of worlds to which it does not belong? How can we learn about other worlds by exposing our nerve-endings to our cosmos? (That is, the object *the whole truth about which* is the actual world.)

The answer must be that facts about our cosmos determine which class of worlds settles the truth value of the conditional. We need an analysis according to which the truth value of A>C depends on whether A⊃C is true throughout a certain class of worlds that *relate in a certain way to the actual world*. The relation must be a *grounded* one—a relation R such that whether R(x,y) depends upon monadic facts about x and about y. Thus, for example, '. . . is bigger than . . .' and '. . . is similar to . . .' are grounded; '. . . is ten miles away from . . .' is not. There are no ungrounded relations between worlds, but I mention groundedness for safety's sake.

This could solve the contingency problem. Suppose that the truth of A>C depends upon the truth of A⊃C through a class of worlds having grounded relation R to the actual world. Then although discoveries about α (the actual world) will tell me nothing about how things stand at any other world, they will tell me which other worlds are relevant to the truth value of A>C.

As applied to the conditional 'If you had walked on the ice, it would have broken', the contingency problem asks what the relevance is of the fact—as I am now supposing it to be—that at the time in question the ice was half an inch thick and the hearer had large helium balloons tied to him. Obviously those facts *are* relevant, making the conditional false, even though it does not mention them; but how does this relevance come about? Well, the actual ice and balloons affect which worlds we have to look to in evaluating the conditional, pointing us to worlds at which the hearer walks on the ice with balloons attached to him; and at those worlds the ice does not break.

The grounded relation between worlds that should control how we evaluate subjunctive conditionals is often called 'closeness'. All the analytic theories following the lead of Stalnaker and Lewis have at their heart something like this:

A>C is true ≡ C obtains at every member of some class W of A-worlds such that every member of W is *closer to* the actual world than is any A-world not in W.

More roughly and informally: A>C is true just in case C obtains at all the closest A-worlds. I earlier spoke of the truth of A⊃C throughout a class of worlds, and now I speak of the truth of C throughout that class. The two are equivalent: by definition A is true throughout the class, so within it C stands or falls with A⊃C.

What is closeness? Any theorist in this tradition will say that 'close' means whatever it has to mean for the above formula, or something like it, to come out true. However, the candidates for the role of closeness that have been proposed have all involved *similarity*, going right back to the early work of Todd:

When we allow for the possibility of the antecedent's being true in the case of a coun-terfactual, we are hypothetically substituting a different world for the actual one. It has to be supposed that this hypothetical world is as much like the actual one as possible . . . (Todd 1964: 107)

If there are thick ice and relevant helium balloons at α, we have to evaluate Walk > Break by considering what goes on at worlds at which the ice is thick and the hearer has balloons tied to him—that is, worlds resembling α in those respects. The contingency problem is solved purely by our taking closeness to be *some* grounded relation between worlds; but when we think about subjunctive condi-tionals in a less abstract way, we find that the only viable candidates for the role involve similarity.

We have reached a position that we can roughly state thus:

A>C is true ≡ C obtains at every member of some class W of A-worlds such
                that every member of W is *more like* the actual world than is
                any A-world that is not in W.

We could express this by saying that A>C is true just in case C is true through-out some class of A-worlds that beat all competitors in respect of how like the actual world they are. (According to Lewis, A>C is also true if there are no A-worlds, that is, if the antecedent is absolutely impossible. Please yourself about that.)

It is easy to see how this blocks Antecedent Strengthening. Take a case where it is true to say:

(1) If you had walked on the ice, it would have broken,

and false to say:

(2) If you had walked on the ice while being supported from the shore, the ice would have broken.

To evaluate 1 we consider worlds at which you walk on the ice and that are oth-erwise pretty much like α; to evaluate 2, we consider worlds at which you walk on the ice while being supported from the shore, and are otherwise pretty much like α. They are different classes of worlds; the 2 set of worlds contains members that the 1 set does not, and at some of those the ice does not break.

Notice that in my more precise statement of the theory, I said '. . . C is true at every member of *some* class W . . .'. There may be many such classes for a given value of A. Lewis neatly expounded this matter through a 'Ptolemaic astronomy'—an explanatory model that portrays a system of nested 'spheres' with α, the actual world, at the centre:

Any particular sphere around α is to contain just those worlds that resemble α to at least a certain degree. This degree is different for the different spheres around α. The smaller the sphere, the more similar to α must a world be to fall within it. To say the same thing in purely comparative terms: whenever one world lies within some sphere around α and another world lies outside that sphere, the first world is more closely similar to α than is the second. Conversely, if S is any set of worlds such that every member of S is more similar to α than any non-member of S, then S should be one of the spheres around α. (Lewis 1973*b*: 14)

In these terms, the analysis says that A>C is true just in case A⊃C is true through some sphere of worlds around α, or, what comes to the same thing, just in case C is true at every A-world throughout some sphere around α. (Regarding the label 'Ptolemaic astronomy', Lewis wrote to me: 'It was Mackie who called it that, commenting on a talk I gave at Oxford while writing *Counterfactuals*. He meant it derisively, but I was happy to take it up.')

I have simplified Lewis's 'astronomy', putting the name 'α' where he had the variable '*i*'. He said that *every* world stands at the centre of such a system of spheres, because he wanted to theorize about how to evaluate subjunctive conditionals at any world, not merely at α. I shall explain this briefly.

You might think that the only evaluations of subjunctive conditionals that you and I and our friends care about are ones made at the actual world, that being our locus in logical space. In fact, though, we have serious reason to consider the truth values that conditionals get when evaluated at other worlds. It comes about through the embedding of some subjunctive conditionals in others. Consider this fragment of conversation, occurring at the actual world:

'Granted, when he threw the lighted match onto the ground, it didn't start a forest fire. But it might have done so, for all he knew; so his behaviour was irresponsible.'

'You do him an injustice. He knew his action was safe. *If it had been dangerous, he would have known it was dangerous* and would have behaved differently.'

The italicized clause means something like this:

> If it had been the case that (A) *if he were to throw the match onto the ground, a forest fire would ensue*, then (C) he would have known that this was the case.

Here one subjunctive conditional (A) functions as the antecedent of another. To evaluate A>C we must consider the closest worlds at which A is true (that is, at which Throw > Fire is true), as it is not at α. A typical bit of such an enquiry will consist in considering the non-actual world w—a closest A-world—and asking whether the Throw-worlds that are *closest to w* are Know-worlds. Observe: closest to w, not closest to α. Similarly when one subjunctive conditional has another as consequent: 'If the leaves had been dry, it would have been dangerous to throw a match on them'; 'If we hadn't annealed the glass, it would have been fragile'.

Unlike indicative conditionals, subjunctives can be freely embedded without raising problems of interpretation. Although we need to be aware of this, and of its requiring us to be able to evaluate conditionals from the standpoints of worlds other than α, we need not go on reminding ourselves of it. I shall now set it aside, and—except in §93—attend only to unembedded subjunctive conditionals, and thus only to spheres of worlds with α at their centre.

68. CONDITIONALS WITH DISJUNCTIVE ANTECEDENTS

The analysis of subjunctive conditionals in terms of 'worlds' implies things in the logic of conditionals. We have already seen one of them: the analysis implies and explains the failure of Antecedent Strengthening (and, by implication, of Transitivity). Enemies of the analysis have argued that it implies a logical falsehood and is therefore itself false. They have maintained that the principle Lewis called Simplification of Disjunctive Antecedents:

SDA: $(A \lor B) > C \therefore (A > C) \& (B > C)$

is true, and that the possible-worlds account of subjunctive conditionals implies that it is false—this being 'a fundamental difficulty for any attempt to validate a logic of counterfactuals via a possible-world semantics' (Ellis *et al.* 1977; see also Ellis 1979: 51–2).

There is certainly evidence for SDA. From the statement

D: If there had been rain or frost, the game would have been called off,

one naturally infers both of these:

D_r: If it had rained, the game would have been called off.
D_f: If there had been frost, the game would have been called off.

What validates those inferences if SDA is not valid?

But if it *is* valid, no 'worlds' analysis of subjunctive conditionals can be right; we can establish this without knowing the fine details of the analysis. Suppose that the closest A-worlds are C-worlds, and that the closest B-worlds are not C-worlds; it follows that the closest (A∨B)-worlds are C-worlds, and hence that (A∨B) > C. That is the premiss for SDA. But it also follows that ¬(B>C), which contradicts a conjunct in the conclusion of SDA. So we see that SDA cannot be reconciled with any 'worlds' analysis of subjunctive conditionals.

Lewis (1977) came to the rescue of such analyses by offering a powerful independent argument against SDA. Start with SDA:

(A∨B) > C ∴ (A>C) & (B>C),

and help yourself to the seemingly safe logical principle of Interchange of Logical Equivalents:

equiv(A,B), A>C ∴ B>C.

These, Lewis showed, cannot both be right. Take any P and Q such that P>Q. From that, by Interchange of Logical Equivalents, we can infer

((P&R) ∨ (P&¬R)) > Q

and that, by SDA, entails

(P&R) > Q.

So the two principles have licensed us to infer (P&R) > Q from P>Q, which means that they validate Antecedent Strengthening; yet the latter's *in*validity is the securest thing we know about subjunctive conditionals.

So we cannot have both SDA and Interchange; and this, Lewis reasonably said, is a problem for all of us, whether or not we have a 'worlds' semantics for subjunctive conditionals. He discussed three escapes from the difficulty, of which two are fairly clear cut: deny SDA and deny Interchange of Logical Equivalents. Ellis *et al.* think that the latter denial is especially difficult for a 'worlds' theorist, and I am inclined to agree, though Lewis strongly resisted this view. His own sympathies, however, were with the denial of SDA, as are mine. That is what is needed to rescue the 'worlds' analysis from this difficulty. Denying Interchange undercuts Lewis's disproof of SDA, but it does not help to reconcile SDA with the 'worlds' analysis.

What, then, makes it so natural to infer D_r and D_f from D? If we do not have SDA to back those inferences, then we have only two options: (1) the inferences are logically valid, but do not fall under SDA; (2) the inferences are not logically valid, but are, for known reasons, plausible and natural.

(1) Those inferences are valid, but do not fall under SDA because our original conditional D—'If there had been rain or frost, the game would have been called off'—does not mean anything of the form (Rain v Frost) > Cancel. Despite its superficial verbal form, it really means a conjunction of two conditionals Rain > Cancel and Frost > Cancel in the verbal guise of a conditional with a disjunctive antecedent. This was Lewis's view, and it had earlier been asserted by others. (See Ellis 1979: 69–74; McKay and van Inwagen 1976, which also offers a further argument against SDA. For other discussions of this matter, see Nute 1978, Warmbröd 1981, and Lycan 2001: 42–6.)

This diagnosis attracted me for as long as I thought it was not purely ad hoc. It seemed not to be, because we often use 'or' to express conjunctive thoughts. 'You may have your coffee with cream or without' conjoins two permissions, as does 'The law allows you to count this either as a deduction or as an adjustment'. But this defence against the charge of being ad hoc does not work. If D does not wear its true form on its face, that is not purely because of its use of 'or'. Compare D with this:

D⁺: If it had not been both dry and warm, the game would have been called off.

Taking both D and D⁺ at face value, they are near enough to equivalent; and each seems to lead to D_r and to D_f. If D is really a disguised conjunction of those two conditionals, then presumably D+ is also; but its disguise does not involve 'or'. So this diagnosis starts to look ad hoc after all.

(2) In agreement with Loewer 1975, I conclude that D and D⁺ are equivalent and not disguised—each is a subjunctive conditional with a disjunctive antecedent—and that neither entails D_r or D_f. Because our inference of D_r and D_f from D is therefore not logically valid, we have to explain why those inferences are natural. The explanation is Gricean (§10). D would be a sensible, decent, ver-bally economical thing to say only for someone who did think that D_r and D_f are both true. Consider a person who asserts D because he is confident of D_r, he regards the closest Freeze-worlds as remote, and does not believe D_f. What this person asserts is true if he is right about D_r; but asserting it on this basis is bad behaviour. It is of the same general kind—though perhaps not so bad in degree—as your saying 'If there had been rain or 90 per cent of the world's Buddhist priests had converted to Catholicism overnight, the game would have been called off.' The second disjunct is pointless in this case. There would be a point in including it only if it too had some bearing on the consequent. In short, D means what it seems to mean; someone who asserts it can ordinarily be assumed to be willing also to assert D_r and D_f; but D does not entail either of those. In contrast with this, if someone says 'If Spain had fought on either the Allied side or the

Nazi side, it would have fought on the Allied side' (Warmbröd 1981: 271), we are not in the least inclined to think him committed to 'If Spain had fought on the Nazi side, it would have fought on the Allied side'—because that is absurd, and because in any case he has a quite different reason for making the antecedent of his conditional a disjunction. (For a stronger, deeper version of this approach, see Nute 1980a.)

Grice said that one mark of conversational implicatures is that they can be cancelled: 'They got married and they had a baby, but perhaps not in that order'; 'The meeting will be either on Wednesday or Saturday; don't assume that I don't know which'. Lycan (2001: 43–4) uses this against the approach I have been taking to SDA. The approach does not seem 'promising', he writes, 'because it is hard to hear the implications [in question] as cancellable'. He offers, presumably for our derision: 'If you eat either the broccoli or the Brussels sprouts, you'll get sick; but don't get me wrong—I'm not implying that if you eat the broccoli you'll get sick.' Then he moves on; but let us pause to consider.

It often sounds fishy when someone cancels an implicature, even in cases where the Gricean diagnosis is plainly correct. Lycan's cancelling statement sounds perverse until a suitable context is provided for it:

'She told me that she is resolved *never again to eat broccoli or Brussels sprouts*. Do you think she will stand firm this evening, when she is guest of honour at a vegan banquet?'

'No, I am quite sure that *she will eat broccoli or Brussels sprouts* this evening; it will be socially impossible for her to keep to her resolve. But I am not saying that she may eat broccoli this evening; I happen to know it won't be served.'

Here the respondent uses the disjunctive form because he is answering a question in which a disjunction is highlighted. The more usual reason for speaking disjunctively—namely, uncertainty as between the disjuncts—creates an implicature, and the speaker, knowing this, cancels it.

This, it seems, is in general how it goes with cancellations of conversational implicatures. With that example as a guide, it is a mere five-finger exercise to devise a context in which we sense nothing notably wrong with the cancellation that Lycan cannot 'hear' as legitimate.

Against the Gricean treatment of the intuitive data that I have defended, Ellis (1979: 81 n. 9) objects that the distinction between truth and assertibility 'is too unclear to bear the enormous weight which is now being put upon it'. The claim of unclarity looks weak to me in the light of the work on the distinction by Grice (whom Ellis does not mention); and the 'enormous weight' is, I submit, really just the brushing away of a minor nuisance.

69. WHY THE LOGICS ARE SO ALIKE

The logics of indicative and subjunctive conditionals are strikingly different from the logic of any strict conditional (§65), but are in their main outlines exactly the same as one another. McCawley (1981: 311–12) denied this, saying that the two logics are 'quite different'; but this was because he thought that indicatives obey Antecedent Strengthening and Transitivity.

Gibbard has suggested that the likeness in the logics may be 'little more than a coincidence', and that the two kinds of conditionals 'have almost nothing in common'. (1981*b*: 211). Many of us find this intrinsically implausible, and Stalnaker has added arguments to support us (1984: 111–12). He points out that the crucial word 'if', shared by the two kinds of conditional, is matched by a similarly shared word in 'most if not all other languages'; that the engaging questions about how conditionals combine with such words as 'even', 'only', and 'might' (and, he could have added, 'then') admit of answers that hold for both kinds of conditional; and that certain kinds of paraphrase—for example, ones using 'unless'—work in just the same way for conditionals of both types.

How far one can go in unifying the two sorts of conditionals is still in dispute, and I shall take up the question in Chapter 23. But we already have before us the materials for *explaining* why the two are so alike in their logics, showing it to be more than a coincidence.

First, I should fill out my account of what the logical likenesses are. We saw Contraposition fail for →, and I now add that it fails for > also, and can be shown to do so in much the same way. It can be true that A>C and ¬A>C—if I were to snap my fingers, the truck would go on rolling; if I were not to snap my fingers, the truck would go on rolling—yet if Contraposition were valid, this would entail both ¬C>¬A and ¬C>A, which is contradictory. Here is a plainer example: it might be true that (even) if the British and Israelis had not attacked the Suez Canal in 1956, the Soviets would (still) have invaded Hungary later in the year, without its being true that if the Soviets had not invaded Hungary when they did it must have been the case that the British and Israelis had earlier attacked Suez. This is all intuitively evident, and what makes it true also makes Antecedent Strengthening fail, namely the variable strictness of >. From the fact that the closest A-worlds are C-worlds it does not even dimly seem to follow that the closest C̄-worlds are Ā-worlds.

Then there is the Simplification of Disjunctive Antecedents (SDA). This fails for >, I have contended, and it obviously fails for → as well. Although I would not ordinarily think it proper to *say* this, I assign a high probability to (Tomorrow will be sunny and warm v Tomorrow will be rainy and cold) → (Tomorrow will be a good day to go for a hike), because when I add the antecedent of that to my present belief system, writing on a fine, warm day in July, its first disjunct gets a high probability and its second a low one, leading to a high probability for the consequent. So my accepting that conditional leaves me free to reject—by assigning an extremely low probability to—(Tomorrow will be rainy and cold) → (Tomorrow will be a good day for a hike).

So the two kinds of conditional have this much logic in common: for each of them, Antecedent Strengthening, Transitivity, Contraposition, and SDA are all invalid. Let us start with the first of these. After briefly rehearsing the familiar tales about why Antecedent Strengthening fails for indicative conditionals and why it fails for subjunctives, I shall tell a single story that contains the essence of both accounts. The existence and relevance of this single story explains, as non-coincidental, this much of the logical sameness of the two types of conditionals.

When you accept A→C you are in a frame of mind in which you can extract C from A together with the rest of your system of beliefs, conservatively adjusted to admit A. When you accept (A&B) → C you are in a frame of mind in which you can extract C from A&B together with the rest of your system of beliefs, conservatively adjusted to admit A&B. The reason why you may be in a position to accept A→C but not (A&B) → C is that some of the propositional material you need to get to C from A alone may be unavailable for getting to C from A&B. Part of your initial belief system that is not deleted by the A-admitting adjustment *is* deleted by the (A&B)-admitting adjustment; or something that is provided by the former adjustment is not provided by the latter (§60).

The next step relies on the fact that for C to obtain at every member of a certain set of worlds is for C to be derivable from the strongest conjunction of propositions that is true at all those worlds. I shall explain this in detail in §119.

What makes A>C true is that C is derivable from A in conjunction with a set of propositions that relate in a certain way to the actual world, the relation being constrained by A. What makes (A&B) > C true is that C is derivable from A&B in conjunction with a set of propositions that relate in a certain way to the actual world, the relation being constrained by A&B. The reason why A>C may be true while (A&B) > C is false is that propositions that can legitimately be conjoined with A in deriving C from it may not be legitimately conjoined with A&B in an attempt to derive C from *it*. Truths about the actual world that also obtain at the closest A-worlds may not be true at the closest AB-worlds, and they may be required for getting C (§§65–6).

Those are old, familiar, fairly uncontroversial explanations. Here, now, is a story that covers both, using '⇒' to stand indifferently for either '→' or '>':

What makes A⇒C all right is C's being derivable from A together with other things. What makes (A&B) ⇒ C all right is C's being derivable from A&B together with other things. The reason why A⇒C may be all right while (A&B) ⇒ C is not is that the 'other things' that let you get C from A alone may not all be among the 'other things' that you would need to get C from A&B.

This is the single account of why Antecedent Strengthening fails for both types of conditional. Abstracting from truth versus probability, and from worlds versus beliefs, it brings out that a certain isomorphism between the workings of indicative and of subjunctive conditionals suffices to explain why Antecedent Strengthening fails for both. You will not have much trouble working out how to extend this to cover Transitivity and Contraposition as well.

It is less obvious how it covers the double failure of SDA, so I shall spell that out a little. The point is just that a high probability for (A∨B) → C rests on C's derivability not merely from A∨B but from what happens when that disjunction is added to the person's belief system—which may include a high value for $P(¬B)$; and the truth of (A∨B) > C rests upon how things stand at the closest (A∨B)-worlds—which may all be $A\bar{B}$-worlds. Here again, what does the work for both types of conditional is the derivability of the consequent from the antecedent and 'other things'.

Those four principles all hold for entailment, causal implication, and material implication, because in none of those does one get from A to C with help from 'other things'. They are strict, not variably strict.

The principles also hold for *independent* conditionals, whether subjunctive or indicative—that is, to ones in which the route from A to C owes nothing to any particular contingent fact or belief (§§7, 62). The manifest failures of the four principles must be exhibited through dependent conditionals of various kinds— ones where 'other things' are part of the story.

Two further logical principles should be dealt with here. One is Or-to-if. We saw this fail for →, and it fails just as spectacularly for >. I am perfectly sure that (A friend of mine said that I have little imagination ∨ I am about to write a novel as good as *Bleak House*), but there is not the faintest chance of its being true that if my friend had not said that I have little imagination I would now be poised to write a novel as good as *Bleak House*.

There is a single explanation for the failure of Or-to-if for our two types of conditional. We have seen that ⊃ is the only conditional operator for which Or-to-if is valid; such arguments hold unrestrictedly for material conditionals and no others. (That is why Jackson could infer that → is ⊃ from the premiss that Or-to-if is valid for →. The inference is not sound, because its premiss is false;

but it is valid.) So the reason why Or-to-if fails for indicatives and subjunctives is simply that each of those is stronger than the material conditional—'stronger' in the sense that A⊃C can be true when A>C is false, and that A⊃C can be believed by someone for whom A→C is improbable. The failure of Or-to-if, therefore, has a different source from the failures of Antecedent Strengthening and its three cousins. The latter quartet fail because our two conditionals are variably strict, but Or-to-if fails also for entailment and causal implication, whose strictness is not variable (§67). The entire source of this latest failure is the fact that → and >, like entailment and causal implication, are stronger than ⊃.

This completes my survey of the most striking logical likenesses between the two types of conditional. We see now that they can be *explained*—not merely written off as coincidental—consistently with holding that the two types of conditional are severely and deeply different, neither being reducible to, or a special case of, the other. Thus, I agree with Ellis (1979: 59) that indicatives and subjunctives have a common logic 'which is a logic of variably strict conditionals', but in §140 I shall dispute his stronger claim that the two types 'are usually variant locutions for the one kind of conditional'.

Edgington (1995b: 286) explains the differences in logic between → and ⊃ in terms of the failure of Conditional Proof. For example,

$$(A \rightarrow C), \neg C \therefore \neg A$$

is valid, but

$$A \rightarrow C \therefore \neg C \rightarrow \neg A$$

is not. My less elegant account helps, I think, with the larger project of relating both → and > to classical validity generally.

Unrestricted Modus Ponens is the locus of a logical difference: it is valid for subjunctive but not for indicative conditionals. 'How can this be? Lycan showed us that it fails for indicatives because they are variably strict, that is, for the reason that Antecedent Strengthening fails for them; but subjunctives are also variably strict, which is why Antecedent Strengthening fails for them too. How, then, could unrestricted Modus Ponens hold for them?' Good question; here is the answer. The truth of A>C requires that C be derivable from A and 'other things', and the truth of (A&B) > C requires that C be derivable from A&B and 'other things', but *when A&B is true*—which it must be for Modus Ponens to come into play—the second lot of 'other things' cannot conflict with the first lot. A world's closeness to α depends on its being in some manner, whose details are yet to be explored, similar to α. Now, if A&B is true then the closest A-world is α and so is the closest AB-world , or at any rate no other A- or AB-world is closer. So the move from A to A&B cannot bring in 'other things' that harm the derivability of C, for in this case the only world we have to deal with is α, all the relevant 'other things' are *facts*, truths about the actual world; so there can be no conflicts amongst them.

This is a difference between the two logics, deriving from a solid difference between the two types of conditional—one that in this context over-rides their sameness in both being variably strict.

Although unrestricted Modus Ponens is valid for subjunctive conditionals, our thinking about them is not strongly coloured by the possibility of using them in Modus Ponens, whether restricted or not. That is because of yet another difference between them and indicatives, which I shall expound in §88.

11

The Competition for 'Closest'

70. THE LIMIT ASSUMPTION

In sketching Lewis's theory, I have tied the truth of A>C to the truth of C throughout a certain *class* of worlds. Why should we not simplify the account, saying that A>C is true just in case C obtains at *the* A-world that is most similar to α? Because there may be no such thing as *the* most similar A-world, for either of two reasons: it may be that given any A-world there is another that is more similar to α; and it may be that two or more worlds are equally similar to α and more similar to it than any others are. Maybe no world wins the similarity stakes, or maybe several worlds come in first equal. Thus Lewis. I shall give these topics two sections each.

How could it be that no world comes first or first-equal in the similarity stakes? Lewis illustrated this startling claim by an example: a certain line is less than one inch long; now consider all the worlds at which it is more than one inch long. At each such world the line has a determinate length, which is a determinate amount greater than one inch. Thus, given any such world, there is another that resembles α even more closely, namely one at which the line exceeds an inch by some lesser amount. So we have a nested infinity of worlds, each containing a line more than one inch long and none exceeding that by a least amount.

This example may seem artificial and trivial, but the underlying point is neither. Lewis was right in saying that we should not assume that there are most-similar A-worlds (with or without ties for first place). Doing so is adopting what he calls *the limit assumption*. The opposing view, that on at least some dimensions of comparison there are closer and closer worlds without limit, I call the *density assumption*—borrowing the mathematical term 'dense', in which the series of all fractions is dense because there is no smallest one.

Lewis's density assumption has unpalatable consequences. His treatment of the line-length example implies that for *any* number n, however small, the conditional

> If (A) the line were more than one inch long, (C) it would be less than 1+n inches long

is true. It is easy to see why that implication holds. I take this argument from Pollock 1976: 18–19, and Stalnaker has also informally presented something like it (1978: 98). Pollock has gone even further, accusing the density assumption of implying that *if the line were more than one inch long it would not be more than one inch long*—because it would be less than 1+n inches long, for any positive n. This argument needs a certain logical principle, which might be challenged as part of a defence of the density assumption, but I shall not go into that. For details see Pollock 1976: 19–20; Herzberger 1979.

We may be tempted to fly from the density assumption into the arms of the limit assumption, but it has troubles of its own. It seems to imply that there are *atoms of dissimilarity* for every dimension of comparison. They are needed if two worlds are to differ by an absolutely minimal amount, with no world coming between them along that dimension of comparison. This is a lot to swallow, because Lewis's line-length example is just one of many dimensions of comparison that are not granular.

Still, we may be able to argue that for purposes of evaluating subjunctive conditionals all such dimensions can be treated as granular because not every difference counts. Do not reject this out of hand as ad hoc and opportunist. We have the hypothesis that A>C is true just in case C obtains throughout a class of A-worlds satisfying a condition of this form: *Every member of the class is closer to α than is any A-world outside the class.* Though not completely empty, this is an incomplete theory, because it does not say what closeness is. It becomes somewhat fuller if we take closeness to be some kind of similarity, or similarity along certain dimensions. To discover what dimensions, and thus bring the analysis to completion, we have to see what kinds of comparison will make the theory come out true. With the incomplete theory in one hand, and in the other our intuitive judgements about which subjunctive conditionals are true, we should fill out the former in the light of the latter. This is a right way to go about conceptual analysis.

When we steered by ordinary, unconstrained, intuitive similarity, we were pushed towards density because if the line is actually one inch long then a world at which it is 1.00000400 inches long is *ceteris paribus* more like the actual world than is one at which it is 1.00000399 inches long. If we work with a modified, constrained, tailored notion of similarity, on the other hand, perhaps that will let us avoid such awkward conclusions, drop density, and embrace the limit assumption. Will it in fact do so?

We shall see in §75 that closeness of worlds cannot be plain untailored intuitive similarity. Several analysts of subjunctive conditionals, Lewis included, have variously made it clear that their theories involve similarity along some dimensions and not along others. These constrainings of the similarity relation are of the highest importance, and they will have their day in court; but they do not help us with the problem of limits versus density. The tailoring and constraining of the similarity relation knocks out some dimensions of comparison as irrelevant, but leaves others in as essential parts of the story; and the density issue arises with them. So *those* developments in possible-worlds theories are no help with our present question.

It might seem that we need some basis for holding that, on any dimension of comparison, small enough differences do not count. This was Stalnaker's position (1968). He wanted the limit assumption from the outset. Where Lewis spoke of a triadic relation whose arguments are the proposition A, the actual world α, and a set of worlds, Stalnaker handles the theory in terms of a *function* going from the pair {A,α} to a unique world—the A-world closest to α. He calls it a 'selection function': given A and α, the function selects the A-world closest to α. The difference between relations and functions does not matter here: we could rewrite Stalnaker's theory in terms of a triadic relation, or Lewis's in terms of a function. What matters is the difference between getting from {A,α} to a class of worlds and getting from {A,α} to a single world. Wanting the latter, Stalnaker had to defend the limit assumption.

He did so by contending that some respects of dissimilarity are irrelevant. Which are relevant varies from case to case, he said: the ones that do not count are filtered out by the context—the interests and concerns of the speakers and hearers:

The selection function may ignore respects of similarity which are not relevant to the context in which the conditional statement is made. Even if, according to some general notion of overall similarity, *i* is clearly more similar to the actual world than *j*, if the ways in which it is more similar are irrelevant [to our present purposes], then *j* may be as good a candidate for selection as *i*. In the example, it may be that what matters is that the line is more than one inch long, and still short enough to fit on the page. In this case, all lengths over one inch but less than four or five inches will be equally good.

But what about a context in which every millimeter matters? If relative to the issue under discussion, every difference in length is important, then one ought not to use the antecedent *if the line were more than an inch long*. This would, in such a context, be like using the definite description *the shortest line longer than one inch*. The selection function will be undefined for such antecedents in such contexts. (Stalnaker 1978: 97)

This looks promising; in almost any context, one would think, some dissimilarities are negligible—treatable as nonexistent. This removes the threat posed by dissimilarities along dense dimensions, and also a deeper threat that I have so far suppressed and now explain. Properly understood, it shows us that denseness has almost nothing to do with the real difficulty confronting us here.

Grains of sand are discrete; nothing could be more granular! If the beach at Bowen Bay had less sand than it does, would it have exactly one grain less? Of course not—that is preposterous. Although when it comes to counting grains there are atoms of dissimilarity, namely differences of *one* in the number of grains, these are too small to matter for our normal purposes, and should therefore not normally be allowed to affect the truth values we assign to subjunctive conditionals; which is what Stalnaker said. He was defending the limit assumption as a thesis not about what differences there are but about 'the orderings of possible worlds *which are relevant to the interpretation of conditionals*' (p. 96, my emphasis).

71. THE CONSEQUENT AS CONTEXT

Stalnaker's work on the limit assumption offers help with the deeper problem, the one that does not essentially involve denseness; and that is a strength in it. However, his rescue operation does not clearly solve some further problems in this area. He has written as though he accepted this:

> If Fness is a matter of degree, and x is not F, then it is true that *If x were F it would be minimally F*,

seeking to make it palatable by requiring speakers to have some idea of what they count as minimal, not making subjunctive conditionals vulnerable to tiny grains, or a dense mush, of difference. I object that this minimalness assumption is wrong, even when hedged by constrictions on what counts in a given context. I have four siblings, and when it comes to siblings every one makes a notable difference; so by Stalnaker's apparent standards I ought to accept that had I had more siblings than I do, I would have had exactly five. I am not even faintly inclined to agree. Again: you made an even-money bet, and lost twelve dollars; for you every dollar counts, though smaller amounts are negligible. The minimalness assumption implies that if you had bet less, you would have lost eleven dollars.

Jackson (1977: 16–17) rejects the minimalness assumption. So does Slote, adducing this as one reason for not handling subjunctive conditionals through similarity of worlds (1978: 22–3). But we can drop the assumption while remaining with the worlds framework for analysing subjunctive conditionals. Here is how.

When we come to assign a truth value to anything, what confronts us is a *sentence*, but what we have to evaluate is the proposition its author means to express by it. Often this cannot be read off from the sentence, for example when the speaker understates his meaning—that is, means something that he could fully express in a sentence only by taking more words than he has used. This is a theme of Stalnaker's, as we have seen. He points out that someone who says '... longer ...' or '... richer ...' or '... more ...' may tacitly mean something that helps to narrow down how much longer, richer, more, etc., and that his hearers may be able to pick this meaning up. The only strengthening he talks about, however, is one that sets a *lower* limit to the amount of difference that is meant, this being set by the speaker's regarding smaller differences as negligible. The phenomenon that interests me, on the other hand, can involve *upper* limits; and even when it involves lower ones, they are not set by the thought that a smaller difference would be insignificant. What is at work, rather, is this general rule for hearers:

> As far as you reasonably can, interpret what a speaker says in such a way that it is neither obviously false nor so obviously true as to be not worth saying.

The warrant for this rule is Gricean. We are enjoined to speak truthfully and informatively; so an interpretation of what someone says is likely to be wrong if it makes his assertion glaringly false or boringly true.

The principle is perfectly general, but I shall show it at work on a conditional. Reporting on a beach party, a friend says: 'The party would have been better if it had been able to spread out on a bigger beach.' How are we to understand 'bigger'? Well, she presumably did not mean to be talking about the beach's being larger by as little as a square yard or as much as a square mile. Either of those would make her statement too obviously false: a square yard would not usefully enlarge elbow-room, and a square mile would scatter the party too widely. We can therefore take the speaker to be directing our minds to worlds that are like α except that at them the beach is larger by an amount which, though vaguely delineated, lies well within the limits I have mentioned.

Limits may be needed to avoid too obvious truth, rather than too obvious falsehood, and sometimes one limit is needed for each task. Reflecting on a tough hike, I remark 'If my pack had been heavier, I couldn't have done it'. My hearers understand me to be speaking of weight differences somewhere in the range between one and twenty pounds. If a quarter-pound difference were within the scope of my meaning, what I said would be too implausible; and to the extent that

I was thinking of more than twenty pounds, what I said would be too obviously true. I certainly would not have completed the hike if my pack had been thirty pounds heavier, but that is not part of what I meant. What my hearers take me to mean is still vague, but less so than the conventional meaning of the sentence I uttered.

Have they been enabled to do this by the context in which I have spoken? Well, yes: when my hearers exclude differences of a quarter of a pound, they are relying on their beliefs about me, including what they think I think about myself. How they understand the antecedent of my conditional has, however, another source as well, namely their estimate of what I must mean if the entire conditional is to be neither trivial nor ridiculous. If this is also part of the 'context', then *the consequent is part of the context in which the antecedent is uttered*. To interpret an antecedent we need more than the facts about it, its author, and the environment (human and other) in which he speaks. We need also to know what he is saying, which means that we must take note of the consequent.

Suppose that when preparing for the hike—the one we have been thinking about—I was worried about the weight of my pack, which is why I resisted the temptation to throw in one extra 4 oz. chocolate bar. This was my only such temptation. In that case, I might say afterwards:

If my pack had been heavier, it would have been exactly 4 oz. heavier,

which would be true. But it would be necessarily false if its antecedent meant what it does in the previous conditional. So we have the very same words uttered by one person at one time, with hearers and circumstances just the same, yet bearing different meanings. This must come from the only difference in the two occurrences, namely between their consequents.

My handling of this matter is triply unlike Stalnaker's. His treatment focuses on lower limits, while mine treats of upper ones as well. I emphasize, as he does not, how the interpretation of A may be affected not only by the conversational environment but by the rest of the conditional. Thirdly, he discusses the matter in terms of limits, because he inherited a question about limits from Lewis; but the phenomenon to which I have called attention is more general than that—it arises not merely from the vagueness of comparatives but also from other instances of vagueness and indeed from understating that does not depend on vagueness at all. Stalnaker tells me that he accepts all three of these points.

The consequent also plays a larger than usual role in a 'general theory of the conditional' offered by Gabbay (1972). The data Gabbay wants to accommodate are similar to those I have been discussing, but for him the extra role of the consequent comes into the semantic analysis of the conditional rather than into the pragmatics of its interpretation.

72. CONDITIONAL EXCLUDED MIDDLE

One of Lewis's reasons for not tying the truth of A>C to what obtains at *the closest* A-world was, we have seen, that there may not be one. His other reason was that there might be a tie for closest. This connects with an issue about the logical principle of Conditional Excluded Middle (CEM), which says that (A>C) v (A>¬C) for all A and C. In expounding this matter, as throughout the rest of this work, I shall assume that for no A is this the case: for any A-world w, some other A-world is closer to α than w is.

If there is always a unique closest A-world, then at that world C is either true or false; if true then so is A>C; if false, then A>¬C is true. Thus, one of those two must be true, and so we have CEM. And if there *are* ties for closest, CEM is *not* universally true. Suppose w_1 and w_2 are A-worlds that are tied for closest to α. Since they are distinct worlds, there must be some proposition C that is true at w_1 and false at w_2. So the conditional A>C is false, because w_2 is a closest A-world and C is false at it; and A>¬C is also false, because w_1 is a closest A-world and ¬C is false at it. So (A>C) v (A>¬C) is false in this case because each disjunct is false.

The second of those arguments assumes that if C is false at some closest A-world then A>C is false. Stalnaker does not agree. According to him, if C is true at some closest A-worlds but not all, A>C is indeterminate, neither true nor false; this is what his theory implies, because in such a case his 'selection function' does not select a world. Thus, for example, neither 'If Bizet and Verdi were compatriots, Bizet would be Italian' nor 'If Bizet and Verdi were compatriots, Bizet would not be Italian' is true, but neither is false either. On Lewis's theory, both are false. Stalnaker's shift from 'false' to 'neither true nor false' provides a basis on which he can rescue CEM, in a manner now to be described.

The basic idea underlying it, though quite old, was not developed in a disciplined way until van Fraassen 1966. Van Fraassen's work on this was directed towards sentences that are neither true nor false because they contain singular referring expressions that do not refer to anything—e.g. 'Pegasus has a white hind leg'. He wanted to know how a logic should deal with such sentences—saying for instance that 'Pegasus has a white hind leg' entails 'Pegasus has a leg'— given their lack of truth values?

This entailment holds, van Fraassen answers, because *any* referent for 'Pegasus' making the first sentence true must also make the second true. This can be adapted to other applications also: as well as non-referring names there are indexicals, vague predicates, and definite descriptions that do not refer uniquely. All three of those are involved in the statement:

(1) 'I now see three bald men in the room' entails (2) 'I now see at least two bald men in the room'.

The entailment holds because any assignment of speaker, time, room, and precise meaning for 'bald' that makes 1 true must make 2 true. Each example involves the idea that if S_1 and S_2 are indeterminate, S_1 entails S_2 if any systematic way of extending (amplifying, fixing up, tightening) S_1 that makes it true operates on S_2 so as to make it true also.

Van Fraassen speaks of 'valuations' and 'supervaluations'. A valuation of a sentence is the assignment to it of a truth value. A sentence that is neither true-as-it-stands nor false-as-it-stands may admit of many valuations, some as true, some as false, according to how vagueness is remedied or single referents are supplied for the indexicals or the noun phrase, and so on. Now, suppose that S is such a sentence and that S* is a complex sentence containing S as a part. We may be able to assign a determinate truth value to S* by means of a *supervaluation*. We see what truth value to assign to S* on *each* of the permissible valuations of S: if they all make S* true, then our supervaluation says that S* is true; if they all make it false, our supervaluation says that S* is false; if some make it true and some make it false, we cannot assign it a truth value. Try out supervaluation on 'Either Pegasus has more than two legs or Pegasus has fewer than three legs', and on 'This cubic rock has seven faces', and on 'The man standing in the corner owns a dog'. What results do you get? That the first comes out true because it is necessary, the second is false because it is impossible, and the third is neither true nor false because it is contingent.

Stalnaker looks to this apparatus for help in combining a classical two-valued logic of subjunctive conditionals with the view that many have no truth value because their antecedents do not, just as they stand, select a unique closest A-world. In this theoretical context, asserting CEM—that is, (A>C) ∨ (A>¬C)—amounts to saying that any way of amplifying, fixing up, tightening either disjunct so that it has a truth value will tighten the other so that it has the opposite truth value. This way of handling CEM is not arbitrary or ad hoc, Stalnaker can plausibly claim, because the conceptual apparatus it uses already serves other plainly good purposes.

In §76 I shall question whether supervaluation can serve Stalnaker's turn in defending CEM. Without waiting for that, however, we can ask: Why bother? What reason have we for going to such pains to preserve CEM? Lewis answered this by conceding that it 'does sound like a contradiction' to say, as he did, that

It is not the case that if Bizet and Verdi were compatriots, Bizet would be Italian; and it is not the case that if Bizet and Verdi were compatriots, Bizet would not be Italian; nevertheless, if Bizet and Verdi were compatriots, Bizet either would or would not be Italian. (1973b: 80)

What is at stake here is this so-called 'distribution' argument form:

A > (B∨C) ∴ (A>B) ∨ (A>C).

Substitute ¬C for B in this and you get:

A > (¬C∨C) ∴ (A>¬C) ∨ (A>C).

In the latter argument the premiss is necessarily true, and the conclusion is CEM, which Lewis rejected; so he had to reject that argument form, a rejection that he said 'seems like a contradiction'. It does, he also said, go against our 'offhand opinions' about what follows from what.

Does it really? If so, perhaps our offhand opinions are confused; and Lewis was well placed to diagnose the confusion. The diagnosis he could offer has been well described by Stalnaker:

The failure of the distribution principle . . . is a symptom of the fact that, on Lewis's analysis, the antecedents of conditionals act like necessity operators on their consequents. To assert *If A, then B* is to assert that B is true in every one of a set of possible worlds defined relative to A. (1978: 93)

Stalnaker writes here with characteristic brevity. I shall spell his point out a little. With ordinary necessity, distribution fails: it can be necessary that P ∨ Q without being necessary that P or necessary that Q—try it out with the value Q = ¬P. Lewis's analysis does, as Stalnaker says, treat the antecedent of a subjunctive conditional as a necessity operator on its consequent: the antecedent collaborates with α to pick out a class of worlds, and the whole proposition says that C obtains throughout the selected class. 'If you had walked on the ice it would have broken' means that *The ice broke* at every member of a certain class of worlds, and this is similar in structure to 'Necessarily the ice broke', which also says that *The ice broke* is true throughout a certain class—this time the universal class—of worlds. So distribution fails within Lewis's theory for basically the same reason that it fails for ordinary necessity statements. Lewis had no need to be embarrassed if some people tend to think, offhand, that the distribution principle is valid. People do get into scope muddles where disjunction and necessity are concerned, and this may be an example of that.

Stalnaker, however, having pointed out this escape route for Lewis, claims to block it off. After the passage quoted above, he writes:

Therefore, if [Lewis's] kind of analysis is correct, we should expect to find, when conditionals are combined with quantifiers, all the same scope distinctions as we find in quantified modal logic. In particular, corresponding to the distinction between A > (B∨C) and (A>B) ∨ (A>C) is the quantifier scope distinction between A > (∃x)Fx and (∃x)(A > Fx). On Lewis's account, . . . there is a semantically significant difference between these two formulas of conditional logic, and we should expect to find scope ambiguities in English sentences that might be formalized in either way. (1978: 93.)

We are all familiar with scope ambiguity when existential quantifiers are combined with ordinary necessity: 'Someone must win' could mean merely that there must be a winner—Nec(∃x)Fx—and it could mean that there is someone who is bound to win—(∃x)(Nec(Fx)). Stalnaker rightly says that if Lewis's analysis is correct, we ought to find a similar ambiguity when existential quantifiers are brought into subjunctive conditionals.

He argues that we do not find it, by contrasting three snatches of conversation. In one, North says 'The President has to appoint a woman', South asks 'Which woman does he have to appoint?', and North says

Have-to: 'He doesn't have to appoint any particular woman; he just has to appoint some woman or other.'

In the second, North says 'He will appoint a woman', South asks who it will be, and North says

Will: 'He won't appoint any particular woman; he just will appoint some woman or other.'

In the third, North says 'If there had been a vacancy, he would have appointed a woman', South asks 'Who would he have appointed?', and North replies

Would: 'He wouldn't have appointed any particular woman; he just would have appointed some woman or other.'

North's answer in Have-to shows that he had meant something of the form Nec(∃x)(Wx & Ax), with a narrow scope for the quantifier, whereas South's question seems to presuppose that North had meant (∃x)(Wx & Nec(Ax)), giving the quantifier wide scope. I say 'seems to' because even if North had meant the narrow-scope thing, he *could* have had an answer to South's question. However, if South insists that his question must have an answer, then he has indeed misunderstood; though I don't see why Stalnaker says he has 'perversely' done so.

In the case of Will, there is no room for two readings, no issue about the scope of the quantifier; and North's reply is therefore absurd. It cannot be that he will appoint a woman unless there is a woman whom he will appoint. (Don't deny this on the ground that the appointing lies in the future whereas the quantifier's 'is' relates to the present, the thought being that the woman he will appoint may not yet exist. That *would* be perverse.)

Against Lewis, Stalnaker contends that North's answer in Would is 'as bad, or almost as bad' as his answer in Will, and thus quite unlike his proper answer in Have-to (p. 95).

I cannot think about these examples just as they stand, because even in Have-to North's answer is so sloppy. If the President has to appoint a woman, *of course* he has to appoint a particular woman; there aren't any others. I assume that Stalnaker intends North to mean this:

Have-to*: There is no woman of whom it is true that he has to appoint her.

This is a clean and legitimate answer, pointing to the narrow-scope meaning of what North first said. But then the proper contrast is with this:

Would*: There is no woman of whom it is true that if there had been a vacancy he would have appointed her.

(In each case, I prefer 'such' to 'of whom it is true', but only on stylistic grounds. Stalnaker, he tells me, suspects that the difference matters, and that the 'such that' version of Would* is objectionable though the 'of whom it is true that' version is not.) This uniform amendment, needed to make the Have-to answer respectable turns the Would answer into something that is all right too. It is, I submit, pretty clear that Would* is acceptable; it shows that North had meant something of the form A > (∃x)Fx; and if South had thought North was committed to there being an answer to his question, this would show that he had understood North to mean (∃x)(A > Fx). A simple scope-ambiguity, as in Have-to.

Stalnaker accepts Would*: 'There may be no particular woman of whom it is true to say, President Carter would have appointed *her* if a vacancy had occurred' (p. 95). But he does not draw from this the conclusion that I do. One of his reasons involves a series of epistemic answers to South's questions:

Have-to$_e$: I don't know; I just know it's a woman that he has to appoint.
Will$_e$: I don't know; I just know it's a woman that he will appoint.
Would$_e$: I don't know; I just know it's a woman that he would have appointed.

Stalnaker, I gather, thinks that Have-to$_e$ is legitimate only on the wide-scope reading of the original statement, whereas Will$_e$ and Would$_e$ are legitimate in all circumstances, even when Would* is also true. I disagree. If in the Would case North means something that is consistent with there being no woman of whom it is true that if there had been a vacancy the President would have appointed her, Would$_e$ is an impermissible thing for him to say. He ought not to say that he doesn't know who the woman is if there is no such woman—no woman of whom it is true that the President would have appointed her. I don't know how to resolve this difference of intuitions between Stalnaker and myself.

His other claim about Would* is that when it is legitimate, this cannot be explained in Lewis's way. That there may be no particular woman of whom it is true to say that the President would have appointed her if a vacancy had occurred, he writes, 'does not imply that there is any scope ambiguity in the original statement'. Indeed, it does not *imply* that the statement had a scope ambiguity, but the existence of such an ambiguity yields one possible explanation for what makes Would* all right, this being strictly analogous to the agreed explanation of why Have-to* is all right. Stalnaker rejects that diagnosis in favour of another, to which I shall come in a moment. Even if it succeeds on its own terms, however, this does not count as much of an argument against Lewis's position. At most, he has produced a datum that could be explained through either theory; Stalnaker prefers his, but I don't find in these materials any independent reason to share this preference.

Let us consider Stalnaker's account of why it may be that there is no woman of whom it is true that the President would have appointed her if etc. This is possible, he writes, 'because of the possibility of underdetermination', and has nothing to do with ambiguity of scope.

The situation is exactly analogous to familiar examples of underdetermination in fiction. The question *exactly how many sisters and cousins did Sir Joseph Porter have?* may have no correct answer, but one who asks it in response to the statement that his sisters and cousins numbered in the dozens does not exhibit a misunderstanding of the semantic structure of the statement. (1978: 95)

No indeed, and he may not exhibit any misunderstanding at all, for nothing in what he has been told rules out there being a precise answer to his question; there are some precise numbers in fiction. Someone who hears about the numbering in the dozens and insists that there *must* be an answer to 'Precisely how many?' does indeed exhibit a misunderstanding; specifically, he does not understand that what he has been told comes out of a work of fiction. I do not see how this is 'exactly analogous' with the case of Would*. In maintaining this analogy, Stalnaker has to say—and does say—that the answer 'I do not know . . .' is always appropriate in the fiction case, just as he says it is with Would*. Here is another flat-out difference of intuitive opinion. If you believe that the operetta *H.M.S. Pinafore* contains no answer to the question of exactly how many etc., then—it seems to me—it is seriously misleading and perhaps downright wrong for you to respond to a questioner by saying that you do not know how many. My not being able to say how many has nothing to do with ignorance; it is quite different from the 'I don't know' answer to a question about the cardinality of the Karamazov brothers or the Bennet sisters.

Stalnaker tries to help us grasp the positive analogy between Would* and the fiction example by remarking that 'the possible situations determined by the antecedents of counterfactual conditionals are like the imaginary worlds created by writers of fiction' because 'In both cases, one purports to represent and describe a unique determinate possible world, even though one never really succeeds in doing so'. This is worth chewing on. I do not think it could win me over from Lewis's position on this matter.

73. 'MIGHT'

Lewis had an objection to CEM that we should now examine. I shall use $A>_m C$ to mean 'If it were the case that A, it might be the case that C' or any tensed variant of this, such as 'If it had been the case that A, it might have been the case that C'. Lewis (1973b: 2) held that $A>_m C$ means the same as $\neg(A>\neg C)$. On the face of it, that seems reasonable. If I say 'If he doesn't study on weekends, he'll fail his finals', you can contradict this by saying: 'I do not agree; (even) if he doesn't work on weekends, he might pass his finals', and it is not clear that you have done more than contradict what I have said.

Lewis showed that if we combine this with CEM the result is a collapse of the very distinction between 'might' subjunctive conditionals and 'would' ones. Thus:

1. $(A>\neg C) \vee (A>C)$.   (CEM)
2. $\neg(A>\neg C) \supset (A>C)$ (from 1, by definition of $\supset$)
3. $(A>_m C) \supset (A>C)$ (from 2, by Lewis's definition of $>_m$)
4. $(A>C) \supset (A>_m C)$.   (obvious; entailed by Lewis's def'n)
5. $(A>C) \equiv (A>_m C)$ (from 3, 4 by trivial logic)

This conclusion is patently unacceptable, so something must yield: either CEM or Lewis's account of 'might'. Stalnaker attacks the latter; and my present concern is also with that, considered in its own right rather than as involved in CEM.

Stalnaker observes (pp. 98–9) that Lewis explained 'If . . . might . . .' as though it were an idiom, something to be understood as a single linguistic lump, like 'under way': you wouldn't try to explain 'At 5 p.m. the ship got under way' by explaining 'under' and explaining 'way'. One might reasonably expect the use of 'might' in the conditional 'If we had seeded the clouds last night, it might have rained this morning' to be intelligibly connected with its use in the non-conditional 'It might rain tonight'; but Lewis's account of the former provides for no such connection. Like Stalnaker, I prefer to explain the meaning of 'If . . . might . . .' so that it emerges from the separate meanings of 'if' and of 'might'— if that can be done (§8). Stalnaker undertakes to show that it can.

He contends that 'might' is usually used epistemically: 'It might be the case that P' usually means 'For all I know to the contrary, it is the case that P' or 'P's obtaining is consistent with everything I know'. By this account, $A>_mC$ usually means 'Nothing I know rules out its being the case that $A>C$' or 'For all I know to the contrary, $A>C$'.

This looks right for many cases, but I contend that in many others the meaning of 'might' is not epistemic. This fact lies behind a counterexample that Lewis brought against four suggested accounts of $>_m$; and it can be used against Stalnaker's account, which is a cousin of one of the four (Lewis 1973b: 80–1). At a particular time John knows nothing ruling out the truth of $A>C$, and so by Stalnaker's theory he can truly assert $A>_mC$; yet it is downright impossible that A and C should both hold. John says 'If I had looked in the haystack, I might have found the needle there', and this is true by Stalnaker's theory; but really it is false, because the needle was not in the haystack. Stalnaker's account of 'might' assigns a wrong truth value in such cases, which involve a non-epistemic 'might'.

In response, Stalnaker allows that there is a seemingly non-epistemic sense of 'might', in which John's conditional is false, but he regards it as 'quasi-epistemic':

I think that this sense can also be captured by treating the *might* as a possibility opera-tor on the conditional. Consider not what is, in fact, compatible with my knowledge, but what would be compatible with it if I knew all the relevant facts. This will yield a kind of quasi-epistemic possibility—possibility relative to an idealized state of know-ledge. (1978: 101)

It is essential to Stalnaker's position that this 'possibility operator on the condi-tional'—which I shall symbolize by '$M(\ )$'—can also operate on nonconditionals; that is, we need $M(P)$ for nonconditional values of P, as well as $M(A>C)$. You use it in the former role when you say 'There might be snow tomorrow', meaning not merely that you do not know anything ruling out there being snow tomor-row but more strongly that nothing is knowable—or nothing is the case—that rules it out. The only way to use $M(\ )$ outside conditionals is in such statements about the future, taking the 'relevant facts' to be all the facts about the present. So far, so good; but when we apply $M(\ )$ to subjunctive conditionals, we get results that I think most people will agree with me in rejecting.

Suppose we have an absolutely random coin-tossing device and a fair coin. I did not toss the coin at T. Now I learn that if I had tossed it and it had come down heads, I would have won a fortune, and I torment myself by reflecting

S: If I had tossed the coin, it might have come down heads.

We all agree that S is true; the dispute is over why, and three explanations are to be looked at. (1) S uses a purely epistemic 'might', and means that I do not or did not know anything ruling out the coin's coming down heads. S *could* mean only this, I suppose, though then it could be true even if the tossing device was rigged so that the coin could never come down heads. Let us set this feeble reading aside, and consider what S can mean that reflects the fact that the coin-tossing proced-ure was indeterministic and the coin fair. (2) S means that all the relevant facts—all the ones about how the world was at T—are compatible with the truth of 'If I had tossed the coin at T, it would have come down heads'. This interprets S in terms of the operator that Stalnaker calls 'quasi-epistemic', giving the statement the form $M(A>C)$. This is Stalnaker's account of S, and it strikes me as wrong. The coin's being fair and the tossing device indeterministic, it seems to me, makes it flatly *false* that if the coin had been tossed it *would* have come down heads. I suppose this is another case of a Lewis intuition butting heads with a Stalnaker one. And with an Ellis one. 'It is not false that this coin would have landed heads if I'd tossed it, because, after all, it might have done so. And it is not false that it would not have landed heads, because it might well not have done so' (Ellis 1979: 77). The first conditional, reordered and with an emphasis added for clarity, becomes 'If I had tossed this coin, it *would* have landed heads'. I submit that this is made false by the admitted fact that if I had tossed the coin it *might not* have landed heads. (3) S is true because it means that it is not the case that if I had tossed the coin it *would* have come down tails; or, in the 'worlds' dialect, Toss-worlds at which the coin comes down heads are as close to α as any at which it comes down tails. This is Lewis's interpretation of S; and I find it more credible than either of the other two.

It still has the drawback that it treats 'If . . . might . . .' as an idiom, but we can repair that while retaining the strengths of Lewis's account of 'If . . . might . . .'. Let us retain Stalnaker's supposedly quasi-epistemic M( ), using it however as an operator not on the conditional but on the consequent. Then we can say that S is true because if I had tossed the coin at T a state of affairs would have obtained in which was it was true to say 'The coin might come down heads'. This rescues 'If . . . might . . .' from being an idiom: it understands $A>_m C$ as meaning something of the form $A>M(C)$, where $M(C)$ is the result of applying to C an all-purpose quasi-epistemic 'might' operator of the kind described by Stalnaker.

Happily, although this drops Lewis's account of what $A>_mC$ means, it does not deprive him of his 'might'-using argument against CEM. The argument still stands, because on any reasonable understanding of subjunctive conditionals $A>M(C)$ will be true in exactly the cases where $\neg(A>\neg C)$ is true. Thus, my definition and Lewis's are equivalent, and any argument supporting either will support the other. Or perhaps these are really one definition, not two. Perhaps, that is, Lewis's definition does not—despite appearances—treat 'If . . . might . . .' as an idiom, and I have merely reworded it so as to make this fact plain.

Lewis would not have agreed with this, however, for he implicitly rejected my account (1973*b*: 80–1). He refuted the view that $A>_mC$ means A > Possibly-C where 'possibly' expresses mere logical possibility. On this view, he pointed out, it could be true that *If I had looked in my pocket, I might have found a penny there* even if in fact there was no penny there; because it is not logically or absolutely impossible that one should find a penny in a certain pocket that is in fact empty. So far, I agree. But then Lewis continued: 'Nor would it help to exchange the outer possibility operator . . . for some other sort of possibility, since the contingencies I have noted persist for other sorts of possibility also.' I am not sure what he had in mind; but the contingencies in question do not, I submit, persist for the possibility operator I express with 'M', so that Look > M(find) is false. If the closest worlds at which I look in my pocket are ones at which M(I find a penny there), then at those worlds there is a penny in my pocket, or a real chance that a penny enters my pocket before I look, or the like; in which case Look $>_m$ Find is not plainly false.

Stalnaker holds that Lewis's and my accounts of 'might' subjunctives conflict with certain firm intuitions people have. (I am here guided by his 1984: 144–5, and by personal communications.) Consider these two:

(1) I deny that if he were to compete, he would win, though I accept that if he were to compete, he might win.

(2) If he were to compete, he might win, though I believe that if he were to compete, he would not win.

Stalnaker's account of 'might' condemns 1 and endorses 2, whereas Lewis's and mine do the reverse. Stalnaker has adduced these facts as support for his account: he holds that 1 is a paradoxical thing to say while 2 is not. My own intuitions go with Lewis. I see nothing wrong with 1, and nor will you if you mentally italicize 'would' and 'might'. A medical witness in a murder trial has been reported as saying: 'I cannot say that death would not occur. [Pause] It might very well. But what I would not say is that it *would* have occurred' (Bedford 1958: 211). That strikes me as perfect. As for 2: it seems to me flatly defective, and not rescuable

by emphases—though it might pass in conversation because one took it to mean
'. . . though (I believe that) if he were to compete he would most probably not
win'. The operator 'I believe that' must be being heard as having some such soft-
ening effect. If not, and the speaker is simply expressing one of his naked beliefs
and reporting another, then he could as well have said:

If he were to compete, he might win; if he were to compete, he would not win.

I need not argue for the paradoxical nature of that.

McCawley (1981: 322–5) argued for a certain liberality about which worlds
are relevant to 'If A were the case, it might be that C'; and suggests that this
breaks the link that Lewis contended for between 'might' conditionals and
'would' ones (similarly Mark Heller 1995). Also, DeRose (1994 and 1999) supports a position close to Stalnaker's, with arguments that challenge everything I
have said here.

Stalnaker, from whom I have learned much about how to approach semantic
analysis, has written to me:

I grant that with all these cases, the intuitions are not decisive. Theoretical considerations mix with intuitive judgments, and some idiomatic paraphrases bring out a point
better than others. In the quantifier scope cases, the intuitions about the differences
between the cases are . . . particularly fragile. An artificial regimented paraphrase may
be theoretically clearer (less sloppy), but the theory implicit in the regimentation may
overwhelm the intuitions. It is hard enough even with more colloquial expressions not
to have one's linguistic intuitions distorted by one's theoretical commitments and
inclinations, and nearly impossible when the expressions are filled with 'such that's and
such. . . . It is not entirely clear what hangs on the dispute about conditional excluded
middle. Each side can make adjustments to account for the facts and make all the distinctions made by the other side. I guess it comes down to judgments about whether
some adjustment is an ad hoc fix, or a revealing discovery.

I am glad to include these wise words in my book.

12

Unrolling from the Antecedent Time

74. CLOSENESS AND SIMILARITY

Two theses about the closeness of worlds each generate a logical principle. I shall discuss them in this section. One is this:

C_1: No world is closer to α than α is to itself.

This stands or falls with the logical principle:

P_1: A>C entails A⊃C.

To see why P_1 entails C_1, look at it contrapositively. If C_1 is false, then it can happen that some world w is closer to α than α is to itself; let A be a proposition which is true at α and at w, and let C be a proposition which is false at α and true at w. (There must be such a C if α and w are distinct worlds.) Then it follows that A>C is true and A⊃C false, which contradicts P_1. With the exception of Lycan (briefly noted in §61), nobody believes that A>C can be acceptable when A is true and C false; so we have to accept P_1 and also, therefore, C_1.

Now consider this stronger thesis:

C_2: No world is as close to α as α is to itself.

That also entails P_1, as well as entailing something that does not follow from C_1, namely:

P_2: A&C entails A>C.

Why? Because if A and C are both true at α, and it is the uniquely closest A-world, then the closest A-worlds are C-worlds. This second bit of logic, unlike the first, is not obviously indispensable; in §92 I shall discuss whether it is true, until when the question of whether any other world is as close to α as α is to itself will remain *sub judice*.

This matter of α's closeness to itself forces us to think about what closeness is. So far, we have only this thesis about subjunctive conditionals:

> There is a triadic relation 'x is closer to y than to z' such that this formula is true: A>C is true if and only some A-worlds that are C-worlds are closer to α than any A-worlds that are not C-worlds.

The formula *defines* 'close', which means whatever it has to mean for the formula to be true. The thesis is false if no triadic relation satisfies the formula. So the thesis makes a substantive claim which some philosophers reject, namely that some closeness relation will do the job, that is, that some possible-worlds approach will serve for the analysis of subjunctive conditionals. To test this we must put flesh on the formula's bones, defining a specific relation which, when identified as closeness, makes the formula assign truth values to subjunctive conditionals in ways we are intuitively comfortable with.

Closeness is universally agreed to involve similarity, and I have indicated why. When we think about what would have happened if A had obtained at time T, we attend to states of affairs in which A obtains and things are otherwise *pretty much as they actually were* at T—and the emphasized phrase connotes similarity to the actual world (§67). Now, the idea that closeness is largely a matter of similarity goes nicely with the thesis (C_1) that no world is closer to α than α is to itself; and that is satisfactory, because the latter thesis is one that we want.

What about the stronger thesis (C_2) that α is closer to itself than to any other world? That is not secured by 'Closeness is some kind of similarity' or 'Closeness is largely a matter of similarity', for it might be that α and w are dissimilar only in ways that play no part in the relation of closeness. What *would* yield the result that α is uniquely close to itself is the thesis that closeness is all-in similarity with no respects being excluded. By that standard, every world is closer to itself than any other world is to it; but we do not yet know whether to want that result. It yields P_2, and we do not yet know if we want that either.

However, even if we end up accepting P_2 and thus accepting that each world is uniquely close to itself, that will not come about through pressure from the equation of closeness with all-in similarity. That equation cannot be sustained, as we shall now see.

75. A > BIG-DIFFERENCE

Most early readers of Lewis's book *Counterfactuals* thought he was saying there that closeness is all-in similarity, which attracted criticism. This was a misunderstanding of Lewis's position, as should have been clear from pp. 76–7 of his book, and was made clear to us all by his 1979 'Time's Arrow' paper. Still, the discussions based on the criticism are worth attending to; we need to be clear about why closeness cannot be all-in similarity, even if no one has ever thought it to be so.

If closeness is merely overall similarity, we must declare false all the true subjunctive conditionals that have the form A > Big-difference. *If on July 20 Stauffenberg had placed the bomb on the other side of the trestle, Hitler would have been killed.* That is almost certainly true, but any A-world at which Hitler dies on 20 July 1944 resembles α less closely than do some at which he miraculously survives, so we are threatened with having to call this conditional false. *If at time T, the trajectory of asteroid X had been one second of arc different from what it actually was, the dinosaurs would have survived to the present.* That may well be true for a suitable time T and asteroid X; yet any A-world at which the dinosaurs still roam today is less like α than are some at which X miraculously swerves just after T into a trajectory identical with its actual one (so that it hits our planet and extinguishes the dinosaurs). *If Jesus of Nazareth had bought and worked a farm in Syria at the age of 25, he would not have been crucified in Jerusalem*—that has a fair chance of being true, but world-similarity goes against it. The effects at α of Jesus' crucifixion (including all the effects of the belief in it) are so many and so conspicuous that some worlds at which he settles down in Syria and nevertheless arrives at being executed in Jerusalem resemble α more closely than do any where he settles in Syria and remains safe.

Generalizing, Lewis's theory might seem to be threatened with having to declare false every subjunctive conditional of the form A > Big-difference. Yet pretheoretically we believe in many such conditionals, for we think that at the actual world some effects become amplified, so that some perhaps-small divergences from actuality would have resulted in much larger ones. The diverging roads were initially much alike, but taking the one less travelled by 'has made *all* the difference'.

Lewis's theory evidently needs to be based not on untutored offhand judgements about all-in similarity, but rather on a similarity relation that is constrained somehow—it must say that A>C is true just in case C is true at the A-worlds that are most like the actual world *in such and such respects.* The philosophical task is to work out *what* respects of similarity will enable the theory to square with our intuitions and our usage. For example, we want constraints on the similarity relation that will allow some A > Big-difference conditionals to be true, implying that some of the worlds at which Hitler dies in July 1944 are more like the actual world in the relevant respects than are any at which Stauffenberg puts the bomb within reach of Hitler and the fuse fails. This must be achieved without also declaring true some conditionals that informed people are sure are false.

The A > Big-difference problem received its first public airings in reviews of Lewis's *Counterfactuals* by Kit Fine (1975) and by myself (1974). In my review I discussed a possible solution for it; and the same fairly obvious idea has occurred to Gibbard, Jackson, and Davis, and is indeed clearly adumbrated in Lewis 1973b: 76–7. Something like it can also be found in work by Thomason and Gupta, Slote, and Pollock (though for these last two, as for Jackson, the idea is embedded in an essentially non-worlds approach; I shall explain this in Chapter 20). The proposal is that we base the closeness of worlds on two respects of comparison.

(1) We must compare them in respect of their states up to the time that the antecedent is about—call it T_A. So long as the theory ignores times later than T_A it does not take account of post-T_A dissimilarities between some worlds and the actual world. For example, if we are comparing two worlds at which a crucial button is pressed at T_A, with the current dying in the wire at one of them and a third world war breaking out in the other, the difference between war and no-war makes no difference to how close they are to the actual world, because it pertains to a post-antecedent time.

That could not be the whole theory, for what a world is like up to a particular time implies nothing about what it is like later unless its causal laws enter the story. Alongside the Button-world w_1 which is like the actual world up to T_A and goes on to be the scene of the Third World War, there is the Button-world w_2 which is equally like w_1 up to T_A and does not go on to be the scene of such a war; and nothing said so far lets us choose between them. This holds for absolutely all 'forward' subjunctive conditionals, by which I mean ones about what would have *ensued* if things had been different at a certain moment. Every AC-world that we might want to adduce in support of a forward conditional A>C will be neutralized by an $A\bar{C}$-world that is exactly like the other in respect of its states up to the antecedent time. We need causal glue to hold together a world's states at different times.

The strongest glue is logical, but we learned from Hume that it will not work for us here. Times do connect logically with later times—*He lost his virginity at T_1* entails *He did not lose his virginity at T_2*—but such logical links will not suffice for the general run of forward conditionals.

(2) We need to bring causation into the story, therefore. The closest A-worlds must not only be like α up to T_A but must also conform to the causal laws that govern α. Let us consider what good this constraint will do us—abstractly at first, and then in the Stauffenberg example.

The constraint probably won't guarantee that two worlds that are exactly alike up to T_A will be exactly alike at all future times. It would do that only if the actual world were deterministic, which it is reported not to be. So long as there is some C such that *C is actually the case at T_C and no causally sufficient condition for it existed at T_A*, there is a pair of causally possible worlds that are exactly alike at T_A but differ at T_C because C obtains at one and not at the other.

Still, even if α is not deterministic, it is pretty sternly governed by causal laws, which means that there are many causally sound inferences from earlier times to later ones. Granted that the world's state at T_A does not causally settle every question about its state at T_C, it does settle many of them. The present state of our planet and our vicinity in the solar system causally guarantees that the arctic ice cap won't be melted ten minutes from now and boiling ten minutes after that. (If you think there is a vanishingly tiny probability of even that, wait until Chapter 16, where I shall address that matter.)

Now, let us return to the Stauffenberg example. The bomb, the room, and the people were so structured and interrelated that the bomb's being placed on Hitler's side of the trestle supporting the table would causally suffice for Hitler's death; so that the only way for Hitler to survive is through a miracle, a breach of the causal laws of α. The proposed confining of ourselves to causally possible worlds is, precisely, the exclusion of all worlds at which miracles occur. So we have what we want: a theory that makes it true that if the bomb had been placed a foot to the right Hitler would have been killed.

Taking our two constraints together, then, we have a theory according to which closeness of worlds is similarity in certain specified respects. The theory makes the truth value of A>C depend on whether C is true at the A-worlds that are (1) like the actual world in matters of particular fact up to the antecedent time and (2) perfectly like the actual world in respect of causal laws. That general idea has been accepted by all analysts of subjunctive conditionals in the 'worlds' tradition and by most others as well. The devil, as we shall see, is in the details.

Before coming to those, I shall give a section to unfinished business which I am now better placed to discuss.

76. OBJECTIVE INDETERMINATENESS

It is the use of van Fraassen's supervaluation device (§72) to rescue Conditional Excluded Middle (CEM). The kinds of indeterminateness that originally provided grist for the supervaluation mill involve vague words, names that may fail to refer, pronouns, tenses . . . and perhaps other such features. In each of these the sentence is indeterminate because it is defective or incomplete; there is some part of its story that it does not clearly tell, or tells only with help from an environment; and when supervaluation judges a sentence to be true, that is because it is true on every permissible way of completing or sharpening the story.

That carries over to some subjunctive conditionals. With reference to a normal coin and a strictly deterministic and fair tossing device, neither Tossed > Heads nor Tossed > Tails is true; but one or other of them will be true if the vague 'tossed' is tightened up into something that specifies the finest details of the tossing. Because *every* such tightening makes one of the conditionals true, the disjunction of them—(Tossed > Heads) ∨ (Tossed > Tails)—is supervalued as true.

This involves *repair* work on the antecedent of the two disjuncts, and is continuous with the semantic phenomena that brought supervaluation into play in the first place. In contrast with this, there are cases where neither A>C nor A>¬C is true although neither sentence is in any way vague or incomplete or otherwise in need of repair. That is how things stand when a causal indeterminacy in the world makes each conditional (by Stalnaker's standards) neither true nor false. Suppose that a particular radioactive atom with a half life of two years decays at time T, then consider the conditionals: *If that atom had not decayed at T, it would have decayed within the ensuing year*, and *If that atom had not decayed at T, it would not have decayed within the ensuing year*. Stalnaker says that neither has a truth value, but CEM requires him to assign the value true to the disjunction of them. That, however, cannot be done through a supervaluation of the usual kind, in which one considers all the ways in which the indeterminate sentence can be tightened, disambiguated, completed, or the like. Replace the above conditionals by ones whose antecedents are univocal, precise and complete about the A-world(s) at T, and they still won't pick out a unique world; rather, each will pick out a class of worlds with C true at some and false at others.

Stalnaker and some other writers in this area are content to apply the concept of supervaluation to cases where causal indeterminacy prevents either of the competing conditionals from being true just as it stands. For example, Thomason and Gupta (1980: 316–18) refer to 'the indeterminacy of the future', which they bracket with the indeterminateness that comes from a semantic defect—imprecision, vagueness, ambiguity, and so on. Whenever neither A>C nor A>¬C is true, these writers call each of them not false but indeterminate, whether its lack of truth comes from indeterminacy in the world or 'indeterminacy' in the conditional. On this basis, they defend CEM across the board. Stalnaker wrote to me:

Here is the way I would treat the radioactive decay example: in the actual world, it decayed at T. There is a range of possible worlds eligible for selection (according to whatever substantive constraints our theory comes up with) in which the atom decays at some time later than T, and so a set of acceptable selection functions each of which selects one of those worlds as the selected world in which the atom did not decay at T. Each determinate selection function yields a determinate truth value for the conditional 'If the atom had not decayed at T, it would have decayed within the ensuing year', but different functions yield different ones. So the supervalue is neither true nor false, though the supervalue for the disjunction is true.

This procedure works all right; it can be made to yield CEM in these causal cases, by moves that are verbally the same as those that yield it where what is needed is the tightening of an antecedent. In each case, it is a matter of the selection of worlds.

Unlike Stalnaker and some others, however, I am uncomfortable with this. When I apply supervaluation in the original cases, I can *see what I am doing*. I have a conditional A>C which invites me to select an A-world and consider whether C obtains at it; I find that A as it stands allows me—without infringing whatever constraints my substantive theory lays down—to select many different worlds; so I consider all the legitimate ways of tightening it up, with each selecting just one world; and then I examine how C fares at each of those. Similarly with A>¬C . . . and so on, to a supervaluation of the disjunction of those two conditionals. What I have done, in effect, is to come to the rescue of a disjunction each of whose disjuncts is defective in a certain manner, having an antecedent that falls short of what an antecedent should do; and I have shown that despite those defects the disjunction as a whole should be accepted.

I cannot make anything like this apply in the other set of cases, where the relevant 'indeterminacy' is causal indeterminacy in the world. Perhaps my trouble is a failure properly to get the hang of selection functions and what they are supposed to do: I think of them as guided by the conditional's antecedent, but Stalnaker evidently sees them as also somehow tied in with the consequent. Anyway, I have expressed an uneasiness about this use of supervaluation, and have tried to make it look reasonable.

The troubling kind of indeterminacy 'in the world' that I have been discussing requires that the world not be causally determined. But I do not infer that 'in a deterministic world we have conditional excluded middle' (Appiah 1985: 48 n. 6). Indeterminism, I have suggested, creates a special difficulty for CEM, but determinism does not make it secure. For one thing, it is still challenged by vague or unspecific antecedents. Also, in §72 I gave a reason for resisting CEM even if this part of the defence of it could succeed.

Lewis knew about the 'vagueness' defence of CEM at the time he wrote *Counterfactuals* (see pp. 81–2), and agreed that it gets Stalnaker off the 'no ties for first' hook. He did not mention objective indeterminacy, perhaps because he had not yet focused sharply on the idea that the closest A-worlds are to be thought of primarily in terms of how things stand at them at T_A.

Fodor and LePore (1996) deny that supervaluation is an innocent device for securing necessary truths involving vague or non-referring terms. They contend that a term's vagueness, like other 'conceptual' facts, generates necessary truths: it is *necessarily* the case that someone whose head is 90 per cent hair-free is neither definitely bald nor definitely not bald; and supervaluation involves illicitly supposing the falsity of such necessary truths. The non-referring of some singular terms is also necessary, they say, citing 'the man who is taller than himself'. The pros and cons of this attack on supervaluation are extensive, complex, and considerable, and this is not the place to go into them. I merely note that the objections of Fodor and LePore to supervaluation as it was originally understood do not apply to it as employed by Stalnaker to secure CEM for indeterministic worlds. That is one measure of how different the two are.

David Lewis pointed me to Robert Adams 1987 for a fine discussion of a theological debate in which CEM is at stake. The theological reasons for CEM give me no reason to retract; Adams does not accept them either. Lewis also advised me to look into McDermott 1999, for a defence of CEM in the interests of what the author calls 'realism'. This is a formidable and evidently substantial piece of work, which I have not mastered. I can say, however, that McDermott reaches this topic by a route which does not make the best use of Lewis's work, and espouses some views which I shall argue against in this book—about miracles (§82), about causal chains (§90), and about other things.

13

Forks

We are looking at the theory that the truth of A>C requires that C be true at A-worlds that are (1) like α in matters of particular fact up to the antecedent time and (2) perfectly like α in respect of causal laws. Let us examine those two clauses separately.

(1) From the causal point of view, it makes no difference whether we say 'at T_A' or 'up to T_A'. If two worlds are exactly alike at T_A, and if each unrolls from there in accordance with the laws of α, then either (a) they will be alike for ever after because α is deterministic, or (b) they will become partly unalike because of indeterminacies that work out differently at the two worlds. What will *not* happen is that (c) they will be unalike *after* T_A as a causal consequence of their being unalike *before* T_A in some manner not reflected in any dissimilarity *at* T_A. For that to happen, the laws of α would have to allow action at a temporal distance—an event at one time causing an event later, but not through a temporally continuous causal chain between them. This is not absolutely impossible, but we are all deeply convinced that the causal laws of α do not permit it. Although I cannot defend this conviction, I do have it, trust it, and work with it; so I assume that *so far as causation is concerned* we can safely ignore earlier times and simply require as much likeness as possible *at* T_A.

So much for causation, but logic is different. What is the case at a later time may *logically* involve some fact of pre-T_A time without involving T_A itself. Here is an example, adapted from one of Lewis's. The Marquise insulted the Vicomte in January. In March he was tempted to publish the letters she had written him. The published letters would have led society to despise and ostracize her, so *If the Vicomte had published the letters in March, then by June he would have had his revenge for her insult.* Now, the consequent of Publish > Revenge, though it concerns June, is also about the preceding January, for it speaks of revenge for what the Marquise did then. This conditional can be true, therefore, only if at the closest Publish-worlds the Marquise does insult the Vicomte in January; and to ensure this our theory must constrain what the closest worlds are like before T_A. Such examples are plentiful; we often characterize a state of affairs obtaining at one time in a way that logically reaches back to some earlier time; and when this happens in the consequent of a subjunctive conditional we need the closest worlds to relate suitably to α at the earlier time, even if it is before T_A, the time of the antecedent. This reach back into pre-T_A time is (I repeat) semantic or logical, not causal.

(2) A *legal* world is one conforming to α's causal laws at all times; and I shall use 'Legal' to name the theory—a partial analysis of subjunctive conditionals—that closest A-worlds must be legal. This theory has dramatic consequences if α is strictly deterministic. For then Legal implies that any closest A-world—if it is not α itself—is unlike α not only at all times after T_A but also at all pre-T_A times as well. A legal world at which at T_A Stauffenberg puts the bomb on the other side of the trestle must be unlike α a little before T_A, a little before that . . . and so on backwards through the whole of time. Some of these unlikenesses might be enormous, for all we know to the contrary.

Some physicists deny that α is deterministic, but most of us are unwilling to rely on this denial in analysing subjunctive conditionals. Some philosophers evidently have relied on it, contending that A>C cannot be true unless the state of α causally allowed that A should obtain. This thought seems to have led Spinoza, a determinist, into hostility to subjunctive conditionals as such; and to have led others to think that such conditionals must have antecedents that could have come about through a different legal outcome of an indeterminist transaction. (See Spinoza 1665: 390; Thomason and Gupta 1980: 306–7.) The underlying thought seems to be: 'How can there be a disciplined thought about what would happen if A *did* obtain, given that from the beginning of time it was settled that A would not obtain?'

Against these philosophers, I side with Lewis and some others in holding that counterfactuals can be true at deterministic worlds, so that any proposed analysis of them must survive being combined with the hypothesis that α is deterministic. (By 'counterfactual' I mean, as I announced at the end of §5, 'subjunctive conditional whose antecedent is false'.) For one thing, indeterminism is not *needed* for the truth of counterfactuals, as I shall show later in this section. (2) Furthermore, indeterminism does not *suffice* for the rescue we are looking for, as I show now. Our topic is the theory that the truth of A>C depends on what happens at the closest worlds at which A comes to obtain through an indeterministic causal transaction that also occurred at α but had a $\neg$A outcome. For short: at the closest A-worlds A becomes true at a node of indeterminacy. It sounds pretty; but the mere information that α is indeterministic gives us no hint as to where the nodes of indeterminacy are. David Lewis wrote to me: 'Indeterminism *per se* doesn't say. But the one well worked-out indeterministic fundamental theory, GRW, says that the nodes of indeterminism are everywhere.' Yes, but it does not tell us—and in general we do not know—to what extent and where indeterminism at the quantum level shows up in indeterminism with respect to the macroscopic events forming the subject matter of most of our conditionals. On the proposed theory, therefore, we might be sure that some counterfactuals are true, but would be left in the dark about which ones they are.

Adopting determinism as a hypothesis, then, let us consider these two worlds:

Miracle: This world exactly resembles α for all of time up to T, then becomes progressively unlike it, starting with a small miracle—a neuronal firing in Stauffenberg's brain which the causal laws of α forbid.

No-miracle: This legal world is considerably unlike α through all time. At it, an event occurs in Stauffenberg's brain just like the miraculous one at Miracle, but this one is legal—it arose in accordance with α's causal laws from the preceding state of affairs.

Now, Legal judges No-miracle to be closer to α than Miracle is, however greatly the former differs from α through all the aeons of pre-T_A time. Lewis rejected this, contending that enough factual unlikeness can outweigh 'a small, localized, inconspicuous miracle'. In support of this, he remarked that a non-legal world, the scene of some event that is 'miraculous' in the sense of conflicting with the causal laws of α, need not be lawless: Miracle may have laws of its own that permit the crucial neuronal event. Anyway, Lewis found this position 'plausible enough to deter me from' accepting the view that closest A-worlds must be legal (1973b: 75).

This frees us from the threat of closest A-worlds that are unlike α for the whole of pre-T_A time. Yet it still leaves plenty of room for causal laws to solve the A > Big-difference problem through the demand that closest A-worlds conform to α's causal laws from T_A onwards. Still, the availability of this agreeable solution should not deter us from asking what the problem is about allowing closest A-worlds to be unlike α for the whole of pre-T_A time. An answer based purely on the meaning of 'close' or 'similar' is no answer at all. When Lewis found one approach more 'plausible' than the other, he was concerned with what it is plausible to think about counterfactuals. But he did not say *why* he found it plausible to turn against Legal.

78. TWO SCARE STORIES ABOUT BACKWARD CONDITIONALS

In reviewing Lewis's *Counterfactuals* I mentioned approvingly a previously neglected paper by P. B. Downing that seemed to offer Lewis a glittering gift—a firm, structured reason for holding that closest A-worlds need not be legal, and thus for rejecting Legal (Bennett 1974: 391; Downing 1959). A crucial feature of Legal is its licensing an unlimited range of temporally backward subjunctive conditionals, ones saying that if A had obtained, then C would (have to) have obtained earlier. Furthermore, it places no obstacle in the way of smoothly combining these with forward conditionals, yielding ones of the form *If A had obtained at T, C would have obtained later and D earlier*, which conjoins a forward conditional with a backward one by letting them share an antecedent. Downing's reason for rejecting Legal is a warning, a scare story about troubles awaiting any analysis of subjunctive conditionals that allows one to combine forward counterfactuals with backward ones in such a way. Here is a version of the Downing scare story:

> Mr D'Arcy and Elizabeth quarrelled yesterday, and she remained angry with him this morning. So *If he had asked her for a favour this morning, she would have refused it.* On the other hand, he is a proud man (and a percipient one, who knows anger when he confronts it); he would never risk being turned down; so if he had asked her for a favour this morning, they wouldn't have quarrelled yesterday, in which case Elizabeth would have been her usual accommodating self and would have granted the favour. So *If he had asked her for a favour this morning, she would have granted it.*

The two forward conditionals, Ask > Refuse and Ask > Grant, cannot both be true; so something has gone wrong. According to Downing, the mistake was to admit into the story the backward conditional Ask > No-quarrel. He concluded that backward subjunctive conditionals as such are defective and inadmissible; which in the context of Lewis's kind of theory amounts to saying that a correct account of subjunctive conditionals will not imply that closest worlds are unlike α before T_A.

Lewis in his book had tolerated small miracles at closest worlds, so that they could be just like α until shortly before T_A; and I saw Downing's argument as motivating this, by pointing to a horde of mischievous backward subjunctive conditionals that will beset any analysis that does not have a back-stop such as Lewis's. In subsequent work Lewis used the Downing argument (1979: 33–4), and Jackson, who evidently found it for himself, has also thought it to be cogent (1977: 9).

The Downing argument has no force, I now realize, because the scare story on which it is based is groundless. To evaluate the competing conditionals, we start by looking—among the worlds that obey the causal laws of α—for the Ask-worlds that most resemble α in respect of their states at the time of asking. If at all those worlds Elizabeth is angry, then Ask > Refuse alone is true; if she is not angry at any, then Ask > Grant alone is true. If she is angry at some but not others, both are false. No problem. The Downing story tricks us into searching twice for closest Ask-worlds—once attending to her anger and ignoring his pride and percipience, the other attending to his pride and percipience and ignoring her anger. Out of these conflicting ideas about what the closest worlds are like, we of course derive conflicting conditionals. The scare story associates one half of the bad procedure with temporal backwardness, and not the other half; but this is an arbitrary add-on—not essential to what is going on, and not a contributor to the trouble. Try this variant:

> Elizabeth was angry with Mr D'Arcy this morning; he had no idea why. Because of her anger, *If he had asked her for a favour this morning, she would have refused it.* On the other hand, he is a proud and percipient man, who would never risk being turned down and would never be insensitive to someone else's anger; so if he had asked her for a favour that would have been because he thought she wasn't angry with him, which could happen only if she wasn't angry with him. When not angry she is amiably complaisant, so *If he had asked her for a favour this morning, she would have granted it.*

This yields the same conflicting pair in essentially the same way, namely by looking first at worlds at which she is the same and he is different, and then at ones at which the reverse holds. Only this time we omit the detour through yesterday's quarrel.

The Downing argument tells us nothing about backward subjunctive conditionals, poses no threat to Legal, and provides no reason for tolerating miracles at closest A-worlds. I did a disservice in pushing it into the spotlight.

I also offered Lewis a second reason, of my own devising, and he adopted it too. The Bennett scare story threatens that if we do not have some constraints on backward conditionals, or on combining them with forward ones in single trains of thought, we shall lose our grounds for believing many of our favourite forward conditionals. I shall explain through an example, against this factual background: on 22 June 1941, German armies invaded the Soviet Union; on 6 December of that year they reached the suburbs of Moscow and were beaten back, defeated by Soviet armies and the Russian winter. Now consider this conditional: *If the German army had reached Moscow in August 1941, it would have captured the city.* This conditional—call it August > Capture—may well be true; there must be something wrong with any analysis of subjunctive conditionals according to which we *could* not be entitled to believe it. Now, suppose that to evaluate August > Capture we must apply the causal laws of α not only forwards from August 1941 but also backwards from there: we have to consider worlds at which the German army pushes into the Moscow suburbs in August, and to consider how that came about at those worlds. They must have been different from α in July 1941, and thus in June 1941, and . . . so on backwards to the beginning of the universe, for all we know to the contrary. Even if we cannot share Leibniz's confidence that 'the whole universe with all its parts would have been different from the beginning if the least thing in it had happened differently from how it did' (1686: 73), we must admit that we do not know, and ought not even to guess, how different the universe would need to be for it to have differed in some one respect.

But, I argued in my Lewis review, this means that we ought not to believe August > Capture. The case for it rests largely on facts about the actual German army in August 1941—for example, the activities on the eastern front of the ruthless and talented General Guderian. Now, we start from our antecedent (plus things we know about α) to get the closest scenario in which the Germans reach Moscow in August. All it took, perhaps, was for Hitler not to decide in March to set the invasion of the Soviet Union back by the four weeks he needed for a punitive attack on Yugoslavia; this might require only a few neuronal events in one brain to go differently. But on the assumption of determinism, which forms the backdrop for Lewis's rejection of Legal, even such a 'small' departure from actuality must have been preceded by another, that by yet another, and so on backwards through the whole of pre-T_A time.

What makes this a threat? Well (I argued), if the closest worlds at which the Germans reach Moscow in August 1941 are unlike α—however slightly—thirty million years earlier, we have no guarantee that they will resemble α in the wanted respects in the summer of 1941. For example, if we could work our way back through causal laws to the state of a world thirty million years earlier, and then work forward again from that world-state through causal laws, we might find the course of events going differently in many ways. Perhaps the High Command of the German Army decides not to hold the 1886 summer manoeuvres—the ones through which, at α, Heinz Guderian's parents first met (I'm making this up). But if his parents do not meet at the closest A-world, then at that world he does not attack Moscow, which removes much of our reason for believing August > Capture. This difficulty pertains only to subjunctive conditionals whose chance of truth depends on particular matters of fact, and does not touch independent conditionals.

We cannot actually conduct these causal inferences back into the remote past and then forward again; but if they could in principle be conducted, and if their results could undermine our favourite forward subjunctive conditionals, we are left with no good reason to believe any of the latter. In my review I offered this as further evidence that even if it can be all right to run subjunctive conditionals backwards in time, such a procedure cannot be integrally involved in forward subjunctive conditionals: we need to be able to think about August > Capture without committing ourselves to anything about the condition of the closest August-world thirty million years ago.

This scare story fails as badly as the Downing one, though it is a little more instructive. My story involves *backtracking*—counterfactualizing back in time and then forward again. (That is the sense I gave this term when introducing it into the literature. Others have used it for just the first half of that.) I envisaged this as a procedure in which we infer our way back to some partial state of world w at an earlier time T, combine that with other facts about w's state at T, and start inferring forward again from that combination. Why do I bring in 'other facts about w's state at T'? Because without them we cannot generate the trouble threatened by the scare story. If my entire account of w's state at T_1 is causally implied by an account of its state at T_2, then it cannot causally imply anything inconsistent with the latter.

So the backtracking procedure, if it is to generate the trouble foreseen in my scare story, *must* bring in more facts than those it reaches by inference. What basis can there be for P's being the case at w before T_A other than its being causally required for w's state at T_A? The only possible basis for this is that P is true before T_A at the actual world. The back-tracking procedure envisaged by my scare story, then, must take the results of temporally backward causal inference *and conjoin them with facts about the past of the actual world.*

That is where the scare story fails. The troubles of which it warns us are ones that might come from freely combining forward subjunctive conditionals with backward ones, with help from a mixture of backward causal inference and the history and pre-history books (as it were) of the actual world. The toxic ingredient in this brew is not the combining of forward with backward, but that way of handling the latter, promiscuously mingling causal inference with appeal to actual fact.

With this in mind, consider a theory that I first presented in 1984, a version of Legal that I shall call the Simple Theory:

A>C is true ≡ C obtains at the legal A-worlds that most resemble α in respect
of their state at T_A.

This is temporally symmetrical because it says nothing about 'before' and 'after';
it places no obstacle in the way of freely combining forward and backward subjunctive conditionals within a single argument or even a single proposition. It
avoids the lethal mixture that inspired the Bennett scare story: the theory gets
the past of the closest A-world purely by inferring causally back from that
world's entire state at T_A; you do not compare it with α in respect of any other
time; the history books remain closed. If that entire T_A state includes the existence of General Guderian, then no line of purely causal argument—however
subtly and intricately backward and forward—can imply that at the world in
question Guderian does not exist. The Simple Theory leaves backtracking (in my
sense) with no real work to do: the backward inferences cover the entire territory
of the world's past; if you turn around and come forward again, you can only
retrace your steps.

The Simple Theory attracted me partly because it allows for both forward and
backward subjunctive conditionals within a single unified analysis. I shall return
to that feature of it, and to its contrast with other treatments of backward conditionals, in Chapter 18.

79. BUMPS

The Simple Theory is clearly virtuous in another respect, namely its providing
for causally smooth run-ups to antecedents. This makes it unlike the analysis
advanced by Jackson (1977), according to which a temporally forward conditional A>C is true just in case C obtains at all the A-worlds that are exactly like α up
to T_A and conform to α's laws from T_A onwards. At many of the A-worlds that
Jackson's analysis counts as closest to α, antecedents become true suddenly,
without warning or run-up; a bump occurs at T_A, the time of the antecedent; A
becomes the case through an abrupt lurch in the course of events. This implies
wrong truth values for many subjunctive conditionals, declaring false ones true,
and true false. A single example shows both troubles.

The dam burst at 8.47 p.m., and within two minutes the waters had swept
through the valley, killing nine occupants of cars on the valley road. Reflecting
on the gratifying fact that the dam-burst did little other serious harm, when it
might have been expected to kill thousands, someone remarks 'If there had been
no cars on the road just then, no lives would have been lost'. In the case I have in
mind, Jackson's theory rightly declares the asserted conditional—call it No-cars

> No-deaths—to be true. According to the theory, however, although at the closest A-world the valley contains no cars at 8.47, several cars started to enter the valley at times from 8.30 p.m. onwards, and none stopped or turned around, because none did so at α. At 8.47 p.m.—bump!—suddenly the valley is empty of cars. If that really is the closest A-world, then these are probably also true:

> If there had been no cars on the road just then, we would be investigating the mystery of where they had all gone to.

> If there had been no cars on the road just then, this would be evidence of a miraculous divine intervention—the sudden removal of the cars at the very moment when the dam burst.

If someone seriously asserted one of these in response to No-cars > No-deaths, we would probably interpret his utterance so as to give it a chance of being true. We would do this by supposing him to have understated the antecedent, and to have meant something of the form 'If there had suddenly and inexplicably come to be no cars on the road at that time . . .'. But this would be an act of special charity, taking the speaker to have meant by his antecedent something that outruns its conventional meaning.

Jackson's theory calls those false or suspect conditionals true. It also calls some true conditionals false. The asserter of No-cars > No-deaths might also reasonably assert: 'If there had been no cars on the road when the dam burst, that event would have been an economic disaster and an engineering challenge but otherwise of no great importance.' Jackson's theory makes that false: at world w, at which about six cars suddenly disappear from a road just before the water floods in, the event will obviously be invested with great importance outside the realms of economics and engineering—in natural theology, for example.

A normal, competent speaker who asserts No-cars > No-deaths envisages a state of affairs in which it *smoothly* comes about that the valley lacks cars when the dam bursts. I conclude that the conventional meaning of No-cars > No-deaths involves smoothness and not bumps, and that this holds in general for subjunctive conditionals whose antecedents do not explicitly mention bumps. We *could* handle subjunctive conditionals in the manner of Jackson's analysis: his story describes a possible form of thought and speech, but not one we have in our actual repertoire.

Jackson denies this. He writes: 'When we evaluate [forward subjunctive conditionals] we set aside questions as to what prior conditions might have led to the antecedent. We proceed as if the attribution had been miraculously realized. That is, we ignore causality prior to T_A' (Jackson 1977: 9). The second sentence of this clashes a little with its neighbours, but let that pass. The general tenor of what Jackson says here fits some cases. 'If he had turned left at the end of the lane . . .'—here we have no sense of the causes of his actual right turn, so when we suppose him to have turned the other way we do not think about what might have led to this difference. Here we can counterfactualize as though we believed the person to have absolute 'freedom', in the sense that his action in turning right had no prior determining cause. Some people do believe this; but the rest of us, who think there was a determining cause, can comfortably set it aside. The smallness of the difference between the closest A-world and α, and our ignorance of its nature, lets us treat it as though it did not exist. We might describe this as our tolerating the thought that at the A-world a tiny miracle occurs in the person's head, leading to his turning left instead of right.

Jackson's theory gets other cases wrong, however, including my dam-burst example. And suppose we apply his standards to August > Capture—'If the German army had reached Moscow on 15 August 1941, it would have captured the city'. This might come out true, but so would a host of conditionals we would ordinarily deem to be false, ones concerning what people would say and do at a world at which an army group reaches Moscow on a certain day after being hundreds of miles away the day before; and many true conditionals would come out false.

One last comment on this work of Jackson's must wait until §109.

80. HISTORIES FOR ANTECEDENTS

The Simple Theory does not suffer from this bump defect. If w is a closest A-world according to it, then A becomes true at w through w's smoothly unfolding in accordance with the causal laws of α. This clear advantage can be added to the apparent merit of being unified rather than split along the forwards/backwards plane of cleavage, and to the Simple Theory's being simpler and cleaner than its rivals. A glittering array of merits! I am not much moved by the objections that Woods (1997: 55–7) brought against the Simple Theory; but I am disturbed by its lack of a central virtue—truth. Like Jackson's, my analysis describes a possible way of handling subjunctive conditionals, but not one we actually have.

To see this, return to the Moscow example, specifically to August > Capture: 'If the German army had reached Moscow in August 1941, it would have captured the city.' The closest A-worlds, according to the Simple Theory, are to be identified initially by their similarity to α in August 1941 except for the difference that at them the German troops are reaching Moscow. (The time of the antecedent need not be a durationless instant; it can be more or less long, depending on what the antecedent is.) In August 1941 at those worlds, then, matters stand thus: the German troops reach Moscow, and otherwise things in Russia are pretty much as they were then at α—the layout of the Moscow streets, the weather, the durable aspects of the German and Russian national characters, the small number of Soviet troops (most of them fresh and inexperienced) in the immediate vicinity of Moscow . . .

Stop! Something has gone wrong here. Most of the listed similarities are all right, but not the last one. At α in August 1941 Moscow did indeed contain few defenders (I am supposing), but we will not let that fact affect how we evaluate August > Capture. Most of us will not, anyway. After putting unloaded questions about this to thoughtful informants, I conclude that when evaluating August > Capture most people will assume that if Hitler's troops had assaulted Moscow in August 1941 there would have been more Soviet troops in the vicinity than there actually were, and most would be battle-weary. The Soviet armies did in fact spend the summer and autumn of 1941 falling back before the advancing Germans. If the Germans had reached Moscow by August, the retreating Soviet troops would have been crowded back into its vicinity also. (Frances Howard-Snyder first alerted me to this fatal flaw in the Simple Theory.)

At some legal worlds the German troops attack Moscow in August 1941, opposed only by the few reserve divisions that were actually there then. Many logically possible histories yield that result: invent one to suit your fancy. But when we talk soberly, carefully, about 'what would have happened if they had reached Moscow in August', most of us think not of any of those worlds but rather of ones at which at some time before August 1941 things are nearly or completely as they were at α, and then move off the track of the actual world through some shift: the Germans start earlier or fight harder or have better weather or leadership than at α, so that their eastward drive reaches Moscow sooner, against defenders who are increasingly concentrated into the area around the city. In the Simple Theory, too, there is a history for the obtaining of the antecedent; but that theory gets the history wrong because it is not constructed so as to *start* from a state of affairs exactly like α's.

If some speakers do not standardly think of antecedent histories in the manner I am advocating, I think they are a minority. Be that as it may, it is at least normal and permissible to understand forward subjunctive conditionals as envisaging for each antecedent a history that does not reach counterfactually back into the whole of pre-A time, but rather provides a coherent route to the truth of A from an earlier world state that exactly resembles α's at the time in question. We do not bother to do this for antecedents of the 'If he had turned to the left . . .' or 'If the coin had fallen heads . . .' kind. We suffer no unwanted dissonance when we think of antecedents like those as just coming true with no special causal preparation. But in other cases the dissonance is audible, even deafening, unless a run-up is provided. That is why the Simple Theory fails: it makes no provision for getting to the antecedent from an earlier world state exactly matching a state of α.

In my pleasure at neutralizing the two scare stories, and realizing that backward and forward subjunctive conditionals might be combined without a threat of inconsistency, I fell in love with the Simple Theory, and neglected to check it against actual usage.

We might try to rescue it by adding this claim about what speakers generally mean by the antecedents of their counterfactual conditionals:

> If A in A>C speaks of something's being the case at a certain time, a normal asserter of A>C will mean—and will be understood to mean—an antecedent that concerns A's coming to be the case at that time through a natural-seeming course of events arising from an inconspicuous divergence from actuality a short time before.

According to this, a history for the antecedent is alluded to *in* the antecedent—not as part of the conventional meaning of the clause expressing it, but as part of what speakers would normally mean by that clause. A normal speaker who asserted the sentence I have condensed into 'August > Capture' would on this account mean something like: 'If things had gone differently throughout the summer of 1941 in such a way that the German troops reached the outskirts of Moscow in August, they would have taken it.'

If this were right, the Simple Theory might after all tell the truth about what forward conditionals conventionally mean. We are playing a risky game here: we are defending a certain account of what expression E means, on the plea that seeming counterexamples to it are awkward not because of what E conventionally means but only because of what speakers ordinarily mean by it. How easily one can defend falsehoods in that way! Still, such defences are sometimes right, and this one deserves its day in court.

Once there, it does not fare well. Think about indisputable cases of a speaker's meaning more than his utterance does. For example: when you ask a guest to teach the children a game, and he replies 'I don't know any games', he probably means that he knows no games fit to be taught to children. But if you so understand him and are wrong in so doing, he can easily make this clear by saying 'I meant just what I said: I don't know *any* games'. A comparable move with August > Capture would not have the corresponding effect. Someone who uttered this conditional sentence, adding that he meant it strictly and literally, would not give us to understand that he envisaged the German troops as reaching Moscow in

August and encountering only such Soviet reserves as were there then at α. The relevance of the 1941 mid-summer to 'If the German army had assaulted Moscow in August 1941 . . .', I contend, is laid down compulsorily in the meaning of that kind of conditional (or in how the meaning intersects with the actual world), not optionally in the mind of the individual speaker.

Anyway, an even sterner difficulty besets the Simple Theory—an old, familiar point which I negligently overlooked. Consider someone who in 2003 says: 'If that hill outside Syracuse had not been levelled last year, it would have been a superb site for a memorial to the Athenian soldiers who starved to death in the marble quarries there 2416 years ago.' This cannot be true unless at the closest A-worlds Athenian soldiers *did* die at Syracuse in 413 BCE; but the Simple Theory refuses to let us assume that. We cannot know how different things might be in 413 BCE at the closest legal world at which the bulldozers spare that Syracusan hill in 2003 CE. No thoughtful person would have the faintest sense of this speaker's running any such risk; and that is because we would all hear him as speaking about a world that exactly resembles α until shortly before the landscaping plan was launched in 1999. Similar cases abound. We often characterize a state of affairs in a way that logically reaches back to earlier times; and when this happens in the consequent of a subjunctive conditional, we need the closest worlds to relate suitably to α at the earlier time, even if it precedes T_A, the time of the antecedent.

81. THE NEED FOR FORKS

Getting August > Capture right requires the thought of a run-up to the antecedent, a *ramp* from the actual world to the antecedent of the conditional. The closest antecedent worlds must (1) exactly resemble α right up to some moment shortly before T_A; at that moment they must (2) diverge from α's path without a large, noticeable bump; and from there they must (3) unfold in a causally coherent way so that A becomes true at them at time T_A. (1) If the relevant worlds differed from α through too much of their past, we would be promiscuously mixing history with backward causal inference, and would again confront the Guderian problem, so to label it. (2) If they diverged from α with a conspicuous bump, this would be as bad as having such a bump at T_A. (3) The development from the fork to A must be causally coherent because that is a plain fact about how we do handle subjunctive conditionals. (Discussing the A > Big-difference problem, I said that closest A-worlds must conform to actual causal laws from the time of *the antecedent* onwards. That, we now see, was a temporary expedient, a place-holder. The real requirement is legality from the time of *the fork* onwards.)

Lewis offered something like this theory of subjunctive conditionals—in embryonic form in his 1973 book and more fully developed in his 1979 'Time's Arrow' paper. I shall say more about his handling of these ideas in a moment.

First, let me diagram the possibilities. I represent the history of each world by a line. Parallelism between two lines represents exact similarity between the worlds for that stretch of their histories; lack of parallelism expresses dissimilarity; a vertical segment of line represents a bump, a conspicuous discontinuity in the course of events, a 'big miracle', as one might say. Then we can draw the three possibilities I have been discussing—Jackson's, mine, and Lewis's fork-involving kind of theory (shown in Fig. 6).

Observe that Lewis's theory does not have a bump at the point where w starts to be unlike α. A bump back there would be as troublesome as one at T_A. I should add that in Lewis's account, usually, not much time elapses between the fork and T_A, and sometimes none may elapse—when the antecedent presents its own fork, and so needs no run-up from an earlier divergence of worlds. Jackson's

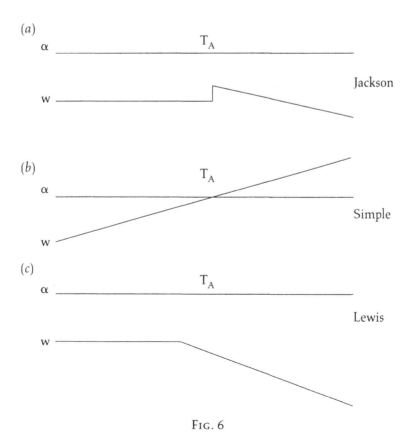

FIG. 6

theory does not imply that the antecedent always comes in with a bump; but it allows that this can happen, and implies that it does so frequently. In the diagram of the Simple Theory (Fig. 6*b*), think of the lines as being on different planes so that they do not intersect; or let them intersect, but do not let that mean anything.

When I speak of a world as branching or forking off from α, I do not mean that one world becomes two. Put more strictly, I mean that two worlds, α and w, are exactly alike up to a moment when something happens at w setting it on a different course from α, this branch-creating event being inconspicuous by the standards that prevail at α at the time when the conditional is asserted.

82. WHAT HAPPENS AT A FORK?

The third diagram (Fig. 6*c*) reflects the fact that when we think about subjunctive conditionals we ordinarily attend only to A-worlds that diverge in an initially modest way from α—worlds that could have become actual through some small difference in the course of events, one whose intrinsic nature will not call attention to itself as would the bumps that Jackson's theory tolerates. The guiding thought is of a world at which something happens that strikes us intuitively as being what 'nearly happened' at α. A correct account of forward subjunctive conditionals should have this as its output: the A-worlds that it deems closest must become unlike α not too long before T_A, the divergence being in itself inconspicuous and unremarkable, and the legal ramp from it up to A being smooth and natural.

Michael Tooley has pointed out to me that this does not cover all the ground, for there are subjunctive conditionals whose antecedents are inherently bumpy. As my discussion of Jackson implies, there are coherent conditionals about what would have ensued if *suddenly* there had been no cars on the road through the valley. To evaluate those, we must look to worlds at which the cars disappear suddenly, that is, with a bump. My non-bumps thesis defines the 'default' position, saying what goes on at closest A-worlds when A does not logically require a bump.

Here is some terminology. In the context of a given counterfactual A>C, a *fork* is an event at an A-world by virtue of which that world for the first time becomes less than perfectly like α. The corresponding verb explains itself. A *ramp* is the segment of that world's history starting at a fork and ending at the obtaining of A; and a world or ramp is *legal* if it conforms to the causal laws of α. Using this terminology: to evaluate a counterfactual A>C we must look to worlds at which A obtains by virtue of a legal ramp running from a fork that occurs not long before T_A. Now we must consider forks.

Lewis pointed to two ways for a world w to fork from α. (1) Through an indeterministic causal transaction that starts out identically but ends up differently at the two worlds, each outcome being legal. (2) Through a causal transaction—deterministic or not—that starts out identically at the two worlds and has one outcome at α and a different one at world w, the outcome at w being in conflict with α's causal laws. There is no limit to how extensive the consequences of such a lawless outcome may be, but the initial breach of actual causal laws must be small—a particle swerving a little, or a neuron firing. It doesn't matter how deeply this tears at the actual world's nomological structure; the notion of smallness of miracle that we need here is just that of an event whose illegality will not obtrude on the thoughts of people evaluating the conditional, as did the extravaganza in which the cars vanished from the valley (§79).

(3) A third kind of fork, not mentioned by Lewis and brought to my attention first by Thomas McKay, is a variant of 1. I call it the 'exploding difference' kind of fork. We have seen that the closest A-world must, until shortly before T_A, resemble α closely enough to be free from the Guderian, Syracuse, and revenge difficulties and their like; but perhaps they need not be exactly like α at any time. So far as anyone can tell, it is not absolutely impossible that a world governed by the same causal laws as α—deterministic or not—should for aeons be unlike α in tiny imperceptible ways and then finally diverge from α in some more conspicuous fashion that supports a subjunctive conditional at α of a kind that might interest us. For example:

At α Hitler decides on 27 April 1941 to delay the attack on the Soviet Union in order first to punish Yugoslavia, being deterministically caused to do so by his state of mind and brain.

At w Hitler decides on 27 April 1941 to let Yugoslavia wait and to attack the Soviet Union in mid-May; he is deterministically caused to do this by his state of mind and brain, which differs from their state at α; those differences arise from earlier ones, those from ones still earlier, back to the beginning of the world. But not until April 1941 does w differ from α in any respect that any human would give thought to.

Some pairs of legal worlds are (so to speak) invisibly unalike for aeons and then part company in some way detectable by the mind's eye; but Lewis held that α does not belong to any such pair: 'It is hard to imagine how two deterministic worlds anything like ours could possibly remain just a little bit different for very long. There are altogether too many opportunities for little differences to give rise to bigger differences' (1979: 45). Still, it is worth remembering that events leading to an 'exploding difference' fork, although they are by the actual world's standards thermodynamically anomalous, do not conflict with α's laws. (I rely here on help from Barry Loewer and Adam Elga.) So they deserve a place in the picture we are trying to draw.

The plain person using a subjunctive conditional has a *vague* thought of a world that does not significantly differ from the actual one until a divergence leading to the truth of his antecedent. We introduce indeterminism and small miracles as two *sharpenings* of this vague thought; and a third way to sharpen it is with the idea of an exploding difference. Though objectionable in a certain way, it is no more so than miracles, including small ones. I think we should add this third item to our little smorgasbord of ways in which the thinker of a vague conditional might tighten his thought: the idea of a world that is like α in every respect we would ever think about and then suddenly, legally, and improbably embarks on a short course of events through which it becomes noticeably unlike α. (This seems also to be the view of Goggans (1992), who allows us to tell stories about little miracles, but denies that we need to suppose they occur at closest A-worlds.)

So let us take a fork to be an event through which an A-world first becomes less than *sufficiently like* α. I stipulate that one item is 'sufficiently like' another if they are alike in every respect we would ever notice or think about. Perfect likeness is the extreme case.

Whether we have two or three kinds of closest world, we need not rank-order them in our account of closeness. If we needed to do so, it must be because a subjunctive conditional that was true relative to the closest worlds in one category was false relative to those in another, and this cannot happen. The three have this in common: the A-worlds they count as closest are all, until shortly before T_A, wholly like α or unlike it only negligibly; and we can safely neglect the difference between 'no differences' and 'only negligible differences'. We can also ignore, in the present context, the difference between small miracles and legal differences in the outcomes of indeterministic processes. (If you are squeamish about miracles, see §86.)

It may do no harm if several ramps meet the requirements, for C may be true at each of those A-worlds. Sometimes, however, the evaluation of a forward conditional will depend upon what ramp is envisaged for the antecedent. For example, many conditionals of the form 'If in 1945 there had been ten times as many Jews in Poland as there actually were, then C' will be unassessable because the latest forks leading to the antecedent are so various: the Germans do not invade Poland, the Germans do not have the extermination of Jews as a policy, the Poles are resolute and skilful in resisting German anti-semitism, the Polish

Jews escape into the forests and survive the war there, they leave Poland in time to save themselves and return as soon as the war ends—these lead to notably different states of Europe in 1945, and the truth of the conditional may depend on which of these obtains at the closest A-world. Faced with this choice of eligible ramps, and seeing how it affects the truth value of the conditional in question, we reject the latter, as unfit for evaluation. We may be willing to consider a successor whose antecedent specifies the ramp.

83. LOCATIONAL CONSTRAINTS ON FORKS

Lewis plausibly held that a subjunctive conditional is answerable to the *latest* inconspicuous fork leading to A's obtaining. We certainly need some constraint on how early the fork can be. If we tried to analyse subjunctive conditionals in terms of antecedent-launching forks without constraining when they are to occur, how could we do this? We might try:

> A>C is true ≡ C is true at *some* A-world reachable by an inconspicuous fork from the actual world.

This makes A>C true much too easily. In infinitely many cases it will be so profligate as to attribute truth both to A>C and to A>¬C. So we are left with this suggestion:

> A>C is true ≡ C is true at *every* A-world reachable by an inconspicuous fork from the actual world.

This makes it too difficult for A>C to be true, and impossible for us ever to have reasonable grounds to believe it to be true. We cannot know at what junctures in α's history an indeterminacy or exploding difference or small miracle could have turned our world on a course towards A's obtaining: some may lie vastly far back in time. Even if God told us when those forks occurred, we would need further news from him to know which forks would lead to the obtaining of C as well as of A. This is a special case of the difficulty discussed in §80 above, about our need to limit how far back in time we must go in providing a causal run-up for A.

So quantifying over forks, whether existentially or universally, does not meet our needs. The only alternative is a locational constraint; but it needs to be vaguer than Lewis's, for a reason that Donald Nute (1980b: 104) learned from John Pollock. The wording is mine:

> My coat was not stolen from the restaurant where I left it. There were two chances for theft—two times when relevant indeterminacies or small miracles could have done the trick. They would have involved different potential

thieves; and the candidate for the later theft is a rogue who always sells his stuff to a pawnbroker named Fence.

If the closest A-world involves the latest admissible fork, it follows from the above story that *if my coat had been stolen from the restaurant, it would now be in Fence's shop.* That is not acceptable. We must protect our analysis from implying that if my coat had been stolen it would have been stolen late rather than early. This is absurd in much the same way as the idea that if anything had been different it would have been minimally so (§71).

The 'latest admissible fork' constraint, then, if taken strictly is too strong to fit our practice. I shall use the phrase 'a latest admissible fork', stipulating that two forks can both count as 'latest' if their times of occurrence are not *considerably* different. This is vague; but then, as Lewis pointed out in his book, our subjunctive conditionals *are* vague. It is for analytic theory to locate and describe the vagueness.

I used to meet Pollock's point by dropping the superlative and settling for 'late admissible fork', but Michael Tooley has warned me of the error in this: A>C can be respectable even when A is reachable only by a marathon ramp starting with a fork that is in no reasonable sense 'late', though it may be the latest that does the job. A latest ramp for any conditional of the form 'If dinosaurs had survived up to today . . .' must start with a small swerve of a certain asteroid and then run for sixty million years to reach today, the time of the antecedent.

Mark Lance wrote this to me: 'We can say no more in general, I think, than something like "the salient admissible fork". Of course *ceteris paribus*, temporally near forks are more salient than others, but in particular cases conversational context, background assumptions, and other things can defeat the *ceteris paribus* rider.' I agree with this. It will come into play when I discuss temporally backward conditionals (§110).

84. DOING WITHOUT FORKS

Forks, we have seen, are the loci of a good deal of theoretical turmoil and complexity. That might make us sympathetic to Lycan's attempt (2001) to dispense with them, and indeed with world-histories. He aims to handle subjunctive conditionals in terms of something a little like Stalnaker–Lewis but much simpler—most notably in its freedom from the concepts of world-history and fork. Where Lewis quantifies over worlds, Lycan quantifies over states of affairs, which he calls 'events'. His core account of A>C is that it is true just in case C obtains in every event in which A obtains. This threatens to imply that A>C is true only if it is absolutely necessary; and so Lycan weakens the analysans to something of the form 'C obtains in every event-in-R in which A obtains', after which the real meat of the theory has to consist in an account of what defines the class R.

Lycan evidently hopes to define it without having recourse to items as extensive as worlds; his 'events' are like worlds, he tells us, except that they are 'incomplete', and 'much smaller than entire possible worlds' (2001: 17). He wants and needs to capture the idea of 'two overlapping neighbourhoods of hypothetical fact, the antecedent state of affairs with its closely related facts, and the consequent with its [etc.]' (p. 22), and he aims to do this without any apparatus of forks from actuality, legality, and all the rest.

However, he offers only the proposal that an event e belongs in R only if 'either it is true in e that C or it is true in e that not-C'. Adding this to the core theory leads to the equation of A>C with 'C obtains in every event in which A *and in which either C or not-C*'. That is logically equivalent to 'C obtains in every event in which A', which is where we started—with an analysis according to which no subjunctive conditional is contingently true.

Lycan wants a theory with roughly the same output as Lewis's, but without all the clutter of worlds, their relations to α, and their causal structure; but the means he allows himself are not adequate for the job. He writes informally about possibilities that are 'related' or 'have [something] to do with' one another, and about 'neighbourhoods' and 'local goings-on', but all his theory offers are propositions and their negations. For more about this, see Bennett 2003.

I should add that for a certain subspecies of subjunctive conditionals, histories and forks really are irrelevant. I shall discuss these in §113, when their time has come, explaining why I regard them as mildly degenerate. Until then, I shall stay with the more respectable subjunctives for which histories—and therefore forks—are of the essence.

14

Reflections on Legality

85. THE PRIMACY OF LAW

In the approach to subjunctive conditionals that I have been exploring, we have needed to insist that the closest A-worlds be causally legal from the time of the fork onwards. This started from the need to prevent an unconstrained notion of world-similarity from subverting hosts of subjunctive conditionals; but there is more to it than this, and the need for legality is just as strong in the approach to subjunctives that does not compare worlds (Chapter 20). Most of the subjunctive conditionals we are interested in are forward or backward ones, saying that if A had obtained at T_A then C would have obtained at some other time; and to get from A's truth at T_A to C's truth at another time we need the 'cement of the universe', causation.

Nicholas Rescher once proposed that laws have a privileged place in the analysis of subjunctive conditionals because we are so sure of their truth that we are unwilling to give them up even when exploring the consequences of some antecedent we believe to be false. 'The nomological use of counterfactuals represents a determination to retain the appropriate [law] at the cost of adapting all else to it.' 'A law . . . is a generalization so secure that we are willing to retain it at practically all costs, and to let all else revolve about it when a belief-contravening supposition is made' (Rescher 1961: 190, 191). I am not comfortable harrying this fine philosopher; but I shall do so because there are things to be learned from seeing three errors in his treatment of this matter.

First, his emphasis on 'belief-contravening suppositions' reflects his handling subjunctive conditionals in terms more fitting for indicatives. When he says that laws have primacy because they are the propositions we hold most strongly and unassailably, Rescher ought to be describing the Ramsey test (§12): in adjusting a belief system to accommodate a new supposition, we shall alter some other probabilities in the light of our causal beliefs, but usually we shall not alter the causal beliefs themselves. Though important when we evaluate indicative conditionals, this is irrelevant to subjunctives.

Second, what Rescher says about our firm adherence to laws is wrong anyway. I have some idea of the laws that make it true that if I had got into the bath a minute ago, the water would now be overflowing; but I am less sure of those laws than of the fact that I did not get into the bath.

Third, Rescher implies that when we assert a subjunctive conditional we have an opinion about what the laws are in virtue of which it is true. We cannot have 'a determination to retain [them] at the cost of adapting all else to [them]' if we are ignorant of what laws they are. In fact, however, we often affirm subjunctive conditionals while having no idea of the laws by virtue of which they are true. This fact is reflected in the 'worlds' approach, which bans big *miracles* and/or says that closest A-worlds are *legal* from T_F onwards—this requires conformity to actual casual laws without implying anything about what they are. The other main approach to subjunctive conditionals is similar: it equates A>C with the statement that C is derivable from A and causal laws and . . .; which requires the speaker to generalize over causal laws but not to know the content of any of them (§119).

Nelson Goodman, who invented that other approach, worried that it might not be legitimate to use the concept of law in an analysis of subjunctive conditionals, because he didn't see how to explain what a law is except by saying that it is a true generalization *that supports subjunctive conditionals*, this being what distinguishes it from accidentally true generalizations such as—perhaps— 'Everything with a bulk of at least ten cubic miles is not a diamond'. If we must explain 'law' in this way, then we are threatened with an explanatory circle that is too small to be helpful. Many writers at the time of Goodman's paper and shortly thereafter shared this worry with him. (Goodman's positive ideas about it, adumbrated in the third section of his 1947, were developed more fully in his 1954.)

This problem must be faced not only by followers of Goodman, who use the term 'law' in their statement of truth conditions, but also by Lewis who wrote of 'miracles', by Thomason and Gupta (1980: 314) who write of a 'causally coherent' selection function (which they presumably could not explain without mentioning laws), and probably also by Stalnaker and Davis, who would have trouble making their analyses come out right in particular cases if they were not allowed to say that conformity to the same causal laws is a dominating respect of similarity when it comes to closeness of worlds.

The problem seems to have lost its urgency. There are psychological reasons for this. Such respect as subjunctive conditionals command these days is muted in comparison with the loud enthusiasm that many philosophers have for the concept of causation (and thus, with most of them, for the concept of law), which they make primary in theories of memory, personal identity, reference, time, classification, and so on. Few philosophers would risk basing this favoured concept on the still suspect notion of subjunctive conditionals.

One can justify this attitude. There are promising alternative ways of explaining what laws are, for example the proposal of Ramsey's that Lewis adopted in 1973b: 73–4 (though he later relinquished it). Furthermore, whether or not we can explain '(causal) law' *without* using or mentioning subjunctive conditionals, van Inwagen (1979) has argued convincingly that we cannot explain 'law' *with* help from subjunctive conditionals, or at least that the standard way of doing this fails. For a helpful short discussion of the issue see Stalnaker 1984: 155–6.

I shall henceforth assume that we have an independent account of the concept of causal law, or that we do not need one, or that our need for one will not be satisfied by anything that uses or mentions subjunctive conditionals in the analysans. Some philosophers think Lewis was in a special difficulty about relating subjunctive conditionals to causal laws. On the one hand, his analysis of the conditionals employs the concept of causal law, in his qualified demand for legality at closest A-worlds. On the other, down the years he developed and polished a counterfactual analysis of causal propositions (Lewis 1973a and, for instance, 1986c). Since he explained subjunctives through causation, and causation through subjunctives, I have heard it alleged, Lewis's position is viciously circular. These critics have failed to distinguish (1) the general concept of causation, as involved in such notions as those of causal law, legal world, miracle, and so on from (2) singular causal statements—the explosion caused the fire, the impact caused the glass to shatter, and so on. Lewis assumed 1 in analysing subjunctive conditionals, which he then assumed in analysing 2. There is no circle here. Those who have missed this point have probably not worked hard on analysing 2 and so do not realize what a tough problem it presents, even with 1 in hand. In §90, however, I shall present one bit of the truth about subjunctive conditionals that seems not to be available to Lewis because of his theory of singular causal statements.

86. MIRACLES

Some writers in this area have been troubled by Lewis's allowing miracles into his analysis of conditionals, which they have regarded as quirky and idiosyncratic. Lewis had some idiosyncratic philosophical opinions, but this is not one of them. In my teaching in the 1960s I used to argue that small miracles may be needed to launch antecedents, and William Todd beautifully defended this view a decade before Lewis did (Todd 1964: 104–6). Nor is it quirky. Critics of small miracles such as Pollock (1981: 242–3) seem not to have grasped what motivates the use of that notion in the analysis of subjunctive conditionals. Let me remind you of the facts that jointly force the concept into our picture—still using 'counterfactual' to mean 'subjunctive conditional whose antecedent is false'.

(1) The facts about our use of counterfactuals show that when we think A>C we do not in general envisage A as becoming true abruptly and discontinuously, with a notable bump (so: not Jackson). (2) The facts also show that we do not envisage A's becoming true out of a past that may be greatly different from α's (so: not the Simple Theory). Putting those two together: the facts about our use of counterfactuals show that we ordinarily think of A as fairly smoothly becoming true out of a past pretty much like the actual world's, which means that (3) they show that we take our counterfactuals to require *forks* from α-like worlds. This is about as far as we can go in describing the frame of mind of someone—not a theorist of conditionals—who thinks A>C. When we ask what the forks might be like, any answers we think up are merely resources for the plain person to appeal to when trying to put flesh on the bones of his 'If it had *somehow* come about that A, then . . .'. It would be unrealistic to pin him down to any of them; and my present point is just that a miraculous fork deserves to be mentioned among the legitimate resources. If we are too squeamish to allow it as something the plain person might include in his meaning or fall back on when challenged, then we condemn him to having to rely on two other kinds of fork—indeterministic, and deterministic exploding difference. That would put our conditional-user into dire straits: he could not responsibly believe A>C unless he had good reason to believe there are close worlds at which A comes to obtain through a fork of one of those two kinds. How could he have reason to believe *that*? We have put an unbearable burden upon him; we should lighten it, and allow him his 'If it had *somehow* come about that A, then . . .' without demanding more in the way of a back-up than a suitable thought-experiment. This involves allowing that one of his possibilities—the catch-all, the backstop, the one requiring no special knowedge—is that A comes about through a small miracle. (Michael Tooley reminded me that an antecedent may require more than one small miracle: 'If Nixon and Haig had each pressed his button . . .'. Such cases raise no extra problems; and I shall continue, for convenience, to write in one-small-miracle terms.)

It is true that determinism entails that for anything to have happened that actually did not happen, the whole previous course of the universe would have to have been different from how it actually was; and it would be perverse to weaken this by adding '. . . unless it was a miracle'. Those remarks concern the exploration of determinism. To force them into our thinking about particular subjunctive conditionals (as in McDermott 1999: 301–3) is to ride roughshod over a patent *fact*, namely that when we think a subjunctive conditional we ask only for a small-departure fork from actuality and do not dig into how it might have come about.

Some writers have fretted at the question of what the metaphysical state of affairs is at an A-world that is the subject of a small miracle, that is, an event conflicting with the causal laws of α. Does such a world have laws of its own that nearly coincide with α's but allow for this one fork-creating event? Are they laws that would have to be expressed in the form 'For every value of x but one . . .'? And so on.

I regret the time I have spent thinking and writing about this. Here is why. Lewis held:

(1) When an ordinary person accepts a counterfactual conditional he or she has a thought which, when pressed down on hard and seriously, may imply that some world exactly matches α up to some time when it forks away through the occurrence of a small miracle.

Suppose—though I do not believe it—that we also had reason to accept this:

(2) No coherent account can be given of the nomological structure of a world that exactly matches α up to some time when it forks away through the occurrence of a small miracle.

To regard 2 as refuting 1, or even as counting much against it, would be unduly optimistic about the conceptual aspects of the human condition. Or perhaps 'optimistic' is the wrong word. When we think A>C, with the thought that a small miracle might have been needed for A to have obtained, why *should* we be committed to any view about the deep-down world-long metaphysics of this? Those who demand such a view misunderstand the analytic enterprise.

Mark Lance made the following comment on that passage:

This seems a bit too easy to me. If the analytic enterprise is just to understand the rules of the linguistic game we are playing by, then perhaps this is the right thing for the analytic enterprise to say. But I take it that a far more interesting thing than merely laying out rules of the game is understanding the point of that game, of explaining what is being understood with subjunctives and why they are important to rational practice. Well there seems a threat. If we take them fundamentally to be reporting what goes on in worlds that we can make no sense of, it appears quite mysterious why we would do this. Indeed, if I became convinced that this was what I was doing, I would resolve to stop. It seems to me that some account is called for, an account of why it is interesting to say things about what happens in such worlds, what that tells us about our own world perhaps.

I do not agree with this; but it clearly deserves respectful attention. I leave it to you to think about this issue between Lance and myself.

87. COUNTERLEGALS

The analysis I am defending tolerates miracles at the fork leading to A, but it insists on strict legality—strict conformity to the causal laws of α—from then onwards. The ramp loses its point if it is not legal; and we need legality also from T_A (which terminates the ramp) onwards, because only causal laws can carry us from a supposition about how a world is before and at T_A to how it is, later, at T_C.

By thus requiring legality, I block the way to counterlegal conditionals, that is, ones whose antecedents are in themselves contrary to actual law; for example, 'If gravity obeyed an inverse cube law, then our months would be shorter'. I am content with this result, because counterlegals need special treatment anyway.

There is no trouble with a counterlegal A>C in which A entails C. An example might be: If the gravitational force between two bodies were not a function of the distance between them, then it would not be proportional to the square root of the distance between them. What makes this manageable is the fact that C is true at *every* A-world, so that the conditional does not require us to sort out the closest from amongst the A-worlds. This is a logically true, and thus independent, conditional (§§7, 95). It is of no interest, and we can set it aside without anxiety.

As we can a counterlegal conditional like this: If A were the case then something contrary to causal law would be the case; which is equivalent to: A > (A miracle occurs). This says only that no A-world is causally possible, or that a miracle occurs at every A-world; it is not established by logic alone, but its truth comes purely from logic together with the causal laws of α. So again no closeness problems arise, and the conditional can be accepted as true, though boring.

The interesting, troublesome counterlegals are those whose consequents are more specific, saying that if causally impossible A were the case then C would be the case, where C obtains at some causally impossible worlds but not at all. To sort these into true and false, we need a suitable way of selecting from among the causally impossible worlds. How can we do this?

If we are to have a single unified analysis that provides for counterlegals as well as counterfactuals, there is only one way to go. The idea we had reached before counterlegals came on the scene was that the truth value of A>C depends on how things stand at a subset of *causally possible A-worlds*. We might see this as a special case of the broader idea that the truth value of A>C depends on how things stand at a subset of *A-worlds that are nomologically more similar to α than are any other A-worlds*—taking nomological similarity to be similarity in respect of laws. Where A is causally possible—so that A>C is not counterlegal—the two versions are equivalent: some A-worlds conform exactly to α's causal laws, so they are nomologically exactly like α; and A-worlds that are not causally possible all drop out of the picture. When A itself is not causally possible, however, it is the causally possible worlds that fall by the wayside, leaving us with a need to find the closest A-worlds among the causally impossible ones; and we might do that on the basis of likeness to α in nomological structure.

I would go along with this if I had a workable concept of nomological similarity; but I have not, and it seems that nobody else has either.

The only philosopher I know of who has worked in detail on counterlegals is Pollock (1976: 56–7, 93–7). He does not speak of nomological similarity: his theory of subjunctive conditionals, although it mentions 'worlds', belongs not to the tradition of Stalnaker and Lewis, but rather to that of Goodman (§130). Pollock thinks of worlds as sets of propositions that are to be constructed by taking the whole truth about α and then modifying it in certain ways. The closest A-worlds are the sets of propositions that include A and can be reached from the truth about the actual world by 'minimal change'. Applying this to counterlegals, Pollock says that if A is causally impossible then A>C is true if C is true at all A-worlds reachable from the actual world by a minimal change in what laws obtain. In giving details, he speaks of 'making deletions' in 'the actual set of basic laws', taking a minimal change to be one that deletes as few of the set's members as possible. This sounds all right until we ask: how can we count basic laws? Pollock's theory needs an objective way of individuating laws, determining what counts as one law rather than more than one (a conjunction in disguise) or less than one (a disjunction in disguise); and nothing in his book provides the means for doing this. Pollock faces up to the analogous problem for propositions that are not laws, presenting an ingenious device for sifting out the conjunctions and disjunctions from amongst them (§126); but that device could not help us to individuate laws. If we can solve the problem, it must be through the physicists' telling us things about the nomological structure of the actual world, as distinct from the propositional structure of their favourite theory. Objection: 'If it takes this kind of information to legitimize counterlegals, that puts them beyond the reach of most of us.' So they are, and so they should be.

Lacking a workable solution along those lines, we might tackle counterlegals from another angle. Consider first how counterlogicals are handled. Most of us think that if A is absolutely impossible then A entails C for every C; and so if A>C is true for some values of C it is true for all. Yet a speaker can say things of the form 'If conjunction were not commutative, then C would be the case,' and be right for some values of C and wrong for others, just so long as he is talking about the power structure of some *system* of logic—some set of rules and independent axioms—and saying that C is a theorem in the system that results from the original one by deleting its commutativity axiom. Such conditionals are saved from triviality by being made relative to some *formulation* of logical truth. They cannot be nontrivially evaluated in terms of worlds, since all their antecedents are false at every world.

We might treat counterlegals in the same way. It is true that for them there are some available worlds, namely those that are merely causally impossible (whereas counterlogicals would require absolutely impossible worlds). But those worlds are of no avail unless we know how to select from amongst them; and it may be that we do not. For counterlegals, then, we may have to turn away from worlds and propositions and have recourse to sentences—the sentences of some theory. Be that as it may, I have nothing more to say about counterlegals. The subjunctive conditionals that crop up in our everyday life all have causally possible antecedents, and they are the ones I care most about.

88. TWO KINDS OF (IN)TOLERANCE

This amounts to saying that subjunctive conditionals conforming to the analysis I am defending are *impossibility-intolerant*. This phrase echoes one I used for a property of indicative conditionals, namely their *zero-intolerance*, meaning that A→C has no role in an environment where A's falsity is beyond question (§23).

In sharp contrast with this, every subjunctive conditional is *zero-tolerant*, that is, seriously usable in a context where everyone regards its antecedent as certainly false. You know I skimmed the broth while it was still hot, and I know that you know; neither of us would call this in question; yet it remains sensible for you to nag me: 'If you had cooled the broth before skimming it, you would have got all the fat.'

Future-tense subjunctive conditionals are also zero-tolerant. Given what we all know about the rain that has fallen and the geology of the catchment area, we assume that the river will rise by at least two feet in the next two days; we do not consider whether we might be wrong about this. In this context you can properly remark 'If the river were to stay at its present level for the next two days, the salmon would be trapped in the rapids'. If someone comments: 'But the river won't—it can't—stay at its present level for the next two days', you can reasonably reply: 'I know that. I spoke only of what *would* happen if it *were* to stay level . . .' etc.

The word 'would' expresses the zero-tolerance, openly maintaining that the conditional holds even if the antecedent is false. Its doing this shows up vividly in something to which Jackson has called attention (1981: 128–9), namely that there is nothing logically or semantically wrong with saying 'If the river were to stay at its present level for the next two days, things would work out differently from how they actually will', and 'If Booth hadn't shot Lincoln, events would have unrolled differently from how they actually did'. To this Dorothy Edgington has added that it makes sense—logically if not historically—to say 'If Booth hadn't shot Lincoln, American history would have continued just as it actually did'. The indicative cousins of these are nonsense. Even a relocator, who puts 'If it rains tonight, the roads will be slippery tomorrow' in the same bin as the subjunctives (§6), must agree that it would be absurd to say 'If it rains tonight, the roads will be different from how they will actually be'.

Or so I thought until I encountered Dudman's recent welcome to the indicative cousins. Of the sentence 'If Booth doesn't kill Lincoln, things will work out differently from how they actually will', he writes: 'Precisely that would be the well-reasoned position of a conspirator convinced that Booth will kill Lincoln' (Dudman (forthcoming)). I have tried this on a number of informants with no theoretical axe to grind, and they have ruled unanimously against it. Dudman's ear for these matters is unreliable. To Edgington's remark that 'it is trivial to say "If it rains, things will be just as they actually will be"', he responds: 'Trivial to say, when only a speaker maintaining it will rain has any right to say it?' On the contrary. I maintain that it will not rain here tomorrow; but I have a perfect right to say that if it rains here tomorrow things will be just as they actually will be. Indeed, I go further and boldly declare: *Whatever* happens, things will be just as they actually will be.

Because a subjunctive conditional is zero-tolerant, one can properly accept it while knowing that one would not be willing to use it in Modus Ponens. Last year I went to Spain; I am pretty sure that *If I had not visited Spain last year I would have visited France.* However, if I consider the implications of my discovering to my amazement that I did not visit Spain, they do not lead to the conclusion that I went to France. On the contrary, if I add 'I did not visit Spain last year' to my belief system with its multitude of memories and other evidences of my having done so, the resulting system makes me unwilling to have any opinion about what I did last year. In contrast with this, it would be improper to assert—and impossible to accept—an indicative conditional while *knowing* that one would not be willing to apply Modus Ponens upon coming to believe its antecedent. (Except for conditionals like the Thomason examples (§12); and even those are not counterexamples in their other-person forms.) You can accept an indicative conditional even though *in fact* you would not be willing to apply it in Modus Ponens, but that is another matter. See the discussion of robustness$_{1,2}$ in §49 above.

The reason why one can accept A>C while fully realizing that one would drop it if A turned out to be true is also the reason why one can properly accept things of the form 'If it were the case that A, such-and-such would not have been as it actually is'. It is just a fact about this use of 'would' that it includes in its meaning a kind of permission to drop the conditional if its antecedent turns out to be true. I have been accused of maintaining that with any subjunctive conditional whatsoever it would be reasonable to avail oneself of this permission, but I have been guilty of no such absurdity.

Returning to my main theme: although they are zero-tolerant, subjunctive conditionals are impossibility-intolerant. In general, A>C is useless, pointless, out of the arena, if A is intrinsically causally impossible. Do not confuse this with A's being causally ruled out *in the circumstances*. That is no impediment to the propriety of A>C.

The impossibility-intolerance of subjunctives is doubly unlike the zero-intolerance of indicatives. The two differ as impossibility from falsehood, and as fact from presupposition. The former concerns what *is the case* at *all* the causally possible worlds, while the latter concerns what *people presuppose* about *one* world, the actual one.

The four main roles of subjunctive conditionals in our lives help to explain their being impossibility-intolerant and zero-tolerant. (1) We use them diagnostically. 'They are not at home. If they had been, the lights would have been on' (Anderson 1951); 'It was arson. If it had been an accidental fire, it wouldn't have broken out in the crypt and the belfry at the same time.'(2) We use them where A concerns someone's behaviour, for broadly moral purposes. They may be guides to ourselves in future practical problems, and bases for applauding or reproaching the person in question because of his causal relevance to some upshot. 'I know he didn't do anything; but if he *had* done something—the right thing—the disaster wouldn't have occurred. So don't tell me he had nothing to do with it.' (3) Whatever A is about, a subjunctive can sketchily report facts about how the world was, is, or will be causally hooked up. 'Without fully understanding the mechanisms, we are convinced that if the Pacific Ocean had been cooler in 1999 there would have been fewer hurricanes.' (4) Subjunctives are used to express, and perhaps also to shape and sharpen, our elations and regrets. 'If just five of my colleagues had forgotten to vote, I would have lost the election.' 'If the belay hadn't slipped, Harry would be alive today.' Some people frown on regret; perhaps some frown on elation; but both are in our repertoire, and we voice them in subjunctive conditionals.

These roles that such conditionals play for us go naturally with zero-tolerance and with impossibility-intolerance. That, I submit, is obvious.

15

Truth at the Actual World

89. SIMILARITY IN MATTERS OF PARTICULAR FACT

To evaluate a forward subjunctive conditional, we must go to A-worlds that (1) sufficiently resemble the actual world until shortly before T_A, (2) fork in an admissible way—through a different outcome of an indeterminacy, a small miracle, or an exploding difference—in a direction that makes A true at them, and (3) conform to the laws of α from the fork onwards. Does this complete the story, or do states of α after T_A also come into the analysis? This raises a problem.

For simplicity, pretend that in evaluating forward A>C we find there is only one admissible fork—its date and its nature are the same at all the candidates for the title of 'closest A-world'. So these worlds are indiscernible up to and at T_F, the time of the fork. All we have to consider is how they might differ in respect of later times, and how such differences affect closeness, and thus the truth values of some subjunctive conditionals. Have we any basis for preferring some over others for the role of closest A-world?

Since our candidate worlds are exactly alike at T_F and are law-abiding from then onwards, they can later become unalike only through indeterminacy. Our present problem arises, therefore, only if α is not strictly deterministic, so that closest A-worlds are not either. In that case, but not otherwise, the candidate worlds could develop differently after T_F even though they are indiscernible at that time. Now we want to know how, if at all, these post-T_F differences bear upon the closeness of worlds. Here is a tempting answer (its name stands for 'particular fact'):

PF: If (1) w_1 exactly resembles w_2 up to T_F, and (2) both conform to the laws of α thereafter, and (3) they first become unalike in respect of one particular matter of post-T_F fact that obtains at α and w_1 but not at w_2, then w_1 is closer to α than w_2 is.

Lewis did not raise this issue in his book *Counterfactuals*; but he discussed it briefly in the 1979 paper in which he presented the book's doctrine in a more developed form. The upshot of the paper is—roughly speaking—that closest A-worlds fork from α shortly before T_A and are perfectly legal from there on. What about post-T_A particular facts? They are 'of little or no importance' in determining closeness, Lewis wrote, adding that when we try to decide between 'little' and 'none' we find that 'Different cases come out differently' (1979: 48). They do indeed. Let us see how and why.

Starting with Lewis's main theory—which determines closeness on the basis of exact likeness up to T_F, smooth parting of worlds at T_F, and strict legality thereafter—should we add PF as a further determinant of closeness? First, here are two arguments against doing so, one logical and the other intuitive.

It seems to be a consequence of PF that if C is true at α, and is not ruled *out* by A, then it is ruled *in* by A. That is:

PF*: C & $\neg$(A>$\neg$C) entails A>C.

One might put this by saying that if C is true at α and at some closest A-worlds, it is true at all the closest A-worlds.

Surprisingly, PF* entails Conditional Excluded Middle (CEM), as I now prove. We start with PF*:

(1) C & $\neg$(A>$\neg$C) entails A>C.

If this is universally valid, then so is what we get from it by replacing C by $\neg$C throughout:

(2) $\neg$C & $\neg$(A>$\neg\neg$C) entails A>$\neg$C.

This has the form 'P&Q entails R', which is equivalent to 'P&$\neg$R entails $\neg$Q'. Apply this equivalence to 2 and you get

(3) $\neg$C & $\neg$(A>$\neg$C) entails $\neg\neg$(A>$\neg\neg$C).

Cancel out the double negations in this and the result is

(4) $\neg$C & $\neg$(A>$\neg$C) entails A>C.

Now 1 and 4 jointly say that A>C is entailed (1) by $\neg$(A>$\neg$C) *conjoined with* C and (4) by $\neg$(A>$\neg$C) *conjoined with* $\neg$C; so A>C is entailed by $\neg$(A>$\neg$C) on its own. That is,

$\neg$(A>$\neg$C) entails A>C,

which clearly entails Conditional Excluded Middle. QED.

So PF* entails CEM (the moves are all utterly secure), and if PF is stronger than PF* then it too entails CEM.

This plainly valid argument comes from Charles Cross (1985). He does not use it against PF, but rather as further support for CEM. This reminds us that the argument, considered as disproving PF, is only as strong as the independent case against CEM—a matter on which able people disagree (§72).

However, there are intuitive obstacles to accepting PF, which counts as true certain conditionals that most thoughtful people, it seems, think to be false. Here is an example. We have a deeply and objectively random coin-tossing machine: pressing a button activates a device that fires a single photon towards two slits; its going through one slit causes the coin to be tossed so that it has to come down heads; similarly for the other slit and tails. Joe activates this mechanism. He presses the button at T_A and the coin comes down heads. Now consider the statement 'If Susan had pressed the button at T_A, the coin would have come down heads.' Without PF added to it, Lewis's main theory makes this conditional false, because it designates as 'closest' some A-worlds at which the coin falls heads and some at which it falls tails; Stalnaker's theory makes it indeterminate; neither makes it true, and I submit that this is as it should be. I count it against PF that it confers truth on that conditional. A minority of people, I find, disagree with the rest of us about this, and accept 'If Susan had pressed the button at T_A, the coin would have come down heads at T_C'. I conjecture that they are pressured by theory, sensing that if they reject this conditional they will be in trouble. I shall remove that pressure.

90. SOLVING THE PARTICULAR-FACT PROBLEM

If we simply delete PF from Lewis's theory, and work purely with Lewis-closeness (as I shall call it for short), we are not embarrassed by the conditional about Susan, for the unamplified theory makes it come out false. Unfortunately, it also classifies as false some particular-fact conditionals that seem true. Examples crop up all over the literature; the earliest I know was due to Pavel Tichý (1976). Here is a variant on it (adapted from Slote 1978: 27 n.):

> Imagine a completely undetermined coin-tossing device. Your friend offers you good odds that it will not come down heads next time; you decline the bet, he activates the device, and the coin comes down heads. He then says: 'You see; if you had bet heads, you would have won.'

According to the unamplified Lewis theory, that conditional is false. At all the Lewis-closest worlds, you make the bet at T_F and (we may suppose) the coin-tossing device is activated in exactly the same way at T_A. Because the device is random, at some of the worlds the coin comes down tails at T_C, which means you lose your bet at some of them, so that Bet-heads > Won is false.

This is a problem for the unamplified theory, because intuitively this conditional seems true. If you are tempted to think it false, be warned of trouble. Here is a likely tale:

> A not fully causally determined event in Hitler's brain at T_2 led to his strange decision not to wipe out the British Expeditionary Force at Dunkirk. Much of that army was rescued from the beach at T_3, by small private craft from England. Mr Miniver had such a craft, but couldn't take part in the rescue because at T_1 he had gone into hospital for elective surgery. He reflected afterwards: 'If I hadn't gone into hospital, I would have taken part in the Dunkirk rescue.'

We are threatened with having to treat this as false, and along with it every subjunctive conditional whose antecedent predates T_2 and whose consequent presupposes that the Dunkirk rescue took place. The reasoning is clear: any conditional of that sort takes us to worlds other than α, at a time before T_2; as well as ones at which the Dunkirk rescue takes place there are others at which it does not; and some No-rescue-worlds are as Lewis-close to α as are their Rescue counterparts.

These reactions of ours are not an unruly mess; we have a disciplined basis for rejecting the false particular-fact conditionals while accepting the true ones. It was exhibited in Johnson 1991: 407–8, and perhaps before that in Thomason and Gupta 1980: 313–15, though I shall expound it in my own way. In so far as we react differently to the two conditionals, we are guided by the thought that in the false one, although the pressing of the button does not *determine* the fall of the coin, it does *cause* it; and we have a sense that a world at which someone else presses the button is a world at which a different causal chain occurs, and that we are not entitled to credit it with the same outcome as the actual causal chain had. In contrast with this, at the closest worlds at which you bet on heads while I press the button, the fall of the coin arises from the very same chain of events: the button-press link in the chain is the very one that occurred at α, with merely a different vocal accompaniment. This seems to be why we reject the particular fact conditional that I call false and accept the ones that I think are true.

If this is indeed how our thoughts are moving, we should be able to capture it in a theory. The job is done by PF with the addition of one clause, which I italicize:

> Causal Chain PF: If (1) w_1 exactly resembles w_2 up to T_F, and (2) both conform to the laws of α thereafter, and (3) they first become unalike in respect of one particular matter of post-T_F fact that obtains at α and w_1—*through the same causal chain at both*—but not at w_2, then w_1 is closer to α than w_2 is.

The added condition gives us the truth values we want, implying that Susan-pressed > Heads is false, and Bet-heads > Won is true. This comfortably handles something that Sanford offers as a difficulty for the 'worlds' semantics for subjunctive conditionals:

'If we had bought one more artichoke this morning, we would have had one for every-one at dinner tonight.' . . . [This is] supported by the fact that the number of people coming for dinner tonight exceeds by one the number of artichokes we bought this morning. Our confidence in the conditional exceeds our confidence about what happens in the closest possible world in which we buy one more artichoke this morning. Who can say about this world just which people in it we impulsively invite for dinner and of those just how many accept? (Sanford 1989: 173).

Causal Chain PF deals with this nicely.

This aspect of our thought involves the concept of an indeterministic causal chain—as defended, for example, in Anscombe 1971 and van Inwagen 1983: 138–41. Most of the time in these studies we handle causal chains only indirect-ly, by saying things about T_1-to-T_2 relations that obtain at all causally possible worlds. This captures territory that has causal chains lurking in it, but it does not isolate them; and anyway they are all deterministic. And when we theorize about indeterminism, we usually focus on causally possible worlds that are exactly alike for a time and then become unalike. This captures indeterminism, but not causal chains. We have to bring in the concept of an indeterministic causal chain, explicitly and separately, if we are to tell the truth about how particular post-T_A facts relate to closeness.

Jason Stanley pointed out to me that Causal Chain PF seems not to be avail-able to Lewis, for a reason that has since been helpfully developed by Dorothy Edgington (2003). Lewis's counterfactual analysis of particular causation state-ments (1973a, see my §§85, 114), though it allows him to use the general notion of causation (or legality, or miracle) in his account of subjunctive condi-tionals, does not allow him—on pain of circularity—the appeal to particular causally related pairs of events that we needed to solve the particular-fact problem.

In presenting that solution, I have taken a causal chain to be a sequence of *events*; so I have to answer questions about whether a given particular event occurs at each of two worlds. I am uncomfortable about this, because reidentify-ing events across worlds is often a murky matter, guided only by unstructured intuitions (see Bennett 1988a: 56–8). Still, we do have such intuitions: we are clear—no, we are *sure*—that a given finger-movement that occurred in silence could have occurred to the sound of a bet's being made, but could not have been made by a different finger; and this seems to give our judgements on particular-fact subjunctives all the grounding they have. For many purposes, I prefer fact- to event-causation, and would like to replace

The landslide caused the damming of the river,

by the likes of

The river was blocked because part of the mountain slid into it.

But I doubt if fact-causation can give us a notion of causal chain that we could use to handle the particular-fact problem: the 'fact' approach to the same-causal-chain concept looks too fancy to be what underlies our intuitive judgements. Rickety and insubstantial though it is, the 'events' approach seems to be what we tacitly use to evaluate conditionals of the kind in question.

91. NON-INTERFERENCE SUBJUNCTIVE CONDITIONALS

The general idea behind Causal Chain PF is this: If at the actual world, A is not the case, C is the case, and these two facts are causally unrelated to one another at α, then C also obtains at the closest A-worlds. From this it follows that A>C. This is unlike the more prominent kind of case where A's being true helps to explain C's being true at the worlds in question. Pollock has put this well:

There are basically two ways that a simple subjunctive can be true. . . . There can be a connection between the antecedent and the consequent so that the truth of the antecedent would bring about [the truth of] the consequent. . . . A simple subjunctive can be true because the consequent is already true and there is no connection between the antecedent and consequent such that the antecedent's being true would interfere with the consequent's being true (Pollock 1976: 26).

A conditional that is true in the second way is a *non-interference* one (§50). When such a conditional is heard out of context, it may sound peculiar. If you overheard someone saying 'If Susan had bet on heads, the coin would have fallen heads', you might suspect the speaker of naive credulity of some sort. But then supply a context. The coin did in fact fall heads, the speaker has remarked that if Susan had bet on heads she would have won, and we ask for his reasons for this, in full. He complies: 'The coin fell heads; if Susan had bet on heads it would (still) have fallen heads; so if she had made the bet she would have won.' The non-interference conditionals, in short, are appropriate and natural in their role as support for other conditionals—ones whose consequents are false, ones that sound natural and reasonable without any setting of the scene.

Consider again my Dunkirk example. Because it is all right for Mr Miniver to think *If I hadn't gone into hospital, I would have taken part in the Dunkirk rescue*, it is all right for him to think *If I hadn't gone into hospital, the Dunkirk rescue would (still) have taken place*. Taken out of context, the latter conditional sounds like a twisted exercise in self-important modesty, but it must be true if the other is.

These remarks apply also to non-interference conditionals that do not involve indeterministic causation. Suppose that the entire causal ancestry of an actual volcanic eruption at T_2 is strictly deterministic, and that no facts about human behaviour have any part in it. Then according to the Lewis-based theory we are exploring, the volcano erupts also at any closest A-world at which A concerns human conduct at T_1. The Lewis theory, then, will count this as true: *If at T_1 I had visited Taormina, the volcano would have erupted at T_2*. That sounds silly until it gets a context, as it might from this: *If at T_1 I had visited Taormina, I would have seen the eruption at T2*. This is a securely true conditional; it is not a non-interference one, because its consequent is false as well as its antecedent; and it seems natural and sensible. But it cannot be true unless the seemingly silly one is true also. For a different defence of Causal Chain PF, see Edgington (2003).

As Pollock's description brings out, the 'non-interference' label does not mark off a kind of conditional, but rather a source for a conditional's truth. If we ask two people who believe A>C why they believe it, one might reply 'Because A would allow C to obtain' and the other 'Because A would make C obtain'. Here is an example.

A village sits near the bottom of a dam that has a lake backed up behind it. An agronomist thinks the village's aridity problem would be solved by cutting channels in the top of the dam so that useful amounts of water would flow to where they would do most good to the crops. Critics worry that cutting the channels will weaken the dam enough for it to collapse and destroy the village. The agronomist reassures them: 'No: if the channels were cut, the village would be safe'. That is Cut > Safe; and this agronomist thinks it is true in the non-interference manner.

Now a new story about the same village, dam, and channels. An engineer fears that the dam, with abnormally high water behind it, may burst and flood the village, but thinks the trouble can be averted by cutting channels in the dam and letting some of the water escape in a controlled way. He proclaims: 'If the channels were cut, the village would be safe.' This is Cut > Safe again—exactly what the agronomist says in the other story—but the engineer believes it to be true in the making-true manner.

If either man speaks truly, then so does the other, for they say the same thing. The engineer asserts it as a making-true conditional, but what he actually says does not express that. If he had said 'If the channels were to be cut into the dam, that would make the village safe', this would be an explicit making-true conditional, and would be false if the agronomist was right. On the other side, if the agronomist had said 'Even if the channels were to be cut into the dam, the village would still be safe', the words 'even' and 'still' would indicate that his conditional was a non-interference one, and thus not something the engineer would say. But the conditional they both assert is, simply, true. Nor is there the faintest reason to think that in the mouth of either of them it is ambiguous.

It follows that one man says something true that he derives from an error: either the agronomist infers it from the false premiss that sufficient conditions exist for the village's safety, and would not be interfered with by cutting the dam; or the engineer infers it from the false premiss that sufficient conditions for the village's safety do not exist but would do so if the dam were cut. We find no problem in this, for truths are often believed on the basis of errors.

The engineer could say 'If the channels were to be cut, then the village would be safe', and the agronomist could not. I learned from Davis (1983) about this use of 'then' to exclude a conditional—whether subjunctive or indicative—from being a non-interference one. Lycan (2001: 35) elegantly explains *why* 'then' is suitable for this purpose. It is, however, just one of many devices we have to do the work, and it seems to me to be a thin and narrow basis for the edifice of theory that Davis and Lycan have erected upon it.

92. DOES A&C ENTAIL A>C?

Few deny that if A is true and C false, then A>C is false. There is a question, however, about whether A>C is automatically true if A and C are both true. All the main analyses of subjunctive conditionals have it as a theorem, and one easily sees why: if C is true at the closest A-world, what more can one say? Well, there may be more.

If the actual world is deterministic, then certainly A&C entails A>C. For in that case, at T_A there exist causally sufficient conditions for the subsequent truth of C—which secures the truth of A>C. I here rely on the Sufficiency Principle: *If A and C are true, and at T_A sufficient conditions exist for the obtaining of C at T_C, then A>C is true.* Admittedly, many conditionals that come out as true according to this, when asserted at the actual world, 'feel false', but a suitable context dissolves such a feeling, as it does the comparable feeling about non-interference conditionals whose antecedent is false.

In the presence of indeterminism, the picture changes. 'If you were to toss the coin, it would fall heads'—is this automatically true if the addressee does toss the coin and it does fall heads? There is no powerful argument for either answer, but I favour the answer No. If when the toss begins, causally sufficient conditions for heads do not exist, and if the toss is causally relevant to whether the coin falls heads, then I think Toss > Heads should be accounted false. I am appealing here to the general line of thought underlying Causal Chain PF. I applied that in §90 to cases where the antecedent is false; now I stick by it when the antecedent is true. My basis for this is the Irrelevance Principle: *When A and C are both true, and the causation of C is indeterministic, A>C is true just in case A is irrelevant to the causal chain that leads to C's obtaining.*

Here are two consequences of this, each relating to a deeply random coin-tossing device. (1) I say: 'If you were to activate that device, the coin would come up heads'; you do activate it, and the coin does come up heads. I have said something false, despite the truth of both antecedent and consequent. (2) I say: 'If you were to bet on heads on the next toss of that device, you would win'; you do bet on heads, and the coin does come down heads. I have spoken truly. It was based on a sheer guess, and was not a reasonable thing for me to say; but it was true.

Obviously, I do not put those two cheek by jowl in the hope of bustling your intuitions over to my side! In my next section, however, I shall offer a theoretical reason that may incline you my way.

In accepting the Irrelevance Principle, I deny that A&C entails A>C. This commits me to allowing that this can happen: *A and C are both true at α, and C is false at some closest A-world.* (The link between the falsity of A>C and the falsity of C at some closest A-world has been axiomatic—almost definitional—through the past five chapters.) So I have to accept that some other worlds are as close to α as it is to itself, which seems odd when closeness is thought of in terms of similarity. Lewis tried to ease the shock: 'Perhaps our discriminations of similarity are rather coarse,' he suggested, 'and some worlds different from α are enough like α so that such small differences as there are fail to register' (1973*b*: 29). This would block A&C from entailing A>C universally, but not in all the right places: the cases I have been discussing do not turn on differences that are too small to register on our minds.

Since Lewis wrote that, it has become ever clearer that closeness cannot be anything like simple untailored similarity; so we can avoid the unwanted entailment without having to appeal to slender dissimilarities that slip through the net of our attention. All we need is for some respects of (dis)similarity to be irrelevant to closeness.

93. HOME THOUGHTS FROM ABROAD

The two stands I have taken about truth conditions for A>C when A and C are both true imply things about how A>C should be evaluated at closest Ā-worlds.

(1) Take a case where A and C are true at α, and where A>C is true according to the Sufficiency Principle, meaning that at T_A there exist sufficient conditions for the subsequent obtaining of C. Now consider this from the viewpoint of the closest Ā-world, which I shall call w. Given that w is α's closest Ā-world, presumably α is w's closest A-world; so what makes A>C true at α by virtue of the Sufficiency Principle also makes it true at w by the analysis we had before the Sufficiency Principle was introduced. So this follows: *when A and C are both true and C is deterministically caused, A>C is true at α just in case it is true at the closest Ā-world.*

(2) I have also embraced the Irrelevance Principle, which says that when A and C are actually true and C is not deterministically caused, A>C is true just in case A is irrelevant to the causal chain that leads to C's obtaining. Once again, step across to w, the closest Ā-world, again assuming that α is w's closest A-world. At w, A>C comes out as true in just the cases where the Irrelevance Principle makes it true at α; and it does so on the basis of the principle Causal Chain PF, which I defended before looking into cases where A and C are true. So this follows: *when A and C are both true and C is not deterministically caused, A>C is true at α just in case it is true at the closest Ā-world.*

Putting together the conclusions of those two paragraphs, we get an agreeable result:

Home from Abroad: Whether or not C is deterministically caused, if A and C are both true then A>C is true (at α) just in case it is true at the closest Ā-worlds.

Part of my reason for the Irrelevance Principle—given that it does not collide violently with any of our intuitions—is that it yields this result.

In this section I have been much helped by Bigelow 1976a. In that paper John Bigelow set out to falsify the non-interference conditionals that 'feel false' out of context, and he now agrees that this was a misguided project. In the course of it, however, he had some original ideas about evaluating subjunctive conditionals at α in the light of how they should be evaluated at certain other worlds, and I have gratefully availed myself of some of these.

94. STAND OR FALL

In §6 I mentioned the thesis that certain indicative conditionals stand or fall with the corresponding subjunctives. A good many philosophers have asserted this especially for indicatives of the Does-will form: 'If Hamilton behaves fairly, Burr will become President' was true in 1800—they say—just in case 'If Hamilton had behaved fairly, Burr would have become President' is true now. I shall call this thesis Stand or Fall. I now offer three warnings relating to it. Two could have been presented some distance back, but the third relies on §90, which is why I have saved all three until this chapter.

First, do not infer from Stand or Fall that subjunctive conditionals can enter into stand-offs such as we found in §34 with Does-will indicatives. In Gibbard's poker-game example, and mine with the gates and the dam, we saw how one person can be perfectly entitled to accept $A\rightarrow C$ and another to accept $A\rightarrow\neg C$; but this cannot happen with $A>C$ and $A>\neg C$.

Return to the gates and the dam, at a time when both levers are down. Because they are both down, Top Gate cannot open; but later there may be truths of the form 'If Top Gate had opened . . .'. Their truth requires a recent inconspicuous divergence from actuality—this is deliberately and healthily vague. Suppose we find that several A-worlds are about equally close to actuality: each diverges inconspicuously from exact likeness to α shortly before T_A—the time to which A pertains. If C obtains at all those worlds, the conditional is true. But there might instead be several suitably close worlds with C obtaining at only some of them; in which case neither $A>C$ nor $A>\neg C$ is true. In one scenario, west lever has been rusted into the down position for months, while well-oiled east lever was moved at 11.55 a.m.; so that 'If Top Gate had been opened at noon, all the water would have run westwards' comes out as true. We can easily devise a story in which Opened > Eastwards is true instead; or one where neither is true. Never can both be true or fully acceptable, as conflicting indicatives in a Gibbardian stand-off can be.

How can this be? There is certainly some some truth in Stand or Fall; so what stops it from implying that Does-will stand-offs stand or fall with corresponding Had-would ones? Well, I introduced Stand or Fall in terms of the *truth* of some Does-wills and the truth of Had-woulds, but now we know better. To give it a better chance of being true, Stand or Fall should say that the items that stand or fall together are these:

(1) There being facts that would make it proper for someone who knew them to accept $A\rightarrow C$ at T_1, and none making it equally proper for someone to accept $A\rightarrow\neg C$ at T_1, and (2) the truth of $A>C$ at T_2.

In this, 1 is the nearest we can get to the notion of the truth of A→C. And from this version of Stand or Fall it does not follow that because Gibbardian stand-offs occur with indicatives they can occur with subjunctives. For the latter conclusion to be drawable, the items that stand or fall together would have to be:

(1) There being facts that would make it proper for someone who knew them to accept A→C at T_1, and (2) the truth of A>C at T_2.

But this, when you think about it, is incredible. In my example, Wesla may later *believe that* if Top Gate had been open the water would have flowed to the west, and Esther may *believe that* if Top Gate had been open the water would have flowed to the east; but if so, at least one of them errs.

This point does not cut very deeply into the thesis that Does-wills stand or fall with the corresponding subjunctives, because—for reasons I gave in §35—there is no great abundance of stand-offs between pairs of Does-wills. Still, they are possible; so this first warning is appropriate.

The second warning concerns cases where Stand or Fall does not apply for a reason to which Mark Lance has drawn my attention. When there are two recent inconspicuous forks from actuality to A, the slightly later one leading to C while the earlier does not, we do not count A>C as true. We *could* award the 'closest' palm to the world with the more recent of the forks—we could but we do not, as Pollock's example showed (§83). However, at a moment between the two forks there is a sound basis for accepting A→C. Here is an example. Sheep are checked first for weight and then for health; if they fail for weight they go into the meadow, if for health into the barn; if they pass both they go to the slaughter-house. Consider now a sheep that squeaks through on weight and on health; we do not say that if it hadn't been picked for slaughter it would have gone to the barn; yet during the minute between the two checks there is a sound basis for saying that if it isn't picked for slaughter it will go to the barn, and no basis for saying that if it isn't it won't.

The third warning about Stand or Fall arises from the discussion of §89, which shows how A>C can be true even though at no time was A→C even slightly plausible for any reasonable person. If you had bet on heads you would have won, but there was never any basis for accepting 'If you bet on heads, you will win'. Another example: perhaps not even Laplace's archangel had grounds to assure me 'If you embark on that plane you will be killed'; but after the plane has improbably crashed, I accept as true that if I had been on it I would have been killed.

Each of those Had-woulds is a true non-interference conditional. In each case, C is actually true, and nothing in the supposition of A interferes with that. But just because A is *not* connected with C, there may be nothing to support the corresponding Does-will (Heads → Win, Embark → Killed) in advance. (This point came to me from Stephen Barker via Dorothy Edgington. I shall discuss her response to it in §142.)

So we have two ways for a Does-will to be acceptable although the corresponding Had-would is false, and one for a Had-would to be true although at no earlier time was the corresponding Does-will acceptable.

In §135 it will appear that Stand or Fall—even when qualified so as to steer around these three pockets of falsity—is grandly and globally false, so there is no substance in the main use that philosophers have wanted to make of it, namely arguing that Does-wills belong in the same hopper with subjunctives. Still, its more local failures have been worth noting.

95. INDEPENDENT SUBJUNCTIVES

My main account of subjunctive conditionals is now complete. Let us now consider, within the subjunctive framework, how dependent conditionals differ from independent ones (§7), and decide what to do about this.

As I noted in §69, various special features of subjunctive conditionals are not possessed by the subclass of them that are 'independent' in my sense. That is because the truth of an independent subjunctive does not depend on any particular facts about how things stand at α. If A>C is logically true, its truth comes from C's obtaining at *all the A-worlds*; if causally true, on C's obtaining at *all the causally possible A-worlds*; if morally true, on C's being judged to apply at *all the A-worlds*. In none of the three cases does the truth of the conditional involve its being variably strict (§67).

That is why independent subjunctive conditionals do not afford counterexamples to the 'classical' logical principles such as Antecedent Strengthening and Transitivity; and do not raise any of the lovely problems about what exactly closeness is—problems that have occupied Chapters 11–15.

Should we conclude from all this that when A>C is an independent conditional, the closest-A-world kind of analysis that I have been presenting does not apply to it? For example, should we conclude that when A entails C, what A>C means is that A entails C, or that C obtains at all the A-worlds? This would introduce a certain disunity into our account of subjunctive conditionals; and we should consider whether that price is worth paying for whatever it brings us. This question runs parallel to one I discussed regarding independent indicative conditionals in §62, and some of the present discussion will echo that earlier one.

Someone who thinks that independent subjunctives have a special meaning will have to choose: A>C conventionally means that A entails C if (1) the speaker thinks that A entails C, or (2) A does entail C, or (3) both of the above. I shall not linger on the choice amongst these, because nothing is gained by accepting any of them. We encounter no special difficulties if we suppose the analysis of A>C to be the same for these 'entailment' cases as it is for subjunctive conditionals generally. Even when A entails C and you know it does, your statement A>C can perfectly well mean that C obtains at all the closest A-worlds—that is, at each member of a set of A-worlds each of which is closer to α than any A-world at which C does not obtain. This will be true because in fact C obtains at all the A-worlds, close or not; but there is no good reason to suppose that A>C says that this is so. We can quite well take it as meaning something about the closest A-worlds, though the entailment makes the closeness constraint idle.

This holds good even when A is itself contrary to law. If such an A logically entails C, then every A-world is a C-world; all these worlds are illegal (that is, they infringe the causal laws of α); but because C obtains at *all* of them, we can judge the conditional to be true without having to sort out some illegal worlds as closer to α than others. This is why logically true subjunctives are impossibility-tolerant. Other subjunctives are impossibility-intolerant just because we have no objective, agreed standards for closeness-to-α among worlds none of which obeys the causal laws of α.

The story is essentially the same for morally independent subjunctive conditionals. If he had tortured someone purely for the fun of it, he would have acted badly: he acts badly at every world, and *a fortiori* at every closest world, at which he tortures someone purely for fun.

For causally independent subjunctive conditionals things go slightly differently. If that particle had been a light year from Calgary at time T, it would not have been in Calgary a month later; for this we look not to all worlds but to all that obey the causal laws of α. But this again is a simple matter, involving none of the complexities that come in when some legal worlds have to be declared closer than some others.

16

Subjunctive Conditionals and Probability

96. UNWANTED FALSITY

Throughout six chapters I have gradually presented a theory about the truth conditions for subjunctive conditionals, without commenting on the fact that according to this theory we are seldom entitled to be even moderately confident that a given counterfactual conditional is true. For A>C to be true, the theory demands that C be true at *all* the closest A-worlds; and we hardly ever have good reason to believe this about counterfactuals that we favour and would like to call true. There are two reasons for this.

(1) One of them obtains if, but only if, the actual world is indeterministic. Consider a false proposition A pertaining to some past time T_A, and suppose we have selected a T_A-closest world. I mean by that: a unique world-segment S_A that ends at T_A and is the best candidate for the role of 'T_A-ending segment of a closest A-world'. If α is not deterministic, then S_A is not deterministic either, and so it has many causally possible futures. This means that it is the initial stage of an infinity of worlds that are unalike in respect of their states at later times. I shall call these complete worlds the 'extensions' of S_A. We can loosely think of S_A as a *temporal part of* each of its extensions; or, staying faithful to the idea of a world as a complete state of affairs, or a maximal consistent proposition (§64), S_A is a *conjunct in* each of its extensions.

Now consider A>C, where C is a proposition which is, at segment S_A at time T_A, probable but not inevitable. This implies that C obtains at most but not quite all of the extensions of S_A. On the analysis of subjunctive conditionals that I have defended up to here, A>C is false in this case. If the closeness of A-worlds is judged by their states up to T_A, then no AC-world can be accounted a closest A-world, because some $A\bar{C}$-worlds are equally close.

I am guessing that α's indeterministic nature has the result that many of the upshots that we confidently think of as inevitable are not really so, but are merely enormously probable. If this is right, we risk finding—or at least being obliged to accept—that hardly any of our favourite counterfactuals are true, except for independent ones. There is virtually always some tiny chance that our procedures (and our world) pick out a world-segment at which the obtaining of C is overwhelmingly probable but not quite inevitable. The Lewis-type analysis that I have been approving speaks of *all* the closest A-worlds, so it demands perfect inevitability.

(2) Even if determinism holds at α and thus at all closest A-worlds, we may seldom have reason to think that A>C is true according to our theory. Granted, no one world-segment is (given determinism) the initial stage of several legal worlds that differ in their states at later times. But what are the chances that our A suffices to pick out a unique world-segment? I have generally written as though A and C were fully determinate propositions, but they are never so. When we entertain counterfactuals in our daily lives we do it with sentences that lack detail, so that many different world-segments may qualify as initial segments of a closest A-world. For example, 'If I had thrown this brick at it, the window would have broken'; there are trillions of trillions of closest Throw-worlds, and indeed of Throw-world-*moments*, because of the different possible times, trajectories, and velocities of the throw, and orientations of the brick. Now, there may be one mixture of time, trajectory, velocity, and orientation such that if the brick had been thrown exactly *thus* it would have passed through the window without breaking it, this being the upshot of an astronomically improbable set of relationships between the brick's atoms and the window's. (For more on this see the discussion of determinist statistical mechanics in Elga 2000.) According to the unrevised theory, Throw > Break is false because C does not obtain at *all* the closest A-worlds.

Unwanted falsity will enter the picture when, among a multitude of acceptable forks leading to A, a stray few do not lead on to C's obtaining. But those ramps will lead to different world states at T_A from the others; if they didn't, we would have action at a temporal distance—that is, differences at T_F causing differences at T_C without causing differences at the intermediate time T_A. So troubles from forks are a subset of the troubles from coarse or undetailed antecedents, not additional to them.

Troubles from coarse antecedents are serious. If an ice cube were dropped into boiling water, you could safely bet on its melting within a few seconds; but its remaining ice-cold for several minutes is not physically impossible, merely astronomically improbable. So at some of the closest worlds where the ice is dropped in the water, it does not rapidly melt; and so Dropped > Melt is false according to our theory. All this can be rerun in terms of the possibility that an ice cube should be formed spontaneously in a pot of boiling water. Given that such things are possible, how can we be sure of any of the appeals to inevitability that we are tempted to make in defence of our favourite counterfactuals?

The first source—actual indeterminism—is probably serious too. Whether it really is so depends on the extent to which the indeterminism which is said to exist at the quantum level shows up at the macro level at which we formulate most of our counterfactuals. Not how far it *can* show up; how far it *does*. I am not entitled to an opinion on this.

97. HOW PROBABILITY COMES INTO THIS

So it can happen (1) that A pinpoints a unique world-segment, which can legally continue in different ways, a few of which do not involve C's obtaining; or (2) that A throws a net over a number of world-segments (each with a unique legal continuation), a few of which do not continue to C's obtaining.

Two kinds of probability are involved here; both are objective, but one is absolute, the other relative (§20). We should pause to get clear about this, before moving on to consider remedies for the trouble.

The trouble arising from (1) determinism is a simple matter of *absolute probability*. We evaluate A>C by considering the closest A-worlds; we find a uniquely closest world-segment S_A terminating at T_A; but we have to accept that at some worlds whose initial segments match S_A, the probability at T_A that C will obtain later is < 1. At any of those worlds it is true to say, even after the obtaining or non-obtaining of C is past, settled, 'The probability that C was going to obtain was, at T_A, high but < 1'.

The second source of unwanted-falsity does not involve absolute probability; it can exist at a deterministic world, where the only absolute probabilities are 0 and 1. In 2 we have *relative probability*. It does not confront us with an actual or possible reality which could unfold *thus,* and could unfold *so,* with each unfolding having a certain absolute objective probability or chance. Rather, we have a proposition, the antecedent A, and the probability that a given world will be a C-world *given that it is a closest A-world*. Even if every world-segment (up to T_A) that A selects has only one legal continuation, it may be that a tiny proportion of the worlds that A selects are $\bar{C}$-worlds. Of any world at all, therefore, we can say that the probability of its being a C-world, *given that it is a closest A-world*, is very high but < 1.

In many contexts, absolute and relative probability are horses of different colours, which is how I treated them in §20; but in our present context they will run in a single harness. All we need for that is to avail ourselves of the crucial idea in John Bigelow's 1976*b* analysis of probability in terms of relative numbers of worlds. Let us equate

The probability at time T_A at world segment S_A of C's coming to obtain is n ÷ m

with

Of all the legal continuations of S_A, the ratio of those at which C comes to obtain to those at which it does not is n ÷ m.

And let us equate

The probability that C obtains at a given world, given that A is true about it, is n ÷ m

with

Of all the worlds of which A is true, the ratio of those at which C comes to obtain to those at which it does not is n ÷ m.

Then for our problem of unwanted falsity we can give a single account which holds for its sources in absolute and in relative probability. Either way, we are threatened with wanting to endorse A>C, to call it true, when we ought to believe that *a small proportion of the closest A-worlds are not C-worlds.*

I could have said this at the start; but I thought it better to confront the diversity of sources of the trouble before going on to unify them through the idea of size-comparisons between classes of worlds. I shall return to the latter idea in §101.

98. ONE SOLUTION: THE NEAR-MISS PROPOSAL

One remedy for the problem of unwanted falsity is to weaken the truth conditions for subjunctive conditionals, ruling that A>C counts as true if

The number of closest A-worlds at which C obtains ÷ the number at which it does not obtain is high enough.

This, which covers both the sources of the unwanted-falsity threat, proposes that we count A>C as true if C obtains at an astronomically high proportion of the closest A-worlds.

In adopting this near-miss proposal, as I call it, we save ourselves from having to call false many (perhaps most) of the subjunctive conditionals we ordinarily regard as true. The proposal draws support from the fact (as I believe it to be) that most people, having asserted A>C and been challenged because of the vanishingly small but real probability of ¬C at the closest A-worlds, would impatiently dismiss this as irrelevant to what they had meant.

The near-miss proposal would weaken the meaning of A>C, but let us be clear about what weakening it is. It does not count as sufficient for the truth of A>C what we would otherwise count as sufficient only for the high probability of A>C. On the contrary, we are trying to confer truth on statements which we might otherwise have to reject as *certainly false*. The near-miss idea is not that we retreat from certainty to probability, but rather that we back away from a non-probabilistic reading that makes the conditionals false, towards a probabilistic one that makes them true. Nothing is said about the probabilities of conditionals.

In §73 I contended that a 'might'-conditional A $>_m$ C is true just in case A>¬C is false. If we combine that with the near-miss proposal, we get the result that just as it has become easier for A>C to be true, it has now become harder for A $>_m$ C to be so. For we shall now reject 'If A were the case, C might be the case' if the probability of an A-world's being a C-world is *nearly* zero. In the old days rejection demanded zero. (For a different handling of this matter, which I do not agree with but shall not discuss, see Lewis 1986d: 63–5.)

However, the near-miss proposal needs repair. According to it, A>C is true if C obtains at an enormously high proportion of the closest A-worlds; so A>C can be true when A is true and C false. That will be so when something almost unthinkably improbable actually happens, putting α into the tiny minority. For example, I say 'If the lead plates were to be inserted at T_A, the radiation would stop getting through by T_C'; the near-miss proposal counts this as true, because at quintillions of closest Insert-worlds the radiation stops getting through by T_C, and at only a few dozen does it not do so. But right here at the actual world the plates are inserted at T_A and, improbably, the radiation does not stop by T_C. We should all agree that T>F = F absolutely; so in the case described, my conditional is false. Our revision led to a theory implying that it is true, so it must be wrong.

Given that there are vastly many closest A-worlds at the vast majority of which C comes to obtain, does it follow that A>C is true? The answer we are pushed towards is:

If α belongs to the majority, Yes.

If α does not belong to the majority, No.

We can accept placidly this wrinkle in the analysis. It is expectable that the conceptual structures we use in subjunctive conditionals should make a special case of the actual world. The best way to express this is probably just to announce first that T>F = F with no exceptions; and then to offer the rest of the account as true subject to this constraint.

One item that would be constrained by it is the thesis I called Home from Abroad (§93): *if A and C are both true then A>C is true just in case it is so at the closest Ā-worlds.* We now find that this cannot be accepted just as it stands. At Ā-worlds, the only way to evaluate A>C is through probabilities; so at the closest Ā-worlds A>C is judged to be true—by near-miss standards—if at α it is overwhelmingly probable at time T_A that C will ensue. But that is consistent with C's improbably turning out to be false at α, in which case we should judge A>C to be false. We need, therefore, to pass the wrinkle along to Home from Abroad also.

If the proportion of C̄-worlds amongst the closest A-worlds is large enough to be appreciable, we should not call A>C true, though we may say that if A had obtained C would probably or almost certainly have obtained. In such a statement, probability governs the consequent, not the whole conditional. Strictly speaking, to say that (1) probably A>C is to say it is probable that C obtains at all (or in the near-miss version, at all but a tiny proportion) of the closest A-worlds. This could be all right too, but it must be sharply distinguished from (2) C's really obtaining at most of the closest A-worlds. Either could be true while the other was false.

Thus, probability relates to subjunctives differently from how it does to indicatives. Our Adams-based analysis does not distinguish A → Probably-C from Probably (A→C): it treats these as equivalent because each assigns a high value to $\pi(C/A)$ and does nothing else. I tacitly equated them throughout my discussion of indicatives, and this did not call for comment because there was no strain in it. That fact is further evidence for (NTV) the thesis that indicative conditionals lack truth values and are in that sense not propositions. If they were propositions, it could not be the case that Probably (A→C) is equivalent to A → Probably-C. That we *can* distinguish those two for > shows that A>C is a proposition with a truth value.

Admittedly, we often find it natural to say things like 'There's only a small chance that if he had entered the lottery he would have won', and 'It's 50% likely that if he had tossed the coin it would have come down heads'. In remarks like these, *the speaker* means something of the form A > (P(C) = n)—if the antecedent were true, the consequent would have a certain probability; yet *the sentence he utters* means something of the form P(A>C) = n. According to me, these have different meanings. When we use one to mean the other we employ a usage that is idiomatic but not strictly correct.

99. A MORE RADICAL SOLUTION: DROP TRUTH

Having carefully protected the turf of subjunctives that are *true*, either strictly or by the near-miss standard, I shall now state the case for an alternative view. Most of the reasons for it were given to me by Dorothy Edgington, though the formulations are partly mine.

Forget the strict-standard true subjunctives; there are virtually none of them, and we hardly ever know which they are. With them out of the way, we can drop truth from our repertoire of evaluations of subjunctive conditionals. Our concern will always be with facts about what would have been probable if A had obtained, and there is now no longer any point in picking out a subclass of these—ones where the probability is high enough—and dubbing the conditional in question 'true'. Once strict-standard truth is banished, the concept of near-miss truth becomes pointless.

We are left, then, with a spectrum of propositions of the form $A > (P(C) = n)$, with values of n ranging from ≈ 0 to ≈ 1. We can think about these, and decide which of them meet which of our needs or interests, without listening for a *click!* as we reach a value of n that is high enough to entitle us to call the conditional 'true'. Among other advantages of dropping the near-miss proposal is that we thereby spare ourselves the embarrassing question 'How high is "high enough"?'

Also, we now need not apologize for things we say about the probabilities of subjunctive conditionals. When truth disappeared from this region of thought and talk, it took probability of truth with it; so now we can *comfortably* say 'There is a 50 per cent chance that if I had tossed the coin it would have fallen heads', meaning by this that if I had tossed the coin there would have been a 50 per cent chance of its falling heads. We do not have to admit, apologetically, that the sentence strictly means something different, namely that there is a 50 per cent chance of its being true that if I had tossed the coin it would have fallen heads. With probability of truth off the scene, such locutions need not be explained or apologized for.

In assessing the virtues of this drop-truth proposal, as I call it, bear in mind that many subjunctive conditionals that we would ordinarily regard as *acceptable* would not pass the near-miss standard for truth. Without having specified how near is near enough (because I have no idea of how to), I have implied that near-miss 'truth' belongs only to conditionals whose chances of falsity are like the chance that an ice cube should form spontaneously in a flask of hot water. For convenience of discussion, I shall suppose that near-miss truth for $A>C$ kicks in when the probability of a closest A-world's being a C-world is 0.999999 or higher. Now, plenty of conditionals strike us as acceptable—worth asserting, communicating, and taking seriously—although in them the probability of a closest A-world's being a C-world is lower than that. I should guess that vastly many of the subjunctive conditionals that we accept fall well short of the near-miss standard for truth that I have proposed; they have probabilities of going wrong that we recognize as such; they are not probabilities that come within our ken only through instruction by experts on statistical mechanics. The drop-truth proposal gives us a comfortable way of fitting these conditionals into our scheme of things; they are simply ones that are high on a continuum on which lie all the subjunctive conditionals that interest us.

Objection: 'When A logically or causally or morally implies C, *every* closest A-world is indeed a C-world. Those conditionals, at least, raise no problem of elusive truth or unwanted falsity; so the drop-truth proposal has no excuse for snubbing them.' I reply that such independent conditionals are not interesting uses of the conditional form, are bad guides to theory, and deserve to be snubbed.

100. WHY DROP-TRUTH DOES NOT MATTER MUCH

I have done my best for the proposal that we banish the notion of truth for subjunctives as for indicatives, and treat the asserting, accepting, disputing, and communicating of subjunctive conditionals entirely in terms of probabilities. I am strongly inclined to accept the drop-truth proposal, because the case for it is good, and there is little to be said against it.

It has no big theoretical consequences. In particular, it does not imply that any part of our exploration of subjunctive conditionals, in Chapters 10–15 and 18–19, is wasted labour. Even if we accept the drop-truth proposal, and let our evaluations be guided always (except for the wrinkle) by the probability that a closest A-world is a C-world, this cannot happen in a disciplined, controlled manner unless we have explored closeness, seen the need for forks, wrestled with future particular facts, and so on.

Furthermore, although accepting the drop-truth proposal might make our informal talk using subjunctive conditionals sound more like talk with indicatives, it does not narrow the theoretical gap between the two kinds of conditional. Here is why.

One reason for dropping truth for indicative conditionals was that we could find no way of according truth values to them. It was not the case that we had a clear notion of what it would be for F→C to be true, but relinquished it because too few conditionals answered to it. The objective truth value of F→C was not difficult to instantiate; rather, it was impossible to conceive. We could not have the idea of it even as a *focus imaginarius* for our thoughts.

In contrast with that, we have a fairly clear idea of what it would be for a subjunctive to be true by the strictest Lewis-type standard. We can set out the theoretical requirements for truth, without using any probability concept. Even if in practice we cannot formulate any conditionals satisfying those requirements, we can use them as guides, and see our actual performances as slight softenings of them.

Dorothy Edgington makes the drop-truth proposal in the course of a project of narrowing the gap between indicatives and subjunctives (§141). The terms in which she offers the proposal, however, debar it from supporting the narrowing project: '. . . Counterfactuals are best evaluated probabilistically. A true/false cut-off point would not serve us well' (2003). This doubly expresses a *preference* for handling subjunctives in terms of probability, a judgement that this would be *better*; but such a handling of indicatives is not merely preferable—it is the only workable way of evaluating them.

As well as being unable to devise credible truth conditions for indicative conditionals, we have encountered four lines of argument for the denial that such conditionals always have truth values. Let us ask whether those apply also to subjunctives.

I start with the sharp little argument of Edgington's that I applauded in §41—the best of a cluster of similar ones. Its premisses are these:

(a) Being certain that A∨C, without being certain that A, is sufficient for being certain that ¬A→C.

(b) It is not necessarily irrational to disbelieve A yet also disbelieve that A→C.

Replace → by > in these, and *b* remains true but *a* becomes false. (I am certain that either I lent the book to Guy or I lent it to Sara; I am pretty sure, though not certain, that I lent it to Guy; I am far from certain that if I hadn't lent it to Guy I would have lent it to Sara.) So this argument does not put pressure on us to deny truth values to subjunctive conditionals, nor do any of its near kin.

Formidable arguments, reported in Chapter 5, count against the Equation:

$$P(A{\to}C) = \pi(C/A).$$

The Equation could escape those attacks, finally, only through a denial that $P(A{\to}C)$ is the probability of a proposition; which led to our treating $P(A{\to}C) = n$ as the most basic kind of thing to be said about an indicative conditional, denying that A→C has a truth value, and so on. But nothing like the Equation holds for subjunctive conditionals. I am pretty sure that if I had not become a philosopher, I would have become a physician; but if I add 'I did not become a philosopher' to my belief system, suitably adjusting to make room for it, the result is not a high probability for 'I became a physician'. Clear evidence for this comes from the fact that subjunctives include in their meanings a permission to with-draw, suspend, or deny them if the antecedent turns out to be true (§88). So the argument from Lewis-type triviality proofs counts against truth values for A→C but not for A>C.

The third line of argument comes from the existence of Gibbardian stand-offs between some pairs of indicative conditionals (§34). The members of a stand-off pair contradict one another, so they cannot both be true; they are equally satis-factory, each from its author's point of view, so neither is false; and the only alternative is to say that neither has an objective truth value, the value of each lying in the reasonableness of the subjective probability it expresses. Not every indicative conditional can enter into a stand-off; but if many can do so, and there-fore do not have truth values, it will not be easy to find a way of conferring truth values on the rest. This is why the existence of stand-offs provides some reason for (NTV) the thesis that F→C never has a truth value.

Edgington (1995b: 294–6) has adduced examples in which, she says, one per-son's A>C and another's A>¬C are equally good: neither false, but not both true either. If there are such stand-offs between subjunctive conditionals, this provides at least some reason for thinking that all subjunctives lack truth val-ues. Her examples of this, however, have all involved conditionals of a margin-al and uninteresting sort that I cheerfully relinquish to any philosopher who wants to spend time on them. They are conditionals that are evaluated in the *direct* manner, with no thought of what leads to A at the closest A-worlds— 'That's a diamond; if it were a ruby it would be red'. I shall discuss these in §113, where I shall bring out how greatly they differ from subjunctive condi-tionals of the history-involving sort—ones that seriously consider how the world would have unfolded if A had obtained.

Adam Morton (1997) challenged Edgington on this matter, and invited her—in effect—to look at her stand-off subjunctives in the history-involving rather than in the directly evaluated way. She has done so (Edgington 1997b: 112–13), contending that even when possible histories for antecedents are taken into account, the stand-off she described still remains. She undertakes to 'apply Lewis's proposed criteria of closeness' to the case under discussion, and to show that with various stories about what goes on at the closest A-worlds, the Lewisian way of resolving the stand-off involves questionable judgements. The whole exercise, she concludes, counts against Lewis's theory rather than against the possibility of a stand-off between counterfactuals.

In arguing for this, Edgington rightly says that a stand-off cannot be resolved by different sizes of small miracles, or by relatively small differences in lateness of fork (§83). But her treatment of the case where one relevant fork is very much later than another seems to me perfunctory, and more dismissive than it earns any right to be. I do not think it should convert us from the reasons I gave in §83 for taking lateness of fork to bear upon closeness of world.

Also, why in the given example are the conflicting subjunctive conditionals not both false? When Edgington turns briefly to this (p. 114) she seems to return to direct evaluations.

The fourth argument for NTV is the one of Richard Bradley's that I reported in §41. One premiss of that is that it is never right to give a probability > 0 to A and to A→C while giving a probability = 0 for C. It would be absurd to think that there may be rain in the desert this month, and that if there is rain in the desert this month there may be a good display of flowers, but that there is no chance of there being a good display of flowers. The subjunctive analogue of this is patently wrong. I give a tiny positive probability to my having walked in my sleep last night, and to the proposition that if I had walked in my sleep I would have had a fatal accident; but I give a zero probability to my having had a fatal accident last night.

There are our five sources of pressure towards NTV for indicative conditionals: four arguments, and our inability to formulate credible truth conditions. None of the five applies to subjunctives; which means that the drop-truth proposal for them, though a reasonable way of managing some of the data, has no tendency to make them in any deep way like indicatives.

Whether the chasm between the two kinds of conditional can be partly or wholly closed by other considerations will be the topic of the last two sections of this book.

101. CLUMPING

Whichever way we jump with regard to the drop-truth proposal, we need to be able to assign probabilities to subjunctive conditionals and/or to their antecedents. I have treated these as ratios between numbers of worlds: the value of n in $A > (P(C) = n)$ is given by the proportion of all the closest A-worlds that are C-worlds, or so I have suggested.

However, if there are infinitely many closest A-worlds, these numerical ratios may not be available. Although it seems intuitively obvious that there are more even numbers than primes, we can pair the evens off with the primes, one for one, with no remainder on either side; which means that by the only clear criterion of equal numberedness that we have, there are as many primes as evens. By that criterion, $N + 1 = N$ for any infinite N. This is not a contradiction, or even an oddity; it is merely a partial definition of 'infinite'.

An unequal split can be performed if one of the subclasses is finite. It is not just intuitively plausible but sternly true that there are more primes than there are even numbers $< 10^{10}$. In the context of our present investigation, however, we have no reason to think that such infinite/finite splits will be available. You might think they are available across the whole range of the unwanted falsity problem: in contrast with the infinitely many closest worlds at which I throw this brick at that window which then breaks, perhaps (you may think or hope) there are just a few dozens or hundreds or millions at which I throw the brick in a special way that enables it to pass through the window without breaking it. Even if this were right, it would not meet all our needs; for we want probability for more purposes than just to discuss unwanted falsity.

And, anyway, the reason why there may be infinitely many closest Throw-worlds altogether is equally a reason why they divide into infinitely many Break-worlds and infinitely many Nonbreak-worlds. The reason comes from the thought of space as infinitely divisible, so that any thinkable proposition about a thing's moving in a certain manner can be subdivided into infinitely many stronger propositions, specifying its movements to ever larger numbers of decimal places; and if that can be done for the range of movements in which the brick shatters the window, it can also be done for the range of movements in which it slips through the window harmlessly.

That may be the whole source of the trouble. That is, it may be that whenever two closest A-worlds differ in a manner that interests or concerns us, they differ only in the locations and movements of things in space, or in ways that supervene on such differences. If that is so, our infinity trouble is easily remediable. If space and time are granular rather than continuous, the solution is notably easy and obvious. At the root of it is the finitude, after all, of the number of possible worlds.

Even retaining continuity of space-time and infinity of worlds, we can solve the problem. Put the worlds in question into *clumps* on this basis: w_1 and w_2 belong to a single clump only if the whole unalikeness between them consists in, or supervenes on, differences of less than n in where some particulars are at some time. Set n as small as you like—perhaps 10^{-10} cm. It needs to be small enough so that differences of less than n are irrelevant to our concerns and interests. However small that is, it suffices to replace an infinity of worlds by a finite set of clumps of worlds. Then the probabilities of subjunctive conditionals or of their antecedents can be understood in terms of comparative sizes of sets of clumps.

That account of clumping is rough and ready, but I think it should satisfy you that the infinity problem is soluble. For more careful and thorough assaults on it, see Bigelow 1976b or Bennett 1996: 92–6.

17
'Even If . . .'

102. 'EVEN': PRELIMINARIES

The literature includes work on the semantics of conditionals that use 'Even if', such as 'Even if you ask me on bended knees, I won't marry you'. The first philosopher to attend to 'Even if . . .' conditionals, so far as I know, was Pollock (1976: 29–31). He treats them as one species of conditional, and seeks to give their truth conditions. Much of his labour on this has to do with how to evaluate A>C when C is true (§§91–3). I shall not resume that topic. My present concern with Pollock focuses on his statement that the subjunctive 'Even if A, C' is true only if C is true, so that in saying 'Even if channels were to be cut into the dam, the village would be safe' one asserts, among other things, that the village will be safe.

Here is a conditional—with some scene-setting—which makes that plausible:

She's going to fire him. If he carries on as in the past she'll fire him; if he becomes more punctual, polite and accurate, she'll fire him; (1) *Even if he were to perform perfectly, she would fire him.*

However, Lewis offered examples like the following as evidence against Pollock's thesis:

If she has any reason to think he is not a teetotaler, she'll fire him. (2) *Even if he were to drink just a little, she would fire him.*

Conditional 2 in the context I have given it does not entail or even suggest the truth of the consequent. Pollock gives 2 the back of his hand, saying: 'We are not attempting to analyze all possible uses of "even if". We are merely analyzing what is in some sense "the standard use" of "even if"' (p. 31). But 2 is perfectly 'standard', and the difference between it and 1 is straightforward. I shall explain it in this chapter.

Pollock took 'Even if' to be an idiom—understanding it as a single semantic lump, rather than as an upshot of the separate meanings of 'even' and of 'if'. (Like

Lewis's treatment of 'If . . . might . . .'—see §73 and §8.) Nobody who has worked on 'even if' in recent years takes it to be an idiom.

Strictly speaking, then, a treatise on conditionals need not discuss 'even' at all, any more than a theory of time and tense needs to attend separately to 'even when'. Still, the present chapter may serve as prophylaxis against mistakes relating to 'even if'. The linguists have worked hard and long on 'even [if]', and I have not absorbed their results. However, I gather from Dancygier 1998: 160–7 that there is a consensus amongst them on at least some of the points I shall be defending.

Among philosophers, a start on getting straight about this was made by Hazen and Slote (1979); I took the story further, writing in culpable ignorance of their work (1982); and Lycan (1991) made yet further progress, partly building on my work though also dissenting from some of it; papers by Barker (1991, 1994) have thrown more light still, in relation to Lycan's work and mine but also rejecting parts of each.

103. LYCAN'S ACCOUNT

Lycan starts by comparing 'even' with 'only'. Each word is what he calls a 'floater': it can occur in many positions in a sentence, each bringing a difference in 'focus' (as the linguists call it). For example:

(1) Only the goats graze on the hillside in the afternoons.
(2) The goats only graze on the hillside in the afternoons.
(3) The goats graze only on the hillside in the afternoons.
(4) The goats graze on the hillside only in the afternoons.

The meanings are different: 1 focuses on the goats (not the sheep), 2 on grazing (not sleeping), 3 on the hillside (not the valley floor), 4 on the afternoons (not the mornings). Many people would use 2 to mean what 4 properly means, and the context would save them from misunderstanding. Sometimes, indeed, the correct placing of 'only'—as of 'even'—can sound a little pedantic. Still, any literate person will agree with me about what is strictly correct, and thus about the proper focus of 'only' in 2.

Now, the word 'even' has the same range of positions, with corresponding differences of focus. Thus:

(1) Even the goats graze on the hillside in the afternoons.
(2) The goats even graze on the hillside in the afternoons.
(3) The goats graze even on the hillside in the afternoons.
(4) The goats graze on the hillside even in the afternoons.

I think you will agree, before hearing detailed explanations, that these differ in meaning because the word 'even' somehow acts in 1 on 'the goats', in 2 on 'graze', in 3 on 'on the hillside', and in 4 on 'in the afternoons'.

This likeness of 'even' to 'only' has long been familiar, but Lycan was the first to turn it to account in an original and illuminating way. Given that 'only' is a quantifier, he conjectures that 'even' is also a quantifier, or at least that it 'reflects a universal quantifier in logical form' (1991: 132). In his 2001 book Lycan proposes a slightly different account from that of the 1991 article; but all the features I shall discuss are the same in both.

Lycan starts from this fact: when we use a universal quantifier, its range is tacitly restricted by the context or by a mutual understanding between speaker and hearers. 'Why aren't you going to the baseball game? Everyone else is going.' This does not mean that every other person in the universe is going, but everyone in some roughly understood group. Sometimes there may be a misunderstanding about the range of the quantifier, as when I say to you 'Michael has always admired Nietzsche', meaning to generalize over times since Michael first heard of Nietzsche (fifty years), and you wrongly think I am talking only about times since he became a philosopher (forty years). Anticipating such a misunderstanding, I might continue '... and that includes his years as a schoolboy'. Similarly, someone might say 'Every Catholic rejects papal infallibility now', and then clarify the intended range of his quantifier by saying '... and that includes the priests'.

Now, either of those clarifications could have been expressed using 'even'. 'Michael has always admired Nietzsche, even when he was a schoolboy.' 'Every Catholic rejects papal infallibility now, even the priests.' What about statements in which 'even' occurs without being prefaced by a clause using 'always' or 'every' or the like? According to Lycan, such statements do themselves mean something universally quantified. He would say that the unadorned 'Even the priests reject papal infallibility' means something along the lines of 'Everybody rejects ... etc., and that includes the priests'. By the same reasoning, (1) 'Even the goats graze on the hillside' means 'Everything (in some envisaged group) grazes on the hillside, and that includes the goats'; and (2) 'The goats even graze on the hillside' means 'The goats do everything (in some envisaged class of activities) on the hillside, and that includes grazing'. Similarly with 3 and 4.

Barker's 1991 paper appeared just three months earlier; evidently it and Lycan's owed nothing to one another. Barker's account of 'even' is basically like Lycan's, minus the comparison with 'only'. Barker stipulates that what is being asserted (minus 'even') is 'an extreme instance' of the relevant universal quantification. Lycan does not say this, but something like it follows from his account.

Whenever there is a point in saying explicitly that the focus item (the one referred to by the focus of 'even') is included, this must be because hearers might otherwise understand the quantifier to exclude it; so the focus item must be thought of as near the edge of the quantifier's likely range, and in that sense to be an extreme instance.

Despite its elegant handling of many cases, the Barker–Lycan account fails for others. Plenty of relevant occurrences of 'even' do not involve universal quantification, even implicitly:

> 'How was the Brahms?' 'Pretty good, I guess. Otto was ecstatic. Even Ben quite liked it.'

> 'Isn't it too late in the season for swimming in the sea?' 'No. I'm going to swim today. I may swim even tomorrow.'

(Or, to avoid sounding pedantic, 'I may even swim tomorrow'.) There are countless such examples, and the Barker–Lycan approach cannot lay a finger on them, so far as I can see. This trouble of theirs seems to be irremediable.

What, then, should we do with the comparison of 'even' with 'only'? Before we just walk out on it, we should note that other words also come into this comparison. 'Other floaters', Lycan writes, 'are *just* . . . , *at least/most, maybe, too*, and *also*. Notice that all have reasonably clear quantificational or otherwise referential values' (Lycan 1991: 134 n. 16). Are we to dismiss all of this as irrelevant to the semantics of 'even'?

Yes. I believe it to be a mere historical accident of our language, and in no way necessary, that (nearly) all of our one-word floaters involve something quantificational. We do have other floaters that are not 'quantificational or referential'. In each member of the 'even' series about the goats, remove 'even' and after its focus insert '(I'm afraid)':

> The goats (I'm afraid) graze on the hillside in the afternoons,
> The goats graze (I'm afraid) on the hillside . . .

and so on. Also 'I'm proud to announce', 'You'll be sorry/glad to hear', and so on. Unlike Lycan's favourite floaters, however, these need commas or parentheses, and that may disqualify them from the comparison I am offering, because it may show that 'they are discourse markers of some sort rather than genuine constituents of the sentences "in" which they occur' (Lycan 2001: 110).

Well, then, consider the role of spoken emphasis, or of the written equivalent, namely italics and a terminal exclamation mark:

The goats graze on the hillside in the afternoons!

The goats *graze* on the hillside in the afternoons!

The goats graze *on the hillside* in the afternoons!

The goats graze on the hillside *in the afternoons*!

In these, the effect of the italics (aided by the exclamation mark) is to express some kind of surprise or impressment about the role of the focus item in the entire truth that is expressed. So does 'even', but it means more than that, so that in some cases where italics would be appropriate 'even' would not. I submit that it is a mere accident that English does not have a single word with exactly the same significance as emphasis/italics, doing a part of what 'even' now does. Then that word and 'only' would also be 'syntactic soul-mates', but it would be obvious that one was a quantifier and the other not. In the light of all this, we should not be flustered by the idea that although most English one-word floaters have something quantificational in their meaning, 'even' does not.

104. AMENDING BENNETT'S 1982 ACCOUNT

My 1982 paper came at things differently. The core of it, now slightly amended, consists of two technicalities and a little doctrine.

Given any sentence S containing 'even', used in the manner I am concerned with, a *simplified* sentence S* can be formed by dropping 'even' from S. Thus, if S is 'Even the children laughed at him' then S* is 'The children laughed at him'.

S has countless 'neighbours', as I call them. A neighbour of S is a proposition that could naturally be expressed, at least approximately, by a sentence formed out of S* by an operation on (Focus) that part that constituted the focus of 'even' in S: the operation may be (1) replacing Focus by something else that yields a sentence or (2) by dropping Focus without replacing it by anything else. Examples of 1: eligible neighbours of 'Even the children laughed at him' include the propositions that everybody laughed at him, that the adults were amused by him, that his grandmother giggled at him, and so on. An example of 2: an eligible neighbour of 'Even *allegations of* conflicts of interest make him angry' could be 'Conflicts of interest make him angry'.

Now for the doctrine. When S uses 'even' in the manner we are studying, S is true if and only if S* is true; and an asserting of true S is felicitous, satisfactory, well-put, if and only if there is a neighbour P_n of S such that:

(a) P_n is true and mutually believed by speaker and hearer, and salient for them (perhaps having just been authoritatively asserted);

(b) the truth of S* and that of P_n can naturally be seen as parts of a single more general truth;

(c) it is more surprising that S* is true than that P_n is true.

I abbreviate the whole of condition *a* to 'P_n is salient', and *b* to 'P_n is related'—but remember that these are mere shorthand. Then the whole story is that S is true and happily asserted if and only if

S* is true, and
S has a neighbour that is salient, related, and less surprising.

Of the two ways in which a neighbour of S may relate to S*, the more usual one is (1) replacement of Focus by something else; but (2) the simple dropping of Focus also deserves a place in my account. Lycan mocks the account for containing it, saying that it commits me to 'compar[ing] the expectedness of allegations ... with that of nothingness' (2001: 100). It does no such thing. The needed comparison, which my account supplies, is between allegations of conflicts of interest and conflicts of interest.

Originally I took sentences as neighbours, rather than propositions. Vic Dudman warned me against this, and he was right. If the account stays with *sentences* formed according to my recipe—replace the focus of 'even' by something else in S*—it does not cover such innocent examples as this: 'The children laughed themselves sick. Even the adults were amused.' In that context the difference between 'laughed themselves sick' and 'were amused' is nugatory, and I have stopped my account from implying otherwise by moving from 'sentence' to 'proposition'. I should add that the salient proposition need not be openly asserted:

'Isn't it too late in the season for swimming in the sea?' 'No.' He dives into the sea, surfaces, and with shivering bravado says: 'I may even swim tomorrow.'

He gives salience to the proposition that he is swimming today, without putting it in words.

I contend that S is true if S* is true. The further constraint on the neighbour proposition is, according to me, a matter of conventional implicature as distinct from outright truth-affecting assertion (§15).

Lycan and I agree that our accounts have much in common. For 'Even Granny tried on the coat' to be all right on my account, there has to be a salient neighbour proposition that naturally combines with 'Granny tried on the coat' to form a single unified truth; and a good way to satisfy this is with a proposition about other people trying on the coat—which gives Lycan his quantification. My requirement of a single unified truth is also provided for in Lycan's account by the inclusion of Granny and the others in the scope of a single quantifier. As for my requirement that the truth of S* must be more surprising than that of P_n: Lycan's analysis provides for this too. It is reasonable to use 'even' for the Lycan purpose only if one thinks that otherwise the range of a certain quantifier might be misunderstood. When I say 'Even granny tried on the coat', rather than merely saying 'Everyone tried on the coat' and trusting you to understand Granny to be included, that should be because I could reasonably have said 'everyone' meaning to exclude Granny; so it must be somewhat surprising or notable that Granny should have tried on the coat—and more so than that the others did. This is not a special feature of this example; it applies to them all.

Barker (1991: 4–5) contends that the concept of 'more surprising' does not do the job, failing in cases where universal quantifiers succeed. He points to this exchange:

> South: 'Only three people out of a hundred won prizes. Brain and Smart won prizes, of course, but so did Smith, the worst student in the class.'
>
> North: 'Even Smith won a prize!'

This plainly infelicitous use of 'even' satisfies my conditions, Barker says, taking it that my requirement for a 'single more general truth' is satisfied by *Three of the students won a prize*. In offering my analysis I did not mean anything as feeble as that, but I am not sure what exactly I did mean. Rather than trying to stiffen that part of the analysis, therefore, I shall accept this as a counterexample to it, and agree with Barker that what is needed is something more, or something other, than mere surprisingness.

Universal quantification could provide it: what North says in that remark would be happier if there were a salient, known, neighbour proposition to the effect that *all the Fs won a prize* for some suitable F that applies to Smith. For example, *All the students with decent attendance records won a prize*. If there is a point in specifying that Smith is included, this must be for a reason that makes it especially surprising that he won a prize; so that condition is satisfied, but no longer by the mere, bare surprisingness that brought down my account.

Because it is wrong to tie 'even' to universal quantification, however, we must look further. I submit that the needed ingredient in the analysis is one Barker considers, by discussing the use of it in Fauconnier 1975, namely the notion of the focus item's *place on a scale*. Suppose the news—the neighbour proposition—was that many students won prizes because the adjudicators had reached a long way down the ability scale; against *this* background it might be reasonable to say 'Even Smith got a prize'. The simplified sentence 'Smith got a prize' says something more surprising than the neighbour proposition; but now it is the surprisingness of their having reached *that far down*, that far along the scale.

The scalar notion is also missing from another of Barker's counterexamples to my analysis:

> Looking out the window expecting to find only family members in the front yard, I see three figures and remark truly, 'There's Pa and Grandma outside and even *Ronald Reagan*!' My audience rejoins 'Even *Reagan* is outside!'

This fits my 1982 conditions for felicity, but it is a downright silly use of 'even'. What is missing, I now suggest, is a relevant scalar thought. Change the example to one where the effective neighbour proposition was that guests at my surprise party included not only my immediate family but also my nieces, nephews, cousins, colleagues, former colleagues, . . . Against this background, I could properly say 'Even Ronald Reagan was there' if, for instance, I had met Reagan a few times and occasionally worked with him on small tasks. The neighbour proposition is that the list of invitees who came to the party stretched a good distance along the remoteness-of-relationship scale; and 'even Ronald Reagan was there' reflects how far along the scale he is. Or the effective neighbour proposition might concern a scale not of closeness of relationship but rather of public importance and fame; that too could make it felicitous to say 'even Reagan was there!', however well I knew him.

My account needs, then, to be modified by strengthening

> (c) it is more surprising that S^* is true than that P_n is true

to something like this:

> (c*) both S^* and P_n involve some single scale, the focus item lies further along that scale than any items referred to in P_n, and for that reason the speaker and the hearers find it more surprising or striking or noteworthy that S^* is true than that P_n is true.

This is on the right lines, I submit. The relevant scale is not merely that of sheer surprisingness, but rather of something upon which—in the given context—surprisingness supervenes. In my first Reagan example, the scale concerns remoteness of relation to me; in the second, public importance and fame. If this is not to include the Reagan example with which Barker challenged my original account, we must deny that my immediate family and Ronald Reagan (whom I have never met or corresponded with) lie at opposite ends of a single scale of closeness of relation to me. Intuitively the denial seems all right; but I would like to support it with explicit rules for the 'scale' concept, and have not been able to devise any.

I now say 'surprising or striking or noteworthy' because 'surprising' is too narrow. 'There has not been proof of any miracle, or strong evidence for any miracle, or even prima facie evidence of any miracle'—this might be said, prop-erly enough, in a group of people none of whom is *surprised* by the final clause; but it is a more striking claim than the ones that go before—which is to say that S* is more striking than P_n—which is what my present analysis makes room for.

The analysis applies well enough to the examples I have used in this chapter. 'I shall swim today; I may even swim tomorrow'—here the focus item is tomor-row, which is lower than today on the scale of early-enough-in-the-year-for-a-swim. 'Otto was ecstatic about the Brahms. Even Ben quite liked it'—the focus item is Ben, who is lower than Otto on the scale of receptivity to Brahms. In this example, the scalar idea is somewhat recessive, but it is present all the same. To see this, consider an example from which it is absent. I hear music on the radio, I enjoy it, and have a sense that my dog enjoys it too, though I don't think the enjoyments are related. The dog, I suspect, is responding to some rhythmic features of the piece that contribute nothing to my aesthetic appreciation of it. Here it is not appropriate for me to say, except as a joke: 'I enjoyed it. Even my dog enjoyed it.' It is not the case that the music was *so attractive* that it reached not only me but the dog.

Barker's objection to the scalar approach (pp. 8–10), though it holds against the version he considers, does not apply to mine. His target version requires merely that there be a relevant scale with the focus item at one end of it; mine requires that relevant scalar fact be implied by the salient, known neighbour proposition, *and that it helps to make S* more surprising etc. than P_n.* The example that Barker uses against the scalar approach involves a scale at one end of which sits the focus item; but that fact is idle, silent, not part of anyone's thought. This does no harm to my version of the scalar approach, which requires that the neighbour proposition be seen by all concerned to involve the relevant scale.

My handling of the scalar notion differs in two other ways from the one that Barker considers. His requires that the item in the focus of 'even' be at 'the low-est point on the scale' (p. 8). I see no need for that, and nor does Lycan (2001: 120). All that is required is that it be low enough for the reported fact—that the simplified sentence is true of it—to be notable. 'They really stretched the criteria for the winning of prizes; even Smith won a prize' could be felicitous although Jones, who is stupider than Smith, also won a prize.

Also, Barker seems to inherit from Fauconnier the idea that if the simple sentence is true of the focus item then it is true of everything higher up the scale. I do not see why. In the prize-winning example, the relevant scale could be that of unworthiness (by correct standards) to win a prize; the examiners went far along that scale awarding prizes. They did so intermittently, so that plenty of lowish-level students did not win prizes. Still, in their erratic way they went pretty far down; even Smith won a prize. Here again, incidentally, universal quantification is absent.

105. 'EVEN IF . . .'

As for the two conditionals that Pollock mentioned (§102), Lycan and I tell essentially the same story about how they differ, namely in the focus of 'even'. My way of showing this was defective in some of its details, as Lycan and Barker have proved, and Delgardo (1999: 114–16) has further illustrated. I wrenched my analysis into an ugly shape through trying to make it imply that one of the two kinds of conditional entails its consequent. In this I was following Pollock's lead, which was an error. I ought not to have struggled to preserve the 'entailment of consequent' idea; my account looks more comely when not crushed under that burden of error.

On the most natural reading of it, 'Even if he were to perform perfectly, she would fire him' is true and felicitous just in case (1) If he were to perform perfectly she would fire him, and (2) Some neighbour proposition of 1—that is, something expressible in the form 'If . . . were to be the case, she would fire him' is (in my shorthand) salient, related, and less surprising because of some scalar fact. Of these, 1 is required for the conditional's truth, 2 for its felicity.

Lycan's treatment could fit the case, for the neighbour proposition might be something implying that for any value of P (within some envisaged range), if P she would fire him. But it might not fit: 'She doesn't think he is yet ready to play Hamlet, and has forbidden him to do so. If he defied her about this, she would fire him. Even if he performed perfectly, she would fire him.' That fits my analysis, not Lycan's. In countless possible scenarios—including many that fit Lycan's analysis as well as ones that fit only mine—the conditional has not the faintest appearance of entailing its own consequent—that is, entailing *She will fire him*.

Now for the other of the two conditionals with which we started: 'Even if he were to drink just a little, she would fire him.' Pollock thought that its special feature, stopping it from involving 'the standard sense' of 'even if', was that it does not entail the truth of its own consequent. In fact, as we have just seen, the other example does not do this either; the idea of entailing the consequent was an *ignis fatuus* that I followed into a swamp. Still, this second conditional differs from the other in a way that Lycan and I can describe.

On its most natural reading, the conditional would be better expressed in the form 'If he were to drink even just a little . . .', and my account deals smoothly with this. The simplified sentence is 'If he were to drink just a little, she would fire him' and the eligible neighbours are such propositions as that if he were to drink more than she does she would fire him, that if he were to drink as much as he would like to she would fire him, and so on. The given conditional is true and felicitously uttered if the simplified sentence is true, and if some neighbour proposition is salient, related, and less surprising or noteworthy because of some scalar fact.

Here again, Lycan's apparatus might be put to use: If he were to drink any (envisaged) amount she would fire him, and that includes the amount just-a-little. But it is not always available.

The two conditionals differ formally, according to both Lycan and me, in that the focus of 'even' is the whole antecedent in one, something within the antecedent in the other.

Having discussed 'even', I should mention 'still'. 'Even if he performed perfectly, she would still fire him.' 'Even if channels were cut into the dam, the village would still be safe.' We use 'still' to mark the idea of something's being the case that might naturally be thought not to be the case, given what has been said before or what is assumed in the context. This plainly fits the *OED*'s examples of sense 6 of the word: 'Ventilation would improve it, but still it would be unhealthy.' 'He is a rogue in many ways. Still, I like him.' (The same adversative idea is present, I suggest, in uses of 'still' falling under the *OED*'s sense 4—'indicating the continuation of a previous action or condition', of which it gives the example '. . . one of those harmless prejudices that still linger round the person of the sovereign'. In that example, and in general, something is said to have 'still' continued because one might have expected it to have stopped.)

The use of 'still' in subjunctive conditionals resembles that. 'Even if the dam were weakened, the village would still be safe' has the same adversative thought buried in it, because such a conditional would ordinarily be asserted only in a context where there was some thought of the antecedent's ruling out the consequent. In such uses of it, 'still' affects what is conventionally implied but not what is outright asserted: the prejudices still linger if and only if the prejudices linger; he still waited for her if and only if he waited for her.

106. TRUTH OR FELICITY?

My 1982 and present accounts of 'even' both say that for the *truth* of S (containing 'even') all that is needed is the truth of S* (that is, what you get by deleting 'even' from S), the remainder of the account bearing on felicity, not truth. Barker agrees about this: his 'remainder' differs from mine, but we agree about what it is an account *of*. Lycan, on the other hand, holds that the truth of a relevant universally quantified proposition etc. is required for the *truth* of the statement using 'even'. He is encouraged in this by the comparison between 'even' and 'only':

An *only*-sentence is true if and only if none but the mentioned member of the reference class satisfies the schema that results from deleting *only* itself and the mention, while an *even*-sentence is true if and only if every member of the reference class including the mentioned member satisfies that schema. (Lycan 1991: 135)

In short, just as the truth of 'Only Susan left' requires more than that Susan left, so does the truth of 'Even Susan left'.

This pays an intuitively high price for the bracketing of 'even' with 'only'. Suppose you are recounting a family's visit to a clothing store. You report that most members of the family tried on many garments while Granny sat in the corner and watched. You believe that everyone, including Granny, tried on the coat, but you are wrong about this: the younger girl went to the bathroom instead. In reporting the coat episode, you say: 'When it came to the coat, even Granny tried it on.' Lycan's analysis implies that this statement, under those circumstances, is *false* because the corresponding 'Everyone tried on the coat'—the proposition you had in mind, the one that fixes your 'reference class' and that you would have asserted if asked—is false. This is hard to swallow.

According to my analysis, you have in this case said something true, and indeed felicitous, although the neighbour proposition lying behind it is not quite true. My line of analysis left me free to go either way on this: the requirement for a neighbour proposition that is salient etc. could have figured either as a truth-condition or a felicity-condition; and I chose the latter because I found it intuitively more plausible. Lycan acknowledges the intuition, but rightly does not regard it as decisive. Judgements about whether a feature of an expression bears on truth or only on conventional implicature are inherently fragile, having no basis except in superficial intuitions (§15). Against the intuition, Lycan brings his comparison of 'even' with 'only'. The latter obviously affects truth-conditions, he says; and the two are so alike in so many ways that he finds it reasonable to think that 'even' does the same.

He remarks that 'few words in English can float so freely' as these two, and mentions other floaters—'just', 'at least', 'at most', 'maybe', 'too', and 'also'— and remarks on the 'quantificational or otherwise referential values' that they share (Lycan 1991: 134 n. 16). He does not say outright that each of these floaters affects truth value in the way 'only' does, but if he allows that some do not, nothing remains of his reason for his counter-intuitive view about the truth-conditions for sentences using 'even'. For then we can liken 'even' not to 'only' but rather to one of the floaters that does not affect truth values. If on the other hand Lycan lumps all floaters together in the respect we are now considering, the intuitive price rises steeply. Consider the force of 'too', which floats as 'even' and 'only' do (try it out on the grazing goats). I awake in a flowery meadow, look around, and murmur *I too am in Arcadia*; it is indeed Arcadia, but I am alone there; so Lycan must say I have spoken falsely. I do not believe it. In statements like this, I submit, 'too' affects only what is conventionally implied, not what is outright asserted, and in this respect it resembles that other floater, 'even'.

107. TWO WORDS?

Consider these two sentences:

(1) Jane is even heavier than Rita.
(2) Even Jane is heavier than Rita.

Noticing that 1 implies that Rita is heavy and Jane heavier, while 2 implies that Rita is light and Jane heavier, some people have wondered by what trick the placing of 'even' (syntax) affects what is implied about a woman's weight (semantics). In my 1982 paper I answered that the difference comes not from syntax but from the fact that these 'even's are distinct words, spelled the same way. *OED* makes a bad job of explaining 2, I contended, because it tries to stretch its account to cover 1 as well. As prima facie evidence that they are two, consider the fact that neither of English's nearest living neighbours has a single word for both. French expresses 1 with *encore* and 2 with *même*. German expresses 1 with *noch* or *sogar*, and 2 with *selbst*. I have since learned that the Spanish, Korean, and Bulgarian languages also use distinct words for these two purposes.

However, the two words must have something to do with one another: it can hardly be a coincidence that both are spelled the same way in English, in Turkish, and presumably in other languages as well. Having noted this, I ought to have dug for a single account to cover both. I might have done so had I noticed that 1 is strictly equivalent to

(1*) Even Rita is lighter than Jane.

This uses 'even' in the manner I associate with *même* and with *selbst*, yet it says just the same thing as 1; their conditions for truth and for felicity are identical. Each implies that Rita is heavy, says that Jane is heavier than Rita, and exclaims over the latter fact. It is hardly credible that two lexically different 'even's are at work in 1 and 1*.

Not credible, and not true. My 1982 view, which has found favour with some writers, was demonstrably wrong, as I learned from Barker (1991: 12–13). Abstracting from details that reflect his theory's reliance on universal quantification, we can learn from Barker the crucial point, that the difference between

(1) Jane is even heavier than Rita
(2) Even Jane is heavier than Rita

lies purely in the focus of 'even'. I have given my account of 2, in which the focus is 'Jane', and have no more to say about that. The right way to understand 1 is as having the form:

Jane is even heavier-than-Rita,

with focus of 'even' being 'heavier than Rita'. This is felicitous if there is a salient neighbour proposition, a milder one, about Jane's degree of heaviness; for then 1 serves to put Jane's weight further along the heaviness scale than the neighbour proposition does.

18

Backward Subjunctive Conditionals

108. BANNING BACKWARD CONDITIONALS

P. B. Downing, thinking he had shown that forward subjunctive conditionals interact fatally with backward ones, banned the latter. We should not join him in drawing this conclusion from his unsound scare story (§78). Also, someone who objects in principle to backward subjunctive conditionals ought to explain why many of them seem innocent.

The only philosopher I know who has tried to meet that requirement is Wayne Davis (1979). He observes that backward conditionals such as this:

If the plane had arrived at 2:00 p.m., it would have left at noon

are more naturally and happily worded like this:

If the plane had arrived at 2:00 p.m., it would *have to* have left at noon.

This verbal point has been frequently noticed, seldom explained. Morton (1981: 141) says that 'have to' is needed 'to indicate that there is something unusual about the conditional'. Davis offers something sturdier than that, and seeks to turn it to theoretical account. According to him, only the second wording is correct, and in it the consequent speaks of the relevant world's state at a time later than T_A: the conditional says that if A had obtained at T_A what would have *ensued* or *followed* is a modalized-past-tense state of affairs. Put it this way:

The plane arrived at 2:00 p.m. > The plane must have left at noon,

and read the consequent as 'some sort of tensed modal statement'—a statement about a modal state of affairs that obtains *after* T_A. According to Davis, the conditional says that at the closest worlds at which the plane arrives at 2 p.m. its doing so *leads on* to the world's being in a the-plane-must-have-left-at-noon state. So really there are no backward subjunctive conditionals, he concludes.

This account misunderstands the force of the modal element in the consequent of a backward subjunctive. Its real point is to register the thought that (C) the consequent is acceptable as the *best explanation* for (A) the antecedent. If the plane arrived at 2 p.m., that would *have to have been because* it left at noon—the modal 'have to' expresses the compulsion in our being forced to that explanation for lack of any other as good. The essence of this is not the 'backward' element in the thought but rather its 'best explanation' element. Among subjunctives those two go together, but among indicatives they do not. For example, 'If you returned the book to me, I must be losing my memory' is not a backward conditional, but it does involve the best-explanation thought (§133).

Woods (1997: 52n.) arrived independently at something like this view of Davis's. Edgington's refutation of that (1997a: 119–20) is a basis for a second objection to Davis.

Even if Davis were right about the significance of the 'have to have' phenomenon, it still would not follow that really there are only forward conditionals. A world at which

It is the case at T_2 that: it must have been the case that P at T_1

is a world at which

It is the case at T_1 that: P.

Therefore, the 'have to have etc.' conditionals that Davis accepts *do* say things about what obtains before T_A at the closest worlds; indeed, Davis has opened the door to an unlimited array of conditionals that are temporally backward so far as their meanings are concerned, even though they are verbally expressed in a 'forward' way; and he has made no theoretical provision for them. This argument relies on the principle that if A>C and C entails P, then A>P.

109. BACKWARD CONDITIONALS AND THE FUTURE

Jackson liberally allows for backward subjunctive conditionals, and offers an analysis for them. An argument like Downing's deters him from combining backward and forward conditionals in a single thought, and his analysis reflects this. Still, we can learn something from an aspect of it that is not connected with the Downing matter.

What Jackson says about backward subjunctive conditionals mirrors his account of forward ones. Here they are, side by side:

Forward: If T_A is earlier than T_C, then A>C is true just in case C is true at worlds that are exactly like α *before* T_A and obedient to the laws of α *after* that.

Backward: If T_A is later than T_C, then A>C is true just in case C is true at worlds that are exactly like α *after* T_A and obedient to the laws of α *before* that.

For Jackson, then, the closest worlds for evaluating A > Earlier are not the closest for evaluating A > Later, even with the same A; and no sense can be made of a mixture of the two. To be quite accurate, I should qualify that. The analysis does allow A > Later to be combined with A > Earlier-same, that is, with conditionals about how if A had been the case the world would not earlier have been unlike how it actually was. The worlds that are closest for purposes of evaluating A > Later do have pre-T_A histories, information about which is available for use in conditionals; but because those histories precisely match α's, those backward conditionals will all be of the form A > Earlier-same. Downing's supposed threat came from A > Earlier-different. However, I shall say no more about the supposed Downing-type troubles. Nor shall I return to the 'bump' problem (§79): according to Jackson's analysis, there may be a great lurch at the starting edge of T_A at the worlds that are closest for evaluating A > Later, and at the worlds that are closest for evaluating A > Earlier there may be a large bump at the ending edge of T_A.

The second bump comes from a part of Jackson's analysis that is objectionable in a way I have not mentioned. It is his requirement that in evaluating A > Earlier we look to worlds that are exactly like α after T_A. From the roughly correct premiss that A > Later concerns worlds that do not diverge from α until T_A, and the enticing idea of an analysis of backward conditionals that is a temporal dual of the analysis of forward ones, he arrives at the view that A > Earlier concerns worlds that converge on α at or just after T_A. This, I shall now show, is not subtly wrong but loudly, extravagantly so.

Jackson rightly permits the consequent in A > Later to reach back logically to actuality at times before T_A, as in the statement that if the Vicomte had published the letters in March he would by June have had his revenge for what the Marquise had done in January (§77). But his account of backward conditionals goes wrong in maintaining the dual of that, thus allowing that the consequent of A > Earlier can reach forward logically to times after T_A, doing this by faithfully copying how things actually stand at α at those later times. Apply this to examples and you will see the flaw in it.

If there are any respectable backward subjunctive conditionals, then I should think that this is one of them:

If Adlai Stevenson had been the undisputed President of the USA in February 1953, he would (have to) have been elected in November 1952.

According to Jackson's analysis, the closest worlds—for purposes of this conditional—at which Stevenson is President in February 1953 are ones at which Eisenhower is President in March 1953! We are not to infer from this that if Stevenson had been President in February, Eisenhower would have had the job in March, because that affirms a forward subjunctive on the basis of a judgement of closeness that is correct only for backward conditionals. But if this part of his analysis is not to be idle, it must allow us to infer:

> If Stevenson had been President in February 1953, then in November 1952 he would have celebrated a success that was doomed to be short-lived.

This conditional is just as preposterous as its predecessor. I conclude that Jackson's requirement of likeness to α after T_A is wrong. The analysis presupposes that when we think a backward conditional we think of possible worlds that exactly resemble α soon after the time of the antecedent; and we do not. I suppose that the charms of symmetry seduced Jackson into this. Rightly thinking that A > Later can reach back into α's past, he optimistically inferred that A > Earlier can reach forward into α's future. A different symmetry once seduced me into publishing a theory that also flatly conflicts with the intuitive data (§80).

110. A BETTER THEORY OF BACKWARD CONDITIONALS

What, then, should we say about the post-T_A states of the A-worlds that are closest for purposes of evaluating A > Earlier? I submit, as something everyone will accept after reflection, that those worlds conform to the causal laws of α from T_A onwards, and that their post-T_A states are what they legally have to be, given the states of those worlds at times before T_A. In short, the proper handling of post-T_A time for forward conditionals is also right, just as it stands, for backward ones as well. So far as I know, this view first appeared in print in Goggans 1992. Something close to it is propounded by Morton (1981: 143–4), but the idea is more complicated in his hands than it will be in mine.

We have made a start on an analysis of backward subjunctive conditionals. What else should we say to complete it? Well, one candidate stares us in the face, namely Lewis's account of forward conditionals, which I state in my own way:

> A>C ≡ C obtains at the A-worlds that most resemble α at T_A, out of all the A-worlds that become unlike α for the first time at a late modest fork and are legal from then onward.

(I omit, as irrelevant to present purposes, the complications having to do with Causal Chain PF (§90), true antecedents, probability, and so on.) I have been applying this to A > Later, but it also works for A > Earlier. According to this theory, A>C is true not only (forward) if C ensues from A at every world at which A is reached by a legal ramp that starts with a latest fork from actuality, but also (backward) if C belongs in every such ramp.

Unlike Jackson's, this is a unified account of forward and backward subjunctive conditionals; it evaluates A > Earlier in terms of the same class of worlds as A > Later, and therefore allows for conditionals of the form A > (Later & Earlier). But this Latest Fork account is lopsided in its yield of counterfactuals with false consequents: it sets a severe limit on how far back before T_A a backward counterfactual can stretch, but none on permissible stretches forward from T_A. (Recall that in this book a counterfactual is any A>C where A is false.) If Earlier is false, then it can obtain at a closest A-world—according to the Latest Fork theory—only by belonging to a ramp leading to A from a latest fork; everything earlier than that is 'sufficiently like' actuality (in my §82 sense).

The time-span represented by A > Earlier may be quite long. For example, Latest Fork theory might make this true: 'If dinosaurs had been roaming the world today, the trajectory of asteroid X at time T would have to have been different from what it actually was', where T is about sixty millions years ago. Long as this interval is, a small difference back then may be part of the *latest* modest fork from actuality leading legally to the survival of the dinosaurs today. Still, that does not save the Latest Fork account of backward counterfactuals from being lopsided in its output. It provides (in principle) for endlessly many counterfactuals about how reality would differ millions of years into the future if it were different in some tiny fashion now; but with long-span backward counterfactuals, it is much more niggardly. So this account is not symmetrical; it does not deal even-handedly with past and future.

Now that we have backward conditionals in hand, we can raise a different question about symmetry, namely: is > symmetrical? Is it always true that A>C ≡ C>A? No. The analysis does not yield *If A>C then C>A* as a theorem, for it provides plenty of ways for A > Later to be true although Later > A is false. It may be that all the closest A-worlds do eventually become Later-worlds, without A's being on the ramp to Later at any of the closest Later-worlds. If my father had written in his will that he wanted me to walk a mountain trail in memory of him on the 100th anniversary of his birth, I would have done that. In fact, I did not walk a mountain trail on that day. If I had, something would have to have been different in my frame of mind, my work, my family, or the like; there may be a choice of ramps leading from late modest forks to that hike. But a ramp running back to a counterfactual testamentary disposition by my father in 1970 is not among them.

Conversely, it can easily happen that A > Earlier is true while Earlier > A is false. Granted that each eligible fork to A starts a ramp with Earlier on it, so that A > Earlier is true, there may still be many eligible forks leading to Earlier but not to A, in which case Earlier > A is false. For example, if the house had slid into the canyon this morning, there would have to have been constant heavy rain for the past week; but it is not the case that if there had been such rain the house would have slid into the canyon this morning. Quite simply, a necessary condition for the slide need not be sufficient for it.

Thus, although a single set of worlds suffices for evaluating both A > Earlier and its converse, > fails doubly to be symmetrical.

111. LOOKING FOR A MORE GENEROUS THEORY

The Latest Fork theory offers a good way to understand many backward counterfactuals—especially, though perhaps not exclusively, ones that come up in the context of forward counterfactuals. But have we no conceptual structure that would admit a less restricted range of backward ones?

There is one obvious but uninteresting one. Someone's handling of a backward conditional might reflect his having a special liking for, or a special hostility toward, some special kind of fork; and this might drive him back to earlier times than he would be led to by Lewis's theory. How would things have to have been different beforehand for the village not have been swept away by floodwaters at T_A? The disaster arose from:

the bursting of the dam
the blocking of an outlet channel by logs
the falling of trees into the lake
the erosion of a hillside above the lake
a brush-fire on the hillside
the focusing of sunlight through a lens lying on dry leaves
the dropping of the lens.

By normal (Lewisian) standards we may handle 'If the village had not been swept away at T_A . . .' in terms of a fork from actuality at which the uprooted trees fall uphill instead of into the water, or fall into the water and are then grounded on the shore instead floating to the outlet channel. But now consider Albert, who holds that each of these was deterministically caused, who cares only about scenarios where nothing miraculous is involved, who has no thought of exploding differences, and who regards human behaviour—alone among physical events—as not governed deterministically. Albert may think that *if the village had not been swept away, that lens would have to have not been dropped.* We could devise examples going further back in time than that; and they need not concern beliefs about miracles and radical human freedom; that was just an example.

This is a respectable procedure, and someone going through it could make clear what he was doing. But it requires special signals, as must any approach to backward subjunctive conditionals using a fork from actuality other than the one(s) Latest Fork theory would dictate.

A wholly unrestricted theory of backward conditionals would not rely on forks at all. Is that possible? The only Yes answers that I know of come from Jackson's analysis and my Simple Theory (§78). Each of those carries heavy baggage of error, but let us try to jettison that and see what remains. From Jackson's account of backward conditionals, drop the disastrous requirement that closest A-worlds match α from T_A onwards and merely require that such worlds be legal from T_A onwards; and from the Simple Theory, excise the disastrous account of forward conditionals, leaving the backward part to stand on its own. Each of those manoeuvres ends up in exactly the same place:

A > Earlier ≡ Earlier obtains at all the legal A-worlds that most resemble α at T_A.

This looks promising: a corrected version of Jackson's account of A > Earlier is equivalent to the not-obviously-false part of the Simple Theory.

Promising, but still wrong: no credible way of evaluating unrestricted backward counterfactuals could conform to this latest account. If we apply the latter to a counterfactual of the form 'If dinosaurs had been roaming the world in 2001 . . .', it requires us to consider worlds that are as like α as possible in 2001, consistently with dinosaurs roaming through them. Those worlds contain not only dinosaurs but also mammals, indeed humans, nay skyscrapers and the Internet! This is absurd: we would never look at such a conditional in this fashion.

John Hawthorne made me aware of this important matter, by revisiting an example presented in §80 above. In actuality, in July 1941 there were few Soviet soldiers in Moscow or in the area stretched for several hundred miles west of it; most were further west still, battling the Germans. Now, consider a backward counterfactual starting 'If the German army had reached Moscow early in August 1941 . . .' What worlds must we consider in evaluating this? According to the proposed theory, we should look to worlds at which the Germans stroll towards Moscow through countryside devoid of opposing armies. Here, as in the dinosaur case, the insistence on likeness to α at T_A leads to a handling of counterfactuals that does not accord with any of our needs or interests, and it infects backward as well as forward conditionals.

We cannot rectify this defect by simply amputating the demand for similarity to α at T_A. That would yield a theory according to which

> A > Earlier ≡ Earlier obtains at all the A-worlds that conform to the causal laws of α.

This cuts the truth value of A > Earlier loose from any particular matters of fact about α, bringing in α only to fix what causal laws are relevant. It implies that A > Earlier is true only if A-not-preceded-by-Earlier is causally impossible—not merely in these or those circumstances, but absolutely. In our backward counterfactuals, however, we think about what would have to have been the case earlier *if A had actually obtained* (as we might casually say); that is, what did obtain earlier at all the A-worlds *that relate to α thus and so*. We need a candidate for the last clause.

Latest Fork theory supplies the only one I can find. The only defensible procedures for relating backward conditionals to matters of actual fact are ones involving forks from actuality. The only decent *general* theory of backward subjunctive conditionals, it seems, is the Latest Fork one nested within Lewis's account of forward conditionals.

112. COUNTERPARTS

This has an extra advantage. Return for a moment to Lewis's extreme realism about worlds (§63). An individual thing—a thing with 'local or accidental intrinsic properties' (as Lewis explained it to me)—cannot inhabit two distinct chunks of space and rock; so for Lewis each individual exists at only one possible world. This threatens to wreak havoc with counterfactuals about particular things. 'If the bowl had been packed properly, it wouldn't have broken', I say, implying something about worlds at which the bowl was packed properly, as it actually was not; but Lewis holds that there are no such worlds, because *this* bowl exists only at the actual world.

This threatens counterfactuals not merely about how a thing could have been intrinsically different but also about how it could have related differently to other things. Consider a broken bowl; Lewis's rejection of inter-world identity threatens not only 'If this bowl had not been broken . . .' but also 'If we had bought cherries, we could have put them in this bowl'. The non-actual buying of cherries has nothing to do with the bowl; but a world at which it happens is not α; so this bowl does not exist at it.

Rather than concluding that all counterfactuals about individuals are false, Lewis interpreted—or *reinterpreted*—them so they do not fall under the axe of his denial of inter-world identity. For this purpose he introduced the notion of a thing's *counterparts*: myriads of worlds somewhat resembling α contain counterparts of this bowl, that is, objects that play nearly or exactly the same role in their worlds as this bowl has played at our world, in our cosmos; and when we say 'If this bowl had been packed properly, it would not have broken' we should be understood to mean that in certain worlds where the counterparts of this bowl are packed properly they do not break.

(Some scholars have said that Leibniz anticipated Lewis's denial of inter-world identity, but he did not. He held that strictly speaking we can refer to a particular only by enumerating *all* its intrinsic (= non-relational) properties. It follows that if Fness is intrinsic, and if Fx is true, then it cannot be literally true that x—that very thing—could have been not-F; because we have to refer to it through its complete intrinsic description, which includes F. But this gives Leibniz no reason to deny that a particular thing could have had different relational properties from its actual ones; he can allow that while I was exercising this morning there could have been fewer clouds in the sky than there were. For Lewis, the intrinsic/relational contrast was irrelevant because his key idea was that of a *world*, whereas Leibniz's was that of a particular thing's *intrinsic properties*. On this I agree with Cover and Hawthorne 1990. Leibniz does need to defuse counterfactuals about how particular things might have been intrinsically different; sometimes he just denies them, sometimes he gestures towards counterpart theory.)

One might feel a need for counterparts without being an extreme realist about worlds. Help yourself (as I do) to the view that a particular bowl could have been different from how it actually is, understanding this as true of that very bowl, not of its counterparts. Then consider some questions about the bowl. Could it have been unlike how it actually is by being . . .

a little bigger?
fifty times as big?
made by someone else?
packed properly for the move?
0.001 per cent richer in aluminium?
made of entirely different materials?
completed five minutes earlier?
completed five years earlier?
a vase?
a statuette?
a plate of scrambled eggs?

Everyone will answer No to some of these questions, and most will answer Yes to others. Some of the questions will be met hesitantly by thoughtful people. I can find little guidance for our thoughts about how particulars could have differed from how they are. We share some strong positive intuitions and some strong negative ones, but over most of the territory there is little agreement and no underlying conceptual structure to help us settle the debates. Considering a possible world at which there is a bowl, and asking whether that bowl is this actual one (which is to ask whether this bowl could have been as that possible one is), we are often at a loss for an answer, having nothing to steer by.

Our one strong, clear intuition is that this bowl's history could have gone differently; we are sure that after beginning its career as it did in actuality, it could have been packed properly, could have remained unbroken, could have coexisted with Joe's smoking a cigarette. What generates this intuition?

Well, the only worlds we have to consider in connection with 'The bowl could have been packed properly' are ones that are exactly like α up to the time T just before the actual bowl was improperly packed. When we contemplate a world w of this sort—one exactly resembling α up to T—we have no problem about the two-worlds identification of particulars that exist before T. An extreme realist may object that even there no such identification can be literally correct, but if we are—as in this discussion I am—viewing worlds abstractly, we have something firm and definite to steer by. Given w's exact likeness to α before T, we can simply read off the identities of the particulars at w from those at α.

This is a good method for identifying particulars at two or more worlds, not because it is *correct* but because it is *secure*. Such identifications are not based on a metaphysical truth that things have essentially—that is, at every world—the origins they have at α. The secure method is simply a clear, firm, determinate procedure that answers every question about the identity at w of actual things existing before T, and its answers square with our intuitive sense that actual particulars could have undergone vicissitudes different from their actual ones.

What about conditionals of the form 'If this bowl had had slightly more aluminium in its composition, then C'? The relevant worlds fork from α before the bowl has been made, so it cannot be identified at them by the secure method. Some philosophers hold that it cannot be identified at them in any manner: appealing to their intuitions about individual essences, they hold that every particular thing is *essentially* composed of the material that *actually* composes it; from which they would infer that the above form of conditional has an absolutely impossible antecedent. I do not have those intuitions, and would not rest anything much on them if I had.

The following strikes me as a better view. The potter could have used a different mix of ingredients in the bowl she made at that time, while otherwise proceeding as she did at α. In that case, there would have been a bowl like this actual one—made by the same person at the same time, with the same shape, size, and pattern, but with a little more aluminium in its composition. That is the *whole* truth of the matter. In most contexts that is a pretty good counterpart of the actual bowl. The question 'Would it really have been this very bowl?' is empty, pointless: no answer has a respectable basis, nor do our serious intellectual needs or interests require us to find one.

The secure method for identifying things at two worlds fits snugly with the Lewisian semantics of forward subjunctive conditionals that I have been defending. In general, forward A>C should be evaluated by considering worlds exactly resembling α up to shortly before T_A; and those let us securely identify most of the particulars we might be talking about in the conditional. I apply this remark to conditionals whose truth involves indeterministic or miraculous forks. When a conditional is true because of an exploding-difference fork (§82), the closest A-world is (in my sense) sufficiently like α before the fork, but not exactly like it, and this spoils the fit with the secure method, which requires exact likeness between initial segments of worlds. To restore the fit we have only to relax the secure method a little: in my account of it, replace 'exactly resembles α' by 'resembles α in every respect that any human would know or think about'.

The situation concerning backward conditionals is equally comfortable, if I am right in holding that—unless special provisions are made to the contrary—they should be evaluated in terms of the same forks and ramps as forward conditionals. This is the advantage I heralded at the start of this section.

Throughout the present chapter I have assumed that when A>C runs temporally backward, and is true for causal reasons, C causes A. Some philosophers hold that temporally backward causal processes are possible, that is, that causes can post-date their effects; and if this is right, the A>C could run backward temporally while owing its truth to A's being a cause of C. Michael Tooley gave me a nice example: 'If Dr Who had eaten only two burritos, rather than three, before setting off to 1000 BCE, his heartburn would have disappeared before he arrived in England in 1000 BCE.' I share Tooley's hunch that temporally backward causation is not logically possible; but if it is, my treatment of counterfactuals has a gap that I have no idea of how to fill.

113. DISPENSING WITH HISTORIES

There is a mildly degenerate though quite common kind of subjunctive conditional which involves no thought about a possible history for the antecedent, and therefore does not bring in forks through which histories part company; nor does it raise questions of the identity of individuals between worlds. I could have introduced this kind of conditional earlier, in connection with histories and forks, but it was better to postpone it until inter-world identity had been discussed.

Here are some things that a reasonable person might say:

(1) That's not a giraffe; if it were, it would have long legs.

(2) I agree that what you bought wasn't glass. But it wasn't a ruby either. If it had been, it would have been red.

(3) You may be right that 666 is a fascinating number, but stop calling it a perfect number. If it were one, it would equal the sum of its divisors.

(4) Pluto is not a planet. If it had been a planet, it would move on the plane of the ecliptic.

Nobody would mean or understand these as involving possible histories—branchings-off from an α-like world to events through which it comes about that this thing which is actually a zebra is a giraffe, that this thing which is actually an emerald is a ruby, that this number is equal to the sum of its divisors, that this heavenly body is a planet.

In these cases, the speaker infers his conditional *directly*, with no detour through a possible history, from its basis in a generalization that he Trusts, that is, thinks is true and would remain so in a wide variety of circumstances, including those envisaged in the antecedent of his conditional. The speaker goes *directly* from 'All giraffes have long legs' to 1, from 'Rubies are all red' to 2, from 'Every perfect number equals the sum of its divisors' to 3, from 'All (solar) planets move in the plane of the ecliptic' to 4. This involves no thought of a possible history; no thought of how—or even of *whether*—this actual particular thing could have been different as required by the antecedent. The antecedent of 4 has history in its meaning, because 'planet' is defined partly by the thing's way of coming into separate existence; but there is still no thought of how this stretch of history could have been Pluto's, or of how it could have been launched at a world that had hitherto been like α. I was alerted to this phenomenon by some acute unpublished work by Boris Kment, though my account of what happens in examples like these differs from his.

In those examples, the Trusted generalization is the whole grounding for the conditional, which owes nothing to any facts about the animal, the gem, the number, or the heavenly body. Sometimes, a direct grounding of a conditional involves contingent facts as well as the Trusted generalization. For example, Charles's wife remarks sarcastically:

(5) If Charles had been CEO of Enron, the accounting fraud would not have lasted a week,

because Charles is incompetent with money. If this is her whole basis for the conditional, then she is giving it a direct grounding. What it omits, which a Lewis-type grounding includes, is a thought about whether Charles is a financial incompetent not only at α but also at the closest worlds at which he runs Enron. It is reasonable to think he is not, because the closest worlds at which he gets to run Enron fork from α early enough turn him away from the study of ancient Assyrian bas-reliefs and towards business management. However, his wife might be impatient with such ideas, regarding 5 as acceptably making her point, which is an instance of a Trusted generalization to the effect that any such financial fool as Charles *is* could not succeed for long in financial subterfuge. By expressing that in 5, she gives it a direct grounding, one mark of which is her regarding as an irrelevant nuisance the question of whether Charles could have *come to* run Enron while still financially incompetent.

Jackson's semantic theory for subjunctive conditionals allows that an antecedent may at the closest A-world come true with a bump that is not announced in A itself; and I criticized it on this score (§79). I should now add that this aspect of Jackson's account fits pretty well with conditionals that are being evaluated in the direct manner.

Although I have used 'direct' only to characterize *groundings* of conditionals, it does mark off a class of conditionals—not of sentences, but of propositions meant by them. That is because what a person regards as (ir)relevant to the evaluation of what he says dictates what he means by it. Claims of ambiguity in philosophy are usually false, and often harmful, but here they cannot be escaped. It could well be that (5) the conditional about Charles is true when understood in the direct manner yet false when understood in the history-involving manner. There cannot be a clearer mark of ambiguity than that.

Ambiguity across the direct/history-involving line does not force itself upon our attention, or give us much trouble, which may be why it has mainly escaped attention. Many direct conditionals declare themselves as such, because—like my examples 1–4—they would be intolerably stupid and wrong if understood the history-involving way. With others the ambiguity does not matter, because the conditional is true either way. Still, the waters are sometimes ruffled—namely, when A>C is true on some direct understanding and false, but not glaringly so, given the history-involving kind of evaluation. We must deal with these as they arise.

In an extreme subset of those cases, direct evaluation supports A>C while history-involving evaluation supports A>¬C. This can generate a kind of stand-off—a pair of subjunctives, relating as A>C to A>¬C, each true as its author means it. Lowe (1991: 127–8) presents such a case. His comments on it have helped me in this section.

This kind of stand-off is unlike the Gibbardian ones for indicative conditionals (§34), in three ways. It does not depend upon two people's having different information, it does involve a difference in meaning, and (connected with that) it does involve a pair that could—with each suitably interpreted—be accepted by one person at one time. Gibbardian stand-offs between indicatives differ in all those respects.

When a conflicting pair of subjunctive conditionals are both true when taken in the direct manner, we have the chance of a stand-off that resembles the Gibbardian ones in all the three respects I have mentioned. Here is a template for how this could happen. The following are all true and Trustable, and two people Trust the second and third of them:

(1) What is both F and G cannot be H.
(2) What is F and H is High.
(3) What is G and H is Low.

Some item is both F and G (and therefore not H), and is Medium, meaning neither High nor Low. One person knows that it is F and Medium, and rightly concludes that it is not H, because

If it were H, it would be High.

A second person knows that the thing is G and Medium, and rightly concludes that it is not H, because

If it were H, it would be Low.

In these directly grounded conditionals, the first person relies on 2, the second on 3, and each is right in what he says. This stand-off *does* reflect different information on the part of the two people, it *does not* involve ambiguity, and it *does not* concern a pair of conditionals both of which could be accepted by one person at one time.

That is the shape of some stand-offs that Dorothy Edgington has adduced in support of a general view of hers about the likeness of subjunctive to indicative conditionals (Edgington 1995*b*: 294–5, and elsewhere). Such a stand-off is a real phenomenon, with striking similarities to the Gibbardian one with indicative conditionals. But, as I noted in §100, it essentially involves directly grounded conditionals; such stand-offs are not possible for conditionals that are meant, and evaluated, in Lewis's history-involving manner.

From here on, the latter return to the spotlight. The directly evaluated conditionals have to be noticed, lest they get between our legs and trip us up; but otherwise we can safely ignore them. Their use of the conditional form is mildly degenerate, and they are uninteresting—because unchallenging—as a philosophical topic.

19

Subjunctive Conditionals and Time's Arrow

114. EXPLAINING THE ARROW OF TIME

Lewis sought to use his analysis of subjunctives to explain 'time's arrow', our sense that the future is not fixed as the past is, our sense of time as having a direction. This objective affected how he handled the analysis, as I shall explain shortly. First, though, let us consider his account of time's arrow on its own merits.

It develops an idea by Downing (§78), who wrote: 'The past is "inviolable" in that it cannot be true that if something happened now some past event would be different from what it would otherwise have been' (1959: 136). Lewis too held that our sense that the future is open and the past closed comes from our awareness that the future 'depends counterfactually' on the present in a way that the past does not:

We can . . . bring it about that the future is the way it actually will be, rather than any of the other ways it would have been if we had acted differently in the present. . . . The future depends counterfactually on the present. It depends, partly, on what we do now. . . . Something we ordinarily *cannot* do by way of 'changing the past' is to bring it about that the past is the way it actually was, rather than some other way it would have been if we had acted differently in the present. . . . The past does not at all depend on what we do now. It is counterfactually independent of the present. (Lewis 1979: 38)

In Lewis's theory many forward counterfactuals are true while relatively few backward ones are—merely ones reaching back down the ramp towards the fork—and he now offers this as explaining the meaning and securing the truth of the common idea that the future is open, the past closed. (When he said we 'ordinarily' cannot affect the past, he was allowing for temporally backward causation. That, if it existed, would make time less arrowed than most of us believe it to be, but it does not touch our present topic.) The asymmetry of his analysis gives Lewis some prospect of doing this; neither Jackson's analysis nor my Simple Theory, which are in their different ways temporally symmetrical, could explain the arrow of time. Lewis's has a chance.

I am not convinced that it succeeds. It does allow that some backward counterfactuals are true, namely ones about the fork and the ramp from it to the antecedent; and Lewis must stop those from spoiling his account of time's arrow. For example: *If Adlai Stevenson had been the undisputed President in February 1953, he would (have to) have been elected in November 1952.* This is probably true—intuitively, and also by Lewis's theory, because any late, modest fork to that antecedent will start a ramp with Stevenson's election on it. Lewis had to explain why he did not take this to imply that in this instance time's arrow points backwards, by implying that Stevenson's being President in January 1953 would have brought it about that he was elected two months earlier, or—worse—why Stevenson's not being President in 1953 actually caused his not being elected in the previous November.

He addressed this problem. Having described the ramp from the fork up to the time of the antecedent, he continued:

That is not to say, however, that the immediate past depends on the present in any very definite way. There may be a variety of ways the transition might go, hence there may be no true counterfactuals that say in any detail how the immediate past would be if the present were different. I hope not, since if there were a definite and detailed dependence, it would be hard for me to say why some of this dependence should not be interpreted—wrongly, of course—as backward causation over short periods of time [and thus, presumably, as an openness of the recent past] in cases that are not at all extraordinary. (1979: 40)

I do not accept what Lewis says here about the hoped-for lack of 'definite and detailed' consequents in true backward counterfactuals. Any late inconspicuous miracle leading to Stevenson's being President in 1953 would get there through his being elected in 1952. Is not that detailed and definite enough?

Lewis did not say quite what he meant, I think. Properly to grasp his meaning, we have to notice that he switched from 'dependence' to 'causation', and to know a couple of things about his understanding of the latter (Lewis 1973a). (1) He took all particular causation statements to concern the causation of *events* by *events*, never of *facts* by *facts*. He did not provide for 'The house caught fire because the gasoline exploded', but only for 'The explosion caused the fire'. (2) He used subjunctive conditionals in analysing particular causation statements (§90). Putting 1 and 2 together, we get from Lewis an analysis of particular causation statements in which 'e_1 caused e_2' means, roughly, 'If e_1 had not occurred, e_2 would not have occurred'. Throughout the remaining three decades

of Lewis's life his analysis of causation became ever more elaborate; but his initial idea about it remained its cornerstone, and it is all we need for our purposes.

When Lewis wrote of 'definite and detailed dependence', I think he meant to
express the hope that except in extraordinary cases no true counterfactual
implies, for any *event* e_1 and subsequent *event* e_2, that if e_2 had not occurred then
e_1 would not have occurred. I have contended that 'If Stevenson had been
President in February 1953, he would have been elected in November 1952' is
definite and detailed, but I agree that it cannot be expressed in the form 'If e_2 had
not occurred, e_1 would not have occurred earlier'. Stevenson's defeat in
November 1952 is a good candidate for e_1, but what can e_2 be? We might try 'If
Stevenson's non-inauguration had not occurred, then . . .', but Lewis could plausibly deny that there is any such event as that. Well, then, how about Eisenhower's
inauguration? This is a genuine event in anyone's book; so we can say 'If
Eisenhower's inauguration had not occurred, Stevenson's defeat would not have
occurred'. This has the right form, but Lewis could dismiss it as false, because
worlds at which Eisenhower loses are less close than ones at which he wins and
then dies in December, leaving Vice-President-elect Nixon to be inaugurated.

This, however, is a merely local success, depending on special features of the
example. It fails here:

> A competitive runner heads the pack until near the end of the race, when she
> stumbles, falls, and comes in last. I remark: 'If she had won the race she could
> hardly have climbed the steps to the podium to get her medal, she was in so
> much pain from that fall.' You reply: 'Not so, because if she had won the race
> she would not have fallen [or: she would have to have not fallen]'.

In Lewis's preferred terminology: if her loss had not occurred, her earlier fall
would not have occurred. Losses and falls are events if anything is. And there are
many more where that came from.

Even if I am wrong about this, and there are no clear cases of 'If e_2 had not
occurred, e_1 would not have occurred', that allows Lewis to explain only a specifically *event-causation* version of time's arrow, which means that he is not
explaining or justifying my belief in time's arrow or, I suspect, yours. I think the
past is closed and the future open not only with respect to the *events that occur*
in them but also with respect to the *states of affairs that obtain* in them, including indefinite, undetailed, and negative ones. Adding an emphasis to Lewis's
own words, I think that 'the past does not *at all* depend on what we do now'.
According to my version of the time's arrow assumption—which I think to be
the usual one—no fact about the world's state at any time before T depended on
the fact that a certain apple fell from my tree precisely at T. But Lewis must allow

that there may be true counterfactuals running from the negation of the fact back into a nonactual past—the least informative of them being 'If that apple had not fallen at T then the world's previous state would have been somewhat different from what it actually was.' Perhaps we can never parlay those into anything of the form 'If e_2 had not occurred, e_1 would not have occurred earlier', but what of that?

I cannot explain time's arrow; I wish I could. But this does not incline me to settle for a theory that 'explains' part of my time's arrow belief by implying that the part it does not explain—the part not expressible in terms of event causation—is downright false.

The waters became muddied for Lewis by his opinion, which he reported to me in the summer of 2001, that 'there is causation by absences'. This deprived him of the line of thought I attributed to him in connection with the Stevenson example. Denying that absences are events, and refusing to countenance facts as causal relata—'Stevenson's defeat was a cause of *his not being inaugurated*'— Lewis said instead that 'there is causation with no causal relata at all'. On this rather fragile basis he might have rescued the line of thought by explicitly tying time's arrow to event-causation rather than to causation generally; but he did not take that way out, and acknowledged this as an unsolved problem.

115. KEEPING TEMPORAL ORDER OUT OF
THE ANALYSIS

This work of Lewis's concerns me here mainly because of how it affected the shape of his analysis of subjunctive conditionals. For the analysis to ground an explanation of temporal direction, it must not itself employ the concept of temporal direction or, therefore, of temporal *order*. Lewis undertook this bold project: to use subjunctive conditionals to explain time's arrow, analysing them without using 'before', 'after', 'early', 'late', or any of their immediate kin.

In Chapters 12 and 13 I emphasized my agreement with Lewis on the crucial points. He was right, I said, in holding that the closest A-worlds exactly resemble α until shortly *before* T_A, diverge from α in an inconspicuous manner that may be a small miracle, and conform strictly to the causal laws of α *thereafter*. How can I offer as essentially Lewis's an account in which 'before' and 'after' are hard at work? The answer is that he aimed to get this result without using those words or any cognates of them—that is, without using any concept of temporal direction or order. The account I have presented agrees with Lewis's in its intended output, but not in its way of getting there.

His way is of the greatest interest. In his 1979 paper Lewis wrote that w_1 is closer to the actual world than w_2 is if

(1) w_2 contains a large miracle and w_1 does not;

or if neither contains a large miracle and

(2) w_1 exactly resembles the actual world for more time than w_2 does;

or, if neither contains a large miracle and the extent of perfect match is the same, and

(3) w_2 contains more small miracles than w_1 does;

or, if they are not separated in any of those ways, and

(4) w_1 has a greater degree of (imperfect) similarity to the actual world than w_2 has;

though Lewis declared himself uncertain whether 4 has any part in determining closeness (§§89–90). Observe that those criteria for closeness contain no hint of temporal order or direction. The only temporal concept is metrical, not topo-logical—it concerns amount, not order.

(In stating 2, Lewis wrote of maximizing 'the spatio-temporal region throughout which perfect match of particular fact prevails', but I have omitted the 'spatio-' part of this because I do not know what to do with it. Lewis explained to me: '"Spatio" is there to take account of Relativity. How inclusive is the past light-cone of the divergence point?')

Temporal order showed up in my account when I stipulated that closest worlds must fork from α late rather than early; Lewis's analysis deals with this through the requirement that closest worlds exactly resemble α for as long as possible—the same result, with no mention of temporal order or direction. Apply this, for example, to the first conditional I used in discussing A > Big-difference in §75: 'If on 20 July Stauffenberg had placed the bomb on the other side of the trestle, Hitler would have been killed.' Suppose this is true, as it well may be. Then the closest A-worlds fork inconspicuously from α not long before T_A, unrolling legally from then on. Lewis's criterion 2 ensures that there is a fork from actuality and that it is late rather than early (though he doesn't put it like that); his criterion 1 ensures that the fork is not so late as to require a bump, a big miracle. So he does achieve that part of the analysis without bringing in tem-poral order or direction.

My other use of temporal order was the requirement that closest A-worlds be perfectly legal from the time of the fork *onwards*. Lewis's account rules out big post-fork miracles by (in effect) ruling out big miracles altogether. But he did not rule out little miracles altogether, because he tolerated them at forks, and his time's-arrow project would not let him say that a little miracle is all right at a fork but not *thereafter*.

To see the shape of this part of Lewis's problem, return to our assassination conditional. Among the worlds that fork from α through a small miracle not long before T_A, there are some where Stauffenberg places the bomb on the other side of the trestle but Hitler survives through the intervention of another small miracle. That second miracle counts against closeness at level 3; but if it restores perfect match with α, that counts for closeness at level 2, which dominates level 3; so our conditional gets the wrong truth value, as do countless others like it. Lewis cannot dismiss this on the grounds that the recovered perfect match does not count because it pertains only to times *after* T_A.

He coped with this difficulty by maintaining that although a small miracle can make indiscernible worlds diverge, only a large one could make them reconverge to *perfect* likeness. If that is right, his criteria do exclude the worlds at which a miracle intervenes between A and C. If the miracle is a large one, the world is excluded at level 1. If the miracle is small, Hitler survives but the world in question does not get *perfectly* back on track with α; so the occurrence of the miracle at that world counts against the latter's closeness at level 3, and if the countervailing similarity-of-fact feature counts towards closeness at all, it does so only at level 4.

Lewis absolutely needed the thesis that (roughly speaking) *small miracles cannot make worlds converge to perfect likeness*. Without it, he could not exclude from closest A-worlds miracles leading to wrong truth values for many conditionals, except by bringing in the concept of temporal order in the stipulation that at a closest A-world no miracle occurs *after* the time of the fork. Let us then examine Lewis's case for this indispensable thesis.

116. THE METAPHYSICS OF WORLD-CONVERGENCE

He argued for it through an example in which at α a man named Nixon ponders pressing a certain button and then does not, while at the same moment at world w_1 a small miracle intervenes and he presses it. (This generates chilling conditionals about what would have ensued if Nixon had pressed the button.) At a world at which Nixon presses the button, a second small miracle just after this might cause the current to die in the wire; but, Lewis said, it could not also deal with the disturbance of dust particles, the light signals already half-way to the moon, the heat in the wire, and so on. Only a big miracle, he declared, could roll back all those effects (1979: 45–6).

It has seemed to me that the force of this comes from the long time-span that Lewis permitted—his envisaging the convergence miracle as occurring a full tenth of a second after the pressing of the button. Actually, button-pressing is itself a spread-out affair, which hinders me in making my point. So let us address a conditional whose antecedent involves some temporally sharper event— something of the form 'If a photon had impinged on that photo-electric cell, then C would have ensued'. Now consider a world that miraculously forks from actuality so that a photon does impinge on the cell, and where *one nanosecond* later another miracle occurs, snapping the causal chain running from that impingement to the obtaining of C. That, one might think, is not enough time for many other effects to radiate out from the impingement of the photon.

Lewis disagreed. 'The effects ', he wrote to me, 'won't radiate out very far; a light-nanosecond is just under a foot. But they'll be varied, and they'll have had time to become more varied by impinging on other things . . . Better make the interval still smaller . . . But the smaller you make it, the less clear it is that the event mentioned in the antecedent really had enough time to happen at all.'

Tooley (forthcoming) describes two kinds of worlds whose laws allow the healing of a divergence through a small miracle. One kind allows a causal process that leads to the type of branching that Lewis envisaged through an initial stretch in which no branching occurs. A small miracle could intervene in the process before it has branched, snipping it off and mopping up its effects up to there; which means that a small miracle could produce a convergence of worlds. Lewis would say of this, as of Tooley's other example, that such worlds are sufficiently unlike α not to damage his thesis. Though not certain that a result like Tooley's must involve a world whose basic laws are unlike α's, I am disinclined to press the point.

I once attacked Lewis's position on convergence of worlds in a different way, as follows (1984: 63–4). Suppose that α and w_1 are exactly alike up to time T and then diverge because of the occurrence at w_1 of a small miracle—an event that slightly infringes the causal laws of α (assumed in this argument to be deterministic). Now, there is a possible world w_2 that exactly resembles w_1 from T onwards, and differs from it in being perfectly legal, so that no event at w_2 infringes the causal laws of α. So w_1 and w_2 are dissimilar up to T and exactly alike thereafter, this convergence being produced by the occurrence of a small miracle at w_1—that is, an event that slightly infringes the causal laws of w_2. This possibility is shown in Fig. 7 (I give α the thickest line for clarity's sake).

That does indeed prove that a small miracle can make one world converge onto another, though it does not address—as my preceding argument does—the question of whether a small miracle can make one world *re*converge on another.

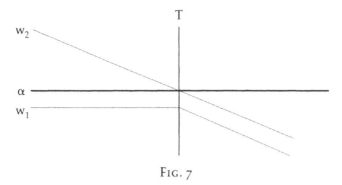

FIG. 7

Lewis replied to my 1984 point by arguing that world w_2, which he called a 'Bennett world', is 'deceptive' in a way that α is not (1986d: 57–8). At least for a while after T the history books, geological and archaeological records, etc. of α are exactly like those at w_1, the world at which through a small miracle Nixon presses the button. (If not, then we can say that if Nixon had pressed the button the history books and other records would instantly have been changed; which is absurd.) And from T onwards w_1 is indiscernible from w_2. So for a while after T the records at α and at w_2 are the same; *but their long-term pasts are grossly different*; so w_2 must be chock-full of deceptive records in a way that α is not. This stops w_2 from being 'a world like ours'; and it is only worlds like ours that Lewis was theorizing about. No lawful world contains records that would deceive a Laplacean archangel; but Lewis was talking about deceptiveness with respect to the likes of you and me.

Why would the long-term pasts of those two worlds be grossly different? Lewis's reason for this came from a view of his that I call Amplify:

> Two deterministic worlds that are somewhat like ours and are slightly different at some time, become greatly unalike at later times.

(This, incidentally, could help to make the emphasis on perfect similarity look reasonable, through the thought that any period of imperfect similarity shrinks to insignificance over the long haul. But the emphasis does not rely upon such help. Lewis's criteria for closeness, and their relative rankings, are justified if they deliver the intuitively right truth values for subjunctive conditionals.)

Lewis could argue from Amplify to the conclusion that Bennett worlds are deceptive as follows. Assuming that α and the Bennett world w_2 are at least a little unalike at every earlier time, we can take a sufficiently earlier time when they are unalike and then apply Amplify to get the result that they are greatly unalike at some intermediate times.

My grasp of all this was helped by correspondence with Lewis, in which he developed something he had hinted at in his 1986d. Setting aside miracles, which do not occur at lawful worlds, the only other basis that has been proposed for the kind of deceptiveness we are considering here is the occurrence of lawful but extremely improbable events, especially ones involving a local decrease in entropy—'counter-entropic fakery', as Lewis called it. For example, a spherical container of gas that is hot at the centre and cool around the outside is excellent evidence that heat was recently released near the centre of the sphere; but the state of affairs could have resulted from a tremendously improbable coincidence in which the movements of the individual molecules happened to produce heat at the centre and not at the edge. If this is the only way in which a lawful world can mislead, then Lewis's argument implies that a Bennett world must be the scene of many such anti-entropic events, this being a deeper account of what makes it not 'a world like ours'.

Arguments put to me by Adam Elga and Barry Loewer encourage me to think that small miracles *can* produce convergences of worlds onto worlds that are as 'like ours' as we are entitled to demand (see Elga 2000). On this remark, David Lewis commented:

I'm not sufficiently expert to see for myself, but I assume Elga and Loewer have it right. However, the worlds that converge onto worlds like ours are worlds with counter-entropic funny-business. I think the remedy—which doesn't undercut what I'm trying to do—is to say that such funny business, though not miraculous, makes for dissimilarity in the same way miracles do. I'll watch for an opportunity to say this, unless Elga or someone makes the point before I get around to it.

I am not equipped to have an independent opinion on this; and my conclusion in §114 leaves me with no reason for caring much one way or the other.

117. FURTHER PROBLEMS FOR LEWIS'S ANALYSIS

It is, then, at least open to question whether a requirement of perfect similarity will do all Lewis needed it to do. There are also two other possible flaws in his account, though each seems to be remediable.

If there can be exploding-difference forks, then Lewis's level 2 demand for perfect similarity is too strong, and should be replaced by a requirement for sufficient likeness, in my sense of that phrase (§82). Presumably a plain person who asserts a subjunctive conditional has no thought of an exploding-difference fork; but nor does his thought rule out such a fork, which therefore merits a place in the story unless the causal laws of α rule it out. It seems easy for Lewis's level 2 to be amended to allow for this, as I have noted, though this change slightly weakens the relevant notion of convergence, thereby adding a little to the burden that has to be borne by his thesis that small miracles cannot produce convergences onto worlds like ours.

In a different way it brings grave trouble to that thesis, by pulling the rug out from under the argument for the gross deceptiveness of Bennett worlds. This argument requires that differences in the remote past are bound to have amplified, producing gross differences in the semi-remote past; but this is not so if exploding differences are possible.

Now for the second of the two flaws I announced. Set aside perfect or near-perfect similarity, and think about small miracles as producers of temporal stretches of partial similarity between worlds—likeness in respect of some matters of particular fact. This is Lewis's level 4. He was hesitant about it, but it does play a part in our handling of subjunctive conditionals (§90), and he did not deny this. Well, now, consider two candidates for closest A-world with respect to our assassination conditional: 'If on 20 July Stauffenberg had placed the bomb on the other side of the trestle, Hitler would have been killed.'

w_1: A small miracle at T_1 leads to his placing the bomb on the other side etc., and Hitler dies.

w_2: A different outcome of an indeterminacy at T_2 leads to his placing the bomb on the other side etc., then a small miracle intervenes in the working of the bomb, and Hitler survives.

In these, we are to understand the times T_1 and T_2 as separated by mere microseconds: at w_1 the miracle intervenes a split second before an indeterminacy does the job at w_2.

Because the conditional is true (I am plausibly supposing), w_1 should count as closer to α than w_2 is. But on Lewis's account it does not. Lacking big miracles, both worlds are equal at his level 1. They are also equal at level 2. The tiny differences of fork-time make no difference, I have argued (§83); but if they do, they count against w_1 rather than for it, because in my account w_1 parts company with α sooner than w_2 does.

The two worlds are dead equal at level 3 as well, for each involves exactly one small miracle. I give the palm to w_1 over w_2 because it does not have a miracle *after* the fork; but Lewis, preparing the ground for his account of time's arrow, denied himself the use of 'after'.

There remains level 4, at which w_2 has in its favour a substantial particular-fact likeness to the actual world, namely Hitler's survival on 20 July 1944. That is, the worlds are equal at levels 1, 2, and 3, and w_1 loses at level 4.

As for the differences between kinds of fork: those have no role in Lewis's criteria for closeness, nor should they do so. As I have argued in §86, when the plain person entertains a subjunctive conditional, his thought does not pick out a miracle or an indeterminacy or an improbable exploding difference: he merely thinks about a world that is not distinguishable (in his thought) from α until shortly before T_A and then *somehow* forks *smoothly* onto a ramp leading to A. The three kinds of fork are our contributions to the rational reconstruction of the plain person's thought; they are not part of it, and the differences amongst them have no effect on it.

However, Lewis's analysis can be amended so as to steer around this difficulty. His explanation of time's arrow would be compromised if his criteria for closeness included 'not having small miracles *after* the fork', but not if he has instead 'not having small miracles except *at* the fork'. This puts w_1 ahead of w_2 in the closeness race, without bringing in temporal direction or order.

This amendment to Lewis's analysis does not solve or abolish his problem about world-convergence through small miracles.

My preferred way of getting the results Lewis wanted (for I am sure that the intended output of his analysis is correct) is to say that a world close to α must sufficiently resemble α until shortly *before* T_A, have no large miracles, and have no small ones at times other than that of the first divergence from being sufficiently like α. Put in this way, sufficient likeness at times *after* T_A play no part in the story, which is therefore not threatened by the possibility that such likeness might be produced through a small miracle. *That* question arises for Lewis because he wanted to handle (level 2) likeness-to-α purely metrically, so that a further stretch of it starting after T_A would contribute to closeness at level 2.

He took on this burden because, wanting to keep temporal order out of his analysis, he refused to handle level 2 in terms of likeness-to-α *before* the time of the fork. I have argued that this self-denial on Lewis's part was not well motivated, because it was meant to serve his explanation of time's arrow, of which we have reason to be sceptical.

118. ANTECEDENT RELATIVITY

For many years I thought that Lewis's account of closeness differed from mine primarily in that his is absolute whereas mine is antecedent relative. Let me explain. In Lewis's 'Ptolemaic astronomy' of possible worlds, all the worlds lie in concentric shells around α with each one's degree of 'closeness' to α being represented by its distance from the centre. These closeness relations are fixed independently of what conditional one is evaluating. For Lewis, as for Stalnaker, standards of closeness can vary with the context; but they do not vary according to what the antecedent is of the conditional in question.

The account of closeness that I have been defending, on the other hand, seemed to me to make closeness antecedent-relative. I thought I had to express the truth conditions for A>C in terms of the likeness of worlds *up to (or near to) the time of A*, and of freedom from miracles *after the time of A*, which involves a doubly antecedent relative concept of closeness. If that is right, then where Lewis has a single astronomy of worlds with α at its centre, I have one for each pair {α,A}. *That* difference between us, I thought, arose from his desire for a non-circular account of time's arrow.

Barry Loewer woke me up to seeing that this is all wrong, and that my own account of closeness is not essentially antecedent relative after all. I take legal worlds whose initial segments are sufficiently like α's, and that fork from α just once in some smooth and initially inconspicuous fashion; and I order them according to how late the fork occurs, on the principle (understood broadly and roughly): the later, the closer. I also count against a world's closeness its having a miracle that is at a temporal distance from a fork; there is nothing antecedent relative in this either.

It has occurred to me since that my handling of the particular-fact problem (§90) might be antecedent relative, but that turns out to be wrong too. Given that two worlds fork from α at about the same time and that neither contains any subsequent miracles, large or small, I count one as closer than the other if the former (but not the latter) shares with α some indeterministically arrived at particular fact and shares with α the causal chain leading to it. Still no antecedent relativity.

Why does antecedent relativity matter? Well, one might want an absolute theory of closeness so as to be able to prove a logical principle that I shall call Substitution:

A>B, B>A, A>C entail B>C.

The first two premises jointly say that A and B are (as I shall say) >-equivalent: if either were to obtain, then so would the other. So Substitution says that if two propositions are >-equivalent, either may be substituted for the other, *salva veritate*, as the antecedent of any subjunctive conditional. Here is why Substitution holds in a theory with an absolute concept of closeness. The premises, taken in turn, say that as we move out from α to increasingly remote worlds:

(1) the first A-worlds we meet are B-worlds,
(2) the first B-worlds we meet are A-worlds,
(3) the first A-worlds we meet are C-worlds.

Now, 1 and 2 imply that the closest A-worlds and the closest B-worlds are the very same set; 3 tells us that these are also C-worlds; so the closest B-worlds are C-worlds, which means that B>C. QED. In an antecedent-relative theory of closeness this argument does not go through, because it requires a single relation of closeness or 'the first . . . we come to', and antecedent-relative analyses do not provide this. According to them, the first A-worlds we come to when evaluating A>B might be different from the first B-worlds we come to when evaluating B>A.

I have been following Stalnaker's treatment of Substitution and antecedent-relativity (1984: 129–31). He considers whether subjunctive conditionals should be tied to an absolute concept of closeness or rather an antecedent-relative one, and favours absoluteness because he thinks Substitution is valid.

He does not directly defend Substitution, but he does consider a certain consequence of it which, he says, also stands or falls with an absolute theory of closeness. I call it Limited Transitivity:

A>B, (A&B) > C entail A>C.

The derivation goes as follows. The premiss A>B entails A > (A&B); this, conjoined with the necessary truth (A&B) > A, entails that A and A&B are >-equivalent. Conjoin this with the other premiss, (A&B) > C, and Substitution lets you infer A>C. QED.

Stalnaker shows Limited Transitivity looking good in a particular argument, and it often does. When showing students that > is not transitive, I have found it natural—as at the end of §65 above—to explain apparently valid instances of Transitivity as really understated instances of Limited Transitivity. It seems reasonable to infer, given

(1) If you had jumped from the roof, you would have broken some bones,

and

(2) If you had broken some bones, you would have been in pain,

that

(3) If you had jumped from the roof, you would have been in pain;

and to suppose that this shows > to be transitive. But then we find counter-instances like this:

(1*) If Gore had successfully blackened Clinton's name in 1990–1, Clinton would not have tried for the Presidency in 1991–2.

(2*) If Clinton had not tried for the Presidency in 1991–2, he would have supported Gore.

(3*) If Gore had successfully blackened Clinton's name in 1990–1, Clinton would have supported Gore.

The first two might be true, while the third is incredible. One can easily see why Transitivity fails here: when 2* is taken on its own, away from the context provided by 1*, it looks to the closest worlds at which Clinton doesn't try; 1* takes us to worlds which, though the closest at which Gore vilifies Clinton, are quite remote among the worlds at which Clinton doesn't try. Still, if Transitivity does not hold, we should explain why the first inference seemed all right. The most inviting explanation says that we endorsed that inference because we took its second premiss to mean:

(2*) If you had jumped from the roof and broken some bones, you would have been in pain.

Then the inference goes through on the strength of Limited Transitivity. You can easily work out that this rescue of the roof/pain inference does not rescue the Clinton/Gore one. So we have a nice explanation of why > can seem transitive, without actually being so. But it presupposes that > satisfies Limited Transitivity, which is secure if our account of closeness is absolute rather than antecedent relative.

This section up to here has discussed whether closeness depends on the antecedent in any clean, clear, systematic manner. Beyond a doubt, in the hurly-burly of everyday thought and talk, standards of closeness can vary greatly and not systematically, according to the aims and interests of the speaker. Also, a Gricean principle that I deployed in §71 implies that in at least one respect our standard of closeness in evaluating a given conditional depends not upon its antecedent but upon the entire conditional. I applied this to different interpretations of comparative terms ('If my pack had been heavier . . .', 'If the beach had been bigger . . .'), but it could also apply to choices of fork. I have no examples, but it obviously *could* happen that someone soberly asserts A>C when there are three prima facie eligible forks, of which one makes his conditional obviously false, another makes it obviously true, and the third makes it neither. In such a case, Gricean charity will lead us—unless we think the speaker is an idiot or a bore—to evaluate what he says in accordance with the third-mentioned fork.

20

Support Theories

The literature on subjunctive conditionals has one principal line through it. On one side lies the work of Lewis, Stalnaker, and those who have followed them in analysing subjunctives in terms of relations amongst worlds. On the other are analyses that do not rely on the 'world' concept; these all stem, in one way or another, from a famous paper of Nelson Goodman's (1947). When Goodman wrote this, nobody had used worlds to elucidate subjunctives; but much of the best Goodman-derived work has been done since the start of, and in conscious opposition to, the 'worlds' approach. We ought not to be satisfied with the latter until its older rival gets a hearing. (For a somewhat scattered but ingenious and interesting development of Goodman's approach to subjunctive conditionals, see also Sanford 1989: 76–86, 209–24.)

Goodman proposed a form of analysis according to which:

> A>C is true ≡ There is a true proposition *Support* meeting certain constraints such that C is entailed by (A & Support) in conjunction with *Laws*, that is, the conjunction of the causal laws reigning at the actual world.

'Support' is a variable ranging over propositions. I use a whole word rather than a mere 'S' because I want a constant reminder of its role in the analysis. When I speak of what entitles a proposition to be a conjunct in Support, I mean 'to be a conjunct in a value of Support'.

According to this analysis, the conditional says that *there is* a true proposition Support which . . . etc.; it does not say what proposition it is. This goes with the fact that I can believe 'If I had taken aspirin my headache would have gone by now' while having no opinion about what facts about aspirin and my brain make it true. Similarly, the conditional implicitly mentions causal laws but does not state any; which goes with the fact that I can believe 'If I had made the iron white hot, it would have become flexible' without any beliefs about what laws make it true.

In tying the truth of A>C to the proposition that C is entailed by (A & Laws & Support) for a suitably constrained value of Support, Goodman was providing for conditionals of the sort I have called 'dependent' (§7). Support brings in the contingent facts that help to make the conditional true. Drop this and you have C being entailed by (A & Laws), so that A>C is independently, causally true. Drop Laws as well, and A entails C, in which case A>C is independently, logically true.

Goodman's analysis needs to be modified to deal with the probability issues that I discussed in the 'worlds' context in Chapter 16. This can be done, but I shall not go into it; we have enough on our plates already.

We have not invented a good label for theories like Goodman's. Some that have been proposed are misleading about what the essence of these theories is and, in particular, about what chiefly marks them off from theories in the manner of Stalnaker and Lewis.

Lewis characterized Goodman's as a 'metalinguistic' theory of subjunctive conditionals, because it specifies truth-conditions for A>C in terms of 'linguistic entities—arguments and their premises' (1973b: 66). Goodman did indeed write of 'statements' or 'sentences'; but that reflects his hostility to abstract objects such as propositions, an attitude having nothing to do with his assault on the problem of subjunctive conditionals.

I once proposed the label 'Consequence Theory' for Goodman's sort of analysis, because it ties the truth of A>C to C's being a logical consequence of a certain proposition in which A is a conjunct (1974: 386). That is a bad label too. It does not mark a deep difference between Goodman's theory and Lewis's, because the latter could also be expressed in terms of C's being a logical consequence of something in which A is a conjunct. The reason for this depends upon a fundamental and uncontroversial truth of modal logic, namely that for any set W of possible worlds, there is a proposition that is true at every member of W and at no other world. If you securely grasp why this is so, skip the next paragraph.

Each possible world corresponds to a maximal consistent conjunction of propositions, a conjunction uniquely specifying that world and true at no other. (Abstract realists would say that a possible world *is* such a conjunction.) Thus, any set W of worlds corresponds to the disjunction P_w of such infinite conjunctions. Now, P_w is true at each member of W, because at each of them one of its disjuncts is true; and it is not true at any world outside W because none of its disjuncts is true of any world outside W. Thus, P_w is the unique proposition that is true throughout W and true nowhere else. QED.

According to Lewis, A>C is true just in case C is true at every member of a certain class W of A-worlds. There is a proposition that is true at every member of

W and at no other worlds; and to say that C is true at every member of W is to say that C is entailed by that proposition. Thus, a Lewis-type theory can be stated as one about C's being a consequence of a certain proposition in which A is a conjunct. So the label 'consequence theory' is not good for marking off Goodman's kind of theory from Lewis's.

Making things still worse, the Goodman kind of analysis could be expressed in the language of 'worlds'. In such an analysis, the truth of A>C is tied to C's being entailed by a conjunction of A and Laws and a conjunction (Support) of other propositions satisfying certain constraints. There seems to be no reason why those constraints should not be expressed as conditions on worlds; and then the analysans says that legal A-worlds which . . . [and here we work in the constraints on Support] are all C-worlds.

Nevertheless, a significant line can be drawn. Certain features of Lewis's analysis, and of the variant on it that I have defended, *require* the use of the worlds concept, whereas Goodman's kind of analysis does not; it *can* all be expressed purely in terms of logical relations amongst propositions.

On the Lewis side: a Lewis-style theory, as I have pointed out, can be stated in terms of C's being entailed by a certain proposition, and this might seem to imply that the analysis does not have to use the worlds concept. But it does not imply this, for we have no way to characterize the proposition in question except by describing the worlds at which it is true. I shall explain and defend this in §129.

On the Goodman side: When a Goodman theory ties the truth of A>C to C's being entailed by a certain complex proposition A&P, this could be expressed as C's being true throughout the class of AP-worlds. But that would be a mere verbal adornment after the hard work had been done. It would be difficult to put the worlds concept to work in characterizing the proposition in the first place; and, anyway, this being the main point, the 'worlds'-*requiring* elements in Lewis's analysis are absent from Goodman's, as we shall see.

I shall distinguish 'Support theories' from 'Worlds theories'. Those labels point fairly accurately to what goes on in the working-out of the various accounts, as long as you remember how I use the technical term 'Support'. The *word* 'world' rattles around in some of the Goodman-type analyses; Pollock, for one, uses it a great deal, though we shall see that he belongs on the Support side of the line.

120. A MISTAKE OF CHISHOLM'S

For Support Theory, the problem of getting a good analysis of A>C is the problem of saying what tests an actual truth must pass to qualify as a conjunct in

Support (meaning, as always, 'a conjunct in a value of Support'). One part of the test is easy: Support must be logically compatible with (A & Laws), that is, with the conjunction of the antecedent and the totality of true causal laws. There are different ways of producing this result, however, and our choice among these can affect how we evaluate particular subjunctive conditionals.

The scope of the problem can be reduced by appealing to speaker's meaning as distinct from sentence meaning. When someone asserts a subjunctive conditional, questions left open by what his sentence means may be closed by some fact about what *he* means. This happens when the sentence contains a 'this' or an 'it' or the like, but it may also happen in less obvious ways. Various writers have stressed speakers' intentions as a resource for tightening up antecedents, replacing them by something more specific than the words themselves mean. Roderick Chisholm dramatically did this in two papers on subjunctive conditionals (1946, 1955), one of which pre-dates Goodman's famous paper and helps to set the scene for it. In Chisholm's 1955 paper, however, he gave too much power to speakers' intentions, allowing them to firm up antecedents in impermissible ways. This is worth demonstrating for what it can teach us about conditionals.

Chisholm tied the truth of A>C to the truth of something of the form *(A & Laws & Support) entails C, for a value of Support such that . . .*, but he continued in terms not of objective constraints on Support but rather of what the speaker has in mind. Chisholm seemed to assume that when we assert subjunctive conditionals we usually understate the antecedent, leaving it to context to indicate what richer proposition we mean as our antecedent. He said at first that 'We may think of the speaker . . . as having deduced the consequences of a singular supposition, viz. [A], taken with a statement he interprets as a law statement' (p. 101), which suggests that A>C is tied to something of the form *(A & Laws) entails C*, with Support being nowhere in sight. But Chisholm continued: 'We can usually tell, from the context of a man's utterance, what the supposition is and what the other statements are with which he is concerned.' This reference to 'the other statements' shows that Chisholm did think Support has a part to play; and he avoided a theoretical account of what it takes for a proposition to be a legitimate 'other statement'—that is, to be a conjunct in Support—by saying that all that matters is what 'other statements' the speaker has in mind, and that hearers can usually work this out from the context.

There are two objections to this. First, it requires the asserter of A>C to have in mind the value of Support on which he is relying. This knocks out most of the subjunctive conditionals we accept. Someone who asserts or accepts A>C may not be in a position to have in mind or be 'concerned with' any relevant value of Support; and this is not a problem (except for Chisholm), because all one needs is to believe and to mean that *there is* a value of Support meeting certain constraints and relating suitably to A, Laws, and C. I am quite sure that if I had pressed the button again, the red light would have gone on again; yet I know none of the facts about the wiring that make the conditional true. My conditional thought involves the belief that there are facts—there is a value of Support—meeting certain constraints etc.; and this reintroduces the theoretical problem, the one about what the constraints are, that slips out of sight in Chisholm's treatment.

Secondly, Chisholm, by not discussing *entitlement* to occur in Support, implied that there are no limits on what 'other statements' a speaker can legitimately rely on in asserting A>C. Granting him for argument's sake that the speaker's state of mind partly fixes the relevant value of Support, are there not limits to how far this fixing can properly go?

Chisholm implied that there are not. His main example does not involve the Support concept, because it concerns only *independent* subjunctive conditionals (§7), in which C is said to be derivable from (A & Laws) without appeal to any matters of particular fact. Still, his treatment of these materials exhibits a licentiousness—an attitude of 'Anything that you really mean is all right'—that he would have to carry over to dependent conditionals, that is, to the inclusion of conjuncts in Support; and so I want to discuss it.

He started with six truths, but we can get by with four:

(1) All gold is malleable.
(2) Nothing is both malleable and not malleable.
(3) That is not gold.
(4) That is not malleable.

In 3 and 4 the word 'that' refers to a piece of cast iron. As Chisholm said, a speaker who says 'If that were gold . . .' is envisaging a state of affairs in which 3 is false; which logically requires him not to include the truth of 1, 2, and 4 in the envisaged state of affairs. This speaker has three options, Chisholm continued: he can retain 1 and 2, and accept 'If that were gold it would be malleable'; he can retain 2 and 4, and accept 'If that were gold some gold would not be malleable'; and he can retain 1 and 4, and accept 'If that were gold some things would be malleable and not malleable'.

This allows the speaker too much freedom. One is *not* entitled to suppose 3 false while retaining both 1 and 4, thus being led to the negation of 2 as one's consequent. We may debate whether A>C can ever be untrivially true when A and C are both impossible, but it should be beyond question that it cannot be true if A is possible and C is not.

Chisholm might have replied that in this case A is not really possible. The speaker who says 'If that were gold, something would be both malleable and not malleable' is understating the antecedent, which really means: 'If that (while retaining all its non-malleability) were gold (and were therefore malleable) . . .', which is impossible; so we can yoke it to an impossible consequent to get a true conditional. Well, all right; but this is not how we play the game. We have no straightforward ways of handling counterlogical conditionals: they get out of hand unless special provision is made for them (§87); and it would be intolerable if speakers were allowed to assert them as freely as Chisholm allowed.

Something similar holds for the other option that he wrongly offered to the speaker, namely holding 2 and 4 steady and denying 1, thus saying 'If that were gold, not all gold would be malleable'. In saying this I follow Chisholm in taking 1 to be a 'law statement' (p. 102).

Returning to my first complaint: Chisholm assumed that the 'other statements' that bear on the truth of a subjunctive conditional are ones the speaker has in mind. Seeing where this leads can help us to grasp how little the speaker needs to have in mind: he needs only the thought that *there are* truths that satisfy certain conditions and, in conjunction with A, entail C. Chisholm's treatment helps to dramatize the need for quantification and thus for the problem that still confronts us.

121. COTENABILITY *EN BLOC*

What constraints must a truth satisfy to qualify as a conjunct in a value of Support? Goodman (1947) approached this under the heading 'The Problem of Relevant Conditions', but this is a misnomer. If C can be law-derived from (A & Support) for a value of Support that contains irrelevant material, then it can also be law-derived from (A & Support*) where this is what remains of Support after its irrelevant content has been removed. Irrelevant conjuncts are mere clutter: they cannot lead to any conditional's being accorded a truth value that it does not deserve. Worlds analyses take in vast amounts of irrelevant materials, and clearly get away with it. A Worlds theorist will say that the truth value of 'If you had unplugged the computer, it would not have been damaged by lightning' depends upon what obtains at certain worlds that are just like α up to a certain moment . . . *Just* like α? Worlds resembling α in respect of the number of sardines in the Atlantic, the average colour of alpine lilies in Tibet, and the salinity of the smallest rock pool in Iceland? What have those to do with the conditional about the computer? Nothing, but Worlds theories bring them in because they are too much trouble to keep out, and—the main point—they do no harm. Irrelevance is harmless. The real problem is that one may include in a value of Support material that is *illegitimate* because it makes C law-derivable from (A & Support) when in fact A>C is false.

What would make a truth R illegitimate as a conjunct in a value of Support? The most obvious answer is the one that first occurred to Goodman: a true proposition R should not be included in Support if:

If it were the case that A, it would *not* be the case that R.

This seems to generate a simple constraint on Support in addition to its being true, namely ¬(A > ¬Support), which Goodman expressed by saying that Support is 'cotenable' with A.

Let us try to make this serve as a completion of the theory. The simple Goodman theory, then, says that A>C is true if and only if

There is some true proposition Support such that: ¬(A > ¬Support) and (A & Support & Laws) entails C.

Goodman *did* entertain this theory, but saw an acute problem in its having a subjunctive conditional in the analysans. 'To establish any counterfactual,' he remarked ruefully, 'it seems that we first have to determine the truth of another' (1947: 19).

He rightly did not say that to establish one we must *establish* another: the proposed analysis implies that to establish A>C we have to *refute* another subjunctive conditional. This suggests a way of escape from the regress—a way that attracted me for years, though I could never make it work out convincingly. Never mind the details; this was an attempt to rescue something that should be left to die because it makes it too easy for a subjunctive conditional to be adjudged true. The detailed argument for this is also a drag, and I merely report its outcome, which is that this analysis of Goodman's implies:

PF*: C & ¬(A>¬C) entails A>C.

'PF*' is the label I used for this thesis in §89, where I derived Conditional Excluded Middle from it, using a proof by Cross. That is enough, I submit, to show that the proposed analysis is unacceptable.

Pollock (1976: 11) has proved the weaker result that CEM follows from PF* in conjunction with ¬A, offering this explicitly as a criticism of Goodman's theory when 'C is cotenable with A' is understood as meaning ¬(A>¬C). He concludes that Goodman should have defined 'Support is cotenable with A' not as ¬(A > ¬Support) but rather as A > Support, implying that then his theory would have been all right except for its infinite regress. It is indeed nearer right to tie the truth of A>C to C's being entailed by

Strong: (A & Laws) in conjunction with a true Support such that A > Support

than to tie it to C's being entailed by

Weak: (A & Laws) in conjunction with a true value of Support such that ¬(A > ¬Support).

Weak is worryingly reminiscent of PF—the emphasis on particular facts, which Lewis put on his fourth level and thought might have no part in the story about closeness (§89). It seems to imply that random coin-tosses would have come out the same way if someone else had tossed the coin, and so on: the coin *did* fall heads uppermost, and it is not the case that if she had tossed the coin instead of him it would not have fallen heads uppermost; so we can include 'The coin fell heads uppermost' in our value of Support, which amounts to saying that we can assume that the coin fell heads uppermost at the closest A-worlds. This leads to accepting some 'particular fact' conditionals that many of us think are false; so Weak is too weak.

Still, Strong is not right either, because the version of Goodman's theory that uses it makes false some conditionals that we think are true. The result of building Strong into Goodman's analysis ties the truth of A>C to C's being law-derivable from (A & Support) for a value of Support that is law-derivable from (A & Support*) for a value of Support* that is . . . etc. (We are still ignoring the circularity problem.) Now, think about the example of the Dunkirk rescue discussed in §90: 'If I hadn't gone into hospital, I would have taken part in the Dunkirk evacuation.' This requires that if he hadn't gone to hospital, the Dunkirk evacuation would still have occurred; its occurrence will have to be part of Support; but in the story I was telling, its occurrence was caused indeterministically, which means that it cannot be law-derived from anything. So Goodman's analysis, with Strong built into it, would have to condemn that innocent conditional and many others like it. Notice that this objection to Strong, like my second objection to Weak, involves indeterminism.

Goodman would respond to this latest objection that the conditionals it involves are all ones with true consequents, and I tacitly admitted that by writing '. . . would *still* have occurred'. He calls such conditionals 'semifactuals' in contrast to 'counterfactuals' in which A and C are both false (and 'factuals' in which A and C are both true). That is not a useful taxonomy of subjunctive conditionals, and in any case it does not enable Goodman to meet the objection I have raised against Strong.

That is more than enough about Weak and Strong. Each is ruled out anyway because it would involve an infinite regress in the analysis. Let us then follow Goodman in walking away from both, abandoning the attempt to deal with cotenability in one fell swoop. Rather than seeking a single formula to block illegitimate conjuncts from getting into Support, I suggest that we look at kinds of illegitimacy and try to defend the analysis against each separately. Goodman did that. He located two kinds of proposition that it would not be legitimate to include as conjuncts in Support; I shall discuss one in the next two sections, and the other throughout the remainder of the chapter.

122. THE CAUSAL CONTRAPOSITIVE PROBLEM

Some candidates for inclusion in Support are ineligible for causal reasons. I am assuming that any conjunct in Support must be causally compatible with A; but it turns out that we need a further cause-involving constraint. This need arises from 'the causal contrapositive problem', as I shall call it. Goodman illustrated this clearly through a tiny, trivial example, but the problem itself is deep and general. It must be solved if the Goodman approach is to achieve anything. He squarely confronted the problem, but it was left to subsequent writers to solve it.

Think of a typical case where it is clearly true of a certain unlighted match M that *If M had been struck, it would have lit*. (Take the antecedent to be understated: it uses 'struck' as shorthand for something specifying the speed, pressure, chemical composition of the box surface, etc.) We accept this conditional because we think that *M lights* is entailed by a conjunction of causal laws with *M is struck* and a number of other truths such as: *The air is still, M is dry, M is made of phosphorus* and so on. The conjunction of those other truths is the value of Support that makes this conditional true. This particular case is straightforward and unproblematic: we know what we think, and why we think it. For a general analysis of subjunctive conditionals, however, we need to know what entitles this value of Support to be used to support Struck > Lit, bringing this under a rule that we can apply to other conditionals as well. We are now considering this candidate rule: We may include in Support any propositions that are true and causally compatible with Struck—that is, logically compatible with (Struck & Laws).

This gives us the value of Support we need for Struck > Lit, but it also gives us other conditionals that we do not want, including some that conflict with Struck > Lit. Here is how. Take the value of Support referred to above, drop from it the conjunct *M is dry* and add the conjunct *M does not light*. The result is another truth that is causally compatible with Struck, and in conjunction with Struck and the rest of Support it entails *M is not dry*.

For safety's sake, I'll go through that again. Let the original value of Support be expressed as (P & M is dry). Then we have that (A & Laws & P & M is dry) entails M lights. It follows by elementary logic that (A & Laws & P & M does not light) entails M is not dry. This second entailing conjunction is also true and causally compatible with A, so it also qualifies under the rule we are considering. So the latter treats as true not only If M had been struck, it would have lit, which is true, but also If M had been struck, it would not have been dry, which is false. The label 'the causal contrapositive problem' explains itself.

To obviate this difficulty, we need constraints on Support that will admit the match's being dry but exclude its not lighting. The concept of causal compatibility will not do it, and we ran into regress and other troubles when we tried to do it with help from >. Something else is needed. Most subsequent writers on Goodman's causal contrapositive problem have broadly agreed about how to solve it, though their solutions have differed in detail.

The main exception is Rescher, who says that although a law taking us from (Struck & Dry) to Lights is logically equivalent to one taking us from (Struck & Not-lights) to Not-dry, these may nevertheless be *two* laws that are not inter-changeable in all contexts (1961: 193 n.). To back this up, he contends that the so-called 'paradox of confirmation' shows that 'All crows are black' is not interchangeable in all contexts with 'All nonblack things are non-crows', because observations of white snow count only in favour of one and not the other. This is doubly erroneous, as I now show.

Rescher draws the wrong moral from the 'paradox of confirmation', which was in fact perfectly solved in its infancy by Janina Hosiasson-Lindenbaum (1940: 137), 'a promising Polish philosopher who did not survive the Second World War' (Lewy 1976: 44). The key point in her solution is that an observation of white snow *could* be part of a test somewhat confirming that all crows are black (that is, that all nonblack things are non-crows), but the test would be a bad one. It would be the statistically lunatic procedure of identifying things as non-black and then investigating whether they are crows, rather than, with a saner focus, identifying things as crows and then checking their colour. The impression that the two (contrapositive) formulations of the law relate differently to confirming instances is an illusion, which seems to come about as follows. One thinks of a white snowdrift as rotten confirming evidence for 'All crows are black' because it *is* so. One then slides lazily into thinking it would be better evidence for 'All nonblack things are non-crows', dimly applying the idea that the way to test 'All Fs are Gs' is always to find Fs and check them for G-ness. Think about it! Isn't it obvious that the right way to test 'All nonblack things are non-crows' is by finding crows and checking their colour?

Secondly, Rescher thinks he confronts two laws, of which only one supports a certain conditional; but he does not say *which* one. He offers only the highly abstract claim that two laws may be equivalent logically yet not equivalent in some other way. This might in theory rescue us from certain contradictions, but it does not tell us which of the competitors is true.

Wilfrid Sellars (1958) was less far off the main track. He agreed that in the circumstances the match could not be struck and dry but not alight, or be struck and not alight but dry; but he broke up the symmetry by moving from *states* to *entries into states*—not the match's being alight but its catching fire, not its being wet but its becoming so. The causal laws and the rest of the situation clearly do imply

(Struck & Dry) ⊃ Starts to be alight,

and clearly do not imply

(Struck & Not alight) ⊃ Starts to be wet.

This seems to be true and relevant, but it is not general enough to cover conditionals having to do not with a thing's becoming F but rather its continuing to be F—for example, 'If that egg hadn't been washed it would have stayed fresh longer'. Admitting that his 'starting to be F' approach does not help with this last conditional, Sellars simply turned away from it, giving a strange excuse (p. 136).

123. CAUSAL DIRECTION

Buried within Sellars's discussion is a concept that we should now focus on, namely that of causal direction. Sellars pointed out, in effect, that although in the circumstances (Struck & Not-alight) implies Not-dry, it is not true that the match's being struck and not lighting would *cause* it to be wet; whereas its being struck and dry would *cause* it to light. That is the strongest element in his discussion, and he may even have (wrongly) thought of his talk about 'starting' as a way of capturing the notion of causal direction without bringing it in explicitly. It has occurred to nearly all Support theorists to make the concept of causal direction central in their analyses. (The first seems to be Parry (1957: 87–8). Goodman (1957: 443–4) briskly dismissed Parry's treatment, but for a reason that does not get to the bottom of it.) Let us look into how this might be done, what problems it solves, and what ones it creates.

We have required values of Support to be true, and causally compatible with A, and now we require further that a true proposition R is admissible as a conjunct in a value of Support only if

R is not caused to be true by ¬A's being true.

This deals neatly with Goodman's problem about the match. We wanted to keep Not-alight out of Support, and this latest proposal does that: Not-alight may not appear in Support, because the match's not lighting is partly caused by its not being struck, that is, by ¬A. We may still admit Dry into Support, because the match's being dry is not caused by its not being struck.

This relies on the concept of causal or causal-explanatory *direction*, which has not been explained. I have openly helped myself to the notion of a causal law, and thus to statements of the form:

It is causally impossible for P to be the case without Q's being the case.

I am willing to go on availing myself of these, and also of things of the form

In the circumstances, it is causally impossible for P to be the case without Q's being the case,

which can be true even if P and ¬Q are not in themselves causally incompatible. This reference to 'the circumstances' may sound unhappily like the very problem of inclusion-in-Support that we are now wrestling with, but really it is not. All that is involved is the idea that

There is some set F of *facts about the actual world* such that: (1) F is causally sufficient for Q, (2) F includes P, (3) what is left of F after P is removed is not causally sufficient for Q.

In other words, P is an NS condition for Q—a Necessary part of a causally Sufficient condition for Q. I take concept of an NS condition from work by Mackie (1965); see also Bennett 1988a: 44–5. Mackie wrote of INUS conditions, but the vowels are interlopers. He got them in by restricting himself to cases where P alone is Insufficient for Q, and where the actual sufficient conditions were Unnecessary because Q could have come about in some other way; but neither restriction has any philosophical point.

This approach does not involve any of the problems of selecting facts for inclusion in Support. However, it does not deliver causal direction. Given that P is an NS condition for Q, in the above sense, it does not follow that P causes Q to obtain. On the contrary, P might figure in some causally conclusive evidence that Q occurred earlier: for example, certain facts about the environment around Mount St Helens at a certain time were an NS condition of the mountain's having volcanically erupted a few hours *earlier*. So the concept of NS conditions cannot yield an account of *causing* until the entirely distinct concept of causal direction comes to its aid.

I do not know how to analyse the concept of causal direction. We cannot do it with help from >, even if we were willing to stomach the circularity this would involve, because there are backward as well as forward subjunctive conditionals; and I have no other suggestions. I still agree with this:

Causally necessary [conditionals] fall into three subclasses. *Forward*: It is causally necessary that P's being the case leads to Q's being the case. *Backward*: It is causally impossible for P to be the case except as a consequence of Q's being the case. *Mixed*, the simplest mixture being this: It is causally impossible for P to be the case except as a consequence of some R that necessarily leads to Q's being the case.

Given that a conditional is causally necessary, you cannot always tell which species it belongs to just by looking at it. For if Q is dated later than P, (P⊃Q) may be either forward or mixed. Indeed, it may even be a backward conditional if temporally backward causation is somehow possible.

Then what does distinguish one species from the others? Three answers have been offered. (1) The nomological structure of the world distinguishes them: perfect knowledge of Laws would enable us first to pick out the causally necessary conditionals and then sort them into their forward, backward, and mixed species. (2) The notion of causal direction is well grounded, but not in [Laws]: our thinking about causation is based not on the notion of causal laws but rather on our everyday perceptions of things pushing one another around. (3) The line between consequences and prerequisites is not objectively grounded at all; it merely reflects our needs and interests, like the distinction between weeds and other plants or between dirt and other matter. (Bennett 1988a: 43–4)

I hope 3 is not the case, but I still have nothing useful to say about which option is right. I see no clear alternative to simply helping myself to the notion of causal direction—treating it as an unanalysed lump, and applying it on the basis of what seems intuitively right. Though not a disgraceful procedure, it is not a distinguished one either.

We could try to avoid the need for it by specifying temporal rather than causal direction. Assuming that causation never goes backwards in time, we can replace the condition:

No conjunct in Support is caused to be true by ¬A's being true

by:

No conjunct in Support is about any time later than (T$_A$) the time the antecedent is about.

The hope that this will do the job rests on the assumption that if something is causally downstream from ¬A at the actual world then it is not temporally upstream from A at any world; though this is not part of the proposed analysis, which says nothing about causal direction.

Some philosophers question that assumption, holding that temporally backward causation is at least possible. But without taking sides on that issue, we can see that the proposal is in any case wrong for our purposes, because it excludes too much from Support. As we saw in §§89–90, many forward conditionals innocently bring in matters of actual fact pertaining to times later than T_A. 'If you had left home at noon, you would have reached Dunedin in time for the kick-off'—the Support for this would have to include facts about the roads' being clear and usable at times later than T_A. There are countless examples like this, and the temporal constraint threatens to falsify them all. Let us return to the overtly causal constraint.

You may notice that it overlaps the 'causal chain' notion that does a needed service for Worlds analyses of subjunctive conditionals (§90). I am not greatly disturbed by having the notion of causal direction in the analysans. It may well be simply *a fact* about the thoughts underlying our everyday subjunctive conditionals that they involve this notion. 'If so, then that is fairly disgraceful. We should be looking for an analysis that describes our ordinary understanding of subjunctive conditionals while also tidying them up where they are offensively unkempt.' I accept the tidying part of our assignment, but I deny that the concept of causal direction calls for it. Although unanalysed, this concept works pretty well for us; we have fairly firm and agreed intuitions about how it applies in particular cases.

This, then, is where we have got to. A>C is true just in case C is entailed by (A & Laws & Support) where Support is true and no conjunct in it is caused to be true by ¬A. We are not home yet, however, because of a further problem that Goodman uncovered—the other half of the problem of cotenability.

124. THE LOGICAL CLEANSING PROBLEM

We cannot admit into Support anything that entails ¬A, for if we did then (A & Support & ...) would be inconsistent. But that is not enough; for some truths do not entail ¬A yet would combine with A to produce unwelcome results. The problem of devising a constraint to keep these from serving as conjuncts in Support is what I call 'the logical cleansing problem', the idea being that we need to cleanse the totality of true causally eligible propositions by throwing out all the ones that are ineligible for inclusion in Support. The adjective 'logical' distinguishes it from the causal contrapositive problem, which also has to do with cleansing.

The problem of logical cleansing is displayed in an example adapted from one of Goodman's. Take T_1 to be a time at the height of the Korean war and T_2 to be a month or so later. I stipulate that at T_1 Jones did not actually go to Korea. Now, our analysis as so far developed might imply:

If Jones had gone to Korea at T_1, he would have been a prisoner by T_2, on the strength of a value of Support that includes *Jones did not go to South Korea at T_1*. This when conjoined with A yields *Jones went to North Korea at T_1*, and this, together with other eligible truths, could yield the conditional Korea > Prisoner. Something has gone wrong: the thought of Jones's going to Korea has been turned into the thought of his going to North Korea, simply because he in fact did not go to South Korea. This is patently absurd. If we do not solve this problem, we shall have no analysis of any subjunctive conditionals except the independent ones, which need no Support.

Goodman graphically illustrated the absurdity of the suggested basis for Korea > Prisoner. The principles which admit it, he pointed out, would be equally hospitable to the conflicting conditional:

If Jones had gone to Korea at T_1, he would have been fighting with the American army at T_2.

We 'establish' this by including in Support the true proposition that *at T_1 Jones did not go to North Korea*. Combine that with the antecedent of the conditional and you have something that entails that at T_1 Jones went to South Korea, which (let us suppose) could reasonably be thought to lead causally to his being conscripted into the American army by T_2. This is serious. An unguided choice between two incompatible conditionals would be bad enough, but our present analysis commits us to accepting both.

Goodman tried to deal with the logical cleansing problem by focusing on this last upshot of it—the one about having equally good or bad bases for each of a pair of conditionals. He proposed the 'no-rival condition', as we may call it (Goodman 1947: 16–17). This has the effect of turning a theory of the form:

A>C is true ≡ There is a Support such that . . . entails C

into one of the form

A>C is true ≡ There is a Support such that . . . entails C and there is no
            Support such that . . . entails ¬C,

with all the blanks filled in the same way. This says that the best case you can make for A>C is not good enough if an equally good one for (A>¬C) is available. Thus, we do not get either Korea > Prisoner or Korea > US-Army because they kill one another off.

This proposed remedy does not centrally explain why the basis for each Korea conditional is inherently absurd; rather, it looks to the peripheral matter of the face-off between the two. It would be better to focus on the fact that Korea > Prisoner is single-handedly preposterous.

Anyway, the no-rival condition fails in its intended purposes, as Parry showed (pp. 90–1) and Goodman acknowledged (1957: 444). Parry showed that if we add the no-rival condition to the previous analysis and do nothing more, the result will be the falsity of all subjunctive conditionals except independent ones. For dependent conditionals, where Support has work to do, there is always a rival. The trick is simple. If A is false, then A ⊃ R is true for any R, and so is A ⊃ ¬R, and each of these truths is compatible with A. Think of 'He did not go to North Korea' as 'He went to Korea ⊃ He went to South Korea', and analogously for 'He did not go to South Korea'; and that will show you why Parry is right that there is always a rival.

125. PARRY'S REPAIRS

Parry suggested a repair of Goodman's analysis to deal with this problem (Parry 1957: 89–93; see Goodman 1947: 17 n. 6, added in 1991). I shall give it in two parts, though he did not. Its first part requires that no conjunct in Support be entailed by ¬A. This is the logical analogue of Parry's solution of the causal contrapositive problem: the two together require that no conjunct of Support may be actually true as a causal *or logical* consequence of the actual truth of ¬A.

The logical part of this is powerful. Apply it to the Korea troubles, and it knocks out both the bad candidates for inclusion in Support—'Jones did not go to North Korea at T' and 'Jones did not go to South Korea at T'—because both are entailed by 'Jones did not go to Korea at T', which is our current ¬A.

The demand that Support not contain any conjunct that is entailed by ¬A amounts to requiring that, for every conjunct R in Support, $¬A \& ¬R$ be possible. Before working with this, let us set it in context. Because A is actually false and Support true, it is already settled that, for every conjunct R in Support, $¬A \& R$ is possible. Also, the Goodmanian analysis rightly requires that (A & Support) be possible, which entails that, for every conjunct R in Support, $A \& R$ is possible. Furthermore, if, for some R in Support, A & ¬R were not possible, A would entail R, in which case R would be idle in Support, because A could do all the work on its own; so standardly, for every conjunct R in Support, $A \& ¬R$ is possible too. Parry's requirement, then, completes the demand that Support be *strongly independent* of A, meaning that every combination of their truth values be possible. Parry pointed out (pp. 91–2) that we must suppose Support to be expressed without parentheses: a conjunct in a conjunct in Support is itself a conjunct in Support. Otherwise, his proposed repair of the analysis would fail.

(Parry's proposal looks good when taken in terms of worlds. R is true at α and at w_1 but not at w_2; and the question is whether that makes w_1 closer to α than w_2

is. Parry says in effect that it does not do so if it is a logical consequence of the truth of ¬A. That seems just right. At α there is a reason for R's truth, namely the truth of ¬A; and this reason is absent from every A-world. No A-world is *an R-world for the reason that α is an R-world*; so an A-world's being an R-world should not count towards its closeness to α.)

We are still not finished, however. Returning to the Jones-Korea example, consider the following suggested conjuncts in Support:

> Jones is left-handed ⊃ Jones did not go to North Korea at T,
> Jones is left-handed.

Each is true and strongly independent of (A) 'Jones went to Korea at T', and neither contains conjuncts that fail the strong independence test. Yet if we allow both into Support, we are back in the mire.

This smuggles 'Jones did not go to North Korea at T' back into Support. It looks like a sneaky trick, because it is one; but how can we keep it out? Here is a natural response:

> As well as not *containing* any conjuncts that fail the strong independence test, Support must not *entail* anything that fails it. The value of Support that is now making trouble for us, though all of its conjuncts pass the test, is ineligible because it entails something that fails the test, namely that Jones didn't go to North Korea at T_1, which is entailed by ¬A.

No: because *every* prima facie eligible value of Support will entail *some* things that are also entailed by ¬A. Given any two contingent truths, there is a contingent truth that they both entail, namely the disjunction of them.

Parry meets this latest difficulty (p. 92) by applying the strong independence test not only to every conjunct in Support, but, more demandingly, to every truth-functional component of it. So now the analysis has reached this form:

> A>C is true ≡ C is entailed by (A & Laws & Support) for a value of Support that is true and none of whose truth-functional components is entailed or caused to be true by ¬A. ˌ

(Slote's 1978 paper, apparently written without knowledge of Parry's work, offers similar solutions to the same difficulties, though its surface is very different. Slote's independent run at this problem area is worth studying, but I shall not report on it here.) Goodman pointed to difficulties that this proposal does not cover; but Parry could easily adjust his account to avoid them. I shall spare you the details.

A more important difficulty may have been at the back of Goodman's mind, and seems indeed to have been at the front of Parry's (pp. 92–3). If Parry's

constraint concerned what *sentences* could be comprised in Support, it would be
of no avail; for we could easily coin words that would let us devise a Support
which, though containing no verbal apparatus of 'if' and 'or' and so on, contained
the materials for generating unwanted conditionals of the old familiar sort. This
is why Parry states his constraint in terms not of the sentences that Support ver-
bally contains but rather of the propositions that it logically contains—he speaks
of truth-functional compounds that Support is logically equivalent to. This,
however, seems to make the constraint fatally strong. Support, we are now told,
must not logically contain anything entailed by $\neg A$; but anything that Support
entails is logically contained in it as a conjunct, because if P entails Q then P is
equivalent to Q & (Q$\supset$P); so the latest version of Parry's constraint implies that
Support must not *entail* anything that is entailed by $\neg A$. That is no good, we
have seen, because, for any true $\neg A$ and any true candidate for the role of
Support, some truth is entailed by each of them. We are still in trouble.

126. SIMPLE PROPOSITIONS

We have to stop the likes of *Jones is left-handed ⊃ Jones did not go to North
Korea at T* from being a conjunct in Support. If it were merely a matter of keeping that sentence out, the job would be easy; but a purely verbal constraint does
not meet our needs. Let 'snig' mean 'not both left-handed and going to Korea';
then we can include 'Jones was snig at T' in Support, where it will make the
familiar trouble. On the other hand, if we exclude whatever is logically equivalent to a material conditional, we shall be excluding everything.

So we need some criterion intermediate between the verbal and the logical
ones. This may be extractable from Pollock's treatment of subjunctive conditionals, through his concept of *simple proposition* (1976: 91–3). According to
this, *Jones is left-handed ⊃ Jones did not go to North Korea at T* is not a simple
proposition, and we can hope to find in this a basis for disqualifying that material conditional from occurring as a conjunct in Support. Can it be done?

The commonest way of handling propositions these days, and the most secure
and comfortable, is to credit them only with features concerning what they
entail and are entailed by. For most of us, this credits them only with features
that determine what worlds they are true at. On this view, there is only one necessary proposition, and only one impossible one; but most of us are willing—
though the 'relevance logicians' are not—to live with those conclusions and
explain away the seeming evidence against them. Nor is the denial of structure
to propositions merely a symptom of undue attachment to the concept of *worlds*.
Before we get to logic or metaphysics, the concept of proposition is put to work

in philosophical psychology: our most fundamental use of the form . . . *that P* is in attributing contentful states of mind to humans and perhaps other animals, as in saying 'He [it] thinks that the cat is up the tree'. This context also is unfriendly to the idea that propositions have structure. (The first four chapters of Stalnaker 1984 contain a superb attack on propositional structure in logic and philosophical psychology.)

In our present context, however, we need propositions to have structure, so that we can pick out some as conjunctions, others as material conditionals, and so on. We need, that is, some basis for saying not merely what worlds P captures but also *how*, by virtue of what structural features, it captures them. Three ways of grounding the notion of propositional structure have been proposed.

One says that propositions are intrinsically structured: each proposition is a complex abstract object whose parts are less complex abstract objects called 'concepts'. This was Frege's view. It is an attractive line of thought; but no one has succeeded in saying—to the satisfaction of the rest of us—what a concept is, or how we know what concepts there are and how they are combined in propositions. Every attempted epistemology of concepts seems to make them, after all, aspects of how we talk or think.

Or we might attribute structure to propositions in a derivative way, through the structures of the sentences in which they are expressed. This may help in some contexts, but not here. We are trying to develop a Goodman–Parry–Pollock analysis that *quantifies* over simple propositions. It says that Support, viewed as a conjunction of simple propositions, must not have any conjunct entailed by ¬A. This requires us to make sense of '. . . is a simple proposition' as a general predicate that propositions can satisfy. The verbal approach that I am now examining gives us only two options:

P is simple ≡ P can be expressed without 'if' etc.
P is simple ≡ P cannot be expressed with 'if' etc.

On the former definition, everything is simple, on the latter nothing is; so both are useless.

The third approach is to attribute structure to propositions derivatively, according to how our minds come to grips with them. Thus Pollock: 'A simple proposition is one whose truth can be known non-inductively without first coming to know the truth of some proposition or propositions which entail it' (1976: 92; see also 73–5). Thus, 'Jones is left-handed ⊃ Jones did not go to North Korea at T'—word it how you will—is not the sort of thing one could know observationally except by observing that Jones is not left-handed or observing that Jones did not go to North Korea at T.

This concept of 'simple proposition' is epistemic, being defined in terms of what could be known. This has to mean: what could be known by the likes of us; it could not be denied that somewhere in logical space there are beings that could know observationally ('noninductively', as Pollock puts it) that *Jones is left-handed ⊃ Jones did not go to North Korea at T* without knowing anything stronger that entails this. We may have hoped for an analysis of subjunctive conditionals in terms more sternly metaphysical than this, with no special relations to human capacities; but we are not entitled to insist that the best analysis will realize these hopes. Pollock's notion of 'simple proposition' is humanity-relative, and is also a bit loose, a little soft around the edges (thus Bigelow 1980: 135); but for all that it might play an essential part in the daily life of subjunctive conditionals.

We could use it to rescue the line of analysis we have been pursuing through Goodman and Parry. The result would be this:

A>C is true ≡ C is entailed by (A & Laws & Support) where Support is a conjunction of truths that are (1) not caused to be true by the truth of ¬A and (2) simple and strongly independent of A.

This analysis withstands all the batterings of this chapter so far. Its clause 1 solves the causal contrapositive problem, while 2 solves the logical cleansing problem.

This seems to be the best we can do by way of a Support theory; and it does solve two main problems that those philosophers recognized. In §129 below, however, we shall find other problems that they overlooked—requirements for a good analysis of subjunctive conditionals that cannot even be asked for, let alone satisfied, within the confines of Support theories. For this reason, I am sure that the palm must be given to the Stalnaker/Lewis way of analysing A>C. Still, it was worthwhile to give the Support approach a run for its money.

21

The Need for Worlds

127. COMPARISONS AMONGST WORLDS

What is basically at issue between Worlds and Support analyses of subjunctive conditionals? I shall lead into this by considering Jackson's discussion of the matter—the only useful treatment I know of (1977: 18–19). It appeared before Lewis's 'Time's Arrow' paper, which puts some of it out of date. Also, Jackson has since declared himself as no longer resistant to a Worlds approach to subjunctive conditionals, though without saying what fault he finds with his criticism of it a decade earlier (1987: 62). I shall examine the criticism anyway, because of what we can learn from it. We must start with Jackson's distinction between two notions of *possible world*.

One of them he calls 'realism'. The only adherent of it whom he names is Lewis, yet it seems not to be extreme realism but rather the disjunction of that with abstract realism (§§63–4). Jackson discusses an argument of Lewis's for some kind of realism, starting from the premiss 'There are many ways things could have been besides the way they actually are' and going on to say 'I call these ways things could have been *worlds*'. It has often been pointed out that this argument cannot lead to extreme realism, because ways things could be are not lumps of space and rock, any more than the way things are is the cosmos we inhabit. Jackson, however, discusses this argument of Lewis's without commenting on the jump from abstract to concrete that it seems to involve, which confirms that he is not concerned with the extreme/abstract difference.

The other position that Jackson mentions is a reductive one, according to which possible worlds are merely 'maximally consistent sets of sentences'. If Jackson had said 'propositions' rather than 'sentences', one might think this was meant to be abstract realism, in which case the other might be extreme realism after all. But Jackson really does mean *sentences*, as we shall see. I do not know what actual philosophers he has in mind here, but we shall find that this does not matter much.

Jackson writes this:

> Lewis is . . . committed to possible worlds . . . by his theory of counterfactuals. For the similarity between possible worlds, which is central in his theory, cannot be reduced to a relation between sets of sentences. . . . The kinds of similarities relevant on Lewis's theory do not hold between the actual world—even if rendered as the set of all the true sentences—and sets of sentences. . . . Structural syntactic similarities and similarities in sound . . . are not the sort of similarities that Lewis thinks are relevant to the truth-conditions for counterfactuals. (1977: 18)

For Jackson, then, the crucial point concerns quantifying over possible worlds and treating them as items that can be described, compared, and contrasted in certain ways; whether they are understood concretely or abstractly does not matter.

In Jackson's own 'causal theory', things are said about likenesses between worlds. The core of them, for forward subjunctive conditionals, ties the truth of A>C to C's obtaining at all the A-worlds satisfying this:

> (1) Their causal laws at and after T_A are identical with ours, (2) their T_A time-slices are the most similar in particular facts to ours, and (3) they are identical in particular fact to our world prior to T_A. (Jackson 1977: 9)

This uses 'similar' in 2, and in 3 it uses 'identical' to mean 'exactly alike'. But these similarity judgements do not put Jackson into the Worlds camp, he says, because they are dispensable:

> A causal theorist about counterfactuals can avoid ontic commitment to (non-actual) possible worlds, for he can specify how to judge similarities of the kind that are relevant on the causal theory without slipping back into talk putatively about possible worlds . . . . The relevant similarities will be in factors like the mass of one object, the position of another, the magnitude of a force, and so on. And similarities of this kind can be read off from the sentences themselves; there is no need to 'go behind' the sentences to what would obtain if they were true. (p. 19)

We can see what this means in application to analyses like Goodman's. When he tied the truth of A>C to C's being entailed by (A & Laws & Support) for a value of Support satisfying certain constraints, we *could* see him as saying that A>C is true just in case C obtains at all the legal A-worlds that resemble α in certain respects. But we are not obliged to read him in that way, because the respects of likeness are *specified* by the stated constraints on Support. The worlds—if we insist on dragging worlds into the story—are characterized by the particular propositions that are true at them. Bringing in the worlds is a needless luxury: the analysis can do its work in terms of those propositions or sentences, without 'going behind' them to talk about what a world would be like at which they were true.

It is less clear that the same applies to Jackson's analysis. I cannot see how the truth value of 'their T_A time-slices are the most similar in particular facts to ours' could be 'read off from the sentences [or propositions] themselves'. Jackson assures us that 'the relevant similarities will be in factors like the mass of one object, the position of another, the magnitude of a force, and so on', and that those can be 'read off from the sentences'. I still don't get it. Jackson writes as though for each subjunctive conditional we can *list* the respects of similarity—the worlds are alike in the position and velocity of x, the mass of y, the gravitational force exerted on z, and so on—and if this were right we could no doubt do the work by specifying the sentences or propositions that are true at α and at the other relevant world. But it is not right. Subjunctive conditionals are useful to us largely because we can have reason to believe them without having so much as an opinion about what their factual basis is.

Perhaps Jackson came to think so too, which might explain his more recently declaring himself to belong in the Worlds camp, apparently without changing his analysis. Anyway, he raised a good question, which should be discussed on its merits.

We can break it into two. (1) Granted that Lewis and others make copious use of the worlds concept, is it indispensable to their analyses? (2) If some of those uses are ineliminable, are they needed for the analyses to be right? Question 1 is partly exegetical, while 2 is wholly philosophical.

The answer Yes to 1 must have seemed obvious to Jackson in 1977. At that time he understood Lewis on the basis of his book, which seemed to equate closeness with over-all intuitive similarity of worlds; and any analysis like that certainly commits itself to using the world concept. But when Lewis elaborated his position in his 'Time's Arrow' paper, in the light of the A>Big-difference difficulty, the result was an account of closeness in which overall comparisons play no overt part.

Well, strictly, they play one overt part, but it is not a problem for Support theorists. The analysis in Lewis's 'Time's Arrow' paper—or the derivative of it that I have defended—globally compares worlds in one obvious way: it requires the closest A-worlds to be exactly like α until shortly before T_A. This kind of global comparison can easily be secured without using the world concept; in a Support type of analysis it could be achieved by requiring that no falsehoods may occur in Support except ones that are dated close to T_A. The perfect likeness before that is secured by requiring that all the earlier-dated propositions in Support are true.

Still, the defended analysis might involve world-comparisons of some subtler and less obvious kind. Does it? One plausible reason for saying Yes misled me for so long that I suppose it is worth exposing. It concerns trade-offs.

128. TRADE-OFFS

Global comparisons of worlds would enter into the analysis if it required trade-offs. Consider these two instructions for partially copying a table:

Make a new table that differs from the old one in respect R, and is otherwise as much like it as possible.

Make a new table that differs from the old one in respect R, and that resembles it exactly in respects $r_1, \ldots, r_n$.

Obviously, the former involves an overall comparison between the two tables, while the latter does not, and this shows in the fact that the former allows for trade-offs while the latter does not. Suppose the first order is for a table resembling this oaken one as much as possible except for being made of mahogany; and the carpenter can, with the available materials, make either a table whose legs are an inch shorter or one whose top is two inches narrower; he must consider which of these counts as being as more like the original. In contrast to this, the second work-order picks out the respects that count, and demands perfect likeness in them; it provides no work for trade-offs, balancing of some dissimilarities against others.

Let us now apply this to the difference between the two kinds of analysis of subjunctive conditionals. A Support analysis, taken as specifying the worlds at which C must obtain for A>C to be true, does so in terms of perfect likeness in named respects, and not in global terms inviting trade-offs of one dissimilarity against another. Every true conjunct in Support corresponds to a perfect similarity (in some respect) between α and the worlds being characterized. This stands in contrast with some Worlds analyses—those of Stalnaker and Wayne Davis, for example, and also the one we thought was offered in Lewis's book—where global comparisons of worlds are in play, inviting trade-offs between some dissimilarities and others.

The contrast between two uses of the concept of similarity is less obviously relevant to the analysis I have derived from Lewis's 'Time's Arrow' paper. According to it, when we are comparing two A-worlds, w_1 and w_2, the relevant questions to ask about each are these:

(1) Is w_i exactly like α until some time T_F not long before T_A?

(2) Does w_i diverge from α at T_F in an inconspicuous way?

(3) Does w_i conform to the laws of α from T_F onwards?

(4) Is it the case that, for every two events e_1 and e_2: if e_1 causes e_2 at α, and e_1 occurs at w_i, then e_1 causes e_2 at w_i?

You will recall that 4 is included to deal with events that are non-deterministically caused, since these are not secured by 3 but evidently do have a role in our thoughts about closeness (§90).

Items 3 and 4 are all-or-nothing affairs, admitting of Yes or No answers, with no room for trade-offs. It might seem to be different with 1 and 2. Together they identify the concept of an acceptable fork from α leading to a ramp to the antecedent, and one might think that w_1 could do better than w_2 in one of these respects and worse in the other, making a trade-off judgement necessary.

That is not how Lewis presented them. The account in his 'Time's Arrow' paper seems to mean that the later the fork the better, period; but we saw in §83 why this is not right. It generates the principle that if some nonactual event had occurred, it would have occurred as late as possible; which is not credible. That is why I have relaxed this element in Lewis's account of closeness, requiring only that closest A-worlds diverge from α at *latest* forks, with this understood vaguely, weakly, not strictly.

The analysis I have defended, like Lewis's own, allows that a fork may be created by a miracle, but it must be a small one. Without rejecting his metaphysical account of smallness of miracle, I have stressed what I see as the essential idea, namely that the miracle must not call itself to the attention of hearers of A>C, generating unintended other conditionals and perhaps even the rejection of A>C itself. Thus, I have said that miracles must be 'inconspicuous' rather than 'small'. Either way, however, this property of some miracles is a matter of degree, just as lateness is. Perhaps this opens the way to trade-offs between lateness and smallness (or inconspicuousness).

For example, someone says 'If at noon the tanks had started advancing along the *west* side of the valley, the defence would have crumbled before the day was over'; and the best candidates for closest A-world are w_1 at which the divisional commander made a slightly different decision from his actual one the night before, and w_2 where the battalion commander disobeyed orders on the morning of the attack. It seems that w_1 has a longer ramp from a less obtrusive fork from actuality; in w_2 the ramp is shorter, but the fork-making event departs more conspicuously from how things went at α. If ever trade-offs are appropriate, they are so here, one would think. But we have no idea of how to proceed. How much of a bump (or click) is a fair trade for a twelve-hour shortening of the ramp? As soon as the question is asked, one sees its absurdity. It has nothing to do with our actual uses of subjunctive conditionals.

To put teeth into the example, let us suppose that the choice of world affects the truth value of the conditional. If the tanks had advanced up the west side of the valley because the battalion commander had disobeyed orders, the divisional commander would have dismissed him on the spot, throwing the attack into confusion and enabling the defence to regroup; whereas if they had advanced on the west because it was so decided higher up the night before, they would indeed have wiped out the defence.

If such a case arose, the sensible reaction would be to ask the speaker what he had in mind. Usually, his only thought about the ramp will be that it should not intrude on his thoughts about the link between (A) the route of the tank attack and (C) the outcome of the battle. If some permissible ramp stays out of the way as he desires, 'listener's charity' requires us to interpret what he says in terms of it. Charity does not require us to interpret his conditional so that it comes out true, for that policy would trivialize subjunctive conditionals generally. But charity does demand that we not reject the conditional because of interference from some permissible ramp, if another is also permissible. I do not say 'equally permissible'; that is not how this game is played.

There are no firm rules for selecting forks. Often the most plausible fork involves a non-actual decision made by some person; often it is something else; and when no objectively right or clearly indicated answer presents itself, the author of the conditional should explain what kind of ramp to the antecedent he envisages. These casual remarks fit the looseness of our thinking about the fork aspect of our subjunctive conditionals. Analysis based on ordinary usage shows that—if there is no warning to the contrary—the author of a subjunctive conditional does not think of it as involving a world that is notably unlike α for the whole of previous time or one that diverges from actuality in an initially conspicuous manner. But what he positively has in mind, subject to those constraints, seems to be fairly loose and vague.

So trade-offs between (dis)similarities of different worlds are not needed in good analyses of subjunctive conditionals. It follows that they cannot be a source of any need for such analyses to employ the world concept.

129. SOME REAL OBSTACLES TO SUPPORT ANALYSES

The Lewis-based analysis that I have defended can be partly expressed in the Support fashion. (1) 'Closest A-worlds are lawful from T_F onwards' appears on the Support side of the line as '. . . only if C is entailed by (A & Laws$_F$ & . . .)' etc., where 'Laws$_F$' refers to the conjunction of all α's causal laws taken as quantifying over all times from T_F onwards. (2) A similar treatment can be given to 'Closest A-worlds are lawful until just before T_F'. (3) 'Closest A-worlds are exactly like α up to T_F' goes over into 'Support may not include any falsehood pertaining to a time before T_F'. (4) 'A fork occurs at T_F' goes over into 'Support includes no falsehoods pertaining to times earlier than T_F and contains a false-hood pertaining to T_F'. (5) 'The fork is late' goes over into 'The earliest-dated falsehood concerns a time only a little earlier than T_A'.

This rich harvest still does not exhaust the contents of the Worlds analysis. Some parts of it elude capture in Support terms.

Unless the author of the conditional specifies otherwise, the fork must be either a non-actual legal outcome of an indeterministic process, or an inconspicuous miracle, or an exploding difference (§82). There seems to be no prospect for stating any of these disjuncts purely as a constraint on a proposition rather than on the state of affairs that would obtain if the proposition were true.

A second shortfall in the Support approach concerns this (§90):

Causal Chain PF: If (1) w_1 exactly resembles w_2 up to T_F, and (2) both conform to the laws of α thereafter, and (3) they first become unalike in respect of one particular matter of post-T_F fact that obtains at α and w_1—*through the same causal chain at both*—but not at w_2, then w_1 is closer to α than w_2 is.

This was needed so that, when an indeterministic coin-toss is in question, 'If you had bet heads you would have won' comes out true while 'If she had tossed instead of you it would have fallen heads' does not. This defeats Support analyses, because they cannot provide for the notion of a causal chain. This seems to be the notion of a chain of *events*; so our analysis requires us to consider whether in such and such a state of affairs the events that occurred would be the very ones that did cause C to be the case in actuality. This cannot be expressed as a constraint on sentences or propositions. It plainly gives us, in Jackson's good phrase, a 'need to "go behind" the sentences to what would obtain if they were true'. This need not involve global talk about whole worlds, but it does involve talk about the state of affairs expressed in the analysans; that is basically Worlds talk; it lacks the essential feature of Support analyses, namely a handling of everything in terms of relations amongst sentences or propositions. The net cast by Support theory is too coarse to catch this fish.

The coin-tossing example came from a note at the end of a paper of Slote's, which offers 'an account of counterfactuals that is strikingly at variance with the presently dominant Stalnaker–Lewis "similarity" theory of counterfactuals [and] is something of a throwback to Goodmanlike "cotenability" treatments of counterfactuals' (1978: 3). Slote declares the coin-tossing example to be 'trou-blesome', says 'I know of no theory of counterfactuals that can adequately explain why such a statement seems natural and correct', and concludes hope-fully that 'perhaps it simply *isn't* correct and the correct retort to it is "no, you're wrong; if I had bet heads, the coin might have come up differently"' (p. 27 n.). This befits one who pins his hopes on Support theory.

The difficulty might be overcome if causal chains were made of facts or states of affairs rather than of events; but I do not think that that approach can be made to work; and I guess the chances for that are even slimmer under the constraints imposed by the Support approach.

I conclude, with moderate confidence, that Support analyses cannot say what needs to be said about indeterministic causation, causal chains, and inconspicuousness of forks. The case for preferring Worlds to Support is strong, therefore; and now I shall strengthen it further.

Every follower of Goodman's opening moves has found the (logical) cleansing problem to be hard. In §§124–6 I offered to solve it, using ideas from Goodman and Parry, aided by Pollock's concept of a simple proposition. It was a laborious business, though, and its end-product is not pretty, though it seems to do what the Support theorists wanted. Nothing like the logical cleansing problem arose in the Worlds context—and not because we missed something there, as Support theorists missed the need for forks. For a good Worlds analysis, the main task in identifying closest A-worlds is to decide which {time, event} pairs constitute acceptable forks; solve this and the cleansing problem does not arise. 'If Jones had gone to Korea at T, . . .'—we evaluate this by considering the eligible latest forks from actuality leading to Jones's going to Korea at T. We then develop most of the remainder of our account of what happens at those worlds on that basis: given this or that fork from actuality, what follows causally? There is not even a prima facie threat of coming to grief by combining 'Jones goes to Korea' with 'Jones does not go to South Korea', or any such nonsense as that.

130. POLLOCK'S ANALYSIS OF SUBJUNCTIVE CONDITIONALS

When contrasting Support and Worlds analyses of subjunctive conditionals, we should take special note of Pollock. He freely uses the term 'world', tying the truth value of A>C to C's being true at each member of a certain class of A-worlds. At its core, however, as Jackson has noted (1980: 414), Pollock's account belongs to the Goodman tradition: according to him, a suitably close A-world is 'one that is obtained from the real world by making minimal changes which suffice to make A true'; and his account of those 'minimal changes' is Goodmanian in spirit. Where Lewis got his closest A-worlds by looking for latest modest forks from actuality, Pollock gets them by specifying which sorts of actually true propositions are false at them. This piecemeal approach, proposition by proposition, stands in stark contrast to the global talk about worlds that characterizes the work of Lewis and his like.

Pollock's concept of *simple proposition* helps us to solve Goodman's cleansing problem (§126); he develops it because he has the problem too, which is one mark of the likeness of his approach to Goodman's.

In this sketch I omit some of Pollock's careful details, which are aimed partly at solving esoteric problems that I do not mind ignoring, and partly at achieving a level of formal rigour that I cheerfully forgo.

Pollock handles the cleansing problem pretty much as I did, with his help; though his treatment is complicated by a recherché problem which I am willing to ignore (it concerns 'If there had been infinitely many Fs . . .' when in fact there are only finitely many Fs). His solution of the causal contrapositive problem, involving something he calls 'undercutting', is at the bottom line exactly the one that I accepted in §123, following Parry, and that has occurred to many other Support theorists, including Jackson and Slote.

As for the other requirements of a good analysis: Pollock provides for indeterministic causation (p. 82), and his concept of 'undercutting' enables him—unlike other Support theorists—to make good use of the concept of sameness of causal chain. I cannot see that he can provide for the idea that a fork may involve an inconspicuous miracle. But then he evidently sees no need for forks. In the course of re-presenting his 'undercutting' idea in terms that are temporal rather than causal, he clearly implies that the closest A-worlds may be unlike α for the whole of pre-T_A time. He writes, for example, that 'in deciding what is true in [a world] at time t, we must first decide what is true for all prior times' (p. 80), with no suggestion that up to a certain point there must be complete conformity with α. Pollock seems to have done this work without noting the reasons there are to espouse Lewis's 'latest fork' kind of analysis, the reasons that killed my Simple Theory (§80).

So much for preliminaries. Now I come to what most concerns me here in this work of Pollock's. Although his analysis belongs to the class of Support theories, he expresses it using 'worlds', which lets him contrast it with the accounts of Lewis and others on a certain significant point of detail. Pollock's side of the difference comes about through his Support approach, but it can be evaluated independently of that.

In Lewis's theory, and in my variant on it, the relation '. . . is at least as close to α as is . . .' is *connected* in the set of all worlds. That is, given any two worlds, that relation holds between them in at least one direction. This does not hold in Pollock's theory, in which it can happen that the 'distances' of two worlds from α are incomparable: neither is at least as great as the other.

To grasp Lewis's side of this contrast, consider his Ptolemaic-astronomy model. The actual world sits at its centre, and around it all the other possible worlds are organized in spheres, with every world in a given sphere being closer to α than any world outside the sphere. Given any two worlds w_1 and w_2, either some sphere contains w_1 and not w_2, or some sphere contains w_2 and not w_1, or every sphere containing either contains the other. In the first case, w_1 is closer to α than w_2 is, in the second case w_2 is the closer, and in the third case they are equally close. There are no other alternatives, and so the relation '. . . is at least as close to α as . . .' is connected.

We can express Pollock's contrasting account through a model in which there are rays, lines, extending out from the actual world: any given ray is constituted by a linear sequence of worlds of which α is the first and each subsequent member is defined by the falsity at it of exactly one simple proposition that is true at every preceding member. You move out along a ray from α by taking simple propositions that are true at α and switching them to false, one at a time, one per world.

We can compare two worlds that are on the same ray, saying that one is further from the actual world than the other. But two A-worlds that are not on the same ray, even if one is intuitively more *like* α than the other, cannot differ in closeness in any way that Pollock's theory recognizes. What puts them on different rays is that each falsifies at least one simple proposition that the other verifies—which makes them Pollock-incomparable.

Thus, for a given false proposition A there could be indefinitely many rays running out from α to minimally reached A-worlds. A given world can occur on more than one ray, so the model is not simply a system of rays but a lattice (Pollock 1976: 23). There are two minimal journeys from α to a world at which grass is blue and snow is black—one through a world at which grass is blue and snow is white, the other through a world at which grass is green and snow is black. A diagram with α and those three worlds on it will be shaped like a diamond (Fig. 8).

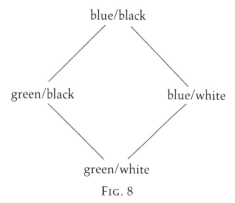

blue/black

green/black   blue/white

green/white

FIG. 8

I stress this matter of connectedness because a possibly important point of logic hangs upon it. We saw in Chapter 10 how differences of opinion about closeness can generate different logics for conditionals, and this is another example of that, because a certain logical principle that holds on Lewis's theory fails on Pollock's.

131. LIMITED ANTECEDENT STRENGTHENING

The principle is Limited Antecedent Strengthening (LAS), which endorses the following as valid:

A>C, ¬(A>¬B) ∴ (A&B) > C.

Borrowing Lewis's essentially correct account of 'might' (§73), we can put this by saying that if

If A obtained, C would obtain, and
If A obtained, B might obtain,

then

If A&B obtained, C would obtain.

We know that unlimited Antecedent Strengthening—

A>C ∴ (A&B) > C

—is not valid on any tenable theory of subjunctive conditionals (§65); and now LAS will be argued to be unacceptable also.

This is somewhat surprising. In thinking about it intuitively, be careful to distinguish it from *Very* Limited Antecedent Strengthening, which says that this:

A>C, A>B ∴ (A&B) > C

is valid. There can be no doubt about that, but it is much safer than LAS. In thinking about this, I find it helpful to take LAS contrapositively, as saying that this:

¬(A>¬B), ¬((A&B) > C) ∴ ¬(A>C)

is valid. To get a sense of the intuitive plausibility of this, think of the premises as 'might' conditionals: if (A) I walked on the ice, I might (B) have helium balloons attached to me; and if (A&B) I walked on the ice with large helium balloons attached to me, the ice might not (C) break. Do not those two seem clearly to make it wrong to say that if I walked on the ice (no mention of balloons) the ice *would* break?

Yet Pollock has argued against LAS. He did this first through a difficult example (1976: 43–4), which he later improved (1981: 254–5). In presenting the latter argument, I shall vary its narrative details, but preserve its form.

Although Pollock does not say this, his example is a case where C is actually true, so that A>C is a non-interference conditional and the only chance (A&B) > C has of being true is also as a non-interference conditional. If LAS does indeed fail, I suspect that it does so only for non-interference conditionals; and one might hope it would look less convincing when applied to them. Unfortunately, it does not. A case where LAS failed for a non-interference conditional would be one in which these three were all true:

> A's obtaining would not interfere with C's obtaining.
> If A obtained, B might obtain.
> (A & B)'s obtaining might interfere with C's obtaining.

This, upon reflection, seems to be impossible. If B might go with A, and if ¬C might go with A&B, how can it be true that if A obtained C *would* obtain? If it cannot, then LAS holds good even for non-interference conditionals. And yet . . .

When electricity flows to the house, the living-room is warm, because the under-floor electrical heating system is always turned on. The room can also be warmed in another way: by heat from the airtight stove and from a natural gas heater, neither being sufficient on its own. The versatile kitchen range can work either on electricity or on natural gas. The gas and electricity supplies are causally independent of one another, and on this cold morning neither supply is working and the airtight stove is unlit. (The only person who ever lights it is a neighbour, who follows his whims in this, paying no attention to how things are in the house.) The living-room is icy.

Given all this, we should accept *(Even) if the kitchen range had been working this morning, the airtight stove would (still) not have been lit*, as a true non-interference conditional. That is,

(1) K>¬A.

(If you are uncomfortable with this, provide it with a context, in the manner of §91; for example, by supposing it to be part of a defence of '(Even) if someone had got the range to work, we couldn't have cooked a meal and burned up what we didn't eat, because the airtight stove was not [and therefore would not have been] lit.') We also have the *falsity* of *If the kitchen range had been functioning, the room would have been cold*. This is false because one way for the range to function is for electricity to flow to it, and that would warm the room. So we have

(2) ¬(K>C).

Now, from 1 it follows by elementary logic that if the kitchen range had been working, it would not have been the case that: the airtight stove was lit and the gas supply was on:

(3) K > ¬(A & G).

This looks tricky but it is valid. If K's truth would leave ¬A standing then it would also leave standing every weaker proposition ¬(A & X), for any X.

Now look again at 3 and 2, in that order:

K > ¬(A & G).
¬(K>C).

Get these by substitutions in the premises of LAS, and out rolls the conclusion:

(K&¬C) > ¬(A & G),

which means that (even) if the kitchen range had been working and the rooms had been warm, it would (still) not have been the case that the airtight stove was lit and the gas supply was running.

This is unacceptable. In the scenario I have given, there are two ways for it come about that the kitchen range works and the rooms are warm; and the conclusion of the above argument implies that only one of the ways obtains at the closest K$\bar{\text{C}}$-worlds. There is no reason for that in the scenario I presented. (Do not say: the electrical solution to the house's problems requires only one change, while the other requires two. That is an accident of the example.)

Yet LAS holds within Lewis's analysis. The premises of LAS say:

(1) Some AC-worlds are closer to α than any A$\bar{\text{C}}$-world is,
(2) Some AB-worlds are as close to α as any A$\bar{\text{B}}$-world is.

So 1 says that as you move out from α through ever-larger spheres of A-worlds measured by their closeness to α, you reach C-worlds before reaching any $\bar{\text{C}}$-worlds; and 2 says that as you move out from α through the same system of spheres you meet B-worlds at least as soon as you meet any $\bar{\text{B}}$-worlds. Now, consider the largest set of C-worlds that are all closer than any $\bar{\text{C}}$-world. Some of those must be B-worlds; for if none were, that would mean that as we move out through the A-worlds, we encounter some $\bar{\text{B}}$ worlds before meeting any B-worlds—which contradicts 2. It follows that some class of ABC-worlds are closer to α than is any AB$\bar{\text{C}}$-world. This means that (A&B) > C, which is the conclusion of Limited Antecedent Strengthening. QED.

In a theory in which '. . . is at least as close to α as . . . is' is not connected, this proof does not go through, and there is no other basis for declaring LAS to be valid. In the context of Pollock's analysis, the first premiss A>C says that all minimally reached A-worlds are C-worlds; and the second says that some minimally reached A-worlds are B-worlds. These plainly do not imply that all minimally reached AB-worlds are C worlds. The point is that on *some* ray where the closest A-world is a C-world, the closest AB-world may be a remoter affair, existing much further along the ray where there are $\bar{C}$-worlds. A minimally reached AB-world is an A-world, but it may not be a minimally reached A-world.

Lewis (1981), in response to Pollock's earlier version of this argument, suggested a way of backing off a little from connectedness while still preserving the essence of his analysis. But the backing off concerned pairs of worlds that are too unlike one another for there to be much sense in asking which if either is closer to α. Pollock (1981: 255–6) replied that when the details of this proposal of Lewis's are brought to bear on Pollock's example, they do not remove the difficulty which it poses. I agree.

This looks like a victory for Pollock's analysis over Lewis's. Given the problems besetting Support analyses, even when developed at Pollock's high level of sophistication, I hope this difficulty can be resolved, but I do not see how to do it.

22

Relating the Two Kinds
of Conditional

132. BASES FOR ACCEPTING INDICATIVE
CONDITIONALS

Through twenty-one chapters I have respected the traditional line dividing supposedly subjunctive 'would' conditionals from indicative 'would'-less ones. In §6
I sketched the 'relocation thesis', which challenges this classification, presenting
two reasons that have been given for putting Does-will indicatives such as 'If it
rains tonight, the roads will be slippery tomorrow' into the same category as the
subjunctives. I undertook to disprove the relocation thesis, which I shall now do.

My disproof starts with a set of facts about bases one may have for accepting
an indicative conditional. Someone who regards A→C as probable has a belief
system which, after being adjusted to admit and assimilate $P(A) = 1$, accords a
high probability to C. That is the Ramsey 'test' or procedure for evaluating
indicative conditionals. It worked hard throughout Chapters 3 and 5–6 above;
but now we must dig into it, *under* it, considering what goes on when your adop-
tion of $P(A) = 1$ elevates your value for $P(C)$.

The materials out of which your value for $P(C)$ must emerge are these:

A, the antecedent of the conditional;

E (for 'evidence'), conjoining all that you believe about particular matters of
fact, minimally adjusted to assimilate A;

P (for 'principles'), containing whatever basic doctrine you use in inferring C
from A&E.

The principles always include some logic, taking this broadly to cover mathematics, abstract probability theory, and other *a priori* aids to the mind.
Sometimes they contain nothing else: 'If the child lived, the family now has as
many boys as girls' could be accepted on the strength of (P) simple arithmetic

together with (E) the belief that the child was a boy and the remainder of the family consists of one boy and two girls. More often P also includes causal doctrine ('If you put one more block on the girder, it will bend') or moral principles ('If he paid for the child's upkeep, that was noble of him') or both ('If you give him the injection, you will be behaving wrongly'). From here on, I shall be silent about P, audible about A and E.

Sometimes E is not needed, because C follows purely from A and general principles. These are independent conditionals (§7), which I again set aside.

In many and perhaps all cases where someone accepts A→C, through the thought that certainty for A, when combined with her E, yields a high probability for C, this movement of her mind involves the makings of a thought about something's explaining or being a reason for something else, a thought with a *because* in it. Unpublished work by Mark Lance, years ago, first gave me the idea of asking with regard to any given conditional 'What is being thought to explain what?' My answers are mainly my own work, but I had to be prodded towards the question.

One might think that explanations have nothing to do with the likes of these: 'Even if I study from now until the time of the exam, I'll fail'; 'Even if the inspector didn't check it out, the work is up to code'. In such non-interference conditionals, it seems, the speaker accepts C unconditionally, giving no reason or explanation for anything. But perhaps not so. It is reasonable to think that the speaker bases 'I'll fail' upon (E) his not having worked all semester long, and bases 'The work is up to code' upon (E) the workers' being competent and conscientious; so in each case some elements in E give a reason or explanation for C. This rescue fails, however, if the person accepts C as a *basic* truth, not supported by any E and thus not explained by any. An example might be: 'Even if an omnipotent Deceiver is at work, I exist.' If there are such basic acceptances of propositions that can then be used as consequents in non-interference conditionals, then in those cases the basis for A→C does not support any explanation. Another possible class of exceptions will be mentioned in §133.

All I need is that bases for indicative conditionals *often* support explanations. I now observe that the latter are of three types:

A and E explain C.
C explains A.
C explains an element in E.

In the first case, if E were not helping A to explain C, it would have no role; then the person would be accepting the conditional as an independent one. E also has a role in the second case, and A in the third; I shall explain these shortly. At the outset, the main thing to be grasped is that the basis for accepting A→C may include an explanation for C, for A, or for E. *I do not assert that indicative conditionals are explanations*, but only that in many cases the basis for accepting such a conditional includes the makings of an explanation.

This tripartite scheme of bases for A→C turns out to have power, enabling us to bury the relocation thesis and to do much more. I shall now offer some examples, to put flesh on the abstract bones, and also to exhibit complications which I have so far suppressed.

133. THREE PATTERNS OF EXPLANATION

Explaining C. Here the thought is of A and E leading to and explaining C. Example: 'If Checkit Inc. conducted the audit, the audit report is accurate', said by someone whose E includes propositions about Checkit's competence and honesty. Another: 'If Stauffenberg used his bomb, Hitler is dead', said by someone whose E includes propositions about the power of the bomb and the layout of the room. In each of these, the speaker envisages a state of affairs in which A and E explain C: the report's being accurate because E and Checkit wrote it; Hitler's being dead because E and Stauffenberg used his bomb. Cases will vary in how natural it is to pick on A, rather than on some elements in E, as 'the explanation' for C; but I need not go into this.

Explaining A. Here C explains A's supposed truth better than anything else would. 'If my umbrella is not in the coat closet, then I took it to campus this morning.' Here, A has no tendency to explain C; but C helps to explain A. This supports A→C only if C is (essential to) *the best* available explanation for A.

The role of E is to help the C-involving explanation of A to be the best one available. It may do this in either of two ways. One is to enter into the explanation, making it stronger: part of my basis for 'If my umbrella is not in the coat closet, then I took it to campus this morning' might be my belief (E) that I did not bring my umbrella home from campus today. That combines with C to yield a nice strong explanation for A. The other way E can help the C-involving explanation to be the best is not by improving it but by eliminating rivals to it. Thus, part of my basis for the umbrella conditional might be my belief (E) that the umbrella was in the closet this morning. This does not contribute to any explanation for (A) its not being there now; but it helps C to be the best explanation for A by knocking out a rival explanation, namely that I left the umbrella on campus yesterday.

Here is another example of E's two possible roles. You might accept 'If (A) Joe died last week, (C) he had an accident', partly on the basis of your belief (E) that Joe has been climbing the north face of the Eiger. Add *that* to 'Joe had an accident' and you get a strong explanation for 'Joe died'. But your basis might (also, or instead) include your belief that Joe has recently been in excellent health and that he has no enemies. These happy aspects of Joe contribute nothing to explaining his death or his accident, but by eliminating two rival explanations they increase the likelihood that his death arose from an accident.

The two roles that elements in E may play in explaining-A bases are not both open to C. For an explaining-A conditional to be acceptable, C must be involved in explaining A, not merely in eliminating a rival. That is because C is the consequent: it is what one is pushed to, not what helps in the pushing.

When you accept a conditional on an explaining-A basis, you can properly use some cognate of 'must' in the consequent: 'If the umbrella is not in coat-closet, I must have taken it to campus this morning'; 'If Joe is dead, he must have had an accident.' This 'must' expresses a sense of being forced to accept a C-involving explanation because no other is as good.

Now for one of the suppressed complications. I have expounded only *straight* explaining-A bases for conditionals; there are also *V-shaped* ones, in which C does not help to explain A but is a consequence of whatever explains A. James Thomson (1990: 64) invented this beauty:

If there is a copy of *Moby Dick* on that table, then there was at least one very large Great Dane with a solid gold collar in Paddington Station yesterday.

This could be accepted on the grounds that the best explanation for (A) the book's being on the table is (X) that Mary came here from London yesterday and left it there, which would probably involve (C) her coming via Paddington and bringing her Great Dane which . . . etc. This speaker thinks that A is best explained by X which in turn leads to and explains C. This has an explaining-C element in it, but it gets to C through an explaining-A move; so we can classify it as explaining-A, with the special feature that C is a consequence, rather than a part, of what does the explaining. I call this a V-shaped explaining-A basis for A→C. In it the thought runs from (A) the book on the table *to* (X) Mary's having come from London, and then off at an angle *from* X to (C) the dog at Paddington. One half of this is a straight explaining-A basis for the A→X, the other a straight explaining-C basis for X→C. These jointly yield A→C because *in this case* Transitivity holds (as it often does; it takes ingenuity to devise cases where it fails). Elements of E can be involved in either part of this; in two different ways in the move from A to X, and in one way in the move from X to C.

Notice that like other explaining-A bases, the V-shaped one also involves a thought of being driven to something (Mary's trip from London) as the best explanation, so again 'must' is appropriate: 'If there is a copy [etc.], then there must have been at least one Great Dane [etc.].'

What about V-shaped explaining-C bases? They exist too. In them, C is explained by E in conjunction not with A but with something back-inferred from A. Someone might accept 'If (A) Smith was fired, (C) so was Wilson' on the grounds that 'Wilson definitely was or will be the first to be fired. If anyone was fired, Wilson was fired' (Sanford 1989: 192–3). In this case, the thought is that (A) Smith's being fired will have arisen from (X) some state of affairs—perhaps a down-sizing—which also leads to and explains (C) Wilson's being fired. One half of this is a straight explaining-C basis for X→C, the other half a straight explaining-A basis for A→X.

As those two examples show, if the basis for an indicative conditional is V-shaped, it can be classified as explaining-C or explaining-A; given a V, there is no difference between these. In the case I called explaining-A there is also a thought about what explains (C) the dog's presence at Paddington; and in the case I called explaining-C there is also a thought about what explains (A) Smith's being fired.

Explaining E. Here, what is explained is an element in E, something that makes no appearance in the conditional itself. In the simplest case, what explains the E item is just C; what enables an explanation to figure as the consequent is that it is thought of as *the best* explanation for the E item. And the role of A is to help C to have this status by knocking out possible rival explanations of the E item. 'If the umbrella is not in the closet, my memory is failing.' In accepting this I have no thought of explaining either A or C. Rather, I think this: I have (E) a seeming memory of putting my umbrella in the closet and no memory of removing it; this could be because I put and left it there; but the hypothesis (A) that it is not there now eliminates that, and the best surviving explanation is (C) that my memory is failing. In my initial account of the three kinds of basis, explaining-E was the only one that did not mention A. That was because here, and only here, A neither explains nor is explained, though it makes a vital contribution to C's being the best explanation for the E item.

It may take more than one step to get from A to the elimination of the rival explanations of the E item. For example: I feel the cold ashes of what has been an enormous fire, and say, pointing to some drab plants growing nearby, 'If those are desert verbena, then this fire is many days old'. Initially the best explanation for the coldness of the ashes is that there has been heavy rain; but when rain falls on desert verbena they flower immediately, which those plants have not done. If they are desert verbena, therefore, there has not been rain recently; this rules out that explanation, leaving standing the cold-because-old one. This squarely falls within the explaining-E category: the only item that is explained is (E) the fact of the cold ashes; there is no thought of explaining either A or C.

Here again the knocking out of a rival makes it idiomatic to use 'must' in the consequent: 'If the umbrella is not in coat-closet, my memory must be failing'; 'If those plants are desert verbena, this fire must be many days old'.

A second suppressed complication is this. In explaining-E bases, C may enter the story dependently, not as helping to explain the E item but as an explained consequence of whatever explains it. 'If those plants are desert verbena, we'll have no trouble crossing the stream': the plants have no flowers, as desert verbena always do soon after rain; so if they are desert verbena there has not been recent rain, in which case the stream will be low and we'll have no trouble crossing it. Here the E item is the flowerless state of the plants; the hypothesis (A) that they are desert verbena knocks out their being of any species that can remain flowerless even after rain; and that leaves standing the explanation that they are flowerless because there has been no rain recently; from which C follows.

When in an explaining-E basis C is a consequence rather than a part or aspect of what explains E, there is an explaining-C element at work also. In the last example, two things are thought of as explained: the flowerless state of the plants, and the ease of crossing the stream. But it suits me to classify all these as explaining-E because, as will appear in §135, the line of division that interests me has all the explaining-Es on one side of it, whether or not they also involve the explaining of C; on the other side are the bases in which C and/or A is explained and E is not.

C's dependence on the explained E item could be a lengthy, twisty affair. Someone might think 'If those plants are desert verbena, we'll have a European holiday next summer', on this basis: if the plants are etc., there has been no rain recently; so we'll have no trouble crossing the river; so I'll get home tonight; so I'll just have time to beat the deadline for joining the class-action suit; so I'll get money from the suit; so we'll be able to afford a European holiday; so . . . It would be risky to venture such a thing in conversation, but it is a possible *thought* for someone to have.

Some familiar examples fit snugly into the explaining-E frame. Being pretty sure that the gate was locked either by the porter or by the bursar, I accept 'If it was not locked by the porter, it was locked by the bursar'. In this case, (C) the gate's being locked by the bursar is my best explanation for (E) the evidence I have for my disjunctive belief, on the supposition that (A) it was not locked by the porter. I can have this thought without remembering what the evidence was.

'What if the whole story is that you believed someone who told you "Either the porter or the bursar locked the gate"?' If I believed him because I trusted him to have good evidence for what he said, that trust could lead me to think of C as the best explanation, given A, for that evidence of his, whatever it was. 'What if you believed him absolutely, for no reason, with no lurking thought of his being believable because he would have evidence for the disjunction's truth?' In such a case I would, indeed, be accepting A→C on a basis that did not support any explanation. Such cases, if they exist, form a second set of exceptions to my generalization that bases for indicative conditionals support explanations. From now on, I shall focus on acceptances of conditionals that do fit into my tripartite scheme, ignoring any—if there are any—that do not.

In every explaining-E basis for an indicative conditional, the thought goes from A to an element of E and then off at an angle (so to speak) to C; but I shall not call such bases 'V-shaped', reserving that label for the ones I have associated with explaining-C and -A. The V-shaped bases are quite different from the explaining-E ones, despite the latters' back-and-forth aspect. In the former, the item at the angle of the V helps to explain C and A, but there is no thought about what explains *it*—about why Mary came from London, or why there was a down-sizing. In contrast with that, in an explaining-E basis the driving force is precisely an explanation for the item that is neither A nor C, the item that could be said to lie at the angle of the V if 'V-shaped' were not being reserved for the other two kinds of basis.

134. DIFFERENT BASES FOR A SINGLE CONDITIONAL

So we have three species of case in which someone accepts A→C. His basis may be of any one of the types: explaining-C, explaining-A, explaining-E. (Or it can be a V-shaped basis which is *both* explaining-A *and* explaining-C; but I shall not go on about that.) His basis for A→C cannot be read off from the conditional itself, for a single conditional might have one basis for one person and another for another. The following might be accepted on any of the three kinds of basis, by three people:

S: If Booth didn't shoot Lincoln, someone else did.

Christopher accepts S on the grounds that, while not knowing whether Booth succeeded, he believes that reliable plans were made for someone else to take over if Booth failed. His basis for S is of the explaining-C type. Albert accepts S for reasons of the explaining-A type. He thinks that nothing could have deterred Booth from his assassination attempt except finding that Lincoln had already been shot by someone else. Albert gets from A to C on the grounds that C would best explain the truth of A. Edgar accepts S because of all the evidence he has (E) that Lincoln was shot by someone. His basis for the conditional is then of the explaining-E type: C is his best explanation for that E element, given the hypothesis A which eliminates the chief rival.

Every indicative conditional that could have a basis of one of the three kinds could instead have a basis of at least one of the others. Not always of both: when A and C are precisely enough dated, explaining-A and explaining-C cannot both be eligible unless we invoke backward causation. What enabled me to slide bases of each of the three types under the Booth–Lincoln conditional S was its silence about *when* Booth didn't shoot Lincoln and *when* someone else did. We need not struggle on with this topic, however. My focus will be on the fact that any instance of the form A→C that could have an explaining-C or explaining-A basis could instead have an explaining-E one.

The conditional 'If I touch that stove, I shall be burned' may look as though it could only be accepted on an explaining-C basis, and it and its kin have figured in the literature with that assumption tied to them. Here, for example: 'If one says "if you step on it, it'll break" one has already described its breaking as a causal consequence . . . of stepping on it' (Morton 1981: 139). In fact, though, Step → Break could be accepted on an explaining-E basis by someone who does not think of the stepping as causing the break; just as Touch → Burned could be accepted on an explaining-E basis by someone who knows the stove to be cold. Given how naturally one sees each as having an explaining-C basis, an example showing an explaining-E one has to be pretty fanciful; I need not apologize for that. Here goes.

The protagonist K is undergoing a series of mysterious ordeals at the hands of unknown tormentors. He has (E) a strong seeming-memory of being told that he will be subject to a horrible burn; he is sure that whatever he has been told is true; but he thinks the best explanation of this seeming-memory is that it was hyp-notically induced in him, in which case he has no reason to think it to be veridi-cal and thus no reason to expect to be burned. K is also sure that any hypnotism he has undergone has included the notorious *noli id tangere* procedure, which causes the subject to be invincibly unwilling to touch any household items. His touching the stove would knock out the hypnotism explanation for (E) his seem-ing memory, leaving it best explained by the hypothesis that it is veridical, which he thinks implies that he will be burned. So he accepts Touch → Burned, on grounds that have no taint of the idea that touching will cause or explain burn-ing. The core of this basis for the conditional is the explaining of (E) the seeming memory.

Another old favourite is 'If it rains tonight, the roads will be slippery tomor-row'. In the following story, Rain → Slippery is accepted on an explaining-E basis. In my locality, rain does not make the roads slippery; they have been treated so that water increases their coefficient of friction. I have here a docu-ment that includes weather predictions (including a prediction of rain tonight), local-government plans (including a plan to oil the roads tomorrow), and other stuff. It looks official; if it is, the weather forecasts are apt to be reliable, and the announced plans are apt to be carried out. But there are some signs that the entire thing may be a hoax, in which case I should not trust it for anything. If it rains tonight, however, that will incline me to accept the document as genuine: to the untrained eye, rain looks unlikely, so a true prediction of it is apt to come from the official meteorologists. If the document is genuine, the local government will probably carry out its plan to spread oil on the roads tomorrow. Thus, I give a fairly high probability to *If it rains tonight, the roads will be slippery tomorrow* on a purely explaining-E basis. On the supposition that there will be rain tonight, the best explanation for the existence of this document is that official government sources produced it, and one consequence of this is that the roads will be slippery tomorrow.

This unlikely story could be true; and if it were, Rain → Slippery would be acceptable on a basis of the explaining-E kind. There is nothing semantically, syntactically, or conceptually suspect about such a basing of this conditional.

A correspondent has told me that in the case as envisaged it is clearly all right for me to think

(1) If it's going to rain tonight, the roads are going to be slippery tomorrow,

but that I ought to be 'a little doubtful' that

(2) If it rains tonight, the roads will be slippery tomorrow;

and that some others have the same pair of intuitions. He also says that the doubt about 2 comes from doubt about

(3) If it were to rain tonight, the roads would be slippery tomorrow,

which is doubtful, he says, since there is a suspicion that this is a hoax. I report the existence of these intuitions, out of respect for their owner. But I do not myself have them, and indeed cannot connect them with any thoughts that I find natural.

135. INDICATIVES AND CORRESPONDING SUBJUNCTIVES

Does the important line dividing conditionals correspond to that between indicative and subjunctive conditional sentences? Relocators answer No, because of conditionals with a present-tense antecedent and a future-tense consequent, such as:

Does-will: If the rouble falls below 20 to the dollar, the government will intervene in the market.

This has been classified as indicative—it has no 'would' in the consequent—and yet, the relocators say, any adequate basis for asserting it would also support:

> Had-would: If the rouble had fallen below 20 to the dollar, the government would have intervened in the market

at a later time, if in the interim the rouble did not fall below 20. This thesis, which I have called 'Stand or Fall', encouraged some of us to think that Does-will differs from Had-would only in tense (and perhaps in the speaker's attitude to the truth value of the antecedent), from which we inferred that Does-will belongs along with Had-would in the hopper containing all the subjunctives. The other bin was to contain only indicatives lacking the Does-will distribution of tenses.

In §94 I pointed out three repairs that must be made to Stand or Fall if it is not itself to fall. In the present chapter I shall filter those out by tackling a version of Stand or Fall that is silently restricted so as not to be asserted of cases where there are Gibbardian stand-offs, nearby forks, or appeals to indeterministically produced outcomes at α.

With all that set aside, *now* can we say that Does-wills stand or fall with subsequent Had-woulds? No. That still comes far short of the truth, because of these two facts:

> Does-will conditionals can have bases of any of the three types; so can indicative conditionals that are not of the Does-will form.

> The basis for an indicative conditional also supports the corresponding subjunctive if it is of the explaining-A or explaining-C type (whether V-shaped or not), but not if it is of the explaining-E type.

These imply that many supports for Does-will conditionals do not support the corresponding subjunctives, and that many supports for indicatives that are not of the Does-will form do also support the corresponding subjunctives. The announced reason for reclassifying Does-will conditionals, therefore, does not apply to all of them and does apply to many others.

Before examining what my two theses imply for the relocation thesis, I shall try to satisfy you that they are true, starting with an indicative conditional of the Does-will form.

We are watching a black earth-to-sky pillar of cloud approaching your villa outside Marrakesh; I ignorantly remark 'I hope it doesn't rain—that would make our picnic uncomfortable', and you—knowing more—reply sardonically:

> If (A) it doesn't rain, (C) the picnic will be impossible.

Here are two stories about your basis for accepting this conditional.

Explaining-E: Your E is what you see to the east, and some general views implying that the two best diagnoses of what you see are that a rain-cloud approaches and that a sandstorm approaches; that, conjoined with (A) the hypothesis that it will not rain, implies that the best explanation for the cloud part of E is that a sandstorm approaches, which implies that (C) we cannot have a picnic. (Here, as always in Does-will conditionals with explaining-E bases, C is a consequence of what explains E, not a part of it.) In this case, the corresponding subjunctive conditional has no support. If it does rain, none of us will think 'If it hadn't rained, the picnic would have been impossible'. Given that it does rain, the closest worlds at which it doesn't rain contain no dark cloud with that trajectory; they don't contain one with that trajectory but carrying sand. If at the relevant time the weather god had been flipping a mental coin to decide whether to afflict us with a rainstorm or a sandstorm, and it did rain, it *would* have been true that if it hadn't rained the picnic would have been impossible because of the sandstorm. But what would make that true is not the basis on which you accepted your indicative conditional. My thesis is not that if the indicative is acceptable the corresponding subjunctive is false, but rather that an explaining-E basis for the indicative does not support the corresponding subjunctive.

Explaining-C: You believe that unless some cooling rain falls it will be too hot for a picnic. You think that (A) the non-occurrence of rain would contribute to, and in that sense explain, (C) the impossibility of the picnic. If this is how things stand, and it does rain, you will be entitled to think 'If it hadn't rained, the picnic would have been impossible'; and you can base this on the same beliefs as were the basis for your indicative conditional.

Now let us look at an indicative conditional that is not of the Does-will but rather of the Did-did type. Last night I heard party noises from the beach; they didn't keep me awake, but this morning I wonder how long the party went on. I thought I saw a police car heading that way at about 8 p.m., and I think:

If (A) the police arrived at the party at 8 p.m., then (C) then it was over by 9 p.m.

Here are two stories about my basis for this conditional.

Explaining-E: I believe that on our island the police almost never visit parties except (for public relations purposes) ones for elementary schoolchildren, and I also think that such parties nearly always end by 9 p.m. because school officials think that by then young children should be heading for bed. So, given the supposition (A) that the police were there, the best explanation for (E) the noises I heard is that elementary schoolers were having a party, which makes it probable that (C) the party was over by 9 p.m. Thus I accept Police → Early. If it turns out that the police were not there and teenagers partied on into the small hours, my basis for Police → Early does not entitle me to accept 'If the police had been there, the party would have ended by 9 p.m.'. This subjunctive may be true; I may even believe it to be true; but my belief in it could not rationally arise from the beliefs on which I based the indicative conditional.

Explaining-C: I think that if the police intruded into the party, they closed it down before 9 p.m.; they nearly always do. This explaining-C basis for Police → Early plainly supports the corresponding subjunctive.

Finally, I offer an example in which the choice is between explaining-E and explaining-A. I am surveying a mountain from below, wondering how the climbers are getting on. As I start to unlimber my telescope, I think:

If there is a flag on the summit, Edwards got there.

As before, two stories.

Explaining-E: I have (E) visual evidence that either Edwards or Gilson has been climbing the mountain; I am not sure which; not both. I believe that who-ever it is will have reached the summit; and I know that when Gilson reaches a summit he celebrates by removing any flags he finds there, not replacing them with others. Thus, given (A) that there is flag there, the best explanation for (E) the evidence of my eyes is that (C) Edwards has been climbing the mountain, and so I accept Flag → Edwards. There need be no thought of him as planting the flag. Now, suppose that when I look through my telescope I see the summit to be flag-free, and I later learn that Gilson got there and Edwards spent the day at home. In this eventuality, my explaining-E basis for Flag → Edwards gives me no basis for accepting 'If there had been a flag there, Edwards would (have to) have reached the summit'. A better rival to that is 'If there had been a flag there, Gilson would (have to) have omitted his usual cleansing chore'.

Explaining-A: I think that Edwards is the only person who has been attempt-ing to climb the mountain today, and that there was no flag on the summit this morning. This gives me an explaining-A basis for accepting Flag → Edwards, which clearly supports the corresponding subjunctive: 'If there had been a flag there, Edwards would (have to) have got there.' Quite generally, explaining-A bases for indicatives support temporally backward subjunctives.

There is nothing wrong with the latter. I stand by my §110 theory about their truth-conditions. Edwards didn't get there, and there is no flag. The closest worlds at which there is a flag are ones that fork from α at about noon, with Edwards having slightly better luck in negotiating the ice-fall, and reaching the summit. Compare: 'If Stevenson had been President in February 1953 he would have to have won the election in the previous November.' (Backward subjunctives sound better with the 'have to' or the like in the consequent. See §108 and §133 for the reason.)

An explaining-E basis for accepting A→C usually or always supports some subjunctive conditionals, but never the corresponding one, the one with the same A and C. You and I accept 'If Booth didn't shoot Lincoln, someone else did', because of the evidence we have that Lincoln was shot by someone. Our explaining-E basis for accepting this conditional supports *some* subjunctives—perhaps 'If there had been a conspiracy to fake Lincoln's death, it would have been revealed by now'—but it could never support 'If Booth hadn't shot Lincoln, someone else would have'.

Summing up: a forward subjunctive conditional makes a claim about A's power to lead to and explain C, which connects it with the explaining-C basis for A→C; a backward subjunctive makes a claim about C's power to lead to and explain A, which connects with the explaining-A basis for A→C. The explaining-E basis is squeezed out of this story, because in it there is no explanatory relation *between* A and C, which there must be in subjunctive conditionals—except for non-interference ones, where the message is that A's truth would not interfere with whatever facts explain C's truth (§91).

When philosophers adduce examples to show how greatly indicatives differ from subjunctives, they always illustrate the former with ones whose most natural and likely bases are of the explaining-E sort. Now we can see why. While not explicitly aware of the three types of basis, these philosophers have been subliminally guided to examples where the most likely basis for acceptance is of the kind that does not support the corresponding subjunctive.

136. THE ANATOMY OF EXPLAINING-E BASES

The relocation thesis is in trouble right across the range of indicative conditionals, but most acutely with explaining-E Does-wills. Their form is its central topic, yet they refuse to behave as it demands.

A friend of mine who likes the relocation thesis better than I do has put it to me that Does-wills with explaining-E bases are too rare and peculiar to count as a serious obstacle to the relocation thesis. Not so. My stove and road examples in §134 are indeed contorted affairs, but those are special cases—conditionals that I tackled precisely because philosophers have confidently thought they *must* have explaining-C bases. When in a general way we enquire after explaining-E Does-wills, we find that they are neither strange nor sparse. There is nothing exotic, except geographically, about my sandstorm example in §135.

Here is a recipe for constructing plausible conditionals with explaining-E bases:

Take an E for which there are two or more plausible diagnoses, and an A whose truth knocks out all but one of them. Choose as C either the surviving diagnosis or something that would be a consequence of the truth of the surviving diagnosis.

There you have it: A→C on an explaining-E basis. Here is the recipe for explaining-E bases for *Does-will* conditionals:

Take an E for which there are two or more plausible diagnoses, an A *about the future* whose truth knocks out all but one of them, and a C *about the future* whose truth would result from the truth of the surviving diagnosis.

This differs in twice requiring futurity, once each for 'does' and 'will'; and in requiring C to be a consequence of the surviving diagnosis rather than being identical with it (also because of 'will'). Let us apply it to the sandstorm example. E is the presence of a black cloud, diagnosable either as rain or as sand; A is the proposition that there will not be rain tonight, which knocks out the rain diagnosis; and C is the proposition that the picnic will be impossible, which is a consequence of the truth of the sand explanation.

This humdrum stuff reveals no reason why Does-wills with explaining-E bases should not be as common as blackberries. Such bases are, at any rate, squarely within our conceptual repertoire and are at least sometimes of interest to us; and the Does-will form of indicative conditionals accommodates them beautifully. We should not flirt with any theory of conditionals that requires us to push these ones out of sight.

My examples have supplied evidence that explaining-E bases for Does-will and other indicative conditionals do not support corresponding subjunctives. Now I am in a position to say *why* they do not do so.

It is not because of their back-and-forth aspect, because that is also possessed by V-shaped bases for explaining-A/C conditionals. (Recall that when the basis is V-shaped, explaining-A and explaining-C are one.) In a V-shaped basis we have an A that is best explained by supposing X, and a C that X would lead to and explain, with Transitivity holding along this short chain. In such a basis, the belief in X comes from the acceptance of A, which it explains; and the belief in C comes from the belief in X, which explains it. If in fact A does not obtain, we still have here a structure making it reasonable to suppose that at the closest A-worlds X obtains (to explain A), and C obtains (in consequence of X). There was in fact no copy of *Moby Dick* on the table; but if there had been, it would have been because Mary had come from London bringing a dog through Paddington.

In a zigzag explaining-E basis, on the other hand, what connects A with C is something that *does* obtain, not merely something postulated to explain A if *it* obtains. Consider 'If it doesn't rain, there will be a sandstorm'—said on the strength of a big black cloud coming our way. What is inferred from the no-rain supposition is a diagnosis of the cloud, an account of what sort of cloud it is; and that diagnosis leads to the (conditional) prediction of a sandstorm. Now, suppose that rain falls, showing that the cloud contained rain, not sand, and consider what we can think of the form 'If it had not rained . . .'. Such thoughts concern worlds at which this cloud does not appear at this time and place, or where it shows up but retains its moisture. It would be absurd to think that at such worlds there is a different big black cloud—one full of sand—at this place and time. Sand entered the picture only through a *thought of ours* about the cloud. It was a sound thought: the cloud-appearance that we saw was bound to portend either rain or a sandstorm. But there is no eligible fork in the world's history at which with a slight shift in events the ramp leading to this rain-cloud would have led instead to a sandstorm at the same time and place.

As I feel the rain falling, I may think: 'Thank God the other diagnosis was wrong! If it hadn't been—if the cloud hadn't been bringing rain—we would now have sand flaying the skin off our faces.' That, though, is playing with a fantasy, not asserting a subjunctive conditional about what would have ensued if the world had gone differently. The nearest it can come to respectability is as a directly grounded conditional (§113), a non-historical affair derived immediately from a Trusted generalization about the effects of sandstorms.

137. REBUILDING THE RELOCATION THESIS

The relocation thesis says that the Does-wills among indicative conditionals ought to be classified with the subjunctives on the grounds—first and foremost—that each such indicative stands or falls with the corresponding subjunctive: ' "If P were the case, Q would be the case" is true if and only if at some earlier date . . . "If P is the case, Q will be the case" was assertible' (Woods 1997: 84). This bold biconditional has turned out to be false in each direction. The 'nearby forks' phenomenon yields Does-wills that do not go with Had-woulds (§94), and an even richer harvest is provided by the multitude of Does-wills that have explaining-E bases. And Had-woulds that do not go with Does-wills are provided by the 'indeterminacy and actual truth' phenomenon (§94). Further trouble is made for the relocation thesis, though not for Woods's biconditional, by the existence of indicatives that stand or fall with the corresponding subjunctives but are not of the Does-will form. The relocation thesis lies in ruins.

Dudman accepts the thesis, using 'hypothetical' to cover (roughly) indicatives other than the Does-will ones, and 'conditional' for Does-will indicatives and subjunctives. He bases the line he draws on grammatical considerations that I am not persuaded by; I glanced at some of them in §§2–3, and shall not return to them. He also offers this: 'Hypotheticals and conditionals are . . . products of quite different styles of reasoning. A hypothetical is arrived at by arguing from proposition to proposition, a conditional by envisaging a developing sequence of events' (Dudman 1984*b*: 153). I remark that one basis for arguing from proposition to proposition is how one envisages a developing sequence of events; to which I add the reminder that in this chapter I have shown that plenty of Does-wills (supposedly conditionals) do not envisage such sequences, and that plenty of other indicatives (supposedly hypotheticals) do envisage them.

The only way to rescue *some* relocation thesis is by shifting to the position that what should be lumped in with the subjunctives are not the Does-wills but rather the explaining-A and -C subsets of them.

But the members of these sets are not conditional sentences, but rather *bases for the acceptance of* such sentences. The relocator will have to say he is classifying *propositions*—meanings of sentences—and that an indicative conditional sentence means different things when accepted on different bases. Thus, for example, 'If I touch that stove, I will be burned' has one meaning in the mouth of someone who accepts it on an explaining-C basis and another for someone—like my Kafkaesque victim in §134—whose basis for it is of the explaining-E kind. In one of its meanings it goes in with the subjunctives; in the other, not.

Because any indicative conditional (sentence) could be accepted on an explaining-E basis, this new relocation thesis implies that *every single indicative conditional is radically ambiguous*. I cannot believe this.

Suppose you have good evidence that someone has shot Lincoln, which leads you to accept 'If Booth didn't shoot Lincoln, someone else did', on an explaining-E basis. I on the other hand am one of the conspirators; without yet knowing exactly what happened, I believe plans were in place for someone else to take over in the event of Booth's failing. So I too am in a position to assert: 'If Booth didn't shoot Lincoln, someone else did', but on an explaining-C basis. Now, if either of us asserts the conditional and asks 'Don't you agree?', it would be excessively odd for the other to say 'It depends on what you mean'. It is more natural to take the sentence as the vehicle for an agreement between us and to think that we differ only in our reasons for accepting it—just as two people might agree that *Lincoln has been shot*, one because he believes that people planned to shoot Lincoln and trusts them to have succeeded, the other because he found the bullet in the body. I am indebted here to Dorothy Edgington, who pulled me back from the precipice at a time when I *was* disposed to postulate ambiguity—a fact which now embarrasses me.

Here is another argument against ambiguity. The sentence 'If Booth didn't shoot Lincoln, someone else did' certainly has *one* sense in which it implies nothing about the speaker's basis for it. We must be giving it that neutral sense when we understand the statement 'They both accept, though on different grounds, that if Booth didn't shoot Lincoln someone else did', and the question 'Why do you think that . . . [etc.]?', and the injunction 'Unless you have good grounds for it, don't accept that . . . [etc.]'. If there is an ambiguity, then, some instances of this form must *also* have stronger meanings, in each of which their asserted content speaks of the basis on which they are accepted. What could make it reasonable for a speaker to expect to communicate such a stronger meaning—an explaining-C one, for instance?

He would have to be relying on some feature of the context: he and his friends have been discussing reliable causal structures; or his conditional needs an explaining-C basis if it is to answer a question he has just been asked; or nobody in his society would normally accept this conditional on any basis but an explaining-C one because any other basis would be weird (like my 'stove' and 'roads' ones); or the like. The speaker who knows such facts can rely on them to help him communicate that he accepts his conditional on an explaining-C basis. But this help is contextual, which removes any need to load extra meaning onto the sentence itself; and because we *can* handle the data without postulating ambiguity, we *ought to* do so. I say this on the strength of the semantic Occamism that Grice defended by argument and made irresistible by his best uses of it (§11).

This argument threatens to imply that no sentence in any natural language is ambiguous through having two conventional meanings of which one is stronger than the other. That is somewhere near the truth, I think.

Sometimes a conditional's content implies something about its basis. When A pertains to a later time than C does, this pretty well settles it that the speaker does not have an explaining-C basis for accepting A→C; and when A pre-dates C the basis can hardly be of the explaining-A type. Far from showing the conditional to be ambiguous, however, this reinforces the idea that it has only one meaning and that further news about what the speaker has in mind can be gathered from further facts about it. Analogously, George is Helen's uncle if he is a brother of either her mother or her father; some contexts could make clear which ('George is Helen's uncle; having never had any sisters, he feels especially close to her'); but in those contexts 'George is Helen's uncle' does not have a narrowed meaning.

Objection: 'Whatever you may say about ambiguity, isn't it just obvious that someone might assert Rain → Slippery and *mean by it* that if it rains tonight that will result in the roads' being slippery tomorrow? If so, that puts into the meaning of what he says its explaining-C basis and thus also its likeness to a subjunctive. So there is *some* such ambiguity. Perhaps there is a lot of it.'

Well, when someone wants to communicate that if it rains tonight that will result in the roads' being slippery tomorrow, he can do this explicitly in augmented conditionals using 'as a result' or 'that will lead to' and the like. No doubt, someone who asserts the *un*augmented 'If it rains tonight, the roads will be slippery tomorrow' might want by that to communicate that the slipperiness will result from the rain, and he might succeed. But it does not follow that the unaugmented sentence has as one of its conventional meanings the message that if it rains, the roads will be slippery as a result. The speaker can reasonably expect to get that across through the unaugmented conditional because neither he nor his hearers are within miles of thinking of any explaining-E basis for accepting it. But that, far from including the 'result from' part of the message in the meaning of what he says, is a reason for excluding it.

Compare this with something Grice taught us. You ask me when the meeting will be held, and I say 'They scheduled it either for Monday or for Wednesday'. Seeing no reason why I should withhold information (I seem not to be joking, teasing, making a philosophical point, or conducting an intelligence test), you infer that I am not sure of the day. You may even think I have told you so; and so I have, in a way, but not in a way that puts my indecision into the meaning of my sentence. Some philosophers used to think otherwise, but Grice's work on pragmatics, and his use of it to defend semantic Occamism, has cured everyone of this error (§§10–11). All the facts that might be explained by attributing that rich meaning to *some* occurrences of 'either . . . or . . .' can be perfectly well explained by combining a thin truth-functional meaning to 'either . . . or . . .' and attending to what generally goes on in civilized discourse.

Renewed objection: 'But what if he asserts Rain → Slippery and *thinks that* he is not merely *conveying somehow* that his conditional has an explaining-C basis but is actually *saying* that it does so?' I am sceptical about this person who has such a theoretical opinion about what he is doing. People have views about what they mean to get across, but few outside philosophy seminars draw lines between conventional meaning and conversational implicature. However, if there is a person such as I am here challenged with, he is in error about what his utterance conventionally means. Similarly with someone who says 'I could care less' to express indifference, or who says 'No head-injury is too trivial to ignore' meaning that every head-injury, however minor, should be taken seriously. Mistakes like these can be widespread yet still be mistakes, and we know how to show this.

I have argued that the relocation thesis is shipwrecked on the facts about bases for indicative conditionals. It has other troubles as well; see especially the compact and powerful battery of them in Edgington 1995*b*: 317–20.

Before dismissing the relocation thesis, I should confront an argument recently offered in its defence by Dudman. Here is the whole of it:

(1) It is a key tenet of 'the traditional way' [of classifying conditionals] that Doesn't-will, as it might be *that if Oswald doesn't shoot Kennedy someone else will*, is logically indiscernible from Didn't-did, *that if Oswald didn't shoot Kennedy someone else did*, the former merely formulating about the future what the latter formulates about the past. (2) A tenet no less central to the tradition has *that someone will shoot Kennedy* is logically indiscernible from *that someone shot Kennedy*, the former merely formulating about the future what the latter does about the past. (3) Didn't-did follows from the proposition *that someone shot Kennedy*. (4) A conspirator espousing the not untenable view that Oswald will shoot Kennedy in a plot that includes no back-up killer obviously maintains *that someone will shoot Kennedy* but need not accept Doesn't-will. Q.E.D. (Dudman 2000)

Dudman's title for this piece is 'Classifying "conditionals": the traditional way is wrong'. That is what *erat demonstrandum*.

Consider Dudman's claim (3) that (iii) 'If Oswald didn't shoot Kennedy someone else did' follows from (ii) 'Someone shot Kennedy'. He offers this, presumably, as a classically valid entailment, as though iii were a proposition with a truth value. Even within that false framework, this entailment claim is indefensible. There can be no denying that ii is entailed by (i) 'Oswald shot Kennedy', and no denying that entailment is transitive. Presumably there can be no affirming that i entails iii.

When we move to the more realistic and well-defended view that iii does not have a truth value, and must be evaluated in terms of conditional probabilities, Dudman's 3 disappears and his argument collapses in a different way. It is true that someone *might* regard (A→C) 'If Oswald didn't shoot Kennedy, someone else did' as highly probable because he thinks it probable that (E) someone shot Kennedy; but if his only reason for thinking E to be probable is that he thinks it probable that (¬A) Oswald shot Kennedy, that will not lead him to attach a high probability to A→C. In short, the move from ii to iii is not probabilistically valid (§53).

Something similar occurs in one of Lycan's arguments against NTV, the thesis that indicative conditionals lack truth values. 'Many indicative conditionals are logically equivalent to briefer non-conditional sentences', he writes, challenging the friends of NTV to explain this (2001: 77–8; see also p. 147). He gives this example:

(*a*) John murdered Sandra if anyone did.

(*b*) No one other than John murdered Sandra.

If these are logically equivalent (I reply), then any evidence for either counts also in favour of the other. But evidence that nobody murdered Sandra counts in favour of *b* without counting equally in favour of *a*. The non-equivalence of the two shows in how they behave in contexts of imperfect certainty. Suppose I have pretty good evidence that nobody murdered Sandra, tempered only by a few slight pointers to Henry's having done so. This should make me pretty sure of *b* and very *un*sure of *a*—so the move from *b* to *a* is not probabilistically valid, and the two are not logically equivalent.

Lycan is not entitled to object that probabilistic validity is a concept to which he owes no allegiance. Even without accepting Adams's whole theory about it, everyone must agree that if *a* and *b* are 'logically equivalent', any rational person must accord the same level of credence to both. Furthermore, anyone who contends that 'Nobody murdered Sandra' entails *a*, perhaps hoping to explain away our contrary intuitions somehow, must concede that 'Nobody murdered Sandra' entails *every* statement that can be derived from *a* by replacing 'John' by some other name—for example, it entails that *you* murdered Sandra if anyone did. The only way to defend that is by construing the latter conditional as meaning 'Somebody murdered Sandra ⊃ You murdered Sandra', which is true because its antecedent is false. But that defence involves accepting the horseshoe analysis, which Lycan rightly rejects.

Here is Lycan's other 'logically equivalent' pair:

If Reagan is a Russian spy, no one knows he is.
No one knows that Reagan is a Russian spy.

These two also behave differently under uncertainty. You could be pretty sure that no one knows that Reagan is a Russian spy, simply because you are confident that he is not one, while at the same time hesitating to agree that if he is one, no one knows.

23

Unifying the Two Kinds
of Conditional

138. DAVIS'S Y-SHAPED ANALYSIS OF CONDITIONALS

Let us, finally, examine what I think to be the main attempts that philosophers have made to tell a fairly unified story about indicative and subjunctive conditionals, bringing the two together under a single yoke. The extreme anti-unity position was provocatively announced in Gibbard's suggestion that the logical similarities between the two types is 'little more than a coincidence'. In §69 I showed it to be nowhere near as bad as that: each kind of conditional has at its heart a variably-strict structure that explains their shared logic. It also explains why in each of them 'if' can combine with 'then', with 'only', and with 'even', in the same way. Questions remain, however, concerning what else can be said about the likeness of the two types of conditionals. At the other extreme from Gibbard are Y-shaped analyses of conditionals (§4), which start with what is common to both types and then branch into two sequels, one for each type. In this section I shall discuss Wayne Davis's Y-shaped analysis, in the next Robert Stalnaker's. More recently Stalnaker has sought to unify the two kinds of conditionals in a different manner, using an idea that has also been employed by Brian Ellis and—more thoroughly—by Dorothy Edgington. In examining these, I shall bring the book to a close.

Following the analytic tradition defended in Chapters 10–12, Davis connects the truth of A>C with C's being true at the A-world most resembling α in respect of its states at all times up to T_A. Thus, if we want to evaluate this:

C_5: If the British had not invaded Suez early in 1956, the Soviets would have stayed out of Hungary later in that year,

we must consider the possible world w_s which meets these conditions:

At w_s the British do not invade Suez early in 1956.

w_s is more like α in respect of its state up to early in 1956 than is any other world at which the British do not invade Suez at that time.

Considering w_s is tantamount to considering the state of affairs that would have obtained if the British had not invaded Suez in 1956 and things until then had otherwise been as much as possible like how they actually were. The question to be asked about w_s is: *At w_s do the Soviets interfere in Hungary late in 1956?* If they do, C_s is false; if they do not, it is true. Something along these lines is right, though there are problems of detail.

Consider now the indicative conditional:

C_i: If the British didn't attack Suez early in 1956, the Israelis rigged the situation to make it look as though they had.

This is plausible because of all the evidence we have that the British did invade Suez. If they did not, this evidence has to be accounted for in some other way, and an Israeli frame-up is the best bet. That gives Davis his clue. He counts A→C as true if C is true at the A-world most resembling α in respect of its states at all times. C_i takes account of states of affairs obtaining after 1956, whereas C_s does not; which is why C_s may be true although its indicative analogue 'If the British didn't invade Suez, the Soviets didn't interfere in Hungary' is not; and it is why C_i is true although its subjunctive analogue 'If the British hadn't invaded Suez, the Israelis would have rigged the situation to make it look as though they had' is not.

So says Davis (1979; see also his 1983). Observe how neatly Y-shaped his analysis is. For each type of conditional it ties the truth of 'If A, C' to the truth of something of the form:

C is true at the A-world that is most like α in respect of its state at all times . . .

For indicative conditionals, add '. . . whatsoever'; for subjunctives add '. . . before T_A'.

In illustrating and defending this, Davis always contrasts a *forward* subjunctive conditional with an indicative accepted on an *explaining-E* basis. I cannot make it work for backward subjunctives. Davis thinks there aren't any, but we have seen him to be wrong about this (§108).

Nor can I see how Davis's Y-shaped account could work for indicative conditionals accepted on an explaining-C basis. (Or explaining-A; but the ignoring of those goes with rejecting backward subjunctives, so I shall say no more about it.) So far as I can see, Davis's best chance to make true, as said in October 2000, 'If Bush doesn't win, Gore will win' is to look to the Not-Bush-worlds that are most like α up to October 2000, when the conditional is being evaluated. Likeness to α at subsequent times seems not to come into it. However, Davis might roll with this punch by adopting his own relocation thesis: his Y-shaped account, he might say, deals with forward subjunctives and explaining-C indicatives on one limb of the Y, and explaining-E indicatives on the other.

But it still will not work, for a reason I gave in §33. The proposed account of indicative conditionals, even on its home ground of explaining-E bases, owes its seeming success to the use of a biased selection of examples. If A is a falsehood about the past, then the world may easily contain, now, abundant evidence for ¬(A&C) and equally plentiful evidence for ¬(A&¬C); so that one person might reasonably think A→¬C while another equally reasonably thinks A→C. In short, when explaining-E indicatives are involved we can expect subjectivity to come to the fore. Davis avoids it through a selection of examples where there happens to be much evidence for ¬(A&¬C) and little or none for ¬(A&C). As a general account of how to evaluate indicative conditionals—or even just those accepted on explaining-E bases—it fails.

I also hold against the account its providing no basis for making the Ramsey test central to the life of indicative conditionals. What preserves it from Lewis's 'triviality' results and their successors is its lack of anything like the Equation.

139. STALNAKER'S Y-SHAPED ANALYSIS OF CONDITIONALS

In each kind of conditional, according to Stalnaker 1975, the speaker says that C is true at an A-world picked out by a certain 'selection function'. Exactly what the function is will vary with context, though it will always involve *some* kind of 'most similar' notion, so whenever A is true the selected world will be α. In any given context, many propositions are taken for granted as confidently accepted by everyone, or anyway not up for question by anyone; 'the context set' is Stalnaker's name for the set of worlds at each of which all those taken-for-granted propositions are true. If there are no signals to the contrary, we take it that someone who asserts a conditional is using a selection function that picks an A-world belonging to the context set, that is, a world that is not agreed on all hands to be out of the running as a candidate for actuality. When a speaker uses 'would', however, he thereby signals that he regards himself as free to reach outside the context set, selecting a world that nobody in his vicinity thinks might be actual. A speaker might do this because A forced him to do so; but there are other possible reasons as well (Stalnaker 1975: 145–6). The thesis that indicative conditionals are not meant to reach outside the context set is the thesis that such conditionals are zero-intolerant (§23).

There, in brief, is Stalnaker's Y-shaped analysis. 'If A, C' says that C is true at the world selected by a certain selection function involving the notion of similarity; A→C implies that the selected world lies in the context set; A>C cancels this implication, signalling that the selected world may lie outside the context set. This puts the zero-intolerance of indicative conditionals and the zero-tolerance of subjunctives right at the centre. Stalnaker does not claim this to be a full-fledged semantic analysis of either sort of conditional; but he offers it as a full account of how they differ from one another, which means that any fuller account will also be Y-shaped.

Woods objected: 'We see nothing unacceptable about a conditional of the form "If P is the case, certain things are not so that we have been taking for granted"' (1997: 54). Indeed, but Stalnaker could take this on board by contending that someone who asserts such a conditional is *changing* the membership of the context set, bringing into question something that previously was not.

A different objection has been offered by Dorothy Edgington. When discussing conditional speech acts other than assertion (§51), she distinguishes obeying a command from merely not disobeying it: you can obey 'If you go out, take an umbrella' only by going out and taking an umbrella, and you can disobey it only by going out without an umbrella. If you stay at home, you neither obey nor disobey the command. Now, on any account like Stalnaker's, the truth value of A→C depends on whether C obtains at a certain A-world that may not be actual. Apply this to conditional commands, Edgington says, and you get absurd results. Suppose you enjoin me: 'If it rains, take your umbrella', which for Stalnaker means that I am to take my umbrella at the closest world (of a certain kind) at which it rains. Then I might flatly disobey your order—by going out without my umbrella at *that* world—even though at the actual world it does not rain (Edgington 1995b: 288). In short, the 'possible worlds' account implies that if this is the case:

If it had rained, I would have disobeyed your order,

then I do in fact disobey your order; an absurd result. This does not outright refute Stalnaker's account, however. As he has pointed out to me, it relies on the 'assumptions: first, that a conditional command should be regarded as a categorical command to make true (or perhaps to ensure the truth of) a certain (indicative conditional statement), and second, that obeying or disobeying a command should be identified with the truth or falsity of the statement'. Finding both assumptions implausible, Stalnaker can turn his back on Edgington's way of handling conditional commands. I like it better than he does, but shall not take it further now.

Stalnaker's 1975 account of indicative conditionals was supposed to include the Equation (§24), rendering it vulnerable to the disproofs of the latter that Lewis pioneered in 1976 and Stalnaker himself subsequently strengthened (§29).

How well does Stalnaker's account provide for the subjectivity of many indicative conditionals? In a way, quite well: each person's selection function is constrained by facts about what she thinks to be taken for granted in the given context, and people might vary in that. But the other problem remains: if the dependence on the subject is part of what is asserted in the indicative conditional, then the latter becomes a self-report, which we have seen it not to be (§36); and if the subjective element affects what the speaker means without being a part of it, intolerable things ensue regarding communication, questions and answers, and so on. The second of these points has been presented with great force by Stalnaker himself (§37).

In a more recent visit to the neighbourhood of his account (1984), made after the first Lewis 'triviality' result and after Gibbard's work on subjectivity, Stalnaker has been cautious and non-committal, though still resolutely exploratory. He is evidently still drawn to the concepts of selection function and context set, and still interested in finding what unity he can between the two kinds of conditional; but does not offer anything like a Y-shaped analysis. Nor does he now try to differentiate the two kinds of conditional through different constraints on the selection function.

Accepting that true subjunctive conditionals owe their truth to objective (mainly causal) necessities in the world, and that indicative conditionals owe their acceptability to epistemic states of affairs, Stalnaker sees the latter as our best route to an understanding of the former, describing this as 'an important resource for explaining the notoriously problematic objective modal concepts'. He continues:

The empiricist and pragmatist traditions have always found the subjective modal concepts less problematic than their objective counterparts. The possibilities that arise from ignorance and uncertainty are less puzzling than the real possibilities that remain even when we know they are unactualized. The connections between ideas that arise from habits of inference are less puzzling than the connections that seem to hold between events in the world. Similarly, the meaning and role of conditionals that represent our dispositions to modify beliefs in response to evidence are easier to understand than the meaning and role of conditionals that seem to be trying to make objective claims about what might have been, but was not. The recurring strategy of empiricists and pragmatists for treating the cluster of objective modal concepts has been to try to explain them either as illusory reflections or as legitimate extensions of their subjective analogues. Whether such a strategy can work in the case of open [indicative] and proposition-expressing [subjunctive] conditionals remains to be seen . . . (Stalnaker 1984: 112)

This sets the scene for Stalnaker's final two chapters, where he explores his strategic question and tentatively answers Yes. His core idea—offered, I think, as a key to understanding subjunctive conditionals—is that when you accept A>C, a forward counterfactual with A in the past, you are hypothesizing that some fact about the world, back before T_A, would have justified an epistemic policy that could have been expressed by A→C (1984: 116). This idea had already occurred to Brian Ellis, and Dorothy Edgington subsequently developed it at length and in depth. I shall come to their treatments of it shortly.

Leading into the passage I have just quoted, Stalnaker writes that the contrast between indicative and subjunctive conditionals 'can be seen as a special case of a wider contrast between subjective and objective modal concepts'. Lycan accepts this, and uses it against (NTV) the thesis that indicative conditionals lack truth values. Of the 'systematic relation' between the two kinds of modal concept he writes: 'Nowhere else in the modal family is that relation manifested by truth valuelessness of the relevant subjective statements' (Lycan 2001: 80). This scores a hit on anyone who holds that a good account of subjunctives automatically becomes a good account of indicatives when all the objective modalities are systematically replaced by subjective ones. If this were what Stalnaker meant— which it wasn't—we could dismiss his remarks out of hand. I hold that subjunctive conditionals involve a certain structure of objective possibilities, while indicatives involve a *different structure* of subjective ones; and the structural difference explains why one lot have truth values while the others lack them. It *involves* the objective/subjective difference, but it also involves more; so NTV need not regard objective/subjective as the sole source of, and thus as what is 'manifested' in, the difference between having and lacking truth values.

140. ELLIS'S UNIFIED ANALYSIS OF CONDITIONALS

Brian Ellis handles conditionals of both kinds in terms of belief systems. A 'completed belief system', he acknowledges, could be thought of as defining a possible world, but he prefers not to do semantics in those terms (Ellis 1978: 113–14, 122–3). The main thrust of his 'unified account' of conditionals can be grasped without choosing between worlds and belief systems. Its core can be stated in relation to these three:

(a) If X occurs on occasion O, then Y will occur on this occasion.

(b) If X occurred on occasion O, then Y occurred on this occasion.

(c) If X had occurred on occasion O, then Y would have occurred on this occasion. (Ellis 1978: 118–19)

Ellis writes b as 'If X occurred on occasion O, then Y (would have) occurred on this occasion'. Delete the parentheses and the result is ungrammatical; Ellis presumably tolerates it—he has it without parentheses at 1979: 50—but he does not explain why, or why he calls it 'indicative' despite its 'would'. However, although the intrusion of '(would have)' into b may give Ellis rhetorical help, it does not contribute to any argument of his, so I expound him without it.

Ellis classifies a and b as indicative, and c as subjunctive. He holds that a is a 'conditional prediction', that b is the same conditional prediction 'made retrospectively', and that c is 'the same conditional prediction . . . made retrospectively against the background knowledge [that] X did not occur' (pp. 118–19). This, he holds, is a microcosm of how things stand with regard to indicatives and subjunctives generally. 'An indicative conditional is usually a conditional prediction', and a subjunctive conditional says something that could also—at a suitable time and against a suitable background of knowledge—have been said in an indicative. Pretty much the same picture is drawn by Thomason and Gupta 1980: 304–5.

Ellis claims that this, among its other benefits, explains how we can learn to use and understand subjunctive conditionals, an ability that is obscure on the 'worlds' account. 'We understand them because we understand the simple indicative conditionals for which they are, essentially, variant locutions' (p. 121).

The core thesis that every acceptable subjunctive reflects an earlier indicative is not embarrassed by indicatives to which no subjunctive corresponds. But Ellis wants to say something about them too, for he means to be offering an overall account of the two kinds of conditional. He approaches indicative conditionals that do not stand or fall with subsequent subjunctives through the example (i) 'If Oswald did not kill Kennedy, then someone else did', which he says 'is not related epistemically to: (ii) "If Oswald had not killed Kennedy, then someone else would have" in the way that the theory requires' (p. 123). He clearly takes i to be accepted on an explaining-E basis; it could instead be accepted on an explaining-C basis, in which case it would after all be epistemically related to ii in the manner that interests Ellis. He does not remark on this; so he sees no need to decide whether we have here two possible bases for a single conditional or rather two conditionals.

Ellis deals with i—understood as having an explaining-E basis—by saying that it has 'the same acceptability conditions as "Someone killed Kennedy"', from which he concludes that i 'might well be considered to be a material conditional'. This lets him put it in quarantine, thus:

But as such it is an atypical conditional. In an ordinary conditional, whether it is expressed indicatively or subjunctively, there is alleged to be some kind of connection between antecedent and consequent conditions or events. In this case there is none. (p. 124)

At about the same time, Lowe (1979: 139) declared that i is 'a *material* conditional—a relatively rare phenomenon in ordinary language'.

If i really is a material conditional, this does indeed make it atypical among indicative conditionals generally, but Ellis's case for so regarding it is weak. All he offers in its support is its being 'epistemically equivalent' to 'Someone killed Kennedy'. But its probability conditions are nothing like those of the corresponding material conditional: someone who is fairly sure Oswald killed Kennedy and who thinks that otherwise Kennedy's death was probably an accident will give a much higher probability to 'Oswald did not kill Kennedy ⊃ Someone else killed Kennedy' than he will to 'If Oswald did not kill Kennedy, someone else did'. I laid all this out against Lycan in §137. The case for it is stated in Ellis's own pioneering work (1978: 114–17) on why probability considerations kill the horseshoe analysis.

Furthermore, conditionals lying outside the scope of Ellis's core thesis—that is, ones that do not stand or fall with corresponding subjunctives—can hardly be 'atypical', given how numerous they are. They include all the conditionals that are accepted on explaining-E bases. Notice the peculiar fates that befall these innocent, familiar, plentiful conditionals: Davis's theory of indicatives covers them and nothing else; Ellis's does not cover them at all.

We should also note that the phrase 'conditional prediction' does not capture the subset of indicative conditionals Ellis wants to cover in his core theory. Granted, the troublesome i is not a conditional prediction, but plenty of conditionals that *are* are accepted on explaining-E bases, and therefore have no role in his theory. I explained this in §136, and need not repeat it here.

So things go wrong in Ellis's attempt to say something about all indicatives, not just the ones covered by his core theory. This, however, leaves the core theory standing, and we are not yet finished with it.

He returns to this matter in a 1984 paper, in which he ranges Jackson and Lewis against Stalnaker and himself. His reference is to the Y-shaped theory of Stalnaker's discussed in the first part of §139 above. Had he known of Stalnaker's much more Ellis-like approach in his 1984 book, he would presumably have written even more confidently of 'the Ellis/Stalnaker theory'. The troubles I have found in the 1978 paper are also present in this one, but they do not touch the core thesis, which is indeed common to Stalnaker and Ellis: our best understanding of subjunctive conditionals comes from the fact that whenever A>C is acceptable at a certain time, A→C was acceptable earlier.

The core thesis is not quite true, as I shall show. First, though, let us address the broader issue of how to parlay the core thesis—if it is accepted—into a general account of the two kinds of conditional. Stalnaker and Ellis both say things bearing upon this; but it was left to Dorothy Edgington to present a full-scale body of doctrine about it.

141. EDGINGTON ON THE TWO KINDS
OF CONDITIONAL

Most of Edgington's magisterial 1995*b* concerns indicative conditionals, to our understanding of which she has contributed more than anyone else except Adams. Those hundred pages contain a nourishingly rich and helpful exploration of the literature on indicatives and the problems arising from it; my own Index of Persons suggests how indebted I am to the works of its author. In its final section (pp. 311–23) Edgington turns to subjunctive conditionals, which she relates to indicatives in something like Ellis's (and indeed Adams's) manner; and here we part company.

She discusses the relocation thesis, presenting the case for it and offering reasons against. Her overall view is this:

We have ample reason to treat Didn't-did and Doesn't-will as a unified class. I am a traditionalist in that I think the bigger distinction is between Didn't-did and Doesn't-will on the one hand, and Hadn't-would on the other. But the distinction isn't that big— Dudman was right to think it is (mainly) one of tense. (1995*b*: 314)

I agree with Edgington in rejecting the relocation thesis, but her final sentence is another matter. She wrote '(mainly)', she tells me, 'because some counterfactuals have nothing to do with time: If Newtonian mechanics had been correct . . .'. I now set those aside, thus entering a context where for Edgington tense is the whole story.

Her unification of the two sorts of conditional rests on something we have also seen in work by Stalnaker and Ellis. I shall call it the Correspondence Thesis:

CT: For any A and C, if A>C is the right thing to think at a certain time, then at some earlier time A→C was the right thing to think.

What Edgington makes of this is extremely strong. She refers back to her presentation at 1995*b*: 237–8 of the now-standard argument for distinguishing indicatives from subjunctives (§4). Borrowing also from Edgington's p. 311, we can put the argument in terms of these two:

DD: If (it is the case that) Oswald didn't kill Kennedy, (it is the case that) no one else did.

HW: If it had been the case that Oswald didn't kill Kennedy, it would have been the case that no one else did.

I would symbolize this pair by O→N and O>N respectively. Edgington does nothing like this, however. She heads her early section on this matter 'One theory or two?'; and now in her final section she reveals that her answer is One, because the two types of conditional differ only in tense:

If this [thesis about tense] is right, it defeats the argument . . . that there must be two conditional connectives. The argument was: the same two propositions, N and O, conditionally connected, express HW and DD. We accept HW and reject DD. So the conditional connective in HW doesn't mean the same as that in DD. On the above [tense] analysis, we do have the same two propositions, conditionally connected in the same way, but concerning different times. Accepting something as probable now, and accepting the same thing as having been probable then, are mutually independent judgments. (p. 315)

Thus, for example, the truth of HW comes from the acceptability at an earlier time, for any well-informed person, of 'If Oswald doesn't kill Kennedy, no one else will'; this is indicative, and obviously differs only in tense from DD.

The claim that there is only one conditional connective implicitly condemns my strategy of running indicatives and subjunctives separately, treating them as interestingly similar yet also radically unalike. I give more than half of my book to subjunctives considered just in themselves. They are a topic in only about a fifth of Edgington's article, and even there the main issue is how they relate to indicatives. I have a vested interest in her being wrong about this; you have been warned.

Edgington writes of the *probabilities* of subjunctive conditionals, not of their truth (§99). In my initial statement of CT, I straddled the truth/probability gap by adopting Edgington's phrase 'the right thing to think'. A subjunctive conditional could be the right thing to think because it was true, or because it was probable; so this version of CT can be stated and entertained independently of whether subjunctive conditionals can be credited with truth values or only with probabilities. But Edgington opts for 'only probabilities', for subjunctives as well as indicatives. She would be willing to state CT in terms of later and earlier probabilities, denying truth values both to F→C and to F>C—that is, to each kind of conditional when the antecedent is false.

An indicative conditional A→C is 'the right thing to think', I take it, if the world offers good grounds for a high probability for it and none for a high probability for A→¬C. Those are the ones—the right things to think—that CT pairs with subjunctives at a later time.

I have already discussed the idea that subjunctive conditionals should not be assigned truth values, arguing in §100 that the case for this has no tendency to close the theoretical gap between subjunctives and indicatives. But the gap may be narrowable or even closable on some other basis, the best candidate for that role being the Correspondence Thesis.

142. THE CORRESPONDENCE THESIS

Even if we credit counterfactuals with truth values, CT may still have great power. Here it is again:

> CT: For any A and C, if A>C is the right thing to think at a certain time, then at some earlier time A→C was the right thing to think.

If A>C can have a truth value and A→C cannot, these two occurrences of 'right thing to think' have to be unpacked differently. But this does not imply that CT is false; it might still be true, and offer promise of a considerable unification of the two sorts of conditional, with an understanding of indicatives serving as the antechamber to an understanding of subjunctives.

CT is true of many subjunctive conditionals, and not only ones of the Had-would form. At a time when I am utterly sure the comet will hit Jupiter, I can entertain 'If it were not to hit Jupiter, then . . .' but not 'If it does not hit Jupiter, then . . .', the latter being ruled out by the zero-intolerance of indicatives. However, the subjunctive requires the thought of a past fork from actuality, and if the subjunctive is all right, then so would have been the corresponding indicative just before the time of that fork. 'Does-will was the right thing to think at an earlier time. Does-will is not the right thing to think now, given the evidence he now has. But if the comet had not been on a collision course with Jupiter, he wouldn't have the evidence that he does have, that collision is now inevitable' (Edgington 1995*b*: 318).

In §§135–7 I attacked the relocation thesis, pointing out the failures of alignment between Had-woulds and Does-wills. My attack does no harm to CT, or to anything that Edgington maintains; for neither it nor she implies the relocation thesis, which concerns Does-wills only. All she needs is that when a subjunctive conditional—of whatever form—is the right thing to think, there was a past time at which the corresponding indicative was the right thing to think. From this she infers, in the manner of Ellis, that to get the hang of what happens in a subjunctive conditional we need only think about the status of the corresponding indicative at an earlier time.

In §94 I presented three obstacles to any general alignment of subjunctives with indicatives. Two of them, because they concerned indicatives with no corresponding subjunctives rather than vice versa, offer no challenge to CT. The third, however, does seem to ground an objection to CT. It concerns a class of examples involving subjunctives of the 'If you had bet heads, you would have won' variety, asserted on the grounds that the coin *did* fall heads and the bet would have been causally irrelevant to the fall (§90). The corresponding indicative conditional was not, before the bet, something anyone could have reason to accept.

Edgington discusses this problem in a new paper (2003), partly titled 'the Benefit of Hindsight'. She takes an example in which you cancel your booking for a certain flight, in the course of which the plane crashes. The crash was a horrible fluke; its prior probability was extremely low; and your presence or absence in the plane had no bearing on the improbable causal chain leading to it. Only a fool or a knave would have said to you in advance 'If you take flight 007, you'll be killed in a crash'. Yet later it is right to say 'If you had taken flight 007 you would have been killed'.

This is prima facie a problem for CT. Having 'forgotten about this sort of example' in earlier writings, Edgington now confronts it in her forthcoming paper, about two-thirds of the way through. Of the case just described, she writes: '"My God, he was right!", I say, on hearing the news [of the crash]. "If I'd caught the plane, I would have been killed"'. And of a variant case where a fortune-teller warns me that if I take the plane I'll be killed, and in the event 90 per cent of the passengers die in the crash, Edgington again has me saying later: 'She was right! It was very likely that I would have been killed, had I caught that plane.'

This seems to preserve CT. In these cases, A>C is the right thing to think later on, and earlier A→C was the right thing to think, in the sense that we could properly have said later that someone who asserted A→C 'was right'.

Edgington does not here use 'was right' to mean 'was true'. She sticks by her view that F→C never has a truth value, applying this to F→T as well as to the rest. What we have here, she says, is a matter of conditional probabilities, for indicatives and for subjunctives. It is not clear to me what the probabilities are in the light of which the indicatives are judged to be 'right' in hindsight. In the fortune-teller case, we can see where '90 per cent' comes in: hindsight shows us that there was a 90 per cent probability of my being killed given that I was on the plane when it crashed. But for the fortune-teller's conditional to be 'vindicated' (Edgington's word), room must also be found in the story for a nearly 100 per cent probability of the plane's crashing given that I was on it. Similarly with the first version, in which the only relevant probability is the near-certainty one. I cannot find, in either case, anything allowing us to say that the predicter's conditional probability for the plane's crashing given my being on it was, though not 'justified at the time', correct, right, vindicated.

Edgington deals swiftly with this question. Here is the whole of her treatment of it: 'Lucky guesses are sometimes right, and this was one. The value to be assigned to the hindsightful counterfactual trumps the most rational value to be assigned to the forward-looking indicative.' This concedes that the fortune-teller's conditional probability for π(Killed/Take) was not 'rational', but that is an understatement. At the time the fortune-teller spoke there may have been nothing in the world making her conditional probability correct. Edgington would have to agree, for she applies this treatment to cases where the causal chain leading to C's obtaining was indeterministic, and the objective probability of C's ensuing *given the whole present state of the world* is extremely low. She holds firm to her denial that the fortune-teller's conditional was *true*; but it was not *probable* either. So the later declaration 'It was right' has floated free from any theory we have been offered regarding indicative conditionals.

When Edgington writes that the subsequent probability of A>C 'trumps' the earlier probability of A→C—that is, the best probability the world then supported—she ought to mean that the judgement 'She was right!' is not just one that hindsight enables us to *see* to be correct, but one that comes to *be* correct only through subsequent events. This is not merely hind-*sight* but hind-*rightness-making*; and the rightness of the conditional has nothing to do with any rightness in the subjective conditional probability it expressed. In cases like this, the idea of the forward indicative's being 'right' *depends on* the idea of sub-junctive's being right—the explanatory direction runs from subjunctive to indicative, not the other way. Edgington seems to agree: 'He was right! If I had been on the plane I would have been killed.' She evidently offers the subjunctive as the reason or basis for calling the earlier indicative 'right'. It would be weird indeed to run an explanation the other way: 'Why do you say that if you had been on the plane you would have been killed?', 'Because if someone had told me in advance, "If you go on that plane, you will be killed" he would have been right.'

This is no small matter. Those subjunctives are right things to think; we can explain how they work without help from the idea of a previously acceptable Does-will, and there is indeed no help to be got from that source. To map this part of the subjunctive territory, we must walk patiently through the terrain, not distracted by thoughts of how it looks from a distant indicative hilltop. And this bit of mapping fits into a larger chart of the analysis of subjunctive conditionals generally; why should we not avail ourselves of it? Having explained these conditionals through closeness of worlds, there is no good reason to refuse to shine that light on other subjunctives, insisting that we can learn all we need to know about *them* from our theory of indicatives together with CT.

All this has concerned subjunctives whose status does not come from the status of corresponding indicatives. We should think also about indicatives for which there is no corresponding subjunctive—ones accepted on an explaining-E basis (§135) or involving temporally close forks (§94). Their existence does not embarrass CT, which is a sort of one-way conditional running from subjunctives to indicatives. But it would be unphilosophical of us simply to accept that no subjunctive corresponds to certain indicatives, without asking why this should be so. To explain why, I submit, we need to tackle subjunctives independently, on their own account.

In the dance around conditionals—I think Edgington thinks—indicatives call the tune: one theory, not two. Her grounds for this thesis have power, and the thesis is in many ways attractive, mainly for how it promises to simplify the material. I stand by the view, for which I have argued, that if we approach the two kinds of conditional wholly in this manner, we will lose some understanding that we could have had.

REFERENCES

Bibliographical references in the text give each work's date of first publication, and use the pagination of the latest printing of it that is recorded here.

Adams, Ernest W. (1965). 'A Logic of Conditionals'. *Inquiry* 8: 166–97.

——(1966). 'Probability and the Logic of Conditionals', in J. Hintikka and P. Suppes (eds.), *Aspects of Inductive Logic*. Amsterdam: North-Holland, 265–316.

——(1970). 'Subjunctive and Indicative Conditionals'. *Foundations of Language* 6: 89–94.

——(1975). *The Logic of Conditionals*. Dordrecht: Reidel.

——(1981*a*). 'Transmissible Improbabilities'. *Journal of Philosophical Logic* 10: 149–77.

——(1981*b*). 'Truth, Proof and Conditionals'. *Pacific Philosophical Quarterly* 62: 323–39.

——(1983). 'Probabilistic enthymemes'. *Journal of Pragmatics* 7: 283–95.

——(1988). '*Modus tollens* revisited'. *Analysis* 48: 122–8.

——(1996). 'Probability-Preserving Properties of Inferences'. *Journal of Philosophical Logic* 25: 1–24.

——(1998). *A Primer of Probability Logic*. Stanford, Calif.: CSLI Publications.

Adams, Robert M. (1974). 'Theories of Actuality'. *Noûs* 8: 211–31.

——(1987). 'Middle Knowledge and the Problem of Evil', in his *The Virtue of Faith and Other Essays in Philosophical Theology*. New York: Oxford University Press, 77–93.

Akatsuka, Noriko (1985). 'Conditionals and the Epistemic Scale'. *Language* 61: 625–39.

Anderson, Alan Ross (1951). 'A Note on Subjunctive and Counterfactual Conditionals'. *Analysis* 12: 35–8.

Anscombe, G. E. M. (1971). 'Causality and Determination', repr. in her *Metaphysics and the Philosophy of Mind*, 1981, Minneapolis: University of Minnesota Press, 133–47.

——(1975). 'Subjunctive Conditionals', repr. in Anscombe 1981: 196–207.

Appiah, Anthony (1984). 'Jackson on the Material Conditional'. *Australasian Journal of Philosophy* 62: 77–81.

——(1985). *Assertion and Conditionals*. Cambridge University Press.

——(1993). 'Only-ifs'. *Philosophical Perspectives* 7: 397–410.

Bach, Kent (1999). 'The Myth of Conventional Implicature'. *Linguistics and Philosophy* 22: 327–66.

Barker, Stephen J. (1991). '*Even, Still* and Counterfactuals'. *Linguistics and Philosophy* 14: 1–38.

——(1993). 'Conditional Excluded Middle, Conditional Assertion, and "Only If"'. *Analysis* 53: 254–61.

Barker, Stephen J. (1994). 'The Consequent-Entailment Problem for *Even if*'. *Analysis* 17: 249–60.

Bedford, Sybille (1958). *The Trial of Dr. Adams*. Harmondsworth: Penguin Books (reissued under this title, New York: Time Reading Program, 1962).

Bennett, Jonathan (1961). 'On Being Forced to a Conclusion'. *Proceedings of the Aristotelian Society* suppl. vol. 35: 15–34.

——(1974). 'Counterfactuals and Possible Worlds'. *Canadian Journal of Philosophy* 4: 381–402.

——(1976). *Linguistic Behaviour*. Cambridge University Press (reissued Indianapolis: Hackett, 1990).

——(1982). 'Even if'. *Linguistics and Philosophy* 5: 403–18.

——(1984). 'Counterfactuals and Temporal Direction'. *Philosophical Review* 93: 57–91.

——(1988a). *Events and Their Names*. Indianapolis: Hackett.

——(1988b). 'Farewell to the Phlogiston Theory of Conditionals'. *Mind* 97: 509–27.

——(1994). 'Descartes's Theory of Modality'. *Philosophical Review* 103: 639–67.

——(1995). 'Classifying Conditionals: The Traditional Way is Right'. *Mind* 104: 331–54.

——(1996). *The Act Itself*. Oxford University Press.

——(2000) 'Infallibility and Modal Knowledge in some Early Modern Philosophers', in T. Smiley (ed.), *Mathematics and Necessity: Essays in the History of Philosophy*. Oxford University Press, 139–66.

——(2001). 'Conditionals and Explanations', in A. Byrne, R. Stalnaker, and R. Wedgwood (eds.), *Fact and Value: Essays on Ethics and Metaphysics for Judith Jarvis Thomson*. Cambridge, Mass.: MIT Press, 1–28.

——(2003). Review of Lycan 2001. *Philosophical Quarterly* 53.

Bigelow, John C. (1976a). 'If-then Meets Possible Worlds'. *Philosophia* 6: 215–35.

——(1976b). 'Possible Worlds Foundations for Probability'. *Journal of Philosophical Logic* 5: 299–320.

——(1980). Review of Pollock's *Subjunctive Reasoning*. *Linguistics and Philosophy* 4: 129–39.

Blackburn, Simon (1986). 'How Can We Tell Whether a Commitment has a Truth Condition?', in C. Travis (ed.), *Meaning and Interpretation*. Oxford: Blackwell, 201–32.

Bradley, Richard (2000). 'A Preservation Condition for Conditionals'. *Analysis* 60: 219–22.

Carlstrom, Ian F., and Hill, Christopher S. (1978). Review of Adams's *The Logic of Conditionals*. *Philosophy of Science* 45: 155–8.

Carnap, Rudolf (1950). *The Logical Foundations of Probability*. University of Chicago Press.

Carroll, Lewis (1894). 'A Logical Paradox'. *Mind* 3: 436–8.

Chisholm, Roderick M. (1946). 'The Contrary-to-Fact Conditional'. *Mind* 55.

——(1955). 'Law Statements and Counterfactual Inference'. *Analysis* 15: 97–105.

Cover, Jan A., and Hawthorne, John (1990). 'Leibniz on Superessentialism and World-Bound Individuals'. *Studia Leibnitiana* 22: 175–83.

Cross, Charles B. (1985). 'Jonathan Bennett on "Even if"'. *Linguistics and Philosophy* 8: 353–7.

Dale, A. J., and Tanesini, A. (1989). 'Why Are Italians More Reasonable than Australians?' *Analysis* 49: 189–94.

Dancygier, Barbara (1998). *Conditionals and Prediction: Time, Knowledge, and Causation in Conditional Constructions*. Cambridge University Press.

Davis, Wayne A. (1979). 'Indicative and Subjunctive Conditionals'. *Philosophical Review* 88: 544–64.

——(1983). 'Weak and Strong Conditionals'. *Pacific Philosophical Quarterly* 64: 57–71.

Delgardo Lavin, Eva (1999). '*Even* as a Constraint on Relevance: The Interpretation of *even-if* conditionals', in *Proceedings of the Sixth International Colloquium on Cognitive Science*. University of the Basque Country, 112–18.

DeRose, Keith (1994). 'Lewis on "Might" and "Would" Counterfactual Conditionals'. *Canadian Journal of Philosophy* 24: 413–18.

——(1999). 'Can it be that it Would Have Been Even Though it Might not Have Been?' *Philosophical Perspectives* 13: 385–413.

——and Grandy, Richard E. (1999). 'Conditional Assertions and "Biscuit" Conditionals'. *Noûs* 33: 405–20.

Downing, P. B. (1959). 'Subjunctive Conditionals, Time Order, and Causation'. *Proceedings of the Aristotelian Society* 59: 125–40.

Dudman, V. H. (1983). 'Tense and Time in English Verb Clusters of the Primary Pattern'. *Australasian Journal of Linguistics* 3: 25–44.

——(1984a). 'Conditional Interpretations of *If*-sentences'. *Australian Journal of Linguistics* 4: 143–204.

——(1984b). 'Parsing "If"-Sentences'. *Analysis* 44: 145–53.

——(2000). 'Classifying "Conditionals": The Traditional Way is Wrong'. *Analysis* 60: 147.

——(forthcoming). 'Three Twentieth-century Commonplaces about '"if"'. *History and Philosophy of Logic* 22.

Dummett, Michael (1973). *Frege: Philosophy of Language*. London: Duckworth.

Edgington, Dorothy (1986). 'Do Conditionals have Truth Conditions?', repr. in Jackson (ed.) 1991: 176–201.

——(1991). 'The Mystery of the Missing Matter of Fact'. *Proceedings of the Aristotelian Society* suppl. vol. 65: 185–209.

——(1995a). 'Conditionals and the Ramsey Test'. *Proceedings of the Aristotelian Society* suppl. vol. 69: 67–86.

——(1995b). 'On Conditionals'. *Mind* 104: 235–329.

——(1996). 'Lowe on Conditional Probability'. *Mind* 105: 617–30.

——(1997a). 'Commentary', in Woods 1997: 95–137.

——(1997b). 'Truth, Objectivity, Counterfactuals and Gibbard'. *Mind* 106: 107–16.

Edgington, Dorothy (2000). 'General Conditional Statements: A reply to Kölbel'. *Mind* 109: 109–16.

——(2003). 'Counterfactuals and the Benefit of Hindsight', in P. Dowe and P. Noordhof (eds.), *Causation and Counterfactuals*. London: Routledge.

Elga, Adam (2000). 'Statistical Mechanics and the Asymmetry of Counterfactual Dependence'. *Philosophy of Science* suppl. vol. 68: 313–24.

Ellis, Brian (1973). 'The Logic of Subjective Probability'. *British Journal for the Philosophy of Science* 24: 125–52.

——(1978). 'A Unified Theory of Conditionals'. *Journal of Philosophical Logic* 7: 107–24.

——(1979). *Rational Belief Systems*. Oxford: Blackwell.

——(1984). 'Two Theories of Indicative Conditionals'. *Australasian Journal of Philosophy* 62: 50–66.

——Jackson, Frank, and Pargitter, R. J. (1977). 'An Objection to Possible-World Semantics for Counterfactual Logics'. *Journal of Philosophical Logic* 6: 35–57.

Fauconnier, G. (1975). 'Pragmatic Scales and Logical Structure'. *Linguistic Inquiry* 6: 353–75.

Field, Hartry (1994). 'Deflationist Views of Meaning and Content', repr. in his *Truth and the Absence of Fact*. Oxford University Press (2001): 104–56.

Fine, Kit (1975). Review of Lewis's *Counterfactuals*. *Mind* 84: 451–8.

Fodor, Jerry A., and LePore, Ernest (1996). 'What Cannot be Evaluated Cannot be Evaluated, and it Cannot be Supervalued Either'. *Journal of Philosophy* 93: 516–35.

Fowler, H. W., and Fowler, F. G. (1931). *The King's English*, 3rd edn. Oxford University Press.

Gabbay, Dov M. (1972). 'A General Theory of the Conditional in Terms of a Ternary Operator'. *Theoria* 3: 97–104.

Gärdenfors, Peter (1986). 'Belief Revisions and the Ramsey Test for Conditionals'. *Philosophical Review* 95: 81–93.

Geach, Peter (1957). *Mental Acts*. London: Routledge.

Geis, Michael, and Lycan, William G. (1993). 'Nonconditional Conditionals', repr. as an Appendix in Lycan 2001: 184–205.

Gibbard, Allan (1981a). 'Indicative Conditionals and Conditional Probability: Reply to Pollock', in Harper *et al.* (eds.) 1981: 253–6.

——(1981b). 'Two Recent Theories of Conditionals', in Harper *et al.* (eds.) 1981: 211–47.

——(1990). *Wise Choices, Apt Feelings*. Cambridge, Mass.: Harvard University Press.

Goggans, Phillip (1992). 'Do the Closest Counterfactual Worlds Contain Miracles?' *Pacific Philosophical Quarterly* 73: 137–49.

Goodman, Nelson (1947). 'The Problem of Counterfactual Conditionals', repr. in Jackson (ed.) 1991: 9–27.

——(1954). *Fact, Fiction and Forecast*. London: Athlone Press.

——(1957). 'Parry on Counterfactuals'. *Journal of Philosophy* 54: 442–5.

Grice, H. P. (1957). 'Meaning', repr. in his 1989: 213–23.

——(1961). 'The Causal Theory of Perception', repr. in his 1989: 224–47.

——(1967a). 'Logic and Conversation', in his 1989: 22–40.

——(1967b). 'Indicative Conditionals', in his 1989: 58–87.

——(1987). 'Further Notes on Logic and Conversation', in his 1989: 41–57.

——(1989). Studies in the Way of Words. Cambridge, Mass.: Harvard University Press.

Hájek, Alan (1989). 'Probabilities of Conditionals—Revisited'. Journal of Philosophical Logic 18: 423–8.

——(1994). 'Triviality on the Cheap?', in E. Eells and B. Skyrms (eds.), Probability and Conditionals: Belief Revision and Rational Decision. Cambridge University Press, 113–40.

——(forthcoming). 'What Conditional Probability Could Not Be'. Synthese.

Hansson, Sven Ove (1992). 'In Defense of the Ramsey Test'. Journal of Philosophy 70: 522–40.

——(1995). 'The Emperor's New Clothes: Some Recurring Problems in the Formal Analysis of Counterfactuals', in G. Crocco et al. (eds.), Conditionals: from Philosophy to Computer Science. Oxford University Press, 13–31.

Hare, R. M. (1952). The Language of Morals. Oxford University Press.

——(1963). Freedom and Reason. Oxford University Press.

——(1981). Moral Thinking: Its Levels, Method and Point. Oxford University Press.

Harman, Gilbert (1979). 'If and Modus Ponens'. Theory and Decision 11: 41–53.

Harper, William L. (1981). 'A Sketch of Some Recent Developments in the Theory of Conditionals', in Harper et al. (eds.) 1981: 3–38.

——Stalnaker, Robert, and Pearce, Glenn (eds.) (1981). Ifs. Dordrecht: Reidel.

Hazen, Allen, and Slote, Michael (1979). 'Even if'. Analysis 39: 35–41.

Heller, Mark (1995). 'Might-Counterfactuals and Gratuitous Differences'. Australasian Journal of Philosophy 73: 91–101.

Herzberger, H. G. (1979). 'Counterfactuals and Consistency'. Journal of Philosophy 76: 83–8.

Hosiasson-Lindenbaum, Janina (1940). 'On Confirmation'. Journal of Symbolic Logic 5: 133–48.

Jackson, Frank (1977). 'A Causal Theory of Counterfactuals'. Australasian Journal of Philosophy 55: 3–21.

——(1979). 'On Assertion and Indicative Conditionals', reprinted in Jackson (ed.) 1991: 111–35.

——(1980). Review of Pollock's Subjunctive Reasoning. Australasian Journal of Philosophy 58: 413–15.

——(1981). 'Conditionals and Possibilia'. Proceedings of the Aristotelian Society 81: 125–37.

——(1984). 'Two Theories of Indicative Conditionals: Reply to Brian Ellis'. Australasian Journal of Philosophy 62: 67–76.

——(1987). Conditionals. Oxford: Blackwell.

——(ed.) (1991). Conditionals. Oxford University Press.

Jackson, Frank and Pettit, Philip (1998). 'A Problem for Expressivism'. *Analysis* 58: 239–51.

Jeffrey, Richard C. (1983). *The Logic of Decision*, 2nd edn. University of Chicago Press.

Johnson, David (1991). 'Induction and Modality'. *Philosophical Review* 100: 399–430.

Kölbel, Max (2000). 'Edgington on Compounds of Conditionals'. *Mind* 109: 97–108.

Lance, Mark (1991). 'Probabilistic Dependence among Conditionals'. *Philosophical Review* 100: 269–75.

Leibniz, G. W. (1686). Remarks on a Letter by Arnauld, repr. in R. Ariew and G. Garber (eds.), *Philosophical Essays*. Indianapolis: Hackett (1989), 69–77.

Levi, Isaac (1988). 'Iteration of Conditionals and the Ramsey Test'. *Synthese* 76: 49–81.

——(1996). *For the Sake of Argument: Ramsey Test Conditionals, Inductive Inference, and Nonmonotonic Reasoning*. Cambridge University Press.

Lewis, David (1970). 'Anselm and Actuality', repr. in his 1983: 10–20.

——(1973a). 'Causation', repr. in his 1986b: 159–72.

——(1973b). *Counterfactuals*. Cambridge, Mass.: Harvard University Press.

——(1976). 'Probability of Conditionals and Conditional Probability', repr. in his 1986b: 133–52.

——(1977). 'Possible-World Semantics for Counterfactual Logics : A Rejoinder'. *Journal of Philosophical Logic* 6: 359–63.

——(1979). 'Counterfactual Dependence and Time's Arrow', repr. in his 1986b: 32–52.

——(1981). 'Ordering Semantics and Premise Semantics for Counterfactuals'. *Journal of Philosophical Logic* 10: 217–34.

——(1983). *Philosophical Papers*, vol. 1. New York: Oxford University Press.

——(1986a). *On the Plurality of Worlds*. Oxford: Blackwell.

——(1986b). *Philosophical Papers*, vol. 2. New York: Oxford University Press.

——(1986c). Postscripts to 'Causation', in his 1986b: 172–213.

——(1986d). 'Postscripts to Counterfactual Dependence and Time's Arrow', in his 1986b: 52–66.

——(1986e). 'Postscripts to Probability of Conditionals and Conditional Probability', in his 1986b: 152–6.

——(1986f). 'Probability of Conditionals and Conditional Probability II', repr. in Jackson (ed.) 1991: 102–10.

——(1997). 'Finkish Dispositions', repr. in his *Papers in Metaphysics and Epistemology*. Cambridge University Press, 1999, 133–51.

Lewy, C. (1976). '*Mind* under G. E. Moore (1921–1947)'. *Mind* 85: 37–46.

Loewer, Barry M. (1975). 'Counterfactuals with Disjunctive Antecedents'. *Journal of Philosophy* 72: 531–7.

——(2001). 'Determinism and Chance'. *Studies in the History and Philosophy of Modern Physics* 32: 609–20.

Lowe , E. J. (1979). 'Indicative and Counterfactual Conditionals'. *Analysis* 39: 139–41.

——(1984). 'Wright *versus* Lewis on the Transitivity of Counterfactuals'. *Analysis* 44: 180–5.

——(1985). 'Reply to Wright on Conditionals and Transitivity'. *Analysis* 45: 200–2.

——(1991). 'Jackson on Classifying Conditionals'. *Analysis* 51: 126–30.

Lycan, William G. (1991). '*Even* and *Even if*'. *Linguistics and Philosophy* 14: 115–50.

——(1993). 'MPP, RIP'. *Philosophical Perspectives* 7: 411–28.

——(2001). *Real Conditionals*. Oxford University Press.

McCawley, James D. (1981). *Everything that Linguists Have Always Wanted to Know About Logic*. University of Chicago Press.

McDermott, Michael (1996). 'On the Truth Conditions of Certain "If"-Sentences'. *Philosophical Review* 105: 1–37.

——(1999). 'Counterfactuals and Access Points'. *Mind* 108: 291–334.

McGee, Vann (1985). 'A Counterexample to Modus Ponens'. *Journal of Philosophy* 82: 462–71.

——(1989). 'Conditional Probabilities and Compounds of Conditionals'. *Philosophical Review* 98: 485–541.

——(2000). 'To Tell the Truth about Conditionals'. *Analysis* 60: 107–11.

McKay, Thomas and van Inwagen, Peter (1976). 'Counterfactuals with Disjunctive Antecedents'. *Philosophical Studies* 31: 353–6.

Mackie, J. L. (1965). 'Causes and Conditions'. *American Philosophical Quarterly* 2: 245–64.

——(1973). *Truth, Probability and Paradox*. Oxford University Press.

——(1977). *Ethics: Inventing Right and Wrong*. New York: Penguin.

——(1980). 'The Transitivity of Counterfactuals and Causation'. *Analysis* 40: 53–4.

Martin, C. B. (1994). 'Dispositions and Conditionals'. *Philosophical Quarterly* 44: 1–7.

Mellor, D. H. (1993). 'How to Believe a Conditional'. *Journal of Philosophy* 90: 233–48.

Miller, Richard B. (1992). 'Concern for Counterparts'. *Philosophical Papers* 21: 133–40.

Morton, Adam (1981). 'Would Cause'. *Proceedings of the Aristotelian Society* 81: 139–51.

——(1997). 'Can Edgington Gibbard Counterfactuals?' *Mind* 106: 100–5.

Nute, Donald (1975). 'Counterfactuals and the Similarity of Worlds'. *Journal of Philosophy* 72: 773–8.

——(1978). 'Simplification and Substitution of Counterfactual Antecedents'. *Philosophia* 7: 317–26.

——(1980a). 'Conversational Scorekeeping and Conditionals'. *Journal of Philosophical Logic* 9: 153–66.

——(1980b). *Topics in Conditional Logic*. Dordrecht: Reidel.

Parry, William Tuthill (1957). 'Reëxamination of the Problem of Counterfactual Conditionals'. *Journal of Philosophy* 54: 85–94.

Pendlebury, Michael (1989). 'The Projection Strategy and the Truth Conditions of Conditional Statements'. *Mind* 98: 179–205.

Pollock, John L. (1976). *Subjunctive Reasoning*. Boston: Reidel.

——(1981). 'A Refined Theory of Counterfactuals'. *Journal of Philosophical Logic* 10: 239–66.

Ramsey, Frank P. (1926). 'Truth and Probability', repr. in his 1978: 58–100.

Ramsey, Frank P. (1929). 'Law and Causality', repr. in his 1978: 128–51.

——(1978). *Foundations*. London: Routledge.

Read, Stephen (1992). 'Conditionals are not Truth-Functional: an Argument from Peirce'. *Analysis* 52: 5–12.

Reichenbach, Hans (1976). *Laws, Modalities, and Counterfactuals*. Berkeley: University of California Press.

Rescher, Nicholas (1961). 'Belief-Contravening Suppositions'. *Philosophical Review* 70: 176–96.

Rosen, Gideon (1990). 'Modal Fictionalism'. *Mind* 99: 327–54.

——(1995). 'Modal Fictionalism Fixed'. *Analysis* 55: 67–73.

Ryle, Gilbert (1949). *The Concept of Mind*. London: Hutchinson.

Sanford, David H. (1989). *If P, Then Q: Conditionals and the Foundations of Reasoning*. London: Routledge.

Sellars, W. S. (1958). 'Counterfactuals, Dispositions and the Causal Modalities', partly repr. (as 'Counterfactuals') in E. Sosa (ed.), *Causation and Conditionals*. Oxford University Press, 1975: 126–46.

Skyrms, Brian (1980). *Causal Necessity*. New Haven: Yale University Press.

——(1994). 'Adams Conditionals', in E. Eells and B. Skyrms (eds.), *Probability and Conditionals: Belief Revision and Rational Decision*. Cambridge University Press, 13–26.

Slote, Michael A. (1978). 'Time in Counterfactuals'. *Philosophical Review* 87: 3–27.

Spinoza, Benedict de (1665). Letter (23) to Willem van Blijenbergh, repr. in *The Collected Works of Spinoza*, vol. 1, ed. Edwin Curley, Princeton University Press, 387–92.

Stalnaker, Robert C. (1968). 'A Theory of Conditionals', repr. in Harper *et al.* (eds.) 1981: 41–55.

——(1970). 'Probability and Conditionals', repr. in Harper *et al.* (eds.) 1981: 107–28.

——(1975). 'Indicative Conditionals', repr. in Jackson (ed.) 1991: 136–54.

——(1976). Letter to van Fraassen, in *Foundations of Probability Theory, Statistical Inference, and Statistical Theories of Science*, vol. 1, ed. W. Harper and C. Hooker, Dordrecht: Reidel, 302–6.

——(1978). 'A Defense of Conditional Excluded Middle', in Harper *et al.* (eds.) 1981: 87–104.

——(1984). *Inquiry*. Cambridge, Mass.: MIT Press.

Strawson, P. F. (1986). ' "If" and "⊃" ', in R. Grandy and R. Warner (eds.), *Philosophical Grounds of Rationality: Intentions, Categories, Ends*. Oxford University Press.

Thomason, Richmond, and Gupta, Anil (1980). 'A Theory of Conditionals in the Context of Branching Time', repr. in Harper *et al.* (eds.) 1981: 299–322.

Thomson, James F. (1990). 'In defence of "⊃" '. *Journal of Philosophy* 87: 57–70; written in about 1963, and published posthumously.

Tichý, Pavel (1976). 'A Counterexample to the Stalnaker–Lewis Analysis of Counterfactuals'. *Philosophical Studies* 29: 271–3.

Todd, William (1964). 'Counterfactual Conditionals and the Presuppositions of Induction'. *Philosophy of Science* 31: 101–10.

Tooley, Michael (forthcoming). 'The Stalnaker–Lewis Approach to Counterfactuals'.

van Fraassen, Bas C. (1966). 'Singular Terms, Truth-value Gaps, and Free Logic'. *Journal of Philosophy* 63: 481–95.

——(1976). 'Probabilities of Conditionals', in W. Harper and C. Hooker (eds.), *Foundations of Probability Theory, Statistical Inference, and Statistical Theories of Science*, vol. 1. Dordrecht: Reidel, 261–300, 307–8.

——(1980). Review of Brian Ellis, *Rational Belief Systems*. *Canadian Journal of Philosophy* 10: 497–511.

van Inwagen, Peter (1979). 'Laws and Counterfactuals'. *Noûs* 13: 439–53.

——(1980). 'Indexicality and Actuality'. *Philosophical Review* 89: 403–26.

——(1983). *An Essay on Free Will*. Oxford University Press.

——(1986). 'Two Concepts of Possible Worlds', repr. in his *Identity, Ontology, and Modality: Essays in Metaphysics*. Cambridge University Press, 2001: 206–42.

Warmbröd, Ken (1981). 'Counterfactuals and Substitution of Equivalent Antecedents'. *Journal of Philosophical Logic* 10: 267–89.

——(1983). 'Epistemic Conditionals'. *Pacific Philosophical Quarterly* 64: 249–65.

Woods, Michael (1997). *Conditionals*, ed. D. Wiggins. Oxford University Press.

Wright, Crispin (1983). 'Keeping Track of Nozick'. *Analysis* 43: 134–40.

——(1984). Comment on Lowe. *Analysis* 44: 183–5.

Zandvoort, R. W. (1963). 'On the So-called Subjunctive'. *English Language Teaching* 17: 73–7.

INDEX OF PERSONS

INDEX OF TOPICS

Lightning Source UK Ltd.
Milton Keynes UK
UKOW06f0338250315

248483UK00005B/61/P